BIVOUAC

of the

DEAD

Mark Hughes

HERITAGE BOOKS
2008

HERITAGE BOOKS
AN IMPRINT OF HERITAGE BOOKS, INC.

Books, CDs, and more—Worldwide

For our listing of thousands of titles see our website
at
www.HeritageBooks.com

Published 2008 by
HERITAGE BOOKS, INC.
Publishing Division
100 Railroad Ave. #104
Westminster, Maryland 21157

Other books by the author:

Confederate Cemeteries, Volume 1
Confederate Cemeteries, Volume 2

International Standard Book Numbers
Paperbound: 978-0-7884-0260-9
Clothbound: 978-0-7884-7663-1

DEDICATION

Only an idiot would fail to dedicate their first book to their wife.
My wife's name is Patricia McDaniel Hughes. I call her Patty. Without
her patience, understanding, and typing, this book could have never
been written.

AND

To the memory of my father, Sidney Jackson Hughes (1924 - 1994)

CONTENTS

HOW TO USE THIS BOOK

This book was written for two different audiences. My original objective was to write a reference book for genealogists who were trying to locate the burial sites of Civil War soldiers. However the more I researched, the more unpublished history I discovered. For example I discovered why an Union soldier lost the burial register of the Florence, S.C., prison camp. Because of this, the graves of over 2,700 Union soldiers had to be marked simply: "unknown".

Bivouac of the Dead also contains the never before published story of B.B. Dykes. Mr. Dykes' land was taken to construct the Andersonville National Cemetery in 1865. He was not paid for his land until 1875 and then only after he threatened to "plant a vineyard" because "Dead Yankees would make good wine."

This book lists burial locations of United States soldiers from 1860 to 1890. This includes both the Civil War and the various Indian Wars.

This book is divided in three sections. The first is a history of the development of the National Cemetery System. Much of the material in this section has never been published.

After the Civil War tens of thousands of bodies of Union soldiers were exhumed and moved to national cemeteries. Section 2 of this book lists the original site of burial along with the final burial location. A brief history of each final interment location is included in section 3. A "#" following an entry of an original burial site means that information on the original site is also included in section 3. Section 3 is arranged in alphabetical order by states then by cemetery.

Sometimes bodies from one location were moved to more than one national cemetery. For example, bodies from the Pea Ridge Battlefield in Northwestern Arkansas were moved to both the Springfield (Missouri) National Cemetery and the Fayetteville (Arkansas) National Cemetery. A list of soldiers originally buried at Pea Ridge was published by the United States Army's Quartermaster General's Office, so Pea Ridge is marked with a "#" in section 2.

Section 3 of this book gives a brief history of over 500 burial sites of United States soldiers. This information often includes where to find lists of soldiers buried in a particular location. When soldiers were first buried their graves were supposed to be marked with wooden headboards. Often these headboards would decay, leaving the grave unmarked. Then when the body was moved, it would be buried as an unknown soldier. The United States Government did not erect stone headstones until 1873. Many graves in military post (fort) cemeteries were not marked until 1885.

The quality and quantity of information on each cemetery listed varies. An archivist at the Suitland, Maryland, branch of the National Archives expressed it best: "As you know, the material on national before 1920 is incomprehensible." One director of a national turned my query with the note: "....I am sorry that I must tell possible to find (the information you requested). There is not a netery in the United States that keeps records of the type of information you seek." All I asked was the number of Union and Confederate soldiers buried in the cemetery.

No attempt was made to correct or modernize the spellings of towns or battlefields. For example the Quartermaster's records use the names Stone's River although the National Park Service uses the name Stones River. Also the word "colored" is used to designate African-American troops. The term "colored" was used in the 1860's and 1870's on official reports. The term "black" was used on one form used around 1868, however. Burials of colored troops were listed separately and this book uses that format. This format is used to help genealogists, not to discriminate. There is no need to try to locate the grave of a member the United States Colored Troops in the Lexington (Kentucky) National Cemetery. The bodies of U.S. Colored Troops were moved from Lexington to the New Albany (Indiana) National Cemetery after the war.

This book does not attempt to list the hundreds of Confederate cemeteries. The author has located at least 400 Confederate cemeteries, but many more exist. After the war no national effort was made to locate and mark Confederate graves. Not until 1906 did Congress even attempt to mark these graves. Even then only the graves of prisoners of war were marked. Many graves were marked by private groups but no one has attempted to write a history of Confederate cemeteries because no one group was in charge of marking these graves. The time required to research the history of these cemeteries would be enormous. It would be almost impossible to research Confederate cemeteries without a grant. However if you know of a cemetery containing the graves of Confederate soldiers, please contact the author in care of the publisher.

FOR MORE INFORMATION ON HOW TO USE THIS BOOK READ THE NEXT SECTION.

SOURCES CITED IN THIS BOOK

Burial of Federal soldiers was the responsibility of the (Corps. The Quartermaster Corps also provided food, clothing, ... supplies to the army. Care of refugee ex-slaves fell to the Quartermaster Corps. Records of the Quartermaster General (1792-1957) are housed in the National Archives as record group 92. This group consists of 22,942 cubic feet of material.

In 1885 the Adjunct General requested a brief history of each national cemetery. Quartermaster General Samuel Holabird wrote the Adjunct General: "No published reports on this subject (the history of each cemetery) are now reliable or accurate since they do not embrace any of the numerous changes that have been made...in the last ten years." Holabird continued: "...we have not at hand the necessary data upon which to base such descriptions."

Most of the surviving Quartermaster's records are in poor condition. Most of this book was taken from entry E576 in Record Group 92. This is cited as **RG92-576**. This group is labeled: General correspondence and reports relating to National and Post Cemeteries, 1865-90.

This record group is housed in 69 boxes, labeled box 127 to box 196. It's length is listed as 98 feet. The boxes are labeled by cemetery in some attempt at alphabetical order. However many documents are misfiled. For example box 140, labeled Cadwalader to Camp Chase, has reports and letters from Forest Home Cemetery, Fort Crawford Post Cemetery, Prospect Hill Cemetery, and Mound Cemetery.

While I was researching this book, box #187 disappeared. Apparently it was returned to the wrong storage area. One archivist told me the box would be found "When this building gives up the dead at the apocalypse."

The material in these boxes varies in both quality and quantity. The only information on some cemeteries is a cryptic noted scrawled on the back of an envelope. "Abraham Lincoln Remains removed to Custer Battlefield Cemetery" is the only information in the file on Fort Abraham Lincoln Post Cemetery. The records on Chattanooga National Cemetery take up 2 1/2 file boxes.

Little of the records are of lasting historic interest. Most of the records concern improvements (lodges, fences...) to the cemeteries. Six letters in the Vicksburg National Cemetery file are about what to do with a sick mule. Some deal with personal matters. (investigations into superintendent's conduct, superintendents' requests to plant a garden....). Some records are requests to purchase supplies locally. Only about 2% of the material has lasting historical value.

Many of the reports and letters in this record group are incomplete. Many are unsigned copies. Other reports are signed but not dated, limiting their value. Often the writing on a document is too faded to read. General

M.C. Meigs', the Quartermaster General from 1861 to 1882, handwriting is impossible to decipher. Even his biographer complained about his "abominable handwriting characteristics."

Because of the lack of dates, signatures,...this book does not contain footnotes. It would be counterproductive to attempt to footnote the notes scribbled on envelopes.

Other papers in these files are labeled **BRIEFS**. These unsigned and often undated pages summarize actions taken. Sometimes the correspondence referred to in a brief is still in the file. Often it is not. These briefs saved an overworked clerk time.

The only records in the 1907 to 1919 national cemetery file are from six cemeteries. No records from the other seventy some odd cemeteries have been found. No file for records from 1891 to 1906 has been found.

Not all Federal soldiers were buried in national cemeteries. Some were buried in **SOLDIERS' LOTS**. Soldiers' lots were a lot set aside in a public cemetery for the burial of soldiers. Some were owned by the Federal Government, others by private groups or local governments. Today the Department of Veteran's Affairs administers 21 soldiers' lots. The smallest is a 15 foot square lot with eight burials in Green Mountain, Vermont. The largest is Mount Moriah Naval Cemetery in Philadelphia with "5,000 plus" burials. No one knows who owns the other lots. (For an example see the listing for Spring Grove Cemetery in section III.)

In 1873 Congress appropriated $1,000,000 to mark the graves of soldiers buried in national cemeteries with permanent headstones. In 1879 the program was expanded to include veteran's graves in post, public, and private cemeteries. Often local Grand Army of the Republic (GAR) posts or local officials (often the postmaster) applied for headstones. The **LISTS** they mailed the War Department are often the only record of burial of a soldier. In the mid 1880's the War Department sent a circular letter to all active army posts. The acting assistant post quartermaster filled out the attached **HEADSTONE REQUEST** form to order headstones for the post cemetery. Many of these forms still exist. Often no other record of these burials exists.

Some burial rosters for national cemeteries are preserved in RG92-576, however a much better reference is available for researchers. From 1866 to 1871 the Quartermaster General published the 27 volume **ROLL OF HONOR** series. The exact title varies but most begin: <u>Names of Soldiers Who Died in Defense of the American Union Interred in the National Cemeteries</u>... Many large university libraries have at least a partial set of these books. This series lists the names of soldiers buried in national cemeteries, post cemeteries, soldiers' lots, and private cemeteries. The <u>Roll of Honor</u> series is currently being reprinted. Sample pages of the <u>Roll of Honor</u> are reproduced in the appendix.

Not all Civil War National Cemeteries are listed in the <u>Roll of Honor</u>. The series omits the Grafton, West Virginia, and Ball's Bluff, Virginia,

National Cemeteries. Volume 14 lists the names of 10,959 Ur
who died as prisoners of war. Volume 3 of the series lists 12,91
prisoners at Andersonville, Georgia. Another 2,797 unknow
buried at Florence, S.C., are listed in volume 19 of the Roll of H(
makes a total of 26,668 Union soldiers who died as prisoners in   _..in
prisons. This was before Northern authorities "discovered" an additional
9,000 bodies at Salisbury.

The grave site of many soldiers listed in the Roll of Honor series is
unknown. Volume 9 of the series lists a total of 532 soldiers buried "at
Cleveland". Only 39 of these were buried in Cleveland's Woodlawn
Cemetery's Soldiers Lot. No one knows where the others are buried. Some
may have been buried in "private lots." **PRIVATE LOTS** were privately
owned plots in family and public cemeteries.

Sometimes records appear to have been lost. Volume 8 of the Roll
of Honor (1866) lists 16 known and 30 unknown burials in the Fort Marcy,
New Mexico, post cemetery. When volume 19 was published in 1868 only
three different names were listed. There were no unknowns listed. Sixty-
four burials at Fort Snelling, Min., are listed in volume 9 (1866). Volume
19 (1869) lists only nine burials, but they are names that were listed in
volume 9. Private James C. Beard, Co. C, 85th Indiana Infantry, is listed
in three volumes (#12, 14, 15).

Often dead soldiers were identified by letters or names written on
their packs. In The Last Full Measure John W. Busey and David G. Martin
discuss the errors made in identifying dead Union soldiers at Gettysburg.
Busey lists 14 soldiers listed as killed but that are known to have survived the
battle. Pvt. Stephen Kelly, a private in the 91st Pennsylvania, had his
knapsack stolen before the battle. His "body" was identified by this
knapsack. Kelly lived to visit his own grave.

According to Busey, who meticulously researched the compiled
service records of Gettysburg's dead, Pvt. Eli Stalcup of the 20th Indiana
was buried as "E. Stallup". Two headstones for "John Glair" are located
side by side in the New York section. But Bushy can locate no John Glair
who was killed at Gettysburg. Busey's book is a must for anyone interested
in the Gettysburg dead.

Problems with names also exist in the Roll of Honor. Volume 9 of
the Roll of Honor lists Isaiah Packard Co I, 18th Michigan, who was buried
at Jacksonville, Florida. Volume 14 of the series gives Packard's first name
as Hiram. Sometimes the same man is listed to two different units.
According to volume 19 of the series, George Hallam of Company C, 31st
U.S. Infantry is buried in grave 4 of Fort Buford's, DT, post cemetery. The
problem is that grave 5 of the same cemetery is occupied by George Hallam,
Company C, 13th U.S. Infantry. Sometimes even the name of cemeteries
changed. The Quartermaster General's file lists Logan Crossroads National
Cemetery. Today the VA lists the cemetery as Mill Springs National

Cemetery. At one time Memphis National Cemetery was called Mississippi River National Cemetery.

Because state troops were technically under the control of state governments, preliminary copies of the rolls were sent to adjutant generals of the states to be checked. Not all rolls were returned before the Roll of Honor volumes were printed. Adjutant Generals also identified many soldiers who were supposed to be members of units of their state units but no records of enlistment could be found. These names were to be researched further, but no more research was done.

In 1866, Chaplin Thomas Van Horne proposed publishing a brief history of each soldier buried in the Chattanooga National Cemetery. This was not done. Brevet Colonel Charles W. Folsom, Inspector of National Cemeteries, proposed publishing a corrected Roll of Honor series. Although Folsom suggested this several times it was never done. No name index to the Roll of Honor has ever been published. In fact a "place index" was published for only the first thirteen volumes. The index in section 2 of this book is the first published index to the entire Roll of Honor series.

Although the Roll of Honor helped "friends, relatives, and surviving comrades" find the burial sites of known Union Soldiers, there was no way to locate where the bodies of unknown soldiers were buried. In 1868 the Quartermaster's Department produced 4 volumes entitled Statement of the Disposition of Some of the Bodies of Deceased Union Soldiers and Prisoners of War Whose Remains Have Been Removed to National Cemeteries in the Southern and Western States. This series, hereafter referred to as the **DISPOSITION**, listed the "final" resting places of over 200,000 Union Soldiers. The Disposition lists about 1,200 original burial sites of Union Soldiers. This book lists over 2,300 original burial sites.

In 1871 the Inspector of National Cemeteries listed a total of 305,492 burials of Union Soldiers. And this figure omitted burials in post cemeteries in the west whose "...death were (sic) not incidental to rebellion." Most Rolls of Honor issued after 1868 include the original sites of interments. Volume 27 (1871) lists the original sites of interment for 2,655 unknown soldiers in the Beaufort National Cemetery. However no original burial site was listed for the 4,857 known soldiers.

Volume 22 of the series (1869) lists 12,486 known and 3,999 unknown soldiers buried in Nashville National Cemetery. But a list of 4,472 names of soldiers who died or were killed in action in or near Nashville is included. These bodies were either removed by friends and relatives or buried as unknowns in the cemetery.

Volume 15 of the Roll of Honor contains 90 pages of names of soldiers who were buried in Virginia but "all of their remains have, undoubtedly, been removed long ere this..." to the Poplar Grove and Yorktown National Cemeteries.

Although the introductions to the Roll of Honor asked that citizens write the War Department postage free to report graves of soldiers and promised rewards for the return of missing prison camp death rolls, the Quartermaster General did not want a list of the deaths at the Camp Ford, Texas, POW Camp.

Most national cemetery reports list burials in three groups: white soldiers, colored soldiers, and civilians. Because U.S. Colored Troops were led by white officers, these officers were sometimes listed as white officers. Other times they were listed as "colored soldiers." The civilian category includes: employees, women, children, refugees (contrabands), laundresses, and sutlers. Some cemeteries list a miscellaneous category in their summaries. Often these soldiers' names were known, but their units were unknown. Other units in the miscellaneous category included riverboat troops, marines, U.S. sharpshooters, U.S. engineers,...

Two National Archives record groups are supposed to contain General orders relating to national cemeteries from 1866 to 1905. Unfortunately most general orders apparently were never filed away. In 1879 General Order # 78 announced Custer Battlefield as a national cemetery. This order is not in any of these record groups.

The Report of the Quartermaster General to the Secretary of War for the Year 1868 contains the report of Brevet Colonel Charles W. Folsom, Assistant Quartermaster of volunteers. **COLONEL FOLSOM** was a volunteer who remained in service to finish his report. Folsom later owned a landscape business in Boston.

In 1871 Brevet Colonel Oscar Mack served as Inspector of National Cemeteries. **COLONEL MACK'S 1871 REPORT** is the most complete report. It also contains the most accurate figures of soldiers who died during the Civil War. In 1872 Congress approved the burial of "destitute" Civil War veterans in national cemeteries. In 1873 Congress bowed to pressure from the GAR and other veterans' groups and allowed any honorably discharged veteran to be buried in national cemeteries. This means that the burial statistics in **COLONEL MACK'S 1874 REPORT** are not all Civil War casualties.

The figures on the numbers who died during the Civil War are from the Medical and Surgical History of the War of the Rebellion (1861-1865). Besides the data on deaths caused by disease, the 3 volume set also contains field reports from surgeons. These reports often give locations of field hospitals. A researcher can use these reports along with this book to identify where casualties from a battle were reinterred.

Information on the history of forts was adapted from Robin Robert's Encyclopedia of Historic Forts. Unfortunately Mr. Roberts died in 1987 just before his book was published.

At first all national cemeteries were under control of the Quartermaster's Department. In 1933, thirteen cemeteries were transferred to the new National Park Service. In 1973 most of the rest of the cemeteries were transferred to the Veterans Administration (now the Department of Veterans Affairs). In 1994 the VA operated 113 national cemeteries. The National Park Service operated 14 national cemeteries. The Army still controlled two national cemeteries. A list of national cemeteries is included in the appendix.

The Department of Veterans' Affairs has microfilmed lists of veterans buried in cemeteries under VA control. These lists are by year of interment. Because a veteran's body might have been moved to a cemetery not under VA control, it is difficult to verify the burial site of a veteran. The VA does not have records of many soldiers listed in the Roll of Honor series. It appears these lists were made from headstone orders. Headstones were not installed in national cemeteries until 1873. If a soldier's wooden headboard decayed, he was listed as an unknown.

The National Park Service is supposed to be developing a computer data base with the names of veterans buried in cemeteries under NPS control. The Park Service has not answered four requests for information on this system.

The U.S. Army operates both Arlington National Cemetery and Soldiers Home National Cemetery. The Army also operates several post cemeteries. These cemeteries quickly respond to written inquires. Vancouver Barracks, Oregon, and Fort Riley, Kansas, are examples of active post cemeteries. A list of these post cemeteries is in the appendix. Some post cemeteries were abandoned. The bodies from Camp Collins, Colorado, were moved to a new cemetery by the local GAR Post.

The U.S. Navy also operated cemeteries. This book lists some of the cemeteries, however no list of names of sailors buried in these cemeteries has been located.

ACKNOWLEDGMENTS

No one writes a book in a vacuum. Many people helped me during the six years I was researching this book. Really I thought the project would only take a year or two but the birth of our daughter and four major eye surgeries changed my plans. I must thank:

My wife of 23 years, Patty Hughes. Without her understanding, moral support, and typing, this book could never have been written.

The staff at the National Archives. Despite the horror stories I'd heard, I never had a problem. (except the time four archivists sent me on a wild goose chase to the Suitland Branch of the Archives, the records were in the Archives all the time) The entire staff from the archivists to the search room staff to the guards were always helpful. Most horror stories come from people who just drop by the Archives and expect to learn their entire family history in one afternoon.

Two archivists were especially helpful:

Mr. Rodney Ross of the Legislative Archives Branch went out of his way to help me find and copy material. Without his help I never would have identified a major source.

Mr. William Lind of the Military Reference Branch has over forty years of experience. He always had time to help me locate sources despite the fact his branch handles over 2,000 telephone inquiries a month. Mr. Lind never gave me any bad information.

Mr. Larry Freeman, Orangeburg-Calhoun Technical College's reference librarian. He ordered many books on interlibrary loan and provided valuable advice as did Mrs. Carolyn Torrance, reference librarian at Southwestern Oklahoma State University.

Mr. Jim Conallen, former computer science instructor at Orangeburg-Calhoun Technical College, who would patiently explain to me how to use DOS and Word Perfect.

Mr. Harold Green, Chairman of the Industrial-Technology Division, and Mr. Pat Black, Vice-President for Academic Affairs of Orangeburg-Calhoun Technical College, for their support and encouragement.

Dr. David Norris, Professor of History at Southeastern Oklahoma State University, who encouraged me to start this project. Dr. Norris read the introduction and made valuable suggestions. However the errors are mine. Mr. Alan Lamm also made valuable suggestions.

My mother, Clara Humphries Hughes, who helped proofread some of the text. Again the mistakes are mine.

Mr. Hammond Wyle and Mrs. Rebecca Grantland for their help with the idiosyncrasies of the English language.

Mr. Don Cunningham, WB4QAQ, and Mr. Carl Kilgus, WA4DFP, for their help with the pictures.

xv

Finally the faculty and staff of Orangeburg-Calhoun Technical College who patiently listened to my progress and disappointments. Stories about dead soldiers and cemeteries are not normal lunch topics, but they never complained. Thanks.

SECTION 1

BURYING THE UNION DEAD:
An Overview

The muffled drum's sad roll has beat
The soldier's last tattoo

BURYING THE UNION DEAD: AN OVERVIE

The first national attempt to provide for burial of Amei
who were killed in battle was the purchase of land for a ce
Mexico City. The 1850 law appropriated $10,000 for "purchasi ɔ, ..ɑɪɪɪɪɡ,
and ditching" land for burial of casualties of the Mexican War and United
States citizens who died in Mexico. No more money was appropriated for
this cemetery until 1873. By then the country would have spent over four
million dollars on burying the soldiers killed in the Civil War.

A total of 1,733 United States soldiers were killed in action during the
Mexican War (1846-48). In the first Battle of Manassas the Union Army
suffered 481 men killed in action. In April 1862 the Battle of Shiloh cost
Grant's army 1,735 killed outright. Many wounded died later either in field
hospitals or general hospitals in the rear. Many other wounded died en route
to the rear. Other wounded soldiers were sent home to recover. An
unknown number of these died. Some officials estimated that as many as
50,000 soldiers "died at home" during the war.

In 1870 the army's Surgeon General reported a total of 303,504
deaths:

Regular Army Officers	267
Regular Army Enlisted Men	4,592
Volunteer Officers	8,553
Volunteer Enlisted Men	256,427
U.S. Colored Troops - Officers (White)	285
U.S. Colored Troops - Enlisted Men	33,380
	303,504

The best estimate on the number of deaths caused by battle and
disease are:

Killed in Action	44,238
Died of Wounds	49,205
Suicide, Homicide, and Execution	526
Disease	186,216
Unknown Causes	24,184
Total	304,369

These totals are slightly different, but few records pertaining to the
war are exact. Disease was the major killer during the war. It claimed
about two of every three soldiers who died.

3

The Surgeon General reported 5,825,480 "admissions to sick call." The major killers were:

Disease	Cases	Deaths
Typhoid Fever	75,368	27,056
Diarrhea	1,325,714	30,481
Dysentery	259,482	7,313
Consumption	13,499	5,286
Inflammation of the Lungs	61,202	14,738
Smallpox	12,236	4,717
Measles	67,763	4,246

Medical care in the 1860's was primitive at best by modern day standards. Antibiotics did not exist. Almost nothing could be done for soldiers who had been shot in the trunk except maybe probe the wound with unclean instruments trying to find the bullet. Bullets in the arm, leg, or hands normally were treated by amputation. The amputation lessened the danger of infection and lead poisoning but the blood loss often caused fatal shock.

Many soldiers would have rather been killed outright than injured and suffer because of the "state of the medical art." One soldier wrote "hell will be filled with doters (sic)..." One of the author's great-great grandfathers was wounded in the arm at Spotsylvania Court House. He refused to let the surgeon amputate his arm, deciding the risk of infection was less than the risk of surgery. He was lucky. He survived. Many didn't.

Lt. Col. E.B. Whitman, writing in 1868, explained a major cause of death of soldiers in Kentucky: "...when the hospitals at the front were crowded that those least sick, called 'convalescents' (often a sad misnomer) were sent to the rear, compelled to travel in army wagons, and at times over almost impassable roads. Exposure to wet and cold caused them to die by scores. In some cases they froze and died in the wagons, and sometimes they were left at cheerless cabins by the wayside to experience a more lingering fate, and at length to be buried by stranger hands in door-yards, or in rude family burying grounds. On one occasion no less than 19 deaths occurred in a company of convalescents sent from Cumberland Gap, before they reached London, a distance of 50 miles."

Two civilian groups were established to help care for sick and wounded soldiers: the United States Christian Commission and the United States Sanitary Commission. Without the help from these volunteer agencies and thousands of volunteer nurses (including Clara Barton) many more Union Soldiers would have died.

On September 11, 1861, the War Department issued General Order # 75. This order made the commanding officers of military departments and corps responsible for burial of dead soldiers. However very few soldiers

4

killed in battle received any more than a quick burial. Many soldiers killed in action were buried in trenches if at all. Trench burials were quick. A trench was dug, the bodies rolled or thrown in, and then the trench was covered with dirt.

Most Union Army units were made up of troops from one state. These troops were very loyal to each other. Often each state regiment buried their dead comrades. When a reburial party examined the Perryville, Ky., battlefield after the war, they found a total of 20 regimental trenches. Each contained from five to twenty-nine bodies. The 1st Wisconsin Infantry and the 79th Pennsylvania Infantry had built a stone wall around their comrades' graves. Eight hospital trenches contained from 15 to 55 bodies each.

Robert Hoffsommer writing in Civil War Times describes a labor saving technique: "Where bodies lay fairly close, the burial details usually dug a shallow hole for one body, rolled it in; dug another hole beside it, covering the corpse with the excavated earth; rolled another body into the new hole; dug again, covering the second body with earth from the third hole, and so on until all were buried." However photographs from the era seldom show this type of burial.

Sometimes friends of soldiers would bury their dead friends in separate graves. They would often carve the dead soldiers name on a nearby tree. Today a tree stump shaped monument at Shiloh National Military Park reads:

J.D. Putman

CO F 14

WV

Putman's friends had carved his name on a tree stump.

The War Department issued General Order # 33 on April 3, 1862. It read: "In order to secure, as far as possible, the decent interment of those who have fallen, or may fall, in battle, it is made the duty of commanding generals to lay off lots of graves in some suitable spot near every battlefield, and to cause the remains of those killed to be interred, with headboards bearing grave numbers, and when practicable, the name of the persons buried in them. A register of each burial ground will be preserved, in which will be noted the marks corresponding with headboards."

The important phrase in General order # 33 was: "as far as possible." Normally burials were made by fatigue details of soldiers. Because defeating the Confederacy was the goal of the Union Commanders, they seldom detailed large groups of soldiers for burial details. Few battlefield cemeteries were started during the war.

The headboards specified in General Order # 33 were normally supplied by the Quartermaster's Department. Headboards were wooden boards. Captain (later Brevet Colonel) James Moore, described the headboards as being made of white pine. They were painted white and lettered in black. Capt. Moore found that if the headboards were not painted first, the wood would absorb the oil in the paint and the lead (lettering) would wash off. Headboards would also rot and decay. Sometimes people stole them for firewood. Headboards on Confederate graves were often used by exslaves for firewood. Sometimes forest fires destroyed the headboards. At the Shiloh Battlefield the boards were subject to the "annual ravages of fire."

On July 17, 1862, President Lincoln signed an omnibus act that included the following section: "That the President of United States shall have power, when in his opinion it shall be expedient, to purchase cemetery grounds and cause them to be securely enclosed, to be used as a National Cemetery for the soldiers who shall die in the service of the country." Twelve national cemeteries were established in 1862 pursuant to the provisions of this legislation:

Alexandria National Cemetery	Virginia
Annapolis National Cemetery	Maryland
Camp Butler National Cemetery	Illinois
Cypress Hills National Cemetery	New York
Danville National Cemetery	Kentucky
Fort Leavenworth National Cemetery	Kansas
Fort Scott National Cemetery	Kansas
Keokuk National Cemetery	Iowa
Loudon Park National Cemetery	Maryland
Mill Springs National Cemetery	Kentucky
New Albany National Cemetery	Indiana
Soldiers' Home National Cemetery	Washington, DC

Of the twelve cemeteries originally designated national cemeteries, only one, Mill Springs was located at the site of a battle. At Fort Scott and Fort Leavenworth the existing post cemetery was enlarged. The cemetery at Cypress Hills, in Brooklyn, was started to bury Confederate prisoners and their guards who were killed in a train wreck. The rest of the cemeteries were started in areas where large groups of soldiers had died in hospitals or training camps.

Burials of Union soldiers were the responsibility of the Quartermaster Corps. The Quartermaster General was Montgomery C. Meigs. Meigs was a competent administrator with an eye for detail. However his ego had caused him problems earlier in his career. Meigs was a civil engineer. He had worked well with Jefferson Davis while Davis was Secretary of War in the early 1850's. However in the late 1850's a disagreement arose with the new Secretary of War, John Floyd. During this disagreement Meigs was almost court martialed. According to his biographer, Russell Weigley, " he (Meigs) proceeded to demonstrate a nice skill in impaling an enemy upon an acid pen." Unfortunately his penmanship lacked a lot. Even Weigley

complained of Meigs' "abominable handwriting characteristics." ⅃
better luck with the next Secretary of War, Edwin Stanton.

Meigs was breveted Major General of Volunteers on July 5, ⅃
He had became Quartermaster General in 1861. He shaped the developme.
of the National Cemetery System until his forced retirement in 1882 at age
65.

Meigs had strong Southern ties. In fact Jefferson Davis helped his
oldest son win an appointment to West Point in 1859. When war came
Meigs began to hate any U.S. Regular Army officer who "went South".
Meigs seemed to dislike his former commander, Robert E. Lee, the most.
Meigs would soon have a chance to "fix Lee."

Lee's wife, Mary Anne Custis Lee, was a granddaughter of George
Washington. She had inherited the beautiful 1,100 acre Custis-Lee estate in
Arlington, Va. The Custis-Lee Mansion overlooked Washington. Soon after
the war began, Mrs. Lee moved south. The Federal army soon occupied the
estate. In 1862 Congress passed a law that allowed tax commissioners to
collect taxes on property in "insurrectionary" districts. Even though Mrs.
Lee tried to send money to pay the taxes (less than $100) the commissioners
refused to accept payment except from Mrs. Lee. The government then
"purchased" the land at a "tax sale."

After the sale a refugee village was established on the estate. The ex-
slaves (contrabands) had flocked to Washington. Many died and were
buried on the estate.

Soldiers who died in Washington were buried in the U.S. Military
Asylum (Soldiers' Home) National Cemetery. The cemetery filled rapidly.
When it closed on May 13, 1864, a total of 5,211 burials had been made.
Meigs had decided to punish Lee by ruining Arlington. He ordered soldiers
to be buried in the Custis-Lee Mansion's rose garden. At first the order was
not carried out. The first burials were made in the northeastern section of
the estate instead of Mrs. Lee's rose garden. As Meigs wrote later: "This
was an error which I corrected as soon as I discovered it." On June 15,
1864, Meigs recommended to Secretary of War Stanton that the 200 acres
around the mansion be made a national military cemetery. Stanton approved
the recommendation the same day!

The seize of Lee's estate was illegal. In 1877, George Washington
Custis Lee, Robert E. Lee's oldest son, sued to recover the estate. The
United States Supreme Court upheld Lee's claim. It was impractical to
remove the graves, so in 1883 Lee accepted $150,000 as payment for the
estate.

Meigs soon had another reason to hate Southerners. On October 3,
1864, his oldest son, Lt. John R. Meigs was killed in the Shenandoah Valley
of Virginia. Young Meigs had graduated first in his class at West Point in
1863. He was General Philip Sheridan's chief engineer when he was killed
in a chance encounter with three Confederates. General Meigs always

believed that his son was murdered and offered a $1,000 reward for his son's killer. George Skoch, who wrote an article on the younger Meigs' death, believes that Meigs was killed in a "fair fight."

General Meigs did not bury his son in Arlington. He instead had him buried in Georgetown's Oak Hill Cemetery. In 1864 Arlington was not the place of honor it is today. Perhaps Meigs remembered that the Mexico City Cemetery had not received any funding since it was started in 1850. Perhaps Meigs didn't want his son's final resting place to deteriorate as the Soldiers' Home Cemetery had. After General Meigs died in 1892, his son's body was moved to Arlington.

In Meigs' 1864 report to the Secretary of War, Col. James Moore wrote: "The miserable condition of the cemetery in the vicinity of the Old Soldiers' Home, and the frequent complaints of persons respecting (sic) it..." led to improvements. Captain Moore in his report states: "the improvements of the National Cemeteries have been a source of great gratification to all who visit them, and entirely dissipated the prevailing opinion of those living remote from Washington that soldiers were irreverently or carelessly buried." Moore was not correct. In 1864, General Meigs wrote Secretary of War Edwin Stanton that up to forty soldiers a day were buried in Arlington without any religious ceremony. Some grave diggers told General Meigs that they hadn't seen a chaplin in three weeks. Meigs requested that a chaplin be detailed from a local military hospital to handle burials.

Burials at other cemeteries received greater care. Harper's New Monthly Magazine in August 1864 described the procedure followed at the military hospital at Hampton, Virginia. The name, company, and date of death of each soldier was painted on both the inside and outside of the coffin lid. All burials included military honors including the firing of a volley of musketry. The grave was then marked by a headboard with the soldier's name, company, and date of death.

This care included carefully recording the burials. Of 5,129 burials in the Hampton National Cemetery, 4,678 (91.2%) were of known soldiers. This is one of the highest rates of known soldiers in any Civil War era cemetery.

As soon as the war ended, the Quartermaster's department began to bury the Union dead. On June 7, 1865, Captain James Moore was dispatched to the Wilderness and Spotsylvania Court House Battlefields. Moore arrived on June 12th and spent 13 days burying the dead. Moore laid out two cemeteries at the Wilderness Battlefield. The first held 108 men, the second, 534 men. Moore wrote: "The bones of these men were gathered from the ground where they fell, having never been interred; and by exposure to the weather for more than a year all traces of their identify were entirely obliterated."

At Spotsylvania Court House, Moore found that very few soldiers remained unburied. General Sherman while marching to Washington after the war had made an agreement with a Mr. Sandford to bury the Union dead. Moore's group marked over 700 graves at Spotsylvania Court House.

Captain Moore intended to rebury the bodies of soldiers who had been partly buried in a cemetery, "but the weather being extremely warm, and the unpleasant odor from decayed animal matter so great, as to make the removal impracticable. They were, however, carefully re-covered with earth and entirely hidden from view."

Moore also reported that: "Hundreds of graves on these battlefields are without any marks whatever to distinguish them, and so covered with foliage that the visitor will be unable to find the last resting place of those who have fallen until the rains and snows of winter wash from the surface the light covering of earth and expose their remains." These bodies were reinterred in the Fredericksburg National Cemetery some time before 1869.

Most reburials had to wait until the fall of 1865 because of the danger of spread of disease from the decaying bodies. On June 23, 1865, Major General George Thomas dispatched Chaplin William Earnshaw to the Stone's River Battlefield to begin construction of a new national cemetery. However because of the danger of spread of disease, Earnshaw could not begin disinterments until the first of October. Earnshaw then began his work with almost religious fervor. He reported finding "with great difficulty" the remains of every Union soldier who fell at Hoover's Gap. At Guy's Gap his burial party found the exact number of dead that General Rosecrans had reported.

Earnshaw's party placed each body in a separate coffin. Any name found at the burial site was copied on the coffin lid and recorded in Earnshaw's record book. A new headboard was prepared in the field, so the grave in the national cemetery could be marked. Earnshaw felt that preparing headboards in the field helped reduce errors that might be made back at the national cemetery.

Earnshaw's group then followed "each road which our army moved at various times, searching the entire country and tracing obscure by-ways, feeling it our solemn duty to find every solitary Union soldier's grave that marked the victorious path of our men in pursuit of the enemy. We also visited all points where camps or garrisons were stationed." The search extended some 90 miles from the cemetery.

Earnshaw reported: "Many persons who have dear friends buried here will be deeply interested to know whether the work of removal was done with that care actually demanded in such a holy cause. I can only reply that all that true men could do was done. All my assistants were brave soldiers who had served throughout the war-men who could sympathize with those far away who mourn the loss of their loved ones, but who could not be present to perform for them this last sad office. Long as I live I shall remember how tenderly they performed this work amid untold difficulties;

how cheerfully they set out on long and toilsome journeys through rain and storm in search of their fallen comrades, and the proud satisfaction expressed by them when the precious remains were laid in the new made grave.

"From the hundreds of letters and visits of those who have friends in this cemetery I have learned something of the deep solicitude felt by them to be sure that all is right; and the daily inquiry - 'Are you sure that this is the grave of my dear son, husband, father, or brother?' (as the case may be) has very deeply impressed us all with the conviction that we cannot be too vigilant in honoring our sacred trust."

Not all burials of Union soldiers were done by Federal troops. Thousands of bodies were moved by friends and relatives. A brief article in the September 15, 1865, New York Times announced that removal of bodies from Virginia could begin the first of October. If Troops stationed nearby had wagons, the wagons could be used to carry the bodies to the nearest railroad station or port.

A letter from William Leonard, hospital Chaplin at Wilmington, N.C., was printed in the August 13th edition of the New York Times. Leonard stated that no bodies could be moved until November. F.W. Foster, a former agent of the United States Sanitary Commission, would disinter, disinfect, and ship north any bodies in the area. Foster had access to all records and could save relatives the expense of going to Wilmington.

Thousands of soldiers were moved to the North and reburied in family plots or public cemeteries. Some of the names of these burials in "private lots" are recorded in the Roll of Honor series but most are not. Col. Oscar Mack, Inspector of National Cemeteries, wrote in 1871: "There is scarcely a grave-yard in New England, and throughout the North, that does not contain the bodies of Union soldiers." As many as 40,000 bodies may have been moved north.

Congress passed a joint resolution on April 13, 1866, authorizing and requiring the Secretary of War "to take immediate measures to preserve from desecration the graves of soldiers of the United States who fell in battle or died of disease in hospitals...; to secure suitable burial places in which they may be properly interred; and to have the graves enclosed so that the resting places of the honored dead may be kept sacred forever."

On February 22, 1867, Congress passed "An act to establish and protect national cemeteries." This act required the Secretary of War to enclose cemeteries with a stone or iron fence, mark graves with a "small headstone or block", and keep a register of burials.

Superintendents were to be appointed from disabled enlisted men. The superintendents could arrest people who damaged any property in the cemetery. Lodges would be erected to house the potters (superintendents).

The bill also allowed the Secretary of War to purchase any "real estate in his judgment (that) is suitable and necessary for the purpose (of establishing cemeteries)." The act also allowed the Secretary of War to appropriate land for cemeteries. Of course most of the burials during the war had been made in appropriated land. A total of $750,000 was appropriated to establish and improve cemeteries.

More removals to national cemeteries were made in 1867 and 1868. By that time it was difficult to identify the graves that had not been marked by headboards. An updated newspaper clipping in the Antietam file states: "Nothing now remains of most of the bodies but the bones. In some cases the flesh has not decayed, but appears to have dried."

Brevet Major E.B. Whitman described problems in identifying the graves in the Department of the Tennessee. He believed that many problems in mortuary records were due to inexperience. However he wrote: "Doubtless, in many instances, the mortuary records were neglected or left incomplete from the influence of circumstances beyond the control of the officer in charge; but oftener from inexperience and want of forethought, and sometimes, unquestionably, from culpable and inexcusable neglect.

"In several cases a large number of internments were made by contractors, and the records and grave-marks were the work of illiterate or careless employees. Frequently the lists kept by hospital stewards and quartermasters' clerks, intended to be correct, have been rendered of comparatively little value from barbarous spelling and bad or careless penmanship.

"Many burials have been made by troops on detached service or on the march. The regimental returns alone will show any official record of these; and the only source of information within reach is to be found in the inscriptions or marks at the grave itself-sometimes a half-obliterated penciling upon a rough board, or a rude carving upon a neighboring tree."

Whitman used hospital records, quartermaster burial records, undertaker's burial lists, chaplain's reports, and the records of contractors who had reinterred bodies to identify the graves in his district.

Brevet Colonel C.W. Folsom served as Inspector of National Cemeteries in 1868 and 1869. He wrote in the March 25, 1869, issue of Nation about identifying the bodies reinterred in national cemeteries: "Every pains was taken to preserve all memorials of identity, from the scrap of a letter hastily pinned on the breast or buried in a can or bottle with the remains, up to the rudely-ornamented headboard which comrades provided were more time was allowed" Col. Folsom's article is one of very few written about national cemeteries in the late 1800's.

Chaplin Thomas Van Horne served as Superintendent at Chattanooga National Cemetery during 1865-6. He oversaw the reburial of over 8,500 soldiers in the cemetery. He reported removing 1,952 bodies from the Chickamauga Battlefield. Of this only 154 were identified. The Union forces had been driven from the battlefield and Confederates buried all but about 800 of the dead. Some forty officers bodies were found, but their exact rank was unidentifiable. Very few buttons or shoulder straps could be found on the bodies. In fact coats and shirts were sometimes taken from the bodies but the "trowsers" almost always were left. The blue mould left by their decay, usually "furnished corroborative evidence of loyal identity."

"Freshets" (floods) in western rivers and epidemics of yellow fever and cholera slowed removals during the summer of 1867. Work was suspended during the southern "hot season" for "preservation of the public health". Cholera was a major threat. 175 U.S. Colored Troops, stationed at Jefferson Barracks, Missouri, died of cholera during August 1866.

By 1868 a total of 257,533 bodies had been buried in 72 national and 320 post and local cemeteries. A local cemetery could have one or two graves up to several hundred graves. Bodies were still being found but as the unknown writer of the Vicksburg National Cemetery's description in volume 24 of the Roll of Honor wrote: "None but the unknown, however, are now found, and after so long a lapse of time, and in soil like that on the banks of the Mississippi, it must soon become impossible, if it is not already so, to distinguish the remains of a soldier from those of a citizen." By 1871 a total of 305,492 burials of Union Soldiers were reported.

Sometimes burials of soldiers killed in action were made by local residents. The original burials at Perryville, Kentucky, were made by three local farmers: H.D. Bottom, J.C. Russell, and David Wikinson. Their motives may not have been totally humanitarian. They moved the bodies so they could again cultivate their fields without disturbing bodies. However they identified over 31% the bodies they buried, not a bad percentage.

A total of 241 Federal soldiers were buried in Richmond's Kentucky, City Cemetery. Only 38 could be identified after the war. The author of volume 17 of the Roll of Honor attributed this to many burials being made by Confederates who failed to mark the graves and "somewhat to the indifference of people in the vicinity to preservation of any gravemarks left by friends".

Undoubtedly many Southerners did little to preserve the graves of Union soldiers. In August 1866, Henry M. LeDue, superintendent of a U.S. Burial Corps party near Point of Rocks, Virginia, wrote Brevet Lt. Col. James Moore about problems his party had encountered with a Mr. William Perdue. LeDue's men had received reports of bodies buried on Perdue's land and in his garden. Perdue denied knowledge of any bodies on his land. However the next day, LeDue received more information about the locations of the bodies. His party removed six bodies. Believing more bodies were hidden, LeDue questioned the colored residents in the area. After being promised anonymity, a lady told LeDue that the mounds over the graves had been plowed over.

Armed with this information the burial party found forty-seven bodies in a pit under Perdue's pea vines. Perdue later acknowledged that he had seen the mounds, but didn't think anyone would remove the bodies. The "women of the house" told the burial party: "Go and find them (the bodies).

They did not want any 'dammed Yankee bones'." Although LeDue wanted an example made of Perdue, there is nothing in the records to indicate that any action was taken against him.

Volume 16 of the Roll of Honor lists the places that bodies moved to the Richmond National Cemetery were found. Some examples are: five bodies recovered from Johnson's farm near Taylorsville. "No one knew who they were, but their clothing and equipment showed them to be Union soldiers." Five unknown soldiers were found on Green's farm, near Bumpass Turnout. These men had been wounded and taken prisoner. They were left in an outhouse and died there. One mass grave of soldiers was found in a hollow. The bodies were "covered with dirt and rails." Col. Folsom, writing in 1868, wrote: "the indications of graves in very many instances were almost entirely obliterated, being grown over with briers, cane, and other woods; and not unfrequently (sic) the soil had been cultivated and the graves so worked over as to render it impossible to locate them from any indications on the surface.

"These difficulties were increased by the hostile sentiments of the residents in many localities, not only to those engaged in this sacred work, but even to the dead themselves."

Of course some Southerners objected to their land being used without payment. B.B. Dykes, who owned the land at the Andersonville National Cemetery, did not receive payment for the land used for a cemetery until February 1875. Dykes threatened to "plant a vineyard" on the cemetery. He was reported to have boasted "dead Yankees would make good wine".

Not only were some Southerners opposed to burial parties removing bodies from their land, they were also bitterly opposed to locating national cemeteries in their area. The Inspector General of National Cemeteries, Lorenzo Thomas, wrote in 1869 about the Wilmington National Cemetery: "The feeling of the community is not favorable to the cemetery, and shrubbery, though abundant, cannot be obtained except at high prices..."

Partly because of hostile Southerners, but mainly because that no effort was made to bury the dead until after the war, many graves were unmarked. For example in the Memphis National Cemetery 47.2% of the 9,754 white soldiers buried were known. However only 5.9% of the 4,208 colored troops buried there were known. At Wilmington National Cemetery 43% of the 1,469 white burials are known, but only 55 of the 557 colored troop buried there are known. Unfortunately often a very low percentage of burials of colored troops are of known soldiers.

But the problem was not limited to colored soldiers. Sixty two men of the 11th Illinois Infantry who were killed at Fort Donelson, Kentucky, were buried in one trench. Only two bodies were identified. Their names were appended to volume 23 of the Roll of Honor.

On January 3, 1867, Quartermaster General Meigs wrote Brevet Lt. Col. Moore: "...it is the desire of this department, where bodies of soldiers

13

are found separately buried,....that they should be reinterred in separate coffins".

Because of this order, very few mass burials of soldiers were made. In some cases it was almost impossible to separate bodies that had been buried together. Two large mass graves were used. At Arlington National Cemetery bodies from the Bull Run Battlefield were buried under a granite monument with the inscription:

BENEATH THIS STONE REPOSE THE BONES OF TWO THOUSAND ONE HUNDRED AND ELEVEN UNKNOWN SOLDIERS, GATHERED AFTER THE WAR FROM THE FIELDS OF BULL RUN, AND THE ROUTE TO THE RAPPAHANNOCK. THEIR REMAINS COULD NOT BE IDENTIFIED, BUT THEIR NAMES AND DEATHS ARE RECORDED IN THE ARCHIVES OF THEIR COUNTRY; AND ITS GRATEFUL CITIZENS HONOR THEM AS OF THEIR NOBLE ARMY OF MARTYRS. MAY THEY REST IN PEACE! SEPTEMBER, A.D.1866

Two mass graves at Cold Harbor National Cemetery hold the bodies of 889 unknown Union soldiers. A marble Sarcophagus was erected over the bodies in 1877. It's inscription reads:

NEAR THIS STONE REST THE REMAINS OF 889 UNION SOLDIERS GATHERED FROM THE BATTLEFIELDS OF MECHANICSVILLE, SAVAGE STATION, GAINES MILLS, AND THE VICINITY OF COLD HARBOR.

Over 1700 bodies were moved to the Cold Harbor National Cemetery in 1866. However a careful second search of the battlefields in 1867 uncovered almost 1,000 additional bodies. These bodies were moved to the Richmond National Cemetery.

Prisoners of War who died in prison camps were normally buried side by side in long trenches. At Andersonville, Georgia, the bodies could be identified because a copy of the burial register was saved by a former POW. Unfortunately at the Salisbury, North Carolina, and Florence, South Carolina, prisons it was impossible to identify individual graves. However these are not true mass graves, because the bodies were laid side by side, not thrown simply together in a pit.

Normally only bodies of Union soldiers were moved to national cemeteries. Quartermaster General Meigs decided that Colored employees of the Quartermaster's Department who were buried near Alexandria National Cemetery could not moved to the cemetery. The graves were on the property of the OI and M Railroad. The graves could be sodded by the superintendent however, according to the Quartermaster General.

Sometimes the reasoning behind a decision to move graves is unclear. The bodies of eight soldiers whose names were "carved on a large oak tree" at the Tupelo, Mississippi, Battlefield were ordered to be removed to a

14

national cemetery according to an unsigned/undated report filed under "Alabama" in the Quartermaster General's files. The report also states that the other bodies of Union soldiers at the site were to be left "provided the spirit of the citizens is such to allow these graves to remain undistributed when put in good condition. Otherwise, the remains had better be removed to some national cemetery although the distance involved in the removal is so great, that it would be desirable to avoid it if possible." It is unclear if the other bodies were moved. However some bodies from Tupelo were moved to Corinth National Cemetery.

Quartermaster General Meigs tried to hold expenses to a minimum. Often bodies were not moved to a secure national cemetery to save money. As the headboards marking the graves rotted, the graves were lost. Several hundred graves are known to have been abandoned this way.

On the other hand often bodies were shipped long distances when other national cemeteries were closer. Bodies from El Dorado Springs, Missouri, were moved over 300 miles to Memphis National Cemetery. The body of Corporal Louis C. Stockton was moved from Andersonville National Cemetery in Georgia to Chattanooga National Cemetery in Tennessee. No reason for this removal has been found. It was NOT the policy of the War Department to pay for moving bodies "home". That was up to friends and relatives.

The most unusual movement of bodies was that of moving 110 bodies from Springfield, Missouri, to Jefferson Barracks National Cemetery (near Saint Louis) in 1868. These bodies were moved over 200 miles when there was a national cemetery in Springfield! Nothing in the Quartermaster General's files explain this move. However it is possible that these removals were handled by the same contractor who was accused of burying coffins filled with sticks and stones at Jefferson Barracks National Cemetery. The December 29, 1867, edition of the <u>Washington Herald</u> claimed that the contractors had sold the bodied for "anatomical purposes." It would be easy for a contractor to make money by burying one body in two coffins. A Memphis newspaper charged that burial parties in the area were doing this. The paper also claimed that the body of Captain Champion of the 2nd Missouri (Confederate) Cavalry was moved to the Memphis National Cemetery despite the objections of local residents. The paper also claimed that the "party exhumed the remains of a great many Federal soldiers...tore off the coffin-lids, and left the bodies lying there exposed for two weeks and a half to the (sic) plain view of all passers-by, and to the depredations of the hogs and dogs." The Federal officer who sent this clipping to the War Department wrote "the whole article is without foundation."

In July 1867 <u>The Missouri Republican</u> printed a graphic report of a burial party that had dug up a woman's casket, chopped the body into pieces so it would fit into a small box , and moved the body to Jefferson Barracks, despite the protests of the woman's children. The Quartermaster who mailed

15

this article to the War Department stated that he had not authorized any removals from the Commerce, Missouri, area.

John Webb from Laurel, Maryland, wrote the Quartermaster's office in 1866 requesting the return of his sister-in-law's body. It had been moved "by mistake" to Arlington National Cemetery along with five other bodies. After an exchange of letters, it was returned without explanation or apology. Col. William Lamb, the Commander of Confederate forces at Fort Fisher, North Carolina, charged in the November 12, 1881, edition of the Philadelphia Times: "On revisiting Fort Fisher after the war I found that the post burial ground, where my soldiers who died previous to the battle were buried, had been robbed of all its dead, and was told that a contractor for the government had stolen their bodies in order to be paid for supplying them with coffins under any appropriation to bury the dead of the Northern Armies."

The amount contractors were paid to move bodies varied. J.P. Low of Charleston, South Carolina, was paid $6.00 per body to move bodies from Savannah, Georgia, to Beaufort National Cemetery in South Carolina. A Philadelphia Contractor was paid $13.40 to move bodies from one cemetery in Philadelphia to another.

Not all burials of Union soldiers were made by the Federal Government. Sometimes private groups arranged for burials. At Gettysburg, Pennsylvania, Pennsylvania's Governor Curtin was spurred to action when he visited the battlefield a week after the battle. Curtin contacted seventeen other Union states and proposed burying all Union dead in one cemetery. Removal of the dead began less than four months after the battle. F.W. Biesecker, a Gettysburg resident, exhumed the Union dead and reburied them in the new "national cemetery" for $1.59 per body.

"Loyal states" formed the Antietam National Cemetery Corporation in March of 1865. The corporation's goal was to bury the Union dead in and around Sharpsburg. However the group decided to build a stone wall and lodge before moving any bodies. The group quickly ran out of money and in 1866 the Quartermaster's Department took over the unfinished task of burying the dead.

In July 14, 1870, Congress voted to "accept and take charge of the soldier's national cemetery at Sharpsburg, Maryland, and Gettysburg, Pennsylvania, whenever the commissioners and trustees having charge of said cemeteries are ready to transfer their care to the general government." Gettysburg was transferred to the United States in 1870. However Antietam was not transferred until 1877 when Congress agreed to pay the trustees' $15,000 indebtedness.

Bodies of soldiers who died of certain highly communicable diseases posed a problem to workers moving bodies. Soldiers who died of smallpox at Murfreesboro, Tennessee, were buried in a separate cemetery near the "pest house." These bodies were moved to Stone's River National Cemetery in 1867 instead of 1866 when most burials were made.

Yellow fever victims were seldom moved. In 1876, Quartermaster General Meigs disapproved the plan to move the bodies of ten Union soldiers who had died of yellow fever during the Civil War form Santa Rosa Island to Barrancas National Cemetery. Meigs wrote: "...even if it can be done without danger it will disturb men's minds, who do not know that such a transfer is safe". In 1898, twenty two victims of yellow fever were buried in a separate cemetery at Hampton, Virginia. This cemetery, now called Hampton VA Medical Center National Cemetery, is the smallest national cemetery in the country.

When bodies were first buried in national cemeteries, the graves were "mounded" with dirt. Dirt was piled over the grave to form a mound 10 to 12 inches above ground level. As the coffin rotted, the dirt fell in the hole, keeping the bones from being exposed. If the grave settled too much, more dirt was added. This kept the risk of spread of disease. After a year or so, the excess dirt was removed and the graves resodded with grass.

Most of the time bodies were reinterred in cemeteries by regiments or at least by states. As Col. Folsom explained, he thought that friends (ex-comrades) of the soldiers would erect monuments to the dead. That rarely happened. The states instead spent money marking battlefields where the Northern armies won. For example, no Northern state has monuments at Bull Run or Chancellorsville, major Confederate victories. Instead Northern states marked the Gettysburg and Vicksburg battlefields.

At Shiloh National Cemetery, there are 29 regimental group burials. Soldiers from a total of 203 different regiments, not including colored troops, were buried at Shiloh.

The 1867 act that established national cemeteries provided for the purchase of land for cemeteries. During the war burials were made wherever the field commanders felt necessary. After the war land was acquired in various ways. H.G. Cole and his wife donated 20 acres to establish the Marietta National Cemetery. Cole wanted both Confederates and Union soldiers buried in the same cemetery, but a separate cemetery was established for Confederates. W.H. Logan and his wife donated land for the cemetery at Mill Springs, Kentucky. The town of Green Mount, Vermont, donated a soldiers' lot.

Arlington National Cemetery was purchased at a "tax sale", but the Supreme Court eventually ruled that the sale was illegal. The Federal Government purchased land for the Beaufort National Cemetery (South Carolina) at a tax sale for $75.00. The State of South Carolina's reconstruction government did not protest the sale.

Land for the Vicksburg National Cemetery (40 acres) and Stone's River National Cemetery (16 acres) were purchased outright. The Crown Hill Cemetery Association in Indianapolis offered to donate land for a national cemetery to the government if the United States would agree to send a "certain sum" on improvements. Because there were no appropriations designated for improvements, the United States purchased the land and the cemetery association spent the purchase price on the desired improvements.

Not all land for cemeteries was owned by the government. 62 known soldiers were buried in six lots owned by Detroit's Elmwood Cemetery. Huntsville, Alabama, offered to pay one half the cost of burring Union soldiers if the United States would pay the rest. The offer was marked "return". These bodies (perhaps as many as 670-the records were "very imperfect and meager") were moved to the Chattanooga National Cemetery. It is surprising the bodies were moved, considering Quartermaster General Meigs' views on moving the bodies at Tupelo.

The government's policy on land was bury now, pay later. The first burials in the Wilmington National Cemetery (North Carolina) were made on February 1, 1867. The land was purchased 20 days later. The record for not paying for land appears to be held by the Fort Scott National Cemetery. Parts of the Town of Fort Scott's cemetery and the local Presbyterian Church's cemetery were designated a national cemetery in 1862. The land was purchased in 1875.

Col. Folsom wrote in his 1868 report that the appropriation section of the 1867 act that established national cemeteries had failed. The board that appraised the ten acres of land appropriated from John Dameron at Knoxville set the price at $500 per acre even though land in the area was selling from $100 to $150 per acre. The government paid the $5,000.

Sometimes the land purchased was in a bad location. Major General T.J. Wood and Brevet Brigadier General H.M. Whittlely, assistant quartermaster, located the Vicksburg National Cemetery on a hillside. After the burials were made a heavy rain and snow storm caused mud slides on the hillside. Even the fence was carried away. In 1869 a Civil Engineer was hired to try to repair the damage. Two years later he was still at work with a crew of sixty men, fourteen mules, and two horses. He had installed drain tile throughout the cemetery. Then the hillside was rebuilt with gentle slopes. He then rearranged the graves before planting Bermuda-grass roots to hold the dirt. Over $261,000.00 had been spent on the cemetery by August 31, 1870.

Quartermaster General Meigs was not above appropriating land without paying for it. In May 1872, Meigs wrote Secretary of War W.W. Belknap about land appropriated for burial of Federal occupation troops in Charleston's, South Carolina, Magnolia Cemetery. The cemetery official had reserved the land that was appropriated for building a chapel. They offered to donate land for burial of the troops, if the Federal authorities would move the bodies to the new lot.

Meigs wrote: "I am against spending money on moving about the dead, where it is not absolutely necessary in order to collect the victims of the war into national cemeteries."

Meigs continued: "Do the dead bodies of our soldiers offend them"? Meigs' logic was that Charleston had been in revolt and then invested, making "this occupation is sacred." Meigs claimed that the Federal government had paid for the occupation of Charleston; and thus the cemetery, with "millions of money and much blood."

Belknap pointed out that the Act of 1867 could not be used in this case because the land was not needed as a national cemetery. The bodies were moved to the Florence National Cemetery at the "proper season of the year." The removal cost $800.

Meigs didn't approve of moving bodies that were buried in a cemetery either. Once, when asked his opinion on "scattering" the bodies of U.S. Colored Troops among the white soldiers in Arlington, he wrote: "I regret always to move a body once interred in a National Cemetery, believing the dead, once decently buried should have rest."

Not all cemeteries keep the same name. Memphis National Cemetery was once named Mississippi River National Cemetery. Monument National Cemetery near New Orleans became Chalmette National Cemetery.

Sometimes more than the name changed. Volume 18 of the Roll of Honor lists burials in Spring Grove National Cemetery at Cincinnati. The land had been donated to the United States by the state of Ohio. However in 1871 Col. Mack listed 932 burials in the soldier's lot at Spring Grove. However the Department of Veterans' Affairs does not list Spring Grove as a soldiers' lot nor do the files at the National Archives have any more information. However the Spring Grove Cemetery verifies that the United States Government does own the lot.

Why Spring Grove ceased to be a National Cemetery when Ball's Bluff National Cemetery in Virginia remained a National Cemetery is a mystery. Ball's Bluff had only 54 interments. In fact only 25 headstones were placed in the cemetery because in 1873 the War Department thought only 25 burials had been made in the cemetery. The cemetery could be reached by a roundabout, very poor, private road.

Many national cemeteries were in out of the way places. To reach Logan's Crossroads National Cemetery in Kentucky a traveler would take the train from Louisville to Stanford. Then the traveler would have to take a stage to Somerset. There was no public conveyance from Somerset to Logan's Crossroads, some eight miles to the west. The prospective visitor would have to secure transportation from private citizens.

Tompkinsville National Cemetery was a gift from a "loyal citizen", J.B. Evans. But because it was remote and small (only 115 bodies), it was closed and the bodies moved to Nashville National Cemetery. Cumberland Gap National Cemetery and Shreveport National Cemetery were also moved to larger cemeteries.

Prisoners of war were a special problem during the war. Congress passed a joint resolution on December 11, 1861, that requested President

19

Lincoln "be requested to inaugurate systematic measures for the exchange of prisoners in the present rebellion." The resolution also stated that "such an exchange does not invade a recognition of the rebels as a government..."

The exchange program worked well until the fall and winter of 1863. Then the program to fall apart. Part of the problem was the Confederate Government's views on Negro troops. The Confederate Congress's response to Lincoln's Emancipation Proclamation was passed on May 1, 1863. The law had two parts: officers of Negro troops "shall be deemed as inciting servile insurrection." This meant the officers could be hanged. Negro troops were to be delivered to state authorities. Although some officials wanted to make an example of Negro soldiers, the official policy was stated by H.L. Clay, Assistant Adjutant General, on July 13, 1863. Clay wrote: "Considering the Negroes as deluded victims, they should be received and treated with mercy and returned to their owners. A few examples might perhaps be made, but to refuse them quarter would only make them, against their tendencies, fight desperately."

As the exchange cartel fell apart, charges of mistreatment of POW's were made by both sides. General Braxton Bragg (CSA) in May 1863 claimed that Confederate prisoners were robbed of blankets, overcoats, watches, and personal items. General H.W. Halleck (USA) replied that POW's were supplied with blankets and clothes.

Prisoners were crowded in overcrowded, filthy prisons. The Confederate Prison Camp at Cahaba, Alabama, had only one source of water, an artisan well. Water traveled 200 feet along an open street gutter before it reached the prison. One report stated: "In its course it has been subjected to the washings (sic) of the heads, feet, faces, and heads of soldiers, citizens, and Negroes, buckets, tubs, and spittoons of groceries, offices and hospital, hogs, cows, and horses, and filth of all kinds from the streets and other sources."

As the Union naval blockage tightened, food and medicine became more scarce. However packages sent to "our starving soldiers in southern prisons" were returned.

But the South did not have a monopoly on poor prisons. In an 1864 report, William Watson reported on deaths that occurred in January and February, 1864, at the Rock Island, Illinois, prison camp. He wrote: "157 died of 637 cases of smallpox. 173 died in 927 cases of other diseases.... a ratio of mortality almost unheard of in modern hospitals.... It is almost a wonder the mortality was not greater."

A.M. Clark wrote about one Federal prison: "From the utter want of attention to sanitary management...it is only to be wondered at that the sick list and mortality is not much greater than it is." About another prison he wrote: "I can say no word for this building except in unqualified condemnation. It is overcrowded and extremely filthy in every part, and its keeper, a civilian, is utterly unqualified for his post."

In March 1865, 6.9% of the Confederate prisoners at Elmira, N.Y., died in one month. In February 1863, 387 of the 3,884 Confederates help in Camp Douglas, Illinois, died. This is a death rate of almost 10% (9.96%). Exact figures of Union POW death are unavailable. However 127 men died in one day at the Andersonville Prison.

Although Andersonville's commandant, Captain Henry Wirz, was hung for "war crimes", the real cause of death in prison camps was overcrowding. It was impossible to maintain sanitation in overcrowded prisons. Both sides also had their share of poor leadership. But overcrowding was the main cause. A contraband camp was set up on Robert E. Lee's Arlington estate. On July 17, 1862, Congress allocated $50,000 for medicine for these ex-slaves. Still a total of 3,235 died.

According to volume 3 of the Roll of Honor a total of 12,912 prisoners died at Andersonville. Volume 14 of the series lists 10,959 burials at other locations. Volume 19 of the Roll of Honor added 2,797 burials at Florence, South Carolina. This gives a total of 26,668 Union prisoners who died. Sometime between 1868 and 1871, Federal authorities "discovered" 8,000 more graves at the Salisbury, North Carolina, prison camp. The discovery was three additional burial trenches. However it appears that the additional bodies never existed. (For more information see the article on the Salisbury Prison).

Although the proposed treatment of colored troops was an excuse to suspend exchanges of prisoners, the real reason was the Union's realization that exchanged Confederates were returning to front line units while many Union prisoners were leaving the army because their enlistments had expired. As Major James D. Jones, drillmaster at Andersonville, wrote: "And may I ask, whose fault was it that there was no exchange of prisoners? We would gladly have given 10 for 1 (and we had them to give) but no! The policy of the Federal government was to exhaust the South. That was General Grant's policy; and the only one that was a success."

On June 30, 1865, Captain James Moore, just back from the wilderness battlefield, was dispatched to Andersonville to mark the graves of the prisoners. His report is typical of descriptions of Andersonville. He describes the residents: "The inhabitants of this sparsely-settled locality are, with few exceptions of the most ignorant class, and from their haggard and sallow faces the effects of chills and fever are distinctly visible." Moore claimed Andersonville chosen as a prison site because it was in the most unhealthy part of the state. He also describes conversations with ex-Confederates. He found the ex-soldiers as very penitent. The residents who did not go off to war were much less ashamed of Andersonville.

Moore failed to mention that Clara Barton and Dorence Atwater had urged Secretary of War Stanton to have the graves marked as soon as possible. Atwater was a 20 year old former prisoner who had served as Andersonville's Clerk of the dead. He had smuggled a copy of

Andersonville's burial register out of prison. Instead of being hailed a hero, Atwater was sent to prison for attempting to have the roster printed. He was later pardoned and made the ambassador to Tahiti. (For more about Atwater's problems see Andersonville National Cemetery in section 3).

One reason for Captain Moore's descriptions of Andersonville is that the War Department could have saved many of Andersonville's victims by diverting part of Sherman's army there after the fall of Atlanta. Hood took his Confederate army toward Franklin, Tennessee where his army was beaten in late November. Sherman could have sent 10,000 men to the stockade without serious loss of manpower. Instead he set off toward Savannah on his famous march to the sea.

Sherman's march actually cost lives of prisoners. In October, 1864, some 7,000 prisoners were sent from Andersonville to a site near Lawton, Georgia. The site had a good supply of clear water, a major problem at Andersonville. Still 725 men died in two months. As Sherman's army approached, the prisoners were taken back to Andersonville. The graves of the dead prisoners at Lawton were marked by numbered stakes, but the burial register disappeared. It was believed to have been destroyed by fire, however a copy of the register later surfaced in Philadelphia! No one knows exactly how the register escaped the fire, much less traveled to Philadelphia.

Not all burials in national cemeteries were of soldiers. At least sixteen citizen prisoners were buried in the Washington area. These prisoners were not necessarily guilty of any crime. Lincoln had illegally suspended the writ of habeas corpus. Volume 2 of Series II of the Official Records contains a list of 100 "citizen prisoners" who were being held at Old Capitol Prison in Washington. Some were accused of spying or "shooting into camps", but twenty-eight men were being held "without the least record of evidence."

One example of such a "citizen prisoner" was that of W.H. Ward who wrote President Lincoln from Fort Lafayette Prison on October 15, 1861. Ward had resigned from the U.S. Navy on May 26, 1861. He "performed my duty to the government faithfully" until he was informed that his name had been stricken from the "Roll of the Navy" on August 12, 1861. After accepting passage home on a passing vessel, he was arrested without charge on August 31, 1861.

Of course thousands of Confederate prisoners died in Union prison camps. At first the Federal government made no attempt to care for the graves of former rebels. However as time passed, the South was reconstructed, and some Confederate burial sites were protected. The Secretary of War declared Finns Point, New Jersey, as a National Cemetery on October 3, 1875. The Governor of Virginia, James Kemper, had requested the War Department take steps to preserve the graves of 2,436 Confederates who died at Fort Delaware on Pea Patch Island. One hundred thirty-five Union soldiers were also buried there, so it was legal for the

Secretary of War to declare the site a national cemetery. Woodland Cemetery at the Elmira, New York, prison site was declared a national cemetery in 1877. A total of 106 Union soldiers and some 2,950 Confederates were buried there.

Not all War Department employees were in favor of the preservation of Confederate graves. The August 6, 1879, edition of the <u>Washington Post</u> reported that Secretary of War McCrary was "tongue lashed" by the senate committee on military affairs. McCrary had endorsed the report of Quartermaster General Meigs that the Government should not purchase the Confederate burial grounds at Champ Chase. If the site were not purchased, it was to be plowed up. Meigs felt the rebels were "the enemies of the United States." Congress approved the purchase.

In 1906 Congress allocated $200,000 to purchase and mark the graves of Confederate soldiers who died in Northern prisons and hospitals. A commissioner was appointed to oversee the marking of the graves. His report was later published. It contains the only official listing of Confederate dead. No one has published a complete roster of Confederate soldiers who died during the war.

The 1867 Act to establish national cemeteries also required that a register of the dead buried in each cemetery was to be kept at each cemetery and the War Department. In 1912 the Quartermaster General issued orders that the names in a cemetery's burial register could be changed only with approval from the Quartermaster's Department. Too many names were being changed by incorrect information given by visitors to the cemeteries.

Often families wrote Col. James Moore for information on their loved ones. About one hundred of these letters are preserved in the National Archives. Many of these inquiries were for information on soldiers who might have died in prison camps. Most of the time, if a soldier was killed in action, his regimental commander would write the family. Because most companies were formed in the same area, after the war comrades of a deceased soldier would tell the family what happened to their relative. In prison, however, this local tie did not exist. These families did not know the fate of their loved ones until after the war.

Not all the records that Col. Moore had were correct. In June, 1864, Henry Lantz, a clerk in the Indiana Military Agency, wrote Moore about apparent errors in the records. Lantz reported that Private Bennet M. Page of company I on the 126 Ohio Volunteers died on May 26, 1864. The records had Page dying in the wrong hospital. Also Page's leg was not amputated, his injury was to his hip.

At times the War Department had no idea how many soldiers were buried in some cemeteries. Ashland Cemetery near Carlisle Barracks, Pennsylvania, is a good example. In 1866 a total of 35 bodies were believed to have been buried in the cemetery. One undated list reports 53 burials. An 1878 file card states there were 313 bodies at Carlisle. The card includes the note: "I can find no evidence that the lots are owned by the U.S." However a 1890 "brief" reported 41 burials. Today the cemetery is marked with a bronze tablet noting 35 known burials and 500 unknown burials.

In order to allow relatives to find graves, the Quartermaster Department printed the 27 volume Roll of Honor Series. The four volume Disposition of bodies was produced in to allow relatives to locate the bodies of unknown soldiers. Only the first 13 volumes of the Roll of Honor series were indexed by place of burial. Some cemeteries, Grafton National for example, were never listed in the Roll of Honor series. Some cemeteries are listed more than once in the series. A total of 1894 burials (87.8% known) in the Knoxville National Cemetery were listed in volume 11 (1866). Volume 23 (1869) listed 1,256 additional burials (only 32.9% known).

Volume 9 of the series listed 532 burials "at Cleveland, Ohio." Volume 26 of the Roll of Honor lists 38 burials in Westside Cemetery (12 from Woodlawn). No record of the place of burial of the other 494 soldiers can be found. However, the same volume lists 38 burials in Cleveland's Woodlawn Cemetery (including removals from Westside). When Col. Mack inspected the Woodlawn Cemetery in 1870 he found 27 graves in the soldiers' lot and 16 other soldiers' graves in the lot belonging to the City of Cleveland. Mack reported a total 102 burials of soldiers in the cemetery. Most had died after the war but a few had been removed from the South. Apparently the information about the Westside Cemetery was in error. Such errors are not uncommon.

By 1868 the War Department had records of 257,258 burials. Not all were in National Cemeteries. In 1871 Col. Mack reported a total of 305,492 burials of soldiers (53.8% known):

151,237	known white soldiers (56.2%)
117,678	unknown white soldiers
13,176	known colored soldiers (39.7%)
20,043	unknown colored soldiers
3,358	unknown and unclassified
305,492	

A total of 6,741 citizens (about 4,000 contrabands) and 21,533 "rebels" had been buried. A summary of Col. Mack's report is in the appendix.

The 1867 Act to Establish National Cemeteries had required that the cemeteries be enclosed with an iron or stone fence. Most cemeteries had been originally enclosed by a paling (picket) fence. Because most localities had no fence laws the fence was needed to protect the graves from cattle. In 1871 Col. Mack noted that stray hogs had damaged the Danville, Kentucky, Cemetery. Most cemeteries were enclosed by stone walls by the mid-1870's.

Carriage roads and footpaths were graveled. In some Southern

24

localities sea shells were used. Gutters and drains were installed. Sometimes wooden culverts were installed. In a few years they rotted and collapsed. About 150 surplus cannons were erected as monuments. Most were mounted upright with 21 projectiles at each gun.

The 1867 Act to Establish National Cemeteries provided for erecting a "porter's lodge" at the cemeteries. A typical lodge cost between $3,000 and $5,000 to build. The Knoxville lodge was built in 1871 at a cost of $4,450.00.

The 1867 act that established national cemeteries did not specifically require that cemeteries be beautified. Because there was no specific approbation for flowers, trees, or shrubs, in 1868 superintendents were instructed to get trees from neighboring forests. The superintendents were also instructed to accept donations of plants. The 1870 appropriation bill included $20,000 for trees and shrubs. Most descriptions of cemeteries in the Roll of Honor series describe that beauty of the cemetery. An exception is Chalmette National Cemetery, near New Orleans, which is described as "...although naturally not very picturesque."

The superintendent of the Richmond National Cemetery had a small greenhouse attached to the cemetery. Col. Mack described the superintendent as "quite an amateur florist."

In a 1873 circular letter to cemeteries Quartermaster General Meigs outlined his views on plants in the cemeteries: "There should be vines at all lodges, both on the porches and against the brick or stone walls. Each lodge should have at least two good hardy grapevines and some ornamental creepers or climbers."

Sometimes when the cemetery was laid out space was left for a monument. At new Albany the space was "occupied by a cheap wooden structure, in imitation of a monument, erected by some of the citizens of New Albany."

Later metal flagstaffs were erected in the cemeteries. Rostrums were erected in some cemeteries for Decoration Day Programs. Roads were built into some cemeteries.

In 1881 the Rock Island Arsenal cast 275 iron tablets. The tablets replaced wooden signs that had Lincoln's Gettysburg Address, Rules for Visitors, and verses from Theodore O'Hare's Poem, "Bivouac of the Dead." O'Hare wrote the poem in honor of Mexican War dead.

"The muffled drum's sad roll has beat,
the soldiers' last tattoo,
no more on life's parade shall meet,
that brave and fallen few."

"On Fame's eternal camping ground
their silent tents are spread;
And glory guards with solemn round
The bivouac of the dead."

Someone in the Quartermaster's Department liked poetry. Each volume of the Roll of Honor has a verse from the poem on the front cover. Not everyone appreciated "good" poetry. A special correspondent for the Boston Thursday Spectator and Weekly Advertiser filed a report in 1868 on the Andersonville prison. He did not care for the poem which was written on wooden tablets placed in the cemetery. He wrote: "As soon as possible I hope Congress may make an appropriation to have these doggerel verses removed and buried very deep."

These improvements cost a lot of money. The Annapolis file contains a list of 35 workers at the cemetery. The list included the notation "payment should be more prompt." Three farmers who agreed to move bodies to the Knoxville National Cemetery ($3.00 per body) were still trying to collect their money in 1871.

Col. Folsom in his 1868 report listed some typical expenses. A picket fence cost between 30 cents per foot (Chicago) to a high of 95 cents a foot (Beaufort, SC). Headboards cost between 90 cents in the Department of Washington to $2.50 (by contract) in the Military Division Tennessee. However coffins cost only 90 cents (contract price) in Tennessee while they cost $4.00 in Washington. It cost $5.00 to move bodies from Arkansas Post to Pine Bluff, Arkansas. Moving bodies to Rural Cemetery at Chester, Pennsylvania, cost $13.50 each.

A total of $2,801,352.49 had been spent on cemeteries by June 30, 1868. In 1871, a total of $4,165,306.25 had been spent on cemeteries by 1871. Appropriations for cemeteries were:

1864	$50,000
1866	$50,000
1867	$750,000
1869	$600,000
1870	$300,000
1871	$200,000
1872	$200,000

Later money was appropriated to improve old post and soldier cemeteries. This was done cemetery by cemetery. In 1888 $2,500 was appropriated to collect and move bodies to the Mound City Soldiers' Lot in Kansas. This act also provided for a monument. In 1906 two bills were passed. One allocated $1,000 for improvements to the old Fort Mackinac cemetery in Michigan. Two thousand dollars was designated to improve the

old Camp Floyd, Utah, cemetery. Utah was to cede the lanc
those cemeteries are VA soldiers' lots.

An Act to Establish National Cemeteries (1867)
appointment of "a meritorious and trustworthy superintenden
selected from enlisted men of the army, disabled in service, and who shall
have to pay and allowances of an ordinance sergeant, to reside therein, for
the purpose of guarding and protecting the cemetery and giving information
to parties visiting the same." The pay of a superintendent was $48.41 per
month in 1868. Col. Folsom proposed that the superintendent, of the 12
largest cemeteries to be selected from disabled officers and be paid second
lieutenant's pay. Folsom reasoned that the government had invested over
$100,000 in these cemeteries and a higher class of superintendent was
needed. Acting Quartermaster General Rucker disagreed, but by 1874 there
were four classes of national cemeteries, each with a different pay scale.
Examples of each were:

1st Class	$75.00 per month - Arlington, Va.
2nd Class	$70.00 per month - Alexandria, Va.
3rd Class	$65.00 per month - Cold Harbor, Va.
4th Class	$60.00 per month - Grafton, W Va.

The 1876 budget allocated $57,750 to pay the superintendents of 70
cemeteries. In 1882 the pay rate remained the same.

Many superintendents had only one arm. Therefore they needed an
assistant. In 1871 the assistant's pay normally ran $25 to $35 per month,
depending if they received a daily ration.

Superintendents earned their money. As Col. Mark wrote in 1871,
many cemeteries were "in out-of-the way places and unfriendly
neighborhoods." He should have added unhealthy. No superintendent had
been sent to Mobile, Alabama, since the last two had died. In 1871 the
superintendent at Beaufort, South Carolina, had rented quarters outside of the
cemetery instead of living in the "neat brick lodge ... owing to the unhealthy
and malarious climate."

The 1867 act had made it in misdemeanor to deface or damage
anything in the cemetery. As the superintendent of the Salisbury National
Cemetery discovered in 1872, this act did not protect the superintendent. A
neighbor had shot into the cemetery just missing the superintendent. Because
the bullet did not hit a tree, headboard, or any other Government property,
the superintendent's only recourse was to complain to local authorities. Often
local authorities wanted nothing to do with the "Damn Yankees" buried in the
cemetery or the cemetery's superintendent. He was worse, he was still alive.

In 1890 the son of Knoxville's superintendent was arrested for
shooting at a neighbor's chickens when they flew into the cemetery. Even
though the superintendent had ordered his son to shoot the chickens, the War
Department declined to pay for the son's defense. The records do not state
if the son was convicted or not. The superintendent of the Annapolis

cemetery was jailed in 1877 after he shot a robber.

But the superintendent with the worst problems with neighbors was James Burke at Logan's Cross Roads, Kentucky. Burke had been sued by his neighbor, Mr. W.H. Logan, twice but he won both suits. In 1875 Logan sued Burke for trespass because Burke had his laborer cut down some blackberry briers on Logan's land near the cemetery's fence. The War Department asked the Justice Department to defend Burke, but the Attorney General declined. In 1877 a jury awarded Logan one cent in damages but Burke was ordered to pay a total of $155.40 in costs. In 1882 Congress, at Quartermaster General Meigs's urging, voted to reimburse Burke $180.40 to cover his expenses.

Sometimes the superintendent caused problems. The "very worthless superintendent" at Springfield, Missouri, was removed in 1871. The Lexington, Kentucky, superintendent was replaced in 1872. He was accused of making money by cutting hay for area farmers with a government mule and cart. There was also a question of possible missing money.

In 1872 the Grafton, West Virginia, superintendent inquired if his personal effects could be taxed. They could. Then he proceeded to write President Grant and various U.S. Senators asking that the cemetery be made a higher class. The superintendent claimed that the graves of Grant's former soldiers were not properly cared for because he didn't have enough help. Quartermaster General Meigs said that the only effect of making the cemetery a higher class would be to raise the superintendent's salary. He planned to ship the superintendent to a smaller cemetery.

Sometimes people wrote the War Department trying to be paid to care for soldiers' graves. In 1890 a Collinsville, Indiana, resident asked "a small salary to tend graves" of his former comrades. His request was refused. However a Quincy, Illinois, man found an easy job. In 1870 the City of Quincy, Illinois, donated a 150 foot by 200 foot soldiers' lot to the Federal Government. Around 240 soldiers were buried in the lot. Upkeep on the lot cost the government about $25.00 a year.

In July 1882 the Secretary of War declared the lot at National Cemetery "at the request of representatives of the Grand Army of the Republic." A superintendent was appointed and paid $720.00 a year. However soon the War Department learned that the superintendent had received the endorsement of the local GAR post only after he agreed to give the post $520.00 a year. The superintendent lost his job and the original arrangement for the upkeep of the cemetery was used. The Federal Government saved about $700.00 a year. It appears that local politicians had influenced the decision to make Quincy a National Cemetery. One Congressman tried to have another superintendent appointed, but the Secretary of War refused. However he did not rescind his order making Quincy a national cemetery.

The Grand Army of the Republic (GAR) had a strong voice in the politics of the 1870's and 1880's. The biggest day of the year for a GAR post was Decoration Day. The day normally featured a parade, speeches, and decorating the graves in the National Cemetery with flowers.

Sometimes things got out of hand. In June, 1871, a colored excursion party of about 1,000 people marched to the Fredericksburg National Cemetery. The superintendent explained to the marshall of the group that the band could not play in the cemetery. Fighting erupted and several people were injured. In 1889 the superintendent of the Florence, South Carolina, cemetery was investigated after he ejected men from the cemetery after a fight occurred during Decoration Day Services. The Finn's Point, New Jersey, superintendent also had problems with Decoration Day. He had to forcible remove drunks from the cemetery.

In 1883 the War Department issued "very explicit instructions" that the superintendent not the GAR was in charge of Decoration Day programs. Local GAR posts had assumed too much control of the observances with resulting "great injuries to cemeteries." Not all GAR posts were happy with the superintendent's rules. The Little Rock, Arkansas, post complained in 1889 that the superintendent refused to allow the post to drive buggies in the cemetery. The superintendent's decision was upheld.

During the early 1900's, a U.S. Marshall was sent to the Vicksburg National Cemetery to preserve order during Decoration Day. Apparently most of the problems were caused by vendors who catered to the large crowds. It was the custom for the colored GAR to have a program in the morning. Then at 3 PM the members of white GAR post and Confederate veterans meet down town and drove to the cemetery together for a program.

By the 1890's Decoration Day was not an important event as it had been in the 1870's. In 1894 Quartermaster General R.N. Botchelder sent a circular letter to all cemeteries. He wrote that if the local GAR did not plan a Decoration Day observance "the superintendents of National Cemeteries shall see graves are appropriately decorated, and shall assume charge of the decoration ceremonies..." The superintendent was to solicit flowers from people in the area, but they were not to purchase any.

Sometimes crime was a problem. In 1874 two more watchmen were hired at Arlington. Robberies were being committed near the Custis-Lee Mansion. Also people from the freeman's village were cutting down trees.

In 1883 the superintendent of the Antietam National Cemetery requested money to hire extra police for Decoration Day. He had taken over the cemetery in 1879 and stopped the local prostitutes from using the cemetery at night. He had heard that a prostitute from Washington had boasted that she was going to set up shop in the cemetery on Decoration Day. His request was refused.

The 1867 Act to Establish National Cemeteries provided that the graves in National Cemeteries were to be marked with a "small headstone or block", however nothing was done to fulfill this section of the act for six years. The graves had originally been marked with wooden headboards. Often these boards rotted. Sometimes forest fires burned them. Sometimes the paint on the board peeled off, removing the name of the soldier buried there.

Congress debated headstones twice in 1867. The public sentiment was for marble or granite markers but others in the War Department wanted to save money by using cheaper metal. In 1867 D.H. Rucker, the acting Quartermaster General, proposed using cast-iron (zinced) headmarkers. He believed with stonecutter's wages of $5.00 a day, stone markers would be too expensive. National Cemeteries had already cost over $2,000,000. Rucker estimated metal markers would cost $136,000. On December 19, 1867 Secretary of War Stanton ordered: "Do nothing about the markers" - a direct violation of the law.

In his 1871 report Col. Mack discussed the headmarker controversy. Quartermaster General Meigs favored galvanized, cast iron, ten inch high, truncated pyramids. These would weigh about 20 pounds each. They were supposed to cost $1.16 each, but Mack pointed out that each one would have to be cast individually, most likely at a higher cost. Mack believed the metal markers would rust freeze and break, or be stolen. Mack favored granite blocks. He said that the public wanted the graves marked for all time not just for one generation. He also pointed out that stone markers would require no maintenance. Also it would be a lot of work involved in stealing a granite marker. Of course, there was no real reason to steal a granite headmarker. It couldn't be sold like scrap metal could. Mack also warned that the marker would have to be thick enough and buried deep enough that it would not be "heaved" by the ground's freezing.

Surprisingly Mack objected to using upright markers. He described them as "monotonous to the eye when in long rows..." Today any television program about national cemeteries always begins by slowly panning the long rows of upright headstones. Americans seem to feel a deep pride that so many have died in their countries' service. Mack recommended using flat markers.

Several other materials were tried. A few markers of "Ransone's patent concrete" were placed in Arlington as a trial. Because wood was scare, limestone blocks ($3.95 each) were used in San Antonio National Cemetery.

Congress ended the discussion on June 8, 1872. They directed that graves in National Cemeteries were to be marked with "small headstones." The name of the soldier and the soldier's state was to be carved on the stone if known. The act appropriated $200,000 and directed the Secretary of War to act "without delay." At least 164 bids where received. There was a problem in determining the winner because some bids were for less than the total number of stones needed. What appeared to be the lowest bid was $662,999.80, only $462,999.80 over the appropriation. J. Holt, Judge-

30

Advocate General, ruled that a contract could only be let for $200,000.00, so nothing was done. In 1873 Congress appropriated $1,000,000 to mark soldiers' graves. Meigs had to readvertise for bids. (An additional $40,000 was appropriated in 1875.)

Congress also appropriated $10,000 in 1873 to construct a monument at the Salisbury Cemetery where some 11,700 Federal soldiers were supposed to have been buried in trenches. (Less than 4,000 soldiers were actually buried there.)

The War Department advertised for bids on 252,797 markers on June 27, 1873. 148,040 headstones were for known soldiers. The stones were for 73 cemeteries. (only 88 markers at Salisbury)

The specifications called for the headstones for known soldiers to be made of white marble or gray granite. The stone was to be 4 inches thick, 10 inches wide, and 12 inches above the ground. The stones were to be set 24 inches in the ground. But stones for north of the "latitude of Washington" were to be set 30 inches deep. The figures and capital letters were to be 2 inches long and 1/2 inches deep. The background of the letters was in the shape of a shield. No date of death was included, so it is impossible to tell if a headstone is for a casualty of the war or a veteran who died long after the war. (The 1872 bid specifications had required this information.)

Unknown graves were to be marked with 6 inch square blocks. The two and one half foot long block was to be set even with the ground. Each block was to be numbered with the grave number.

Although the original contract called for blocks for 2,799 unknown soldiers' graves at Florence National Cemetery, today only the end of each trench is marked with a stone stating the number of bodies in each trench.

There was no appropriation to mark graves of soldiers not buried in national cemeteries. In both his 1876 and 1877 reports to Congress Meigs asked that he be allowed mark some 17,000 graves of soldiers who died during the war and were buried in soldiers' lots or private cemeteries. Finally in 1879 Congress passed legislation to provide headstones for Union veterans who were buried in "private, village, or city cemeteries." The rest of the $1,000,000 appropriation was to be used to supply the stones. This meant that graves in soldier's lots could be marked. There was no money to erect the headstones. Normally a local GAR post or government official would contact the War Department, order the stones, and erect them.

In 1879 the Greenlawn Cemetery in Columbus, Ohio, offered to deed the United States the soldiers' lot, provided the Government would supply and erect stones for the 495 Civil War dead buried there. Quartermaster General Meigs refused the offer. There was no allocation for erecting the markers. There is a question of ownership of the lot. Col. Mack's report states that the state of Ohio owned the lot.

Unfortunately Quartermaster General Meigs ruled that headstones could not be supplied without the regiment the soldier served in. There was

31

no name index to the Union soldiers who served in the war. There was not any way to prove that a soldier served in the war without the regimental data. The Quartermaster refused to supply headstones for three soldiers who died in a Dunkirk, New York, hospital even though their names were known. No stones would be supplied without a regiment.

For some reason Meigs ruled against supplying headstones for unknown soldiers who were not buried in a lot exclusively for burying soldiers (a soldiers' lot). This decision meant that many graves of soldiers went unmarked. In 1882 Dr. J.M. Spainhour, a Lenoir, North Carolina, dentist, requested headstones for "two sick soldiers who were left here, several humane citizens did all they could to restore them to health, but they died..." The headstones were not supplied because their names were not known. Headstones for unknown soldiers not buried in a soldier's lot were furnished in 1888. By then many graves of unknown soldiers were lost.

Graves of government employees (mainly of the quartermaster department) were marked by headstones in 1884. In 1886 a circular letter was sent to forts and military posts asking if there were any unmarked graves in the post cemeteries. Many of the lists filled out by the acting assistant post quartermaster still survive. Often these lists are the only listing of names of soldiers who died at a post.

In 1904 Congress allocated $5,000 to mark the graves of civilians buried in post cemeteries. These civilians included the wife and children of soldiers, sutlers, and laundress. Sometimes the post cemetery was the only cemetery in the area. Often civilians who died of disease or were killed by Indians were buried in post cemeteries. This practice appeared to gradually end in the 1870's.

In 1906 Congress approved the marking of graves of Confederate soldiers who died in prisoner of war camps or Northern hospitals. The headstones used were like the Union headstones, but they were pointed on top. Why a pointed headstone? One story is that the dead Confederates didn't want any DAMN YANKEES setting on their graves. In 1929 Congress approved the marking of all Confederate graves with markers. By this time many graves had been marked by private groups or lost.

In 1884 the Goshen, Ohio, GAR post requested stones "in memory of those that did not return." The request was denied. However in 1973 Congress approved memorial markers for soldiers whose bodies could not be recovered. The Fort Bliss National Cemetery (Texas) has stones in memory of cavalry troops whose bodies were not recovered. Today headstones for the holders of the Congressional Medal of Honor are lettered in gold.

The major decision that determined the development of the National Cemetery System was the decision to allow veterans to be buried in national cemeteries. This decision did not come easy. Quartermaster General Meigs was opposed to the idea. Apparently he realized that many veterans would want to be buried, thus taxing the resources of his department. He based his arguments on the 1862 act that authorized President Lincoln to establish national cemeteries. The act specifically authorized cemeteries for "soldiers who shall have died in the service of the country." The joint resolution of Congress in 1866 confirmed this. The official policy was that no veteran could be buried in a national cemetery.

This policy had not been completely followed. Miss Carrie E. Cuttere had been buried beside her "betrothed" at Newberne National Cemetery. Unfortunately his name is unknown. An unknown infant was buried at Alexandria National Cemetery. However the problem that changed the policy occurred at Chattanooga National Cemetery. According to Edward Steere, Major General George Thomas had reserved a section of the Chattanooga Cemetery for burial of veterans. Apparently Thomas had allowed burials of veterans for some time before Meigs learned of Thomas's actions and ordered him to cease allowing veterans to be buried in the cemetery.

A large group of veterans in the Chattanooga area petitioned Thomas to appeal the decision. The petition stated: "Many of us...have buried there those who are near and dear to us in this spot, hallowed by the bravery of those whose remains there repose, and are anxious to know whether the same privilege may be expected in the future, or whether those already buried there will be allowed to remain."

Thomas submitted his request for reconsideration to his superior, General-in-Chief Sherman. Sherman turned the matter over to the Secretary of War with the endorsement: "Surely, when practicable these cemeteries should be devoted to the burial of soldiers for all time to come." The Secretary of War referred the matter to Judge Advocate General Joseph Holt.

Meigs restated his views. He had strictly interpreted the act of 1862 and the joint resolution of 1866. The resolution stated that burial was for soldiers who died **during the war of the rebellion.** The 1867 Act to Establish National Cemeteries referred to **burial of deceased soldiers and sailors.**

Judge Advocate General Holt upheld Meigs's actions but he noted the Act of 1862 provided for "soldiers who died in the service of their country." Holt ruled this "clearly includes soldiers dying in the army at any or all times." Holt's decision temporarily ended the burial of veterans in national cemeteries.

On March 3, 1871, Congress appropriated funding to cover the burial expenses of officers, non-commissioned officers, and soldiers who were either killed in action or who died in the service of the country.

Holt's ruling angered many powerful veteran's groups including the Grand Army of the Republic (GAR). At one time the GAR was considered the Republican Party's largest fund raiser. Congress attempted to appease these groups in June 1872 by passing an amendment to 1867 act that allowed honorably discharged soldiers and sailors who "may die in a destitute condition" to be buried in national cemeteries.

This failed to placate the powerful veteran's lobby. Less than a year later (March 3, 1873) Congress relented: "That honorably discharged soldiers, sailors, or marines who served during the late war either in the regular or volunteer forces, dying subsequent to the passage of this act may be buried in any national cemetery of the United States free of cost and their graves shall receive the same care and attention as the graves of those already buried. The production of the honorable discharge of the deceased shall be the authority for the superintendent of the cemetery to permit the interment." As Meigs feared the number of interments increased dramatically. Between 1871 and 1889 the number of burials at the Jefferson City National Cemetery (Missouri) increased by 25%.

The same day Congress authorized care of the Mexico City Cemetery by the War Department. There had not been an appropriation for this cemetery since it's inception in 1850.

Soldiers who died as a result of the Indian Wars were normally buried in post cemeteries. Veterans of the Indian Wars were buried in national cemeteries. No one questioned the burials. On June 11, 1899, the Secretary of War ruled that "existing law and custom" allowed honorably discharged veterans of the Spanish American War to be buried in national cemeteries.

Although veterans were allowed the privilege of burial in national cemeteries, their families could not, at least in theory. The commander of Fort Wilkens, Michigan, ordered that the illegitimate child of the wife of a soldier be buried in the post cemetery with "full military honors."

In September 1873 an orphan of a colored soldier was buried in the Whitehall National Cemetery. Apparently the post commander at Whitehall had allowed burials from the Bridgewater Soldiers' Orphans' Home before contrary to established policy. In 1873 the child of a Federal occupation soldier was moved from Macon, Georgia, to Andersonville National Cemetery. The same year the wife of a soldier was moved from the Fort Blandensburg, Maryland, Post Cemetery to the Military Asylum National Cemetery. In December 1884, Quartermaster General Samuel Holabird ruled that a child could not be buried in post cemeteries. However both soldiers and civilians were buried in the Yellowstone National Park Post Cemetery even after this ruling. On May 14, 1948. Congress voted to allow burial of wives, husbands, widows, and minor children of veterans in national cemeteries.

Colored soldiers were not always welcome in national cemeteries. In 1868 a proposal to move 229 U.S. Colored Troops from Laurel Hill cemetery to Loudon Park National Cemetery was rejected. Instead a man was paid $15.00 a quarter to raise and lower the flag each day at Laurel Grove each day. Because Laurel Grove was not a national cemetery, the graves were not marked with headstones in 1873. In 1879 the superintendent of Loudon Park was ordered to care for the long neglected Laurel Cemetery

34

lot. Because the graves were not properly marked, the superintendent was forced to report in 1883 that no records of burials could be found. The Quartermaster's Department noted "It is presumed... two hundred and forty interments..." These bodies were eventually moved to the Loudon Park National Cemetery and buried as unknowns.

506 Colored soldiers who died in Louisville, Kentucky, were buried in the Eastern Cemetery instead of Cave Hill National Cemetery. After the war these bodies were moved across the Ohio River to the New Albany National Cemetery (Indiana) where they were buried in a separate section. There was room for the bodies in Cave Hill, some 900 bodies were moved there after the war. It appears that the War Department did not wish to move colored soldiers to Cave Hill because it was located in an all white cemetery. The Cave Hill cemetery Association had donated the land to the Federal Government.

New Albany was not the only national cemetery with a "colored section." Fort Scott, Kansas, also had a segregated section. Arlington National Cemetery was also segregated. In 1871 a committee of "loyal citizens" asked the Secretary of War to move the graves of colored soldiers in Arlington. Quartermaster General Meigs explained that colored soldiers had been buried in the Northeastern section of the cemetery near the lodge. A few white soldiers had been buried there also, but later they were removed "to repose with their comrades." As Meigs put it:"The colored soldiers appear to have been left when so large a number of their own race had been interred, and thus, this part of the ground was eventually devoted to the colored people, soldiers, and refugees."

Apparently the committee asked that these bodies be moved and scattered among the white soldiers graves. Meigs objected to the proposed removals "in sentiment as well as in the expense." Meigs argued: "These are buried among their own people.." He concluded: "I believe that hereafter it will be more grateful to their descendants to be able to visit and point to the collected graves of these persons, than to find them scattered through a large cemetery."

Burial records of colored troops are sketchy. Only 50 of 2,484 U.S. Colored Troops (2%) buried in Natchez National Cemetery were ever identified. 175 U.S. Colored Troops were buried in a pauper's burying ground near Saint Louis. In 1874 the United States was asked to repair the fence. Quartermaster General Meigs endorsed the request: "the removal of these remains is not recommended, if deeded to the United States, the United States will care for." This cemetery was lost.

Black soldiers during the Civil War were not paid the same pay as white soldiers. In 1869 Quartermaster General Meigs ordered that "A colored laborer preforming an equal amount of the same kind of work as a white laborer is entitled to an equal amount of pay." Meigs was responding to complaints of unequal pay at the Chalmette National Cemetery.

deral Occupation Troops who died in the South normally were town cemeteries where they died. There is not a listing of Federal who died on occupation duty. Because no date of dead was ⌐⌐ ⌐ ⅃ on headstones furnished by the War Department during the 1800's, it is impossible to determine from a headstone if a soldier died during the war, died on occupation duty, or was a veteran who had moved to the area. Of course there were white Union Units formed from all the Southern States during the Civil War except South Carolina.

In 1879 Thomas Vance, an ex-Union soldier living in Yorkville, South Carolina, wrote the War Department reporting that the graves of eight Federal Occupation troops in the town's cemetery were being desecrated by children playing on them. Vance wanted the bodies moved to the Florence National Cemetery.

The investigating officer found no desecration. He requested the fence around the graves be repaired and the headboards relettered. Why he did not order granite headstones for the graves is unclear. The Yorkville Enquirer wrote: "There is not a South Carolinian in this entire community who would be guilty of the act of desecration the grave of a (sic) United States soldiers; and on occasions of decorating the soldier's graves, in our cemetery, the same floral tributes as were bestowed upon those who fell in the Confederate service."

Less than three years later, bodies of Federal Occupation troops were moved from Odgensville, South Carolina, to the Florence National Cemetery. Odgensville is less than fifteen miles form Yorkville. The records do not state why these bodies were moved. The Lynchburg, Virginia, Postmaster moved the bodies of ten Union occupation troops from an uncared for "private lot" to Lynchburg's Confederate Cemetery where they could be cared for.

Bodies of Civil War soldiers were discovered from time to time. If they could be identified as Union soldiers they were to a National Cemetery. In March 1877 the bodies of ten Union soldiers were discovered at Spotsylvania Court House. After they were identified by cartridge boxes found with the bodies they were moved to the Fredericksburg National Cemetery.

In 1882, a report was received at the War Department of "six or seven" members of Col. Cayton's Cavalry being buried at Monticello, Arkansas. Seven years later the superintendent of the Little Rock National Cemetery investigated and removed thirteen bodies.

The superintendent of the Fayetteville National Cemetery reported it cost $44.00 to move two bodies from Bellefonte, Arkansas, to the national cemetery. The trip took eleven days. Rent of light wagon and a team of horses ran another dollar a day.

Often shifting sands at the ocean would uncover bones of soldiers. Thirty-eight bodies were moved from Fort Fisher to the Wilmington National

Cemetery. Three years later fifty more bodies were uncovered ar.
In June 1890, two students from the Charleston Military Acader.
charged with desecration of graves uncovered on Morris Island,
Carolina.

Not all bodies reported to the War Department were graves of Un ₋n
soldiers. Reports of soldiers at Belmont, Missouri, were false. The
investigator discovered the bodies were those of riverboat deckhands.

Sometimes the superintendent did not bother to visit the site and
investigate. In 1884 the <u>Washington Tribune</u> published a report of bones
scattered on the ground near Franklin, Tennessee, battleground. The
superintendent of Stone's River National Cemetery was requested to
investigate. He did not visit the site, but wrote the War Department that
over 900 bodies had been moved 20 years before, so no more bodies could
be there. That ended the "investigation."

Bodies still turn up from time to time. Nine unknown Federal
soldiers were buried in the Gettysburg National Cemetery on Memorial Day
1991, almost 128 years after the battle!

Sometimes GAR posts requested the War Department's help with
maintenance of their cemeteries. Of course the requests were always denied
because there was no funding for such requests. In 1884 a request was made
to move the bodies of ex-soldiers in Knox County, Missouri, to a common
site. The request was denied. However in 1877 Congress authorized $6,000
to move the victims of the sinking of the United States Steamer Huron from
the North Carolina Coast to the Annapolis Naval Cemetery. Bodies of the
crew of the rescue ship B.and J. Baker who drowned were also to be moved.

Soldiers who died at military forts and camps were buried in post
cemeteries. Life was hard on the frontier and deaths were frequent. A 1873
list of burials in the Fort Whipple, Arizona Territory, post cemetery listed
the following causes of death:

2 killed in action with Indians
2 died of wounds
1 murdered
1 accidental pistol shot
1 wounded by pistol shot in Prescott, A.T.

Volume 17 of the <u>Roll of Honor</u> lists 17 burials in the Camp Cooke,
Montana Territory, post cemetery. The burials were all made in late 1866
and early 1867. The causes of death listed were: morbiss brightes, chronic
diarrhea (2 cases), consumption (3 cases), remittena fever, chronic dysentery
(sic), bronchitis (2 cases), scalded foot, suicide, chronic rheum's (sic),
rheumatism, sybhilis (sic), and gunshot wound. The 17th grave was that
Pitanista who was "killed-Chief of Pirgan Indian Tribe." Five graves were
unmarked by headboards.

The most complete cause of dead recorded in the <u>Roll of Honor</u> series
is that of Private Daniel H. Lee, Company K, 13th United States Infantry.

37

He was "Found dead November 26, 1867, and lying on the prairie about three (3) miles from the post. He was last seen alive on the evening of the 24th, intoxicated, at Sun River Crossing, a place five (5) miles from the post, where liquors are sold to the public. No marks of violence were found on his person; probably died from exposure while intoxicated."

Post cemeteries were not normally as well cared for as national cemeteries. A sergeant at Key West, Florida, paid $25.00 from his own pocket to repair the post cemetery's fence. He didn't wait for local post commander to obtain permission to repair the fence because horses and cows were grazing on the graves.

There was no established policy on the upkeep of abandoned post cemeteries. Sometimes the remains in the cemetery were moved to another post or national cemetery, but this was done on a post by post basis. The official "policy" was stated in a letter to the Camp Collins, Colorado, GAR post. The post wanted help in moving some 25 or 30 graves from the abandoned post cemetery to a newer cemetery in town where the graves would receive better care. The answer was "...there is no appropriation to remove the remains of deceased soldiers, except to a national cemetery in cases where there is danger of disturbance, or desecration of the graves."

The post cemetery at Santa Fe, New Mexico, was designated a national cemetery in early 1875. The idea was to move remains to Santa Fe from abandoned post cemeteries in the Southwest. However when the Atchison, Topeka, and Santa Fe Railroad was completed in 1882, it proved easier to ship bodies from some forts in New Mexico and Arizona to Fort Leavenworth National Cemetery in Kansas than to Santa Fe.

During the 1870's several national cemeteries ceased to exist. In March 1879, 349 bodies were moved from remote, snake infested Fort Saint Phillip National Cemetery to Chalmette National Cemetery at a cost of $1,050.26.

Fort Vancouver's (Washington) Post Cemetery was named a national cemetery in 1881. However the next year the Secretary of War decided that "this is a post cemetery" so it reverted to post cemetery status. It appears that plans were made to remove bodies to Fort Vancouver from much of the West Coast. The cemetery was moved and enlarged, however only about a dozen bodies were ever moved to the cemetery. Fort Vancouver remains an active post cemetery under control of the Army.

Fort Vancouver's proposed function was taken over by San Francisco National Cemetery. In 1882 Brigadier General D.B. Saekeh reported on the poor condition of the old post cemetery at Fort Yuma, Arizona. Saekeh wanted the post cemetery at the Presdio of San Francisco converted into a national cemetery. Saekeh wrote "The Pacific States deserve some such show of consideration." San Francisco National Cemetery was established in 1884.

Custer Battlefield National Cemetery was established in 1879, three years after Custer's defeat. This was the last national cemetery established at an American battlefield. The bodies of soldiers killed in the battle were buried in a mass grave on top of Custer Hill in 1881. Surprisingly, none of the bodies of fifty-three soldiers who died at the Reno-Benteen Battlefield less than five miles away were ever recovered.

In 1890 a total of 338 bodies from abandoned post cemeteries were moved to Custer Battlefield National Cemetery in at a cost of $4,378.10. ($12.95 per body) 145 bodies were moved from Fort Rice, North Dakota. However the bodies of nineteen civilians were left at the abandoned fort.

Bodies from a total of nineteen post cemeteries were eventually moved to Custer Battlefield National Cemetery. In August, 1890, Quartermaster General Richard Batchelder wrote: "...nor is it deemed necessary that full, sized boxes be used except in cases of comparatively recent interments. In the majority of cases, where only the bones are found, boxes 26" X 10" have been found to be sufficiently large for the purpose." Burlap sacks were used to move the "slight remains" from old Fort Belknap, Texas, to San Antonio National Cemetery in 1890. In 1909 bones were shipped by railroad from Madison Barracks, New York, to San Antonio National Cemetery in 10" X 10" X 26" boxes. The boxes were "classified" human bones.

Not all bodies from post cemeteries were moved to national cemeteries. Fort Lapwai, Washington, closed in 1884. In 1890 a total of sixty-four bodies were shipped to the Fort Walla Walla, Washington, Post Cemetery at a cost of $1,298.88. In 1884 Congress transferred nine acres of land, including Fort Bidwell's Post Cemetery, to the Masons Lodge and Oddfellow's Lodge. The two lodges agreed to maintain the old post cemetery for the government.

Several post cemeteries were named national cemeteries in the 20th century. When volume 9 of the Roll of Honor was published in 1866, the Fort Snelling Post Cemetery contained sixty-four graves. (all known) When the Fort Snelling National Cemetery was established in 1939, 680 bodies were moved from the old post cemetery and buried as unknowns. These graves should have been marked in 1886, why they weren't is a mystery. But it points out a major problem with the marking of soldiers' graves. The Quartermaster's Department often failed to follow up on the care of soldier's graves. If a problem was reported to the department, it normally was taken care of. But the department didn't initiate action.

Quartermaster General R.N. Batchelder realized this in 1891 when he sent circular letter to post quartermasters. The post quartermaster was to inform his department of the cost of moving bodies from post cemetery to the nearest national cemetery when the post closed. Batchelder's letter effectively ended the era of hit and miss removals of bodies from abandoned post cemeteries. This practice continued until 1947 when Congress directed the War Department to transfer "historic graveyards in abandoned military posts" to local or state agencies provided the local agency would care for the graves.

Batchelder's letter also ends this book. By 1890 the frontier had disappeared. No major changes were planned in the cemetery system. The Spanish-American War would not fill cemeteries like the Civil War. The National Cemetery System would not make major changes until after the First World War.

Except for one change. There had been racial problems at Fort Brown, Texas. The colored soldiers stationed there did not get along with the local residents. In 1906 Negro soldiers were accused of killing a local bar keeper. Tensions ran high. When Fort Brown closed in 1910, over 3,000 bodies from the Brownsville National Cemetery were moved to the Alexandria National Cemetery in Louisiana.

National cemeteries continued under the War Department until June 10, 1933, when President Roosevelt's Executive Order #6166 transferred 11 national cemeteries to the new National Park Service:

Antietam National Cemetery, Maryland
Battleground National Cemetery, District of Columbia
Chattanooga National Cemetery, Tennessee
Fort Donelson National Cemetery, Tennessee
Fredericksburg National Cemetery, Virginia
Gettysburg National Cemetery, Pennsylvania
Poplar Grove National Cemetery, Virginia
Shiloh National Cemetery, Tennessee
Stone's River National Cemetery, Tennessee
Vicksburg National Cemetery, Virginia
Yorktown National Cemetery, Virginia

All of these cemeteries were later developed into a larger National Military Park, National Battlefield,... except for the Battleground National Cemetery. Chattanooga National Cemetery was later transferred back to the Army.

Chalmette National Cemetery was transferred to the National Park Service in 1939. In 1971 the Andersonville National Cemetery was transferred to the National Park Service.

The Quartermaster's Department continued to operate the other national cemeteries. Other cemeteries were established to bury the casualties and veterans of both World Wars.

After the First World War the American Battle Monuments Commission was established to bury American GI's who died overseas. This agency oversees 24 overseas cemeteries including the Mexico City Cemetery.

On August 1, 1962, the Office of the Chief of Support Services (U.S. Army) assumed control of the 85 national cemeteries from the Quartermaster's Department. On December 31, 1962, the Department of the Army's 85 national cemeteries had 2,171,762 acres developed for cemeterial purposes. A total of 858,047 interments had been made in these cemeteries.

40

During the 1960's no major expansion of the existing national cemetery system occurred. In January 1967, President Johnson asked the Administrator of Veterans Affairs to make a complete study of all veterans' programs. One recommendation was that all national cemeteries administrated by the U.S. Army be transferred to the Veterans Administration. This pleased veterans groups who believed the VA would expand the National Cemetery System.

Most of the administrator's recommendations on burial of veterans were implemented on June 18, 1973, when Public Law 93-43 took effect. All but two of the national cemeteries under Army control were transferred to the Veterans Administration . The 21 national cemeteries all ready established by the Veterans Administration were also incorporated in the National Cemetery System. Twenty-one soldier's lots and several Confederate Cemeteries were also transferred.

In 1992 over 1.8 million veterans were buried in 113 cemeteries and 33 soldiers' lots and Confederate Cemeteries under control of the Department of Veteran's Affairs. The U.S. Army reported 190,000 burials in Arlington National Cemetery and 13,000 burials in the Soldiers' Home National Cemetery. The American Battle Monuments Commission oversaw 24 cemeteries with 125,000 interments. The National Park Services' 14 national cemeteries contained over 97,000 dead.

Theodore O'Hare said it best:
    "On Fame's eternal camping ground
    Their silent tents are spread
    And Glory guards, with solemn round
    The bivouac of the dead."

SECTION 2

INDEX TO THE FINAL BURIAL SITES OF UNITED STATES SOLDIERS

Section 3 contains a brief history of all "final sites" and original burial sites listed with a "#".

No more on Life's parade shall meet
That brave and fallen few

Bodies removed by Friends see Bodies Removed by Friends

BODIES REMOVED FROM LOCATIONS IN ALABAMA

Original Burial Site	Final Burial Site	
"Central Alabama"	Mobile National	Ala
"North Alabama"	Chattanooga National	Ten
Athens	Corinth National	Miss
Athens	Stone's River National	Ten
Barton Station	Corinth National	Miss
Battle Creek	Chattanooga National	Ten
Bellfonte	Chattanooga National	Ten
Bridgeport	Chattanooga National	Ten
Carpenters	Chattanooga National	Ten
Catawba #	Marietta National	Ga
Chatooga	Marietta National	Ga
Cherokee County	Marietta National	Ga
Cherokee Station	Corinth National	Miss
Claysville	Chattanooga National	Ten
Courtland	Corinth National	Miss
De Kalb County	Marietta National	Ga
Decatur	Corinth National	Miss
Demopolis	Demopolis	Ala
Dixon Station	Corinth National	Miss
Dotsonville	Chattanooga National	Ten
Elkmont	Corinth National	Miss
Eufaula	Andersonville National	Ga
Fort Blakely	Mobile National	Ala
Fort Gaines	Mobile National	Ala
Fort Morgan #	Mobile National	Ala
Fort Powell	Mobile National	Ala
Gainsville	Gainsville	Ala
Gurley's Tank	Chattanooga National	Ten
Harris Station	Corinth National	Miss
Huntsville	Chattanooga National	Ten
Jacksonville	Jacksonville	Ala
Jonesboro'	Corinth National	Miss
Judson	Marietta National	Ga
Larkin's Landing	Chattanooga National	Ten
Lebanon	Marietta National	Ga
Leighton	Corinth National	Miss
Livingston	Livingston	Ala
Madison County	Chattanooga National	Ten
Mobile	Mobile National	Ala
Montgomery #	Andersonville National	Ga
Montgomery #	Marietta National	Ga
Morgan County	Chattanooga National	Ten
Moulton	Moulton	Ala
Mount Veron Barracks	Mobile	Ala
Mouterallo	Mouterallo	Ala
Mud Creek Bridge	Chattanooga National	Ten
Navy Cove	Mobile National	Ala
Paint Rock	Chattanooga National	Ten
Pollard	Andersonville National	Ga
Scottsboro	Chattanooga National	Ten
Spanish Fort	Mobile National	Ala
Stevenson	Chattanooga National	Ten
Talladega	Talladega	Ala
Thackers Station	Chattanooga National	Ten
Tuscumbia	Corinth National	Miss
Waterloo	Shiloh National	Ten

BODIES REMOVED FROM LOCATIONS IN ALABAMA

Original Burial Site	Final Burial Site	
Winchester	Chattanooga National	Ten
Woodville	Chattanooga National	Ten
Will's Valley	Marietta National	Ga

BODIES REMOVED FROM LOCATIONS IN ARIZONA

Original Burial Site	Final Burial Site	
American Ranch	San Francisco National	Calf
Beal Spring	San Francisco National	Calf
Camp Beale Springs	San Francisco National	Calf
Camp Date Creek	San Francisco National	Ariz
Camp Goodwin	Fort Leavenworth National	Kan
Camp Hualpi	San Francisco National	Calf
Camp McDowell #	San Francisco National	Calf
El Picacho	El Picacho	Ariz
Fort Bowie #	San Francisco National	Calf
Fort Crittenden	San Francisco National	Calf
Fort Defiance	Fort Leavenworth National	Kan
Fort Goodwin	Fort Goodwin	Ariz
Fort Grant	Santa Fe National	NM
Fort Huachuca	Fort Huachuca	Ariz
Fort Lowell	Fort Lowell	Ariz
Fort Mason #	San Francisco National	Calf
Fort McDowell #	San Francisco National	Calf
Fort Thomas	Fort Leavenworth National	Kan
Fort Verde	San Francisco National	Calf
Fort Wallen #	San Francisco National	Calf
Fort Wingate	San Antonio National	Tex
Lowell	San Francisco National	Calf
Mojave #	San Francisco National	Calf
Phoenix	Fort Leavenworth National	Kan
San Carlos	San Carlos	Ariz
Simmons Ranch	San Francisco National	Calf
Tubac	San Francisco National	Calf
Tucson	Tucson	Ariz
Whipple Barracks #	San Francisco National	Calf
Willows	San Francisco National	Calf

BODIES REMOVED FROM LOCATIONS IN ARKANSAS

Original Burial Site	Final Burial Site	
Arkansas Post #	Arkansas Post	Ark
Arkansas Post #	Devall's Bluff National	Ark
Arkansas Post #	Memphis National	Ten
Arkansas Post #	Vicksburg National	Miss
Austin	Little Rock National	Ark
Batesville #	Little Rock National	Ark
Bellefonte	Fayetteville National	Ark
Benton	Little Rock National	Ark
Bentonville	Fayetteville National	Ark
Black Jack Ridge	Fort Smith National	Ark
Brownsville	Little Rock National	Ark
Camden #	Baton Rouge National	La
Can Hill	Fayetteville National	Ark
Chalk Bluff	Jefferson Barracks National	Mo
Chico County	Vicksburg National	Miss
Cincinnati	Fort Gibson National	In T
Clandestine House	Memphis National	Ten
Clanerrdarr	Little Rock National	Ark
Clarksville	Fort Smith National	Ark

46

BODIES REMOVED FROM LOCATIONS IN ARKANSAS

Original Burial Site	Final Burial Site	
Columbia	Vicksburg National	Miss
Cross Hollow	Fayetteville National	Ark
Des Arc	Little Rock National	Ark
DeValls Bluff #	Little Rock National	Ark
Douglass Landing	Little Rock National	Ark
Dutches Creek	Fort Smith National	Ark
Elkhorn Tavern #	Springfield National	Mo
Elm Spring	Fayetteville National	Ark
Fayetteville	Fayetteville National	Ark
Fitzhughs Woods	Fitzhughs Woods	Ark
Fort Curtis	Memphis National	Ten
Fort Eureka Springs	San Antonio National	Tex
Fort Hindman	see Arkansas Post	Ark
Fort Smith	Fort Smith National	Ark
Fulton	Jefferson Barracks National	Mo
Handises Lake	Little Rock National	Ark
Hawk House	Memphis National	Ten
Helena #	Memphis National	Ten
Hickon Station	Little Rock National	Ark
Hicks Station	Little Rock National	Ark
Horse Head Creek	Fort Smith National	Ark
Hot Springs	Fort Leavenworth National	Kan
Huntersville	Little Rock National	Ark
Huntsville	Little Rock National	Ark
Island # 63	Vicksburg National	Miss
Jacksonport #	Little Rock National	Ark
Jenkins Ferry	Little Rock National	Ark
Keitville	Fayetteville National	Ark
Leetown	see Pea Ridge	Ark
Lewisburg	Little Rock National	Ark
Little Rock	Little Rock National	Ark
Madison	Madison	Ark
Madison County	Madison County	Ark
Mark's Mills	Little Rock National	Ark
Monticello	Little Rock National	Ark
Mouth of White River	Vicksburg National	Miss
Napoleon	Vicksburg National	Miss
Ozark Hospital	Ozark Hospital	Ark
Pea Ridge B.F.	see Pea Ridge	Ark
Pickets Farm	Little Rock National	Ark
Pine Bluff #	Little Rock National	Ark
Poteau Mountain	Fort Smith National	Ark
Prairie Grove #	Fayetteville National	Ark
Princeton	Little Rock National	Ark
Rogers Landing	Fort Smith National	Ark
Sarry Landing	Little Rock National	Ark
Scatterville	Jefferson Barracks National	Mo
Scott County	Fort Smith National	Ark
Sebastian County	Fort Smith National	Ark
Silver Creek	Fort Smith National	Ark
St Charles	Little Rock National	Ark
Sugar Creek Valley	Fayetteville National	Ark
Sunny Side	Vicksburg National	Miss
Temples Plantation	Little Rock National	Ark
Thompson House	Memphis National	Ten
Van Buren	Fort Smith National	Ark
Waldon	Fort Smith National	Ark
Washington	Little Rock National	Ark
Waxhaw Landing	Vicksburg National	Miss
White House	Little Rock National	Ark

47

```
                BODIES REMOVED FROM LOCATIONS IN ALASKA
Original Burial Site            Final Burial Site
Fort Kodiak                     Fort Kodiak                    Ask


               BODIES REMOVED FROM LOCATIONS IN CALIFORNIA
               [ see also the Pacific Military District ]
Original Burial Site            Final Burial Site
Alcatraz Island                 Alcatraz Island                Calf
Angel Island                    Angel Island                   Calf
Auburn                          Fort Leavenworth National      Kan
Benecia Barracks                Benecia Barracks               Calf
Camp Anderson                   Camp Anderson                  Calf
Camp Babbit                     Camp Babbit                    Calf
Camp Drum                       Drum Barracks                  Calf
Camp Independence #             San Francisco National         Calf
Camp Jaqua                      Camp Jaqua                     Calf
Camp Lincoln                    Camp Lincoln                   Calf
Camp Wright                     San Francisco National         Calf
Drum Barracks                   Drum Barracks                  Calf
Fort Bidwell                    Fort Bidwell                   Calf
Fort Gaston                     Fort Gaston                    Calf
Fort Grant                      Fort Grant                     Calf
Fort Humboldt                   Fort Humboldt                  Calf
Fort Iaqua                      Camp Jaqua                     Calf
Fort Independence               San Francisco National         Calf
Fort Long                       Camp Lincoln                   Calf
Fort Point                      Fort Point                     Calf
Fort Winfeild Scott             Fort Point                     Calf
Fort Wright #                   San Francisco National         Calf
Fort Yuma #                     San Francisco National         Calf
Hallick                         San Francisco National         Calf
Long's Fort                     Camp Lincoln                   Calf
Monterry Barracks               Monterry Barracks              Calf
Owens River Valley              Camp Babbit                    Calf
San Diego                       Fort Rosecrans National        Calf
San Francisco                   Fort Leavenworth National      Kan
San Francisco                   San Francisco National         Calf


               BODIES REMOVED FROM LOCATIONS IN COLORADO
Original Burial Site            Final Burial Site
Beaver Creek                    Fort Wallace                   Kan
Camp Collins                    Camp Collins                   Col
Camp on White River             Fort McPherson National        Neb
Camp Rankin                     Fort McPherson National        Neb
Camp Weld                       Denver                         Col
Cantonment on the Uncomphane    Fort McPherson National        Neb
Colorado Springs                Colorado Springs               Col
Denver                          Denver                         Col
Denver #                        Fort Leavenworth National      Kan
Fort Crawford                   see Cantonment on the Uncomp   Col
Fort Garland #                  Fort Leavenworth National      Kan
Fort Gaston                     Fort Gaston                    Col
Fort Lewis #                    Fort Leavenworth National      Kan
Fort Lewis #                    Fort McPherson National        Neb
Fort Lyon #                     Fort Leavenworth National      Kan
Fort Morgan                     Fort Morgan                    Col
Fort Rankin                     see Julesburg                  Col
Fort Sedgewick #                Fort McPherson National        Neb
Julesburg                       Julesburg                      Col
Kit Carson                      Fort Wallace                   Kan
```

BODIES REMOVED FROM LOCATIONS IN COLORADO

Original Burial Site	Final Burial Site	
Pagosa Springs	Fort Leavenworth National	Kan
Pueblo	Santa Fe National	NM

BODIES REMOVED FROM LOCATIONS IN CONNECTICUT

Original Burial Site	Final Burial Site	
Danbury	Danbury	Con
Hawleyville	Danbury	Con
New Haven	New Haven	Con
New Haven #	Cypress Hills National	NY

BODIES REMOVED FROM LOCATIONS IN THE DAKOTA TERRITORY

Original Burial Site	Final Burial Site	
Brule Creek	Fort Dakota	D T
Fort Abercrombie #	Custer National	M T
Fort Abraham Lincoln #	Custer National	M T
Fort Benett	Custer National	M T
Fort Buford	Custer National	M T
Fort Casper	Fort Casper	D T
Fort Dakota	Fort Dakota	D T
Fort Hall	Fort McPherson National	Neb
Fort McKinney	Custer National	M T
Fort Pembina	Custer National	M T
Fort Randall #	Fort Leavenworth National	Kan
Fort Reno #	Custer National	M T
Fort Rice #	Custer National	M T
Fort Sisseton	Custer National	M T
Fort Stevenson	Custer National	M T
Fort Sully #	Fort Leavenworth National	Kan
Fort Thompson	Fort Thompson	D T
Fort Wadsworth	Fort Wadsworth	D T
Fort Yates	Keokuk National	Iowa
Pine Ridge	Fort Leavenworth National	Kan
Yankton	Yankton	D T

BODIES REMOVED FROM LOCATIONS IN THE DISTRICT OF COLUMBIA

Original Burial Site	Final Burial Site	
Fort Stephens	Battleground National	D.C.
Washington	Arlington National	Va
Washington	Congressional Cemetery	D.C.
Washington	Soldiers' Home National	D.C.

BODIES REMOVED FROM LOCATIONS IN DELAWARE

Original Burial Site	Final Burial Site	
Brandywine Hundred	Brandywine Hundred	Del
Wilmington	Wilmington	Del

BODIES REMOVED FROM LOCATIONS IN FLORIDA

Original Burial Site	Final Burial Site	
Appalachicola #	Barrancas National	Fla
Arsenal, US	Andersonville National	Ga
Baldwin	Baldwin	Fla
Barrancas	Barrancas National	Fla
Camp Clinch	Barrancas National	Fla
Chattahoocke	Chattahoocke	Fla
East Pass	Barrancas National	Fla
Euchenana	Barrancas National	Fla
Fort Dade	Barrancas National	Fla

BODIES REMOVED FROM LOCATIONS IN FLORIDA

Original Burial Site	Final Burial Site	
Fort Jefferson	Fort Jefferson	Fla
Fort Myers	Barrancas National	Fla
Fort Pickens	Barrancas National	Fla
Gainsville	Gainsville	Fla
Gunboat Point	Barrancas National	Fla
Hawks Park	St. Augustine National	Fla
Jacksonville #	Beaufort National	SC
Jacksonville #	Saint Augustine National	Fla
Key West	Barrancas National	Fla
Lake City	Lake City	Fla
Lakeland	Saint Augustine National	Fla
Loggerhead Key	Fort Jefferson	Fla
Marianne	Barrancas National	Fla
Miami	Miami	Fla
Mosquito Inlet	St. Augustine National	Fla
Olustee	Barrancas National	Fla
Pensacola	Barrancas National	Fla
Quincy	Quincy	Fla
Saint Andrews Bay	Barrancas National	Fla
Saint Augustine	Saint Augustine National	Fla
Saint Francis Barracks	Saint Francis Barracks	Fla
Saint John's Island	Barrancas National	Fla
Santa Rosa Island #	Barrancas National	Fla
Seminole War Casualties	Saint Augustine National	Fla
Tampa	Saint Augustine National	Fla
Warrington	Barrancas National	Fla
Ybor City	Saint Augustine National	Fla

BODIES REMOVED FROM LOCATIONS IN GEORGIA

Original Burial Site	Final Burial Site	
"Eastern Georgia"	Beaufort National	SC
Abbeville	Andersonville National	Ga
Acworth	Marietta National	Ga
Adairsville	Marietta National	Ga
Atlanta	Marietta National	Ga
Albany	Andersonville National	Ga
Alexander	Lawton National	Ga
Allatoona	Marietta National	Ga
Americus	Andersonville National	Ga
Andersonville	Andersonville National	Ga
Andersonville #	Chattanooga National	Ga
Athens	Marietta National	Ga
Atlanta #	Chattanooga National	Ten
Atlanta #	Marietta National	Ga
Augusta #	Andersonville National	Ga
Augusta #	Marietta National	Ga
Bainbridge	Andersonville National	Ga
Bartow	Andersonville National	Ga
Bear Creek Station	Marietta National	Ga
Big Buckhead Bridge	Lawton National	Ga
Big Shanty	Chattanooga National	Ga
Big Shanty	Marietta National	Ga
Calhoun	Marietta National	Ga
Campbell County	Marietta National	Ga
Carroll County	Marietta National	Ga
Carrollton	Marietta National	Ga
Cartersville	Marietta National	Ga
Cassville	Cassville	Ga
Catesville	Lawton National	Ga

50

BODIES REMOVED FROM LOCATIONS IN GEORGIA

Original Burial Site	Final Burial Site	
Cedartown	Marietta National	Ga
Clinton	Andersonville National	Ga
Columbus	Andersonville National	Ga
Coosa River	Marietta National	Ga
Covington #	Andersonville National	Ga
Crawfords	Chattanooga National	Ten
Cuthbert	Andersonville National	Ga
Dallas	Marietta National	Ga
Dalton	Chattanooga National	Ten
Darien	Beaufort National	SC
Davidsboro'	Andersonville National	Ga
Decatur	Marietta National	Ga
East Point	Marietta National	Ga
Eatenton	Andersonville National	Ga
Eutoy Creek	Marietta National	Ga
Ezra Church	Marietta National	Ga
Fayette County	Marietta National	Ga
Floyd County	Marietta National	Ga
Fort Tyler	West Point	Ga
Franklin	Marietta National	Ga
Gainesville	Marietta National	Ga
Gilmer County	Marietta National	Ga
Gordon	Andersonville National	Ga
Graysville	Chattanooga National	Ten
Griswoldsville	Andersonville National	Ga
Hack's Mills	Lawton National	Ga
Harelson County	Marietta National	Ga
Hawkinsville	Andersonville National	Ga
Hillsboro'	Andersonville National	Ga
Irving's X Roads	Andersonville National	Ga
Irwinton	Andersonville National	Ga
Jonesboro'	Marietta National	Ga
Kenesaw	Marietta National	Ga
Kenesaw Mountain	Chattanooga National	Ten
Kenesaw Mountain	Marietta National	Ga
Kingston #	Marietta National	Ga
Lawton	Lawton National	Ga
Lee's Mill	Chattanooga National	Ten
Lost Mountain	Marietta National	Ga
Lovejoy Station	Marietta National	Ga
Macon #	Andersonville National	Ga
Macon #	Lawton National	Ga
Madison #	Andersonville National	Ga
Marietta #	Chattanooga National	Ga
Marietta	Marietta National	Ga
McDonough	Andersonville National	Ga
Merryfield	Lawton National	Ga
Milledgeville	Andersonville National	Ga
Millen	Lawton National	Ga
Monticello	Andersonville National	Ga
New Hope	Marietta National	Ga
New Hope Church	Marietta National	Ga
Newman	Marietta National	Ga
North East	Wilmington National	NC
Peachtree Creek	Marietta National	Ga
Pine Mountain	Marietta National	Ga
Polk County	Marietta National	Ga
Pulaski County	Andersonville National	Ga
Resaca	Chattanooga National	Ga
Resaca	Marietta National	Ga

51

BODIES REMOVED FROM LOCATIONS IN GEORGIA

Original Burial Site	Final Burial Site	
Ringgold	Chattanooga National	Ten
Rocky Ford	Chattanooga National	Ten
Rome	Marietta National	Ga
Rossville	Chattanooga National	Ga
Roswell	Marietta National	Ga
Rough and Ready Station	Marietta National	Ga
Sandersville	Andersonville National	Ga
Savannah #	Beaufort National	SC
Social Circle	Marietta National	Ga
Stanfordsville	Andersonville National	Ga
Station No. 7 C.R.R.	Lawton National	Ga
Station No. 9 C.R.R.	Lawton National	Ga
Station No. 9 1/2 C.R.R.	Andersonville National	Ga
Stone Mountain	Marietta National	Ga
Stringer's Hill	Chattanooga National	Ten
Sunshine	Andersonville National	Ga
Sweetwater	Chattanooga National	Ga
Sweetwater	Marietta National	Ga
Tennville Station	Andersonville National	Ga
Thomas' Station	Lawton National	Ga
Thomasville	Andersonville National	Ga
Toomsboro'	Andersonville National	Ga
Tracey City	Chattanooga National	Ten
Trenton	Chattanooga National	Ten
Tunnel Hill	Chattanooga National	Ten
Vining's Station	Marietta National	Ga
Washington	Marietta National	Ga
Washington County	Andersonville National	Ga
Waynesboro'	Lawton National	Ga
Wells Valley R.R.	Chattanooga National	Ten
West Point	West Point	Ga
William's Island	Chattanooga National	Ten
Worthville	Andersonville National	Ga

BODIES REMOVED FROM THE IDAHO TERRITORY

Original Burial Site	Final Burial Site	
Camp Lyon	Camp Lyon	Id T
Camp Winthrop	Camp Winthrop	Id T
Fort Boise	Fort Boise	Id T
Fort Hall	Fort McPherson National	Neb
Fort Lapwai #	Fort Walla Walla	Id T
Fort Loproai	see Fort Lapwai	D T

BODIES REMOVED FROM LOCATIONS IN ILLINOIS

Original Burial Site	Final Burial Site	
America	Mound City National	Ill
Bunker Hill	Bunker Hill	Ill
Cairo	Mound City National	Ill
Camp Butler	Camp Butler National	Ill
Carbondale	Carbondale	Ill
Cario	Camp Dennison	Ohio
Carlinville	Carlinville	Ill
Chestnut	Chestnut	Ill
Chicago	Chicago	Ill
Clearlake	Camp Butler National	Ill
Decatur	Decatur	Ill
Dixon	Dixon	Ill
Dundee	Dundee	Ill
Elgin	Elgin	Ill
Galesburg	Galesburg	Ill

52

BODIES REMOVED FROM LOCATIONS IN ILLINOIS

Original Burial Site	Final Burial Site	
Metropolis	Mound City National	Ill
Mound City	Mound City National	Ill
Oakwood (near Chicago)	Chicago	Ill
Rockford	Rockford	Ill
Saint Charles	Saint Charles	Ill
Springfield	Springfield	Ill
Springfield (near)	Camp Butler National	Ill

BODIES REMOVED FROM LOCATIONS IN THE INDIAN TERRITORY

Original Burial Site	Final Burial Site	
Cabin Creek	Fort Gibson National	In T
Durant	Fort Gibson National	In T
Flat Rock	Fort Gibson National	In T
Fort Arbuckle,	Fort Gibson National	In T
Fort Gibson	Fort Gibson National	In T
Fort Gibson #	Fort Leavenworth National	Kan
Fort Reno	Fort Reno	In T
Fort Sill	San Antonio National	Tex
Fort Supply	Fort Leavenworth National	Kan
Fort Towson	Fort Gibson National	In T
Fort Washita	Fort Gibson National	In T
Fort Wayne	Fort Gibson National	In T
Gunther's Prairie	Fort Gibson National	In T
Hayfield B.F.	Fort Gibson National	In T
Honey Springs	Fort Gibson National	In T
Hudson's Crossing	Fort Gibson National	In T
Kilderband's Mills	Fort Gibson National	In T
McKay's Saline	Fort Gibson National	In T
Park Hill	Fort Gibson National	In T
Scullyville	Fort Gibson National	In T
Tahlequah	Fort Gibson National	In T
Twelve Mile Creek	Fort Gibson National	In T
Wolf Creek	Fort Gibson National	In T

BODIES REMOVED FROM LOCATIONS IN INDIANA

Original Burial Site	Final Burial Site	
"various sites"	see various sites	Ind
Camp Carrington	Crown Hill National	Ind
Evansville	Evansville	Ind
Evansville #	Spring Grove, Cincinnati	Ohio
Fort Finney	Jeffersonville	Ind
Indianapolis	Crown Hill National	Ind
Jeffersonville #	New Albany National	Ind
Madison #	New Albany National	Ind
Mount Vernon	Mount Vernon	Ind
New Albany	New Albany National	Ind
Newberg	Evansville	Ind

BODIES REMOVED FROM LOCATIONS IN IOWA

Original Burial Site	Final Burial Site	
"various sites"	see various sites	Iowa
Clinton	Clinton	Iowa
Des Moines	Des Moines	Iowa
Iowa City	Keokuk National	Iowa
Sioux City	Sioux City	Iowa

53

BODIES REMOVED FROM LOCATIONS IN KANSAS

Original Site	Final Burial Site	
"various sites"	see various sites	Kan
Allen County	Geneva	Kan
Allen County	Iola	Kan
Ashland	Fort Leavenworth National	Kan
Atchison Road	Fort Leavenworth National	Kan
Aubrey	Olathe	Kan
Barnesville #	Fort Riley	Kan
Baxter Springs	Baxter Springs	Kan
Bourbon County	Mound City	Kan
Camp Coldwater	Paola	Kan
Camp Denver	Barnsville	Kan
Carlisle	Iola	Kan
Cherokee County	Fort Gibson National	In T
Coffy County	Ottumwa	Kan
Council Grove	Fort Leavenworth National	Kan
Cow Creek	Fort Gibson National	In T
Cox Creek	Fort Gibson National	In T
Crawford County	Fort Gibson National	In T
Crisfield	Fort Leavenworth National	Kan
Drywood	Fort Riley National	Kan
Edna	Fort Scott National	Kan
Fort Aubrey	Fort Aubrey	Kan
Fort Dodge	Fort Leavenworth National	Kan
Fort Downer	Fort Leavenworth National	Kan
Fort Ellsworth #	Fort Leavenworth National	Kan
Fort Fletcher	Fort Fletcher	Kan
Fort Harker	Fort Leavenworth National	Kan
Fort Hays #	Fort Leavenworth National	Kan
Fort Larned #	Fort Leavenworth National	Kan
Fort Leavenworth	Fort Leavenworth National	Kan
Fort Lincoln	Fort Scott National	Kan
Fort Riley	Fort Riley	Kan
Fort Scott	Fort Scott National	Kan
Fort Wallace #	Fort Leavenworth National	Kan
Geneva	Geneva	Kan
Iola	Iola	Kan
Johnson county	Olathe	Kan
Lawrence	Lawrence	Kan
Leavenworth	Fort Leavenworth National	Kan
Linn county	Mound City	Kan
Little Blue B. F.	Olathe	Kan
Little River	Fort Leavenworth National	Kan
Louisville	Louisville	Kan
Mapleton	Mound City	Kan
Marmaton City	Kan	Kan
McCune	Fort Leavenworth National	Kan
Miami county	Paola	Kan
Mine Creek Battlefield	Mound City	Kan
Monument Station	Monument Station	Kan
Mound City	Mound City	Kan
Mound City #	Fort Scott	Kan
Neosho Falls	Geneva	Kan
Olathe	Olathe	Kan
Ossawatamie #	Fort Riley	Kan
Ottumwa	Ottumwa	Kan
Paola	Paola	Kan
Parsons	Parsons	Kan
Platte City	Fort Leavenworth National	Kan
Pleasant Hill	Fort Leavenworth National	Kan
Pottawattamie County	Louisville	Kan

54

BODIES REMOVED FROM KANSAS

Original Burial Site	Final Burial Site	
Rockville	Paola	Kan
Saddler's Crossing	Mound City	Kan
Shawnee Mission	Fort Leavenworth National	Kan
Sheridan	Fort Wallace	Kan
Shiloah Creek	Fort Scott National	Kan
Spring Hill	Spring Hill	Kan
Stone Corral	Fort Leavenworth National	Kan
Topeka #	Fort Leavenworth National	Kan
Towner's Station	Towner's Station	Kan
Trading Post	Mound City	Kan
Turkey Creek	Fort Scott National	Kan
Woodson County	Geneva	Kan

BODIES REMOVED FROM KENTUCKY

Original Burial Site	Final Burial Site	
Ashland	Ashland	Ky
Bacon Creek	Cave Hill National	Ky
Barboursville	Knoxville National	Ten
Barboursville	London National	Ky
Bardstown	Lebanon National	Ky
Bear Wallow	Mill Spring National	Ky
Beaver Post	Mill Spring National	Ky
Belmont Furnace	Cave Hill National	Ky
Belmont Station	Cave Hill National	Ky
Bethel	Lebanon National	Ky
Bethel	Mill Springs National	Ky
Big Hill	London National	Ky
Big Paint Creek	New Albany National	Ind
Big Sandy River	New Albany National	Ind
Boston	London National	Ky
Bowling Green	Nashville National	Ten
Bowling Green	Tompkinsville National	Ky
Boyd County	New Albany National	Ind
Buffalo	New Albany National	Ind
Burkesville	Tompkinsville National	Ky
Calhoun	New Albany National	Ind
Camp Burnside	Mill Spring National	Ky
Camp Dick Robinson	Camp Dick Robinson	Ky
Camp Green	Mill Spring National	Ky
Camp Nelson	Camp Nelson National	Ky
Camp Pitman	London National	Ky
Camp Wickliffe	Lebanon National	Ky
Campbellville	Lebanon National	Ky
Cane Valley	Lebanon National	Ky
Canton	Lexington National	Ky
Casey's Creek	Lebanon National	Ky
Catlettsburg	New Albany National	Ind
Cave City	Nashville National	Ten
Cave Hill	Cave Hill National	Ky
Centre Point	Tompkinsville National	Ky
Centreville	Tompkinsville National	Ky
Chapel Hill	Spring Grove, Cincinnati	Ohio
Colesburg	Cave Hill National	Ky
Columbia	Mill Spring National	Ky
Columbia	Tompkinsville National	Ky
Columbus	Mound City National	Ill
Covington #	Camp Nelson National	Ky
Crab Orchard	Lebanon National	Ky
Crab Orchard	Mill Spring National	Ky

BODIES REMOVED FROM KENTUCKY

Original Burial Site	Final Burial Site	
Cumberland Ford	Knoxville National	Ten
Cumberland Gap	Cumberland Gap National	Ten
Cynthiana	Lexington National	Ky
Danville	Danville National	Ky
Dutton Hill	Mill Spring National	Ky
Elizabethtown	Cave Hill National	Ky
Elkton	Nashville National	Ten
Falmouth	Lexington National	Ky
Fishing Creek	Mill Spring National	Ky
Flat Lick	Cumberland Gap National	Ten
Flemingsburg	New Albany National	Ind
Floyd County #	New Albany National	Ind
Fort Boyle	Cave Hill National	Ky
Fort Heiman	Shiloh National	Ten
Fort Holt	Mound City National	Ill
Fort Sands	Cave Hill National	Ky
Fort Willach	Cave Hill National	Ky
Frankfort #	Camp Nelson National	Ky
Franklin	Nashville National	Ten
Frederickstown	Lebanon National	Ky
Freedom	Mill Spring National	Ky
Gap in the Ridge B.F.	Mill Springs National	Ky
Glasgow	Tompkinsville National	Ky
Greasy Creek	Mill Spring National	Ky
Green River	New Albany National	Ind
Green River Bridge B.F.	Lebanon National	Ky
Greensburg	Lebanon National	Ky
Harrison	Mill Spring National	Ky
Harrodsburg	Perryville National	Ky
Hawe's Ford	New Albany National	Ind
Henderson	Cave Hill National	Ky
Hereford River Bottom	Mill Spring National	Ky
Hickman	Memphis National	Ten
Hodgensville	New Albany National	Ind
Hopkinsville	Fort Donelson National	Ten
Horseshoe Bend	Mill Springs National	Ky
Jackson County	Tompkinsville National	Ky
Jamestown	Mill Spring National	Ky
La Fayette	Fort Donelson National	Ten
Lancaster	Camp Nelson National	Ky
Lebanon	Lebanon National	Ky
Lebanon Junction	Cave Hill National	Ky
Lexington	Lexington National	Ky
Liberty	Lebanon National	Ky
Logan's X Roads	Mill Spring National	Ky
London	London National	Ky
Louisa	New Albany National	Ind
Louisville	Cave Hill National	Ky
Louisville	New Albany National	Ind
Louisville	Spring Grove, Cincinnati	Ohio
Madisonville	New Albany National	Ind
Manchester	London National	Ky
Mansfield	Mound City National	Ill
Marrowbone Creek B.F.	Tompkinsville National	Ky
Maxville	Perryville National	Ky
Maysville	New Albany National	Ind
Meeting House	London National	Ky
Mill Springs	Mill Spring National	Ky
Milledgeville	Danville National	Ky
Monrue County	Tompkinsville National	Ky

Original Burial Site	Final Burial Site	
Monticello	Mill Spring National	Ky
Moore's Creek B.F.	Tompkinsville National	Ky
Mount Moriah	Cave Hill National	Ky
Mount Sterling	Lexington National	Ky
Mount Vernon	London National	Ky
Mundfordsville	Cave Hill National	Ky
Neatsville	Camp Nelson	Ky
Nevada	Perryville National	Ky
New Haven	Lebanon National	Ky
New Haven	New Albany National	Ind
New Market	Lebanon National	Ky
Newell's Ferry	Mill Spring National	Ky
Nicholasville	Camp Nelson National	Ky
Nolin Station	Cave Hill National	Ky
Owensboro'	Cave Hill National	Ky
Paducah	Mound City National	Ill
Paintville	New Albany National	Ind
Paris	Lexington National	Ky
Peach Orchard	New Albany National	Ind
Perryville	Perryville National	Ky
Pisgah Church	Mill Spring National	Ky
Pleasant Hill	Tompkinsville National	Ky
Poor Valley Ridge	Knoxville National	Ten
Prestonburg	New Albany National	Ind
Princeton	New Albany National	Ind
Red Mills	Cave Hill National	Ky
Richmond #	Camp Nelson National	Ky
Ringold Schoolhouse	Mill Spring National	Ky
Rock Hill Station	Nashville National	Ten
Rumsey	New Albany National	Ind
Russellville	Nashville National	Ten
Russelville	Spring Grove, Cincinnati	Ohio
Sacramento	New Albany National	Ind
Salem Meeting House	Mill Spring National	Ky
Scottsville	Nashville National	Ten
Shanhan Station	Lexington National	Ky
Sheppardsville	Cave Hill National	Ky
Shiloh Church	Mill Spring National	Ky
Sinking Creek	Knoxville National	Ten
Smith's Grove	Nashville National	Ten
Smithland	New Albany National	Ind
Somerset	Mill Spring National	Ky
Sonora	Cave Hill National	Ky
Springfield	Perryville National	Ky
Stanford	Camp Nelson National	Ky
Stigall's Ferry	Mill Spring National	Ky
Tabor Church	Mill Spring National	Ky
Tompkinsville	National Ky	
Union Meetinghouse	Mill Spring National	Ky
Waitsboro'	Mill Spring National	Ky
Waitsburg	Mill Springs National	Ky
West Point	New Albany National	Ind
White Cat	London National	Ky
Williamsburg	London National	Ky
Winchester	Lexington National	Ky
Wolf Creek	Mill Spring National	Ky
Woodbury	Nashville National	Ten
Woodsonville	Cave Hill National	Ky

57

BODIES REMOVED FROM LOUISIANA

Original Burial Site	Final Burial Site	
A V Davis's Plantation	Natchez National	Miss
Acklin's Plantation	Natchez National	Miss
Alexandria	Alexandria National	La
Algiers	Chalmette National	La
Baton Rouge	Baton Rouge National	La
Bayou Baxter B.F.	Vicksburg National	Miss
Bayou Boeuf	Chalmette National	La
Bayou Ferry	Vicksburg National	Miss
Bayou Sara	Port Hudson National	La
Bayou Teche	Chalmette National	La
Berwick	Chalmette National	La
Bonnet Carre	Chalmette National	La
Brashear #	Chalmette National	La
Brushy Bayou	Vicksburg National	Miss
Bullet's Bayou	Natchez National	Miss
Camp Moore	Camp Moore	La
Camp Parapet	Chalmette National	La
Camp Stevens	Chalmette National	La
Carroll Parish	Vicksburg National	Miss
Carrolton Avenue	Chalmette National	La
Chacahoula	Chalmette National	La
Chalmette	Chalmette National	La
Cheneyville	Alexandria National	La
Clear Creek	Alexandria National	La
Clinton	Port Hudson National	La
Cloutierville	Alexandria National	La
Colfax	Alexandria National	La
Concordia Parish	Natchez National	Miss
Cotile Landing	Alexandria National	La
Crompton's Plantation	Alexandria National	La
Cross Bayou Ferry	Natchez National	Miss
Cypress Grove (No. 2)	Chalmette National	La
De Soto	Vicksburg National	Miss
Donaldsville	Chalmette National	La
Dr. Lanters Plantation	Alexandria National	La
Duckport	Vicksburg National	Miss
Dumbar's Plantation B.F.	Vicksburg National	Miss
East Branch of Mississippi	Port Hudson National	La
Fontania	Port Hudson National	La
Fort DeRussey	Alexandria National	La
Fort Jackson	Fort Saint Phillip National	La
Fort Livingston	see Grand Terre Island	La
Fort Macomb #	Chalmette National	La
Fort Pike	Chalmette National	La
Fort Saint Phillip	Fort Saint Phillip National	La
Franklin	Chalmette National	La
Goodrich's Landing	Vicksburg National	Miss
Grand Coteau	Chalmette National	La
Grand Ecore	Alexandria National	La
Grand Terre Island	Grand Terre Island	La
Groves (Madison Parish)	Vicksburg National	Miss
Hagaman Bayou	Vicksburg National	Miss
Harris Plantation	Natchez National	Miss
Illawara Landing	Vicksburg National	Miss
Iron's Plantation	Alexandria National	La
Jackson	Port Hudson National	La
Jackson Barracks	Chalmette National	La
Jackson's Sally Port	Port Hudson National	La
Labadieville	Chalmette National	La
Lafayette Parish	Vicksburg National	Miss

58

BODIES REMOVED FROM LOUISIANA

Original Burial Site	Final Burial Site	
Lafourche Crossing	Chalmette National	La
Lafourche Parish	Chalmette National	La
Lake Providence	Vicksburg National	Miss
Madison Parish	Vicksburg National	Miss
Mansfield	Alexandria National	La
Marksville	Alexandria National	La
Matairie's Ridge	Chalmette National	La
Milliken's Bend	Vicksburg National	Miss
Monett's Ferry	Alexandria National	La
Monroe	Monroe	La
Monument	Chalmette National	La
Mooreville	Natchez National	Miss
Morganza	Port Hudson National	La
Mott's Ferry	Alexandria National	La
Mount Pleasant	Port Hudson National	La
Mount Pleasant Landing	Port Hudson National	La
Natchitoches	Alexandria National	La
New Cathage	Vicksburg National	Miss
New Iberia	Chalmette National	La
New Orleans	Chalmette National	La
Olive Branch	Port Hudson National	La
Omega	Vicksburg National	Miss
Omega Landing	Vicksburg National	Miss
Opelousas	Chalmette National	La
Packan Plantation	Natchez National	Miss
Pattersonville	Chalmette National	La
Paw Paw Island	Vicksburg National	Miss
Pettus Farillo Parish	Pettus Farillo Parish (sic)	La
Pineville	Alexandria National	La
Pinhook B.F.	Vicksburg National	Miss
Plantation	Natchez National	Miss
Plaquemine	Baton Rouge National	La
Pleasant Hill	Alexandria National	La
Point Coupee	Natchez National	Miss
Point Coupee	Port Hudson National	La
Ponchatoula	Chalmette National	Va
Port Hudson	Port Hudson National	La
Prophet's Island	Port Hudson National	La
R D Chotard's Plantation	Natchez National	Miss
Red River Landing	Natchez National	Miss
Richmond B.F.	Vicksburg National	Miss
Rondleson	Port Hudson National	La
Roundaway Bayou	Vicksburg National	Miss
Sabine Cross Roads	Alexandria National	La
Saint Francisville	Port Hudson National	La
Saint Mary's Parish	Chalmette National	La
Sandy Creek	Port Hudson National	La
Sedgwick Hospital	Chalmette National	La
Semmesport	Alexandria National	La
Shreveport	Shreveport National	La
Smith's Plantation	Alexandria National	La
Somerset Landing	Vicksburg National	Miss
Springfield Landing	Port Hudson National	La
St. Martin's Parish	Chalmette National	La
Stacey's Plantation	Natchez National	Miss
T B Magruder's Plantation	Natchez National	Miss
Tehsas Parish	Vicksburg National	Miss
Terrebonne Parish	Chalmette National	La
Terrebonne Station	Chalmette National	La
Thibodeaux	Cornith National	Miss

BODIES REMOVED FROM LOUISIANA

Original Burial Site	Final Burial Site	
Tigersville Station	Chalmette National	La
Transylvania	Vicksburg National	Miss
Turnbull's Island	Natchez National	Miss
Upper Springfield Landing	Port Hudson National	La
Vermillionville	Chalmette National	La
Vidalia	Natchez National	Miss
Washington	Chalmette National	La
Waterproof	Natchez National	Miss
Willow Bayou	Vicksburg National	Miss
Wilson's Landing	Alexandria National	La
Yellow Bayou	Alexandria National	La
Young's Point	Vicksburg National	Miss

BODIES REMOVED FROM MAINE

Original Burial Site	Final Burial Site	
Augusta	Augusta	Me
Bucksport	Bucksport	Me
Calais	Calais	Me
Danville	Danville	Me
Euta	Euta	Me
Mackay Island	Portland	Me
Nautucket	Nautucket	Me
Portland	Portland	Me
Wallingford	Wallingford	Me

BODIES REMOVED FROM MARYLAND

Original Burial Site	Final Burial Site	
Annapolis	Annapolis National	Md
Annapolis	Naval Cemetery, Annapolis	Md
Antietam	Antietam National	Md
Baltimore	Laurel Grove, Baltimore	Md
Baltimore	Louden Park National	Md
Berlin	Antietam National	Md
Bladwnsburg #	U S Military Asylum	D C
Bloomington	Antietam National	Md
Boonesboro'	Antietam National	Md
Brownsville	Antietam National	Md
Burkettsville	Antietam National	Md
Camp Parole	Annapolis National	Md
Cavetown	Antietam National	Md
Chappel Point	Arlington National	Va
Claryville	Antietam National	Md
Clear Spring	Antietam National	Md
Cumberland	Antietam National	Md
Elkridge Landing	Loudon Park National	Md
Fort McHenry	Fort McHenry	Md
Fort McHenry #	Loudon Park National	Md
Fort Pendleton	Antietam National	Md
Fort Washington	Fort Washington	Md
Frederick #	Antietam National	Md
Frostburg	Antietam National	Md
Funkstown	Antietam National	Md
Hagerstown	Antietam National	Md
Hancock	Antietam National	Md
Keedysville	Antietam National	Md
Laurel	Laurel	Md
Licksville	Licksville	Md
Little Orleans	Antietam National	Md

BODIES REMOVED FROM MARYLAND

Original Burial Site	Final Burial Site	
Locust Spring	Antietam National	Md
Maryland Heights	Antietam National	Md
Middletown	Antietam National	Md
Monocacy Junction	Antietam National	Md
Montgomery County	Arlington National	Va
Oakland	Antietam National	Md
Oldtown	Antietam National	Md
Point Lookout #	Arlington National	Va
Point of Rocks	Antietam National	Md
Port Tobacco	Arlington National	Va
Preston	Preston	Md
Prince George's County	Arlington National	Va
Relay House	Loudon Park National	Md
Rockville	Arlington National	Va
Rum Point	Arlington National	Va
Saint James College	Antietam National	Md
Sandy Hook	Antietam National	Md
Sandy Point	Arlington National	Va
Sharpsburg	Antietam National	Md
Smoketown	Antietam National	Md
South Mountain	Antietam National	Md
Urbanna	Antietam National	Md
Westernport	Antietam National	Md
Weverton	Antietam National	Md
Williamsport	Antietam National	Md

BODIES REMOVED FROM MASSACHUSETTS

Original Burial Site	Final Burial Site	
Abington	Abington	Mass
Boston	Boston	Mass
Brookline	Brookline	Mass
Cambridge	Cambridge	Mass
Chelsea	Chelsea	Mass
Dedham	Dedham	Mass
Easthampton	Easthampton	Mass
Readville	Dedham	Mass
Roxbury	Roxbury	Mass
Worcester	Worcester	Mass

BODIES REMOVED FROM MICHIGAN

Original Burial Site	Final Burial Site	
Detroit	Detroit	Mich
Elmwood	Detroit	Mich
Flint #	Fort Wayne	Mich
Fort Detroit	Fort Detroit	Mich
Fort Gratiot	Fort Gratiot	Mich
Fort Macinac	Fort Macinac	Mich
Fort Wayne	Fort Wayne	Mich
Fort Wilkens	Fort Wilkens	Mich
Grand Rapids	Grand Rapids	Mich
Jackson	Jackson	Mich
Kalamazoo #	Fort Wayne	Mich
Niles #	Fort Wayne	Mich
Ypsilanti #	Fort Wayne	Mich

Bodies Buried in Mexico   see Mexico City National Cemetery

BODIES REMOVED FROM MINNESOTA

Original Burial Site	Final Burial Site	
Alexandria	Alexandria	Min
Camp Coldwater	Fort Snelling National	Min
Fort Ridgley #	Rock Island National	Ill
Fort Ripley	Rock Island National	Ill
Fort Snelling	Fort Snelling National	Min
Pomme de Terre	Pomme de Terre	Min
Saint Paul	Fort Leavenworth National	Kan
Sauk Centre	Sauk Centre	Min

BODIES REMOVED FROM MISSISSIPPI

Original Burial Site	Final Burial Site	
Abbleville	Cornith National	Miss
Aberdeen	Cornith National	Miss
Baldwin	Cornith National	Miss
Baldwin's Ferry	Vicksburg National	Miss
Big Black River Bridge	Vicksburg National	Miss
Birdsong Ferry	Vicksburg National	Miss
Black Fish Lake	Memphis National	Ten
Bolton	Vicksburg National	Miss
Bovina	Vicksburg National	Miss
Braunar's Plantation	Natchez National	Miss
Brice's X Roads	Cornith National	Miss
Bridgeport	Vicksburg National	Miss
Brookhaven	Vicksburg National	Miss
Brown's Mill	Natchez National	Miss
Brownsville	Vicksburg National	Miss
Buck's Plantation	Natchez National	Miss
Burnsville	Cornith National	Miss
Camp Davis	Cornith National	Miss
Canton	Cornith National	Miss
Carolina Landing	Vicksburg National	Miss
Carroll County	Vicksburg National	Miss
Champion Hill B.F.	Vicksburg National	Miss
Chickasaw	Shiloh National	Ten
Chickasaw Bayou	Vicksburg National	Miss
Claiborne County	Vicksburg National	Miss
Clarke's Graveyard	Vicksburg National	Miss
Clinton	Vicksburg National	Miss
Coffeeville	Cornith National	Miss
Coldwater River	Memphis National	Ten
Columbus	Cornith National	Miss
Corinth	Cornith National	Miss
Davis Bend	Vicksburg National	Miss
Dunlap Springs	Cornith National	Miss
Eagle Lake	Vicksburg National	Miss
Eastport	Shiloh National	Ten
Edwards Station	Vicksburg National	Miss
Egypt Station	Cornith National	Miss
Ellistown	Cornith National	Miss
Farmington	Cornith National	Miss
Flowers	Vicksburg National	Miss
Fort Adams	Natchez National	Miss
Fort Hill	Vicksburg National	Miss
Four Mile Bridge	Vicksburg National	Miss
Glendale	Cornith National	Miss

62

BODIES REMOVED FROM MISSISSIPPI

Original Burial Site	Final Burial Site	
Grand Gulf	Vicksburg National	Miss
Greenwood Island	Greenwood Island	Miss
Grenada #	Vicksburg National	Miss
Guntown	Cornith National	Miss
Hall's Ferry	Vicksburg National	Miss
Hatchie river	Cornith National	Miss
Haynes Bluff	Vicksburg National	Miss
Hinds County	Vicksburg National	Miss
Holly Springs #	Cornith National	Miss
Island # 82	Vicksburg National	Miss
Iuka	Cornith National	Miss
Jacinto	Cornith National	Miss
Jackson	Jackson	Miss
Jenkins Plantation	Natchez National	Miss
Job's House	Cornith National	Miss
Judge Coleman's Plantation	Natchez National	Miss
Kingston	Natchez National	Miss
Kossuth	Cornith National	Miss
Lacopolis	Memphis National	Ten
Lamling's Landing	Natchez National	Miss
Madison County	Vicksburg National	Miss
McMurran's Plantation	Natchez National	Miss
Meadville	Natchez National	Miss
Meadville Road	Natchez National	Miss
Mechanicsburg B.F.	Vicksburg National	Miss
Milldale	Vicksburg National	Miss
Natchez	Natchez National	Miss
Neshoba County	Vicksburg National	Miss
Newton County	Vicksburg National	Miss
Okolona	Cornith National	Miss
Oktibbeha County	Vicksburg National	Miss
Oxford #	Cornith National	Miss
Pass Christian	Vicksburg National	Miss
Philadelphia	Vicksburg National	Miss
Port Gibson	Natchez National	Miss
Port Gibson	Vicksburg National	Miss
Prentiss	Vicksburg National	Miss
Prio's Racetrack	Natchez National	Miss
Quitman's Landing	Natchez National	Miss
Ration Hill	Vicksburg National	Miss
Raymond	Vicksburg National	Miss
Rienzi	Cornith National	Miss
Rocky Springs	Vicksburg National	Miss
Rodney	Natchez National	Miss
Salem	Cornith National	Miss
Saltillo	Cornith National	Miss
Ship Island #	Chalmette National	La
Snyder's Bluff	Vicksburg National	Miss
Sprout Spring	Vicksburg National	Miss
Starksville #	Vicksburg National	Miss
Sunflower County	Vicksburg National	Miss
Swallow's Bluff	Shiloh National	Ten
T B Magruder's Plantation	Natchez National	Miss
Templeton	Vicksburg National	Miss
Tribles	Vicksburg National	Miss
Tupello	Cornith National	Miss
Two Mile Bridge	Vicksburg National	Miss
Union	Vicksburg National	Miss

BODIES REMOVED FROM MISSISSIPPI

Original Burial Site	Final Burial Site	
Vandalia	Vicksburg National	Miss
Vicksburg	Vicksburg National	Miss
Warren County	Vicksburg National	Miss
Warrenton	Vicksburg National	Miss
Washington	Natchez National	Miss
Water Valley	Cornith National	Miss
Wayne County	Vicksburg National	Miss
West Point	Cornith National	Miss
White House	Cornith National	Miss
Winchester	Vicksburg National	Miss
Worthington	Vicksburg National	Miss
Wyatt	Memphis National	Ten
Yazoo City	Vicksburg National	Miss

BODIES REMOVED FROM MISSOURI

Original Burial Site	Final Burial Site	
Adair County	Jefferson Barracks National	Mo
Bailey's Station	Jefferson Barracks National	Mo
Balltown	Fort Scott National	Kan
Barry County	Fayetteville National	Ark
Barry County	Springfield National	Mo
Barton County	Springfield National	Mo
Bates	Jefferson City National	Mo
Baxter Springs	Fort Gibson National	In T
Belmont	Mound City National	Ill
Benton County	Jefferson Barracks National	Mo
Big Blue River	Fort Leavenworth National	Kan
Bird's Point	Mound City National	Ill
Bloomfield #	Jefferson Barracks National	Mo
Bloomfield #	Springfield National	Mo
Blue Spring Road	Fort Leavenworth National	Kan
Bolivar	Springfield National	Mo
Boonville	Jefferson City National	Mo
Brunswick #	Jefferson City National	Mo
Buck Prairie	Springfield National	Mo
Buena Vista Springs	Nashville National	Ten
Butler	Fort Scott National	Kan
Butler County	Jefferson Barracks National	Mo
Byrams Ford	Fort Leavenworth National	Kan
Callaway County	Jefferson Barracks National	Mo
Camden Point	Fort Leavenworth National	Kan
Camden Point Road	Fort Leavenworth National	Kan
Camp Bliss	Springfield National	Mo
Camp Cole	Jefferson Barracks National	Mo
Camp Hunter	Fort Gibson National	In T
Camp John Ross	Fort Gibson National	In T
Cape Girardeau #	Jefferson Barracks National	Mo
Carthage	Springfield National	Mo
Cassville #	Fayetteville National	Ark
Cassville #	Springfield National	Mo
Centralia	Centralia	Mo
Charleston	Jefferson Barracks National	Mo
Chauton County	Jefferson City National	Mo
Chillicothe	Jefferson Barracks National	Mo
Christian County	Springfield National	Mo
Clinton	Clinton	Mo
Columbia	Jefferson Barracks National	Mo
Columbus	Fort Leavenworth National	Kan
Commerce	Mound City National	Ill
Coon Creek	Springfield National	Mo

64

BODIES REMOVED FROM MISSOURI

Original Burial Site	Final Burial Site	
Cooper County	Jefferson Barracks National	Mo
Cooper County	Jefferson City National	Mo
Coursey's Station	Springfield National	Mo
Crane Creek	Springfield National	Mo
Cuntsville	Jefferson Barracks National	Mo
Dale County	Springfield National	Mo
Dallas #	Jefferson Barracks National	Mo
Dallas County	Springfield National	Mo
De Soto	Jefferson Barracks National	Mo
Dent County	Jefferson Barracks National	Mo
Douglas County	Springfield National	Mo
Dry Wood	Fort Scott National	Kan
Dug Springs	Springfield National	Mo
Dunkirk City	Jefferson Barracks National	Mo
Dunklin County	Jefferson Barracks National	Mo
Elk Mills #	Springfield National	Mo
Enterprise	Springfield National	Mo
Evansville	Jefferson Barracks National	Mo
Fayette	Jefferson Barracks National	Mo
Flat Creek	Springfield National	Mo
Forsythe	Springfield National	Mo
Four Mile	Jefferson Barracks National	Mo
Franklin #	Jefferson Barracks National	Mo
Fredericksburg	Fort Leavenworth National	Kan
Freeland	Jefferson Barracks National	Mo
Fremont	Jefferson Barracks National	Mo
Fulbright Springs	Jefferson Barracks National	Mo
Fulton	Jefferson Barracks National	Mo
Gardins Coal Bank	Fort Leavenworth National	Kan
Georgetown	Jefferson Barracks National	Mo
Georgetown	Jefferson City National	Mo
Georgia City	Springfield National	Mo
Glasgow #	Jefferson City National	Mo
Greenbrier Station	Nashville National	Ten
Greene County	Springfield National	Mo
Greenfield #	Springfield National	Mo
Greenville #	Jefferson Barracks National	Mo
Hannibal	Jefferson Barracks National	Mo
Harrisonville	Fort Leavenworth National	Kan
Hartsville	Springfield National	Mo
Hickman Hills	Fort Leavenworth National	Kan
Hickmann's Mills	Fort Leavenworth National	Kan
Hogan's Crossing	Fort Scott National	Kan
Holden	Fort Leavenworth National	Kan
Hoosier Prairie	Springfield National	Mo
Houston	Jefferson Barracks National	Mo
Howard County	Jefferson City National	Mo
Huntsville #	Jefferson Barracks National	Mo
Hutchinson's Farm	Fort Leavenworth National	Kan
Independence #	Fort Leavenworth National	Kan
Ironton #	Jefferson Barracks National	Mo
Jackson #	Jefferson Barracks National	Mo
Jasper County	Springfield National	Mo
Jefferson Barracks	Jefferson Barracks National	Mo
Kansas City	Fort Leavenworth National	Kan
Kirksville	Jefferson Barracks National	Mo
Laclede County	Springfield National	Mo
Lake Springs	Jefferson Barracks National	Mo
Lamar	Springfield National	Mo

BODIES REMOVED FROM MISSOURI

Original Burial Site	Final Burial Site	
Lawrence County	Springfield National	Mo
Lebanon #	Springfield National	Mo
Lexington #	Fort Leavenworth National	Kan
Liberty	Fort Leavenworth National	Kan
Liberty Township	Jefferson Barracks National	Mo
Licking	Jefferson Barracks National	Mo
Lime Creek	Jefferson Barracks National	Mo
Linn Creek	Jefferson Barracks National	Mo
Macon City	Jefferson Barracks National	Mo
Marble Hill	Jefferson Barracks National	Mo
Marionsville	Springfield National	Mo
Marshfield	Springfield National	Mo
McDonald County	Springfield National	Mo
McDowell	McDowell	Mo
Memphis	Keokuk National	Iowa
Mexico #	Jefferson Barracks National	Mo
Minersville	Springfield National	Mo
Moniteau County	Jefferson Barracks National	Mo
Morgan County	Jefferson Barracks National	Mo
Morgan County	Jefferson City National	Mo
Moselle Station	Jefferson Barracks National	Mo
Mount Gilead	Springfield National	Mo
Mount Mora	Fort Leavenworth National	Kan
Mount Vernon	Springfield National	Mo
Neosha	Fort Gibson National	In T
Neosho	Springfield National	Mo
New Madrid	Memphis National	Ten
New Madrid	Mound City National	Ill
Newton County	Fayetteville National	Ark
Newton County	Springfield National	Mo
Newtonia #	Springfield National	Mo
Oliver's Prairie	Springfield National	Mo
Oregon	Springfield National	Mo
Osceolo	Memphis National	Ten
Ottterville #	Jefferson City National	Mo
Ozark	Springfield National	Mo
Palmyra	Jefferson Barracks National	Mo
Patterson #	Jefferson Barracks National	Mo
Perryville	Jefferson Barracks National	Mo
Pettis County	Jefferson City National	Mo
Phelps County	Jefferson Barracks National	Mo
Pilot Grove	Jefferson Barracks National	Mo
Pilot Knob	Jefferson Barracks National	Mo
Pineville	Springfield National	Mo
Platte City	Fort Leavenworth National	Kan
Pleasant Hill	Fort Leavenworth National	Kan
Point Pleasant	Memphis National	Ten
Polk County	Springfield National	Mo
Pomme de Terre Creek	Springfield National	Mo
Poole's Prairie	Springfield National	Mo
Prarrie Holden	Fort Leavenworth National	Kan
Preston	Springfield National	Mo
Pulaski County	Jefferson Barracks National	Mo
Reeves' Station #	Jefferson Barracks National	Mo
Rockport	Jefferson Barracks National	Mo
Rolla	Jefferson Barracks National	Mo
Round Pond	Jefferson Barracks National	Mo
Saint Joseph	Fort Leavenworth National	Kan
Saint Louis	Jefferson Barracks National	Mo
Salem	Jefferson Barracks National	Mo

BODIES REMOVED FROM MISSOURI

Original Burial Site	Final Burial Site	
Sand Springs	Springfield National	Mo
Sarcoxie	Springfield National	Mo
Sedalia #	Jefferson City National	Mo
Shawnee	Fort Leavenworth National	Kan
Shepard Mountain	Jefferson Barracks National	Mo
Shirley's Ford	Springfield National	Mo
Smithton	Jefferson City National	Mo
Springfield	Jefferson Barracks National	Mo
Springfield	Springfield National	Mo
St. Charles	Jefferson Barracks National	Mo
St. Genevieve	Jefferson Barracks National	Mo
St. Joseph	Fort Leavenworth National	Kan
Stevens' Mills	Springfield National	Mo
Stoddard County	Jefferson Barracks National	Mo
Stone County	Springfield National	Mo
Swan Creek	Springfield National	Mo
Syracuse	Jefferson Barracks National	Mo
Taney County	Springfield National	Mo
Texas County	Jefferson Barracks National	Mo
Tipton #	Jefferson Barracks National	Mo
Tyree Springs	Nashville National	Ten
Urbana	Springfield National	Mo
Vera Cruz	Springfield National	Mo
Vernon County	Fort Scott National	Kan
Verona	Springfield National	Mo
Versailles	Jefferson Barracks National	Mo
Warrensburg	Jefferson Barracks National	Mo
Warsaw	Jefferson Barracks National	Mo
Waynesville #	Jefferson Barracks National	Mo
Webster County	Springfield National	Mo
Wellington	Fort Leavenworth National	Kan
West Plains	Springfield National	Mo
Weston #	Fort Leavenworth National	Kan
Westport	Fort Leavenworth National	Kan
White River	Springfield National	Mo
Wilson's Creek B.F.	Springfield National	Mo
Wright County	Springfield National	Mo

BODIES REMOVED FROM THE MONTANA TERRITORY

Original Burial Site	Final Burial Site	
"Custer's Last Stand"	Custer National	M T
Bear Paw Mountains B.F.	see various sites	M T
Big Timber	Fort Wallace	Kan
Camp Cooke	Camp Cooke	M T
Camp Poplar River	Custer National	M T
Camp Sam Fordyce	Custer National	M T
Clark's Fork	see various sites	M T
Custer B.F.	West Point	NY
Custer B.F.	Custer National	M T
Fort Assinniboine	Custer National	M T
Fort Assinniboine	Fort Leavenworth National	Kan
Fort C.F. Smith	Custer National	M T
Fort Custer #	Custer National	M T
Fort Ellis	Fort Ellis	M T
Fort Keogh	Custer National	M T
Fort Maginnis	Custer National	M T
Fort Missoula	Fort Missoula	M T
Fort Shaw #	Custer National	M T
Fort Totten	Custer National	M T

67

BODIES REMOVED FROM THE MONTANA TERRITORY

Original Burial Site	Final Burial Site	
Little Big Horn B.F.	Custer National	M T
Little Big Horn B.F.	Fort Leavenworth National	Neb
Little Big Horn B.F.	West Point	NY
Little Big Horn River	Fort Leavenworth National	Kan
Mispah Creek	see various sites	M T
O'Fallen Creek	see various sites	M T
Pumpkin Creek B.F.	see various sites	M T
Reno-Benteen B.F.	see Custer National	M T
Rosebud Creek B.F.	see various sites	M T
Tongue River B.F.	see various sites	M T
Wolf Mountains B.F.	see various sites	M T

BODIES REMOVED FROM NEBRASKA

Original Burial Site	Final Burial Site	
Camp Sheridan	Fort Robinson	Neb
Crete	Fort Leavenworth National	Kan
Fort Hallock	Fort McPherson National	Neb
Fort Harts	Fort McPherson National	Neb
Fort Hartsuff	Fort McPherson National	Neb
Fort Karney	Fort McPherson National	Neb
Fort Kearny	Fort McPherson National	Neb
Fort McPherson	Fort McPherson National	Neb
Fort Niabrana	Fort Leavenworth National	Kan
Fort Omaha	Fort Omaha	Neb
Fort Robinson	Fort Robinson	Neb
Fort Sidney	Fort McPherson National	Neb

BODIES REMOVED FROM NEVADA

Original Burial Site	Final Burial Site	
Camp Dun Glen	Camp Dun Glen	Nev
Camp McKee	Camp McKee	Nev
Carson	Carson	Nev
Fort Churchill	Camp Dun Glen	Nev
Fort McDermit	Fort McDermit	Nev
Fort Ruby #	San Francisco National	Calf
Granite Creek Station	Camp McKee	Nev
Quinn River Camp Number 3	Fort McDermit	Nev

BODIES REMOVED FROM NEW HAMPSHIRE

Original Burial Site	Final Burial Site	
Candia	Candia	NH
Concord	Concord	NH
Manchester	Manchester	NH
Portsmouth	Portsmouth	NH

BODIES REMOVED FROM NEW JERSEY

Original Burial Site	Final Burial Site	
Beverly	Beverly National	NJ
Bridgeton	Bridgeton	NJ
Burlington County	Burlington County	NJ
Finn's Point	Finn's Point National	NJ
Newark	Newark	NJ
Pea Patch Island	Finn's Point National	NJ
Tuckerton	Burlington County	NJ

BODIES REMOVED FROM NEW MEXICO

Original Burial Site	Final Burial Site	
Albuquerque	Albuquerque	NM
Apache Canyon	Apache Canyon	NM
Camp Boyd	San Antonio National	Tex
Camp Easton	Fort Bascom	NM
Camp Mosby	San Antonio National	Tex
Fort Apache	Fort Apache	NM
Fort Bascom	Fort Leavenworth National	Kan
Fort Bayard #	Fort Leavenworth National	Kan
Fort Bayard #	San Antonio National	Tex
Fort Craig #	Fort Leavenworth National	Kan
Fort Craig #	Santa Fe National	NM
Fort Cummings #	Fort Leavenworth National	Kan
Fort Filmore	Fort Filmore	NM
Fort Lowell	Santa Fe National	NM
Fort Marcy #	Santa Fe National	NM
Fort McRae #	Fort Leavenworth National	Kan
Fort Selden #	Fort Leavenworth National	Kan
Fort Stanton #	Santa Fe National	NM
Fort Sumner #	Santa Fe National	NM
Fort Union #	Fort Leavenworth National	Kan
Fort Union #	Santa Fe National	NM
Fort Wingate	Fort Wingate	Kan
Glorieta B.F.	Santa Fe National	NM
Kozloskis Ranch	Santa Fe National	NM
Las Cruces	Las Cruces	NM
Las Vegas	Santa Fe National	NM
Los Pinos #	Santa Fe National	NM
Pecas	Santa Fe National	NM
Pigeons Ranch	Santa Fe National	NM
Santa Fe	Santa Fe National	NM
Taos	Santa Fe National	NM
Thornton	Santa Fe National	NM
Val Verde B.F.	Santa Fe National	NM

BODIES REMOVED FROM NEW YORK

Original Burial Site	Final Burial Site	
Albany	Albany	NY
Beechwood	New York City Harbor	NY
Brooklyn	U S Naval Cemetery, Brooklyn	NY
Buffalo	Buffalo	NY
Camp Lafayette	Cypress Hills National	NY
Camp Spraque	Cypress Hills National	NY
Cherry Creek	Cherry Creek	NY
David's Island	New Rochelle	NY
David's Island	New York City Harbor	NY
Dunkirk	Dunkirk	NY
Elmira	Elmira	NY
Fort Columbus	New York City Harbor	NY
Fort Hamilton	New York City Harbor	NY
Fort Ontario	Fort Ontario	NY
Fort Wadsworth	Fort Wadsworth	NY
Governor's Island #	New York City Harbor	NY
Hart Island-NYC	New York City Harbor	NY
Ithaca	Ithaca	NY
Jamestown	Jamestown	NY
Lansingburgh	Lansingburgh	NY
Lockport	Lockport	NY
Lodi	Lodi	NY
Madison Barracks	Madison Barracks	NY

BODIES REMOVED FROM NEW YORK

Original Burial Site	Final Burial Site	
New Rochelle	New Rochelle	NY
New York City	Cypress Hills National	NY
Newburg	Newburg	NY
Plattsburg Barracks	Plattsburg Barracks	NY
Rochester	Rochester	NY
Sackett"s Harbor	Madison Barracks	NY
Sandy Hook	New York City Harbor	NY
Seneca Falls	Seneca Falls	NY
Staton Island	Cypress Hills National	NY
Watervliet Arsenal	West Troy	NY
West Point	West Point	NY
West Troy	West Troy	NY
Willett's Point	New York City Harbor	NY

BODIES REMOVED FROM NORTH CAROLINA

Original Burial Site	Final Burial Site	
Ashville	Chattanooga National	Ten
Averysboro	Raleigh National	NC
Bachelor's Creek	Newberne National	NC
Barrettville	Chattanooga National	Ten
Beaufort	Newberne National	NC
Bentonville	Raleigh National	NC
blowing up the Albemarle	Newberne National	NC
Brunswick	Wilmington National	NC
Bryson City	Knoxville National	Ten
Buffalo Swamp	Raleigh National	NC
Camden B.F.	Newberne National	NC
Camp Russell	Raleigh National	NC
Camp York	Salisbury National	NC
Carolina City #	Newberne National	NC
Castle Island	Newberne National	NC
Chapel Hill	Raleigh National	NC
Charlotte #	Salisbury National	NC
Edenton	Newberne National	NC
Elliott's Ferry	Chattanooga National	Ten
Fayetteville	Wilmington National	NC
Fort Clark	Newberne National	NC
Fort Fisher	Wilmington National	NC
Fort Johnson	Wilmington National	NC
Fort Macon #	Newberne National	NC
Franklinton	Raleigh National	NC
Gold Hill	Salisbury National	NC
Goldsboro #	Newberne National	NC
Goldsboro' #	Raleigh National	NC
Grassy Fork	Chattanooga National	Ten
Greensboro' #	Raleigh National	NC
Hatteras	Newberne National	NC
Henderson	Raleigh National	NC
Hilton	Wilmington National	NC
Kinston	Newberne National	NC
Lenoir	Lenoir	NC
Lexington	Salisbury National	NC
Lincolnton	Salisbury National	NC
Louisburg	Raleigh National	NC
Madison County	Chattanooga National	Ten
Marshall	Chattanooga National	Ten
Morehead City #	Newberne National	NC
Morganton	Morganton	NC
Neuse River Road	Raleigh National	NC

BODIES REMOVED FROM NORTH CAROLINA

Original Burial Site	Final Burial Site	
Newberne	Newberne National	NC
Newport Ferry	Chattanooga National	Ten
Old Fort	Salisbury National	NC
Paint Rock	Chattanooga National	Ten
Parretsville	Chattanooga National	Ten
Plymouth	Newberne National	NC
Princeton	Raleigh National	NC
Rainbow Bluff	Newberne National	NC
Raleigh	Raleigh National	NC
Rawles Mills	Newberne National	NC
Roanoke Island	Newberne National	NC
Salsibury	Andersonville National	Ga
Salsibury	Salsibury National	NC
Shelby	Shelby	NC
Smithfield	Raleigh National	NC
Smithville	Raleigh National	NC
Smithville	Wilmington National	NC
Swain County	Salisbury National	NC
Tarboro	Raleigh National	NC
Warm Springs	Chattanooga National	Ten
Washington #	Newberne National	NC
Weldon	Weldon	NC
Whitehall	Newberne National	NC
Wilmington	Wilmington National	NC
Wilson	Wilson	NC
Wilsonville	Chattanooga National	Ten
Wise's Forks (near Kinston)	Newberne National	NC

BODIES REMOVED FROM OHIO

Original Burial Site	Final Burial Site	
Camp Delaware	Camp Delaware	Ohio
Camp Dennison #	Spring Grove, Cincinnati	Ohio
Cincinnati	Spring Grove, Cincinnati	Ohio
Cleveland	Cleveland	Ohio
Clinton Chapel	Greenlawn, Columbus	Ohio
Columbus	Columbus	Ohio
Dayton	Dayton	Ohio
Gallipolis	Gallipolis	Ohio
Harmon	Harmon	Ohio
Johnson's Island	Johnson's Island	Ohio
Marion	Marion	Ohio
Sandusky	see Johnson's Island	Ohio
Walnut Hill	Spring Grove, Cincinnati	Ohio

BODIES REMOVED FROM OREGON

Original Burial Site	Final Burial Site	
Camp C.F. Smith	Camp C.F. Smith	Org
Camp Grant	San Francisco National	Calf
Camp Warner	Camp Warner	Org
Clearwater Indian Terr.	Fort Vancouver	Wash
Fort Dalles #	Fort Vancouver	Wash
Fort Kalmath #	San Francisco National	Calf
Fort Stevens	Fort Vancouver	Wash
Fort Watson #	Fort Vancouver	Wash
Lava Beds	San Francisco National	Calf
Warner	San Francisco National	Calf

BODIES REMOVED FROM THE PHILIPPINES

Original Burial Site	Final Burial Site	
Manilla	Vicksburg National	Miss

BODIES REMOVED FROM PENNSYLVANIA

Original Burial Site	Final Burial Site	
Braddock's Field	(Allegheny) Pittsburgh	Pen
Bristol	Bristol	Pen
Camelton	Camelton	Pen
Camp Cadwalader	Camp Cadwalader	Pen
Camp Curtin	Harrisburg	Pen
Carlisle	Carlisle	Pen
Chambersburg	Chambersburg	Pen
Chester	Chester	Pen
China Hall	Bristol	Pen
Doylesville	Doylesville	Pen
Duncansville	Duncansville	Pen
Easton	Easton	Pen
Elk Creek	Elk Creek	Pen
Fairfield	Gettysburg National	Pen
Fort Chester	San Antonio National	Tex
Fort Mifflin	Fort Mifflin	Pen
Fulton County	Antietam National	Md
Gettysburg	Gettysburg National	Pen
Hanover	Gettysburg National	Pen
Harrisburg	Harrisburg	Pen
Hollidaysburg	Hollidaysburg	Pen
Hunterstown	Gettysburg National	Pen
Lackawaxan	Lackawaxan	Pen
Lebanon	Lebanon	Pen
Mercersburg	Mercersburg	Pen
Orangeville	Orangeville	Pen
Philadelphia	Philadelphia	Pen
Pittsburgh	Pittsburgh	Pen
Reading	Reading	Pen
Scranton	Scranton	Pen
Spring Mill	Spring Mill	Pen
Tamaqua	Tamaqua	Pen
Whitehall	Bristol	Pen

BODIES REMOVED FROM RHODE ISLAND

Original Burial Site	Final Burial Site	
Dutch Island	Dutch Island	RI
Fort Adams	Fort Adams	RI
Portsmouth	Cypress Hills National	NY
Portsmouth Grove #	Cypress Hills National	NY

BODIES REMOVED FROM SOUTH CAROLINA

Original Burial Site	Final Burial Site	
Aiken	Aiken	SC
Anderson	Anderson	SC
Antioch	Florence National	SC
Battery Island	Beaufort National	SC
Beaufort	Beaufort National	SC
Blumtrill	Beaufort National	SC
Bray Island	Beaufort National	SC
Camden	Florence	SC
Cane Island	Beaufort National	SC

72

BODIES REMOVED FROM SOUTH CAROLINA

Original Burial Site	Final Burial Site	
Chaplain Place	Beaufort National	SC
Charleston	see Charleston	SC
Chester	Chester	SC
Cole's Island	Beaufort National	SC
Columbia	Columbia	SC
Cossawhatchie	Beaufort National	SC
Edisto Island	Beaufort National	SC
Florence	Florence National	SC
Folly Island	Beaufort National	SC
Fort Johnson	Beaufort National	SC
Georgetown	Beaufort National	SC
Gillisonville	Beaufort National	SC
Gregory	Beaufort National	SC
Henry Island B.F.	Beaufort National	SC
Hilton Head #	Beaufort National	SC
Honey Hill B. F.	Beaufort National	SC
James Island	Beaufort National	SC
John's Island	Beaufort National	SC
Land's End	Beaufort National	SC
Legare Point	Beaufort National	SC
Lownde's Place	Beaufort National	SC
Morris Island	Beaufort National	SC
Ogdensburg	Florence National	SC
Orangeburg #	Florence National	SC
Otter Island	Beaufort National	SC
Paris Island	Beaufort National	SC
Pawnee Landing	Beaufort National	SC
Pawnee Woods	Beaufort National	SC
Pocaataliago B.F.	Beaufort National	SC
Port Royal Island	Beaufort National	SC
Sea Islands	Beaufort National	SC
Secessionville	Beaufort National	SC
Smith's Plantation	Beaufort National	SC
Spanish Wells	Beaufort National	SC
St. Helena Island	Beaufort National	SC
Stony Creek	Beaufort National	SC
Sullivan Island	Beaufort National	SC
Sumter	Sumter	SC
Tripp Place	Beaufort National	SC
Yorkville	Yorkville	SC

BODIES REMOVED FROM TENNESSEE

Original Burial Site	Final Burial Site	
Adam's Station	Nashville National	Ten
Adamsville	Shiloh National	Ten
Alexandria	Stone's River National	Ten
Anderson	Chattanooga National	Ten
Antioch Church	Fort Donelson National	Ten
Asbury Church	Stone's River National	Ten
Ashton Mill	Stone's River National	Ten
Athens	Chattanooga National	Ten
Battle Hill	Nashville National	Ten
Bean Station	Knoxville National	Ten
Bear Station	Bear Station	Ten
Beard's Ferry	Nashville National	Ten
Bell Buckle	Stone's River National	Ten
Bethel	Cornith National	Miss
Big Creek Gap	Knoxville National	Ten
Blaines Cross Roads	Knoxville National	Ten

73

BODIES REMOVED FROM TENNESSEE

Original Burial Site	Final Burial Site	
Blountsville	Knoxville National	Ten
Blue Springs	Chattanooga National	Ten
Blue Springs	Knoxville National	Ten
Bolivar	Cornith National	Miss
Boyd's Ferry	Chattanooga National	Ten
Bradyville	Stone's River National	Ten
Branchville	Stone's River National	Ten
Bristol	Knoxville National	Ten
Britton's Lane	Cornith National	Miss
Brown's Ferry	Chattanooga National	Ten
Brownsville	Memphis National	Ten
Buck's Lodge Station	Nashville National	Ten
Buford's Station	Nashville National	Ten
Bull's Gap	Knoxville National	Ten
Burns' Station	Nashville National	Ten
Camp Dick Robinson	Perryville National	Ky
Campbell Station	Knoxville National	Ten
Carter's Station	Knoxville National	Ten
Carter's Station	Stone's River National	Ten
Carthage	Nashville National	Ten
Castilian Springs	Nashville National	Ten
Cedar Creek Landing	Shiloh National	Ten
Centreville	Nashville National	Ten
Cerro Gordo	Shiloh National	Ten
Charleston	Chattanooga National	Ten
Charlotte	Nashville National	Ten
Chattanooga	Chattanooga National	Ten
Cheatham's Mill	Nashville National	Ten
Cherry Mound	Nashville National	Ten
Chestnut Ridge	Nashville National	Ten
Chewalla	Cornith National	Miss
Chickamauga	Chattanooga National	Ten
Christiana	Stone's River National	Ten
Cipple Creek	Stone's River National	Ten
Clarksville	Fort Donelson National	Ten
Clarkville	Nashville National	Ten
Claysville	Chattanooga National	Ten
Clear Creek	Knoxville National	Ten
Cleveland	Chattanooga National	Ten
Clifton	Shiloh National	Ten
Clinton	Knoxville National	Ten
Cloud Spring	Chattanooga National	Ten
Collierville	Memphis National	Ten
Columbia	Nashville National	Ten
Columbia	Stone's River National	Ten
Columbus	Cumberland Gap National	Ten
Concord	Knoxville National	Ten
Concord	Nashville National	Ten
Corinth Road	Shiloh National	Ten
Cowan	Stone's River National	Ten
Craven's Landing	Shiloh National	Ten
Crump's Landing	Shiloh National	Ten
Cumberland Furnace	Nashville National	Ten
Cumberland Gap	Cumberland Gap National	Ten
Cumberland Mount	Chattanooga National	Ten
Cumberland Mountains	Stone's River National	Ten
Dahlonego	Marietta National	Ga
Dandridge	Chattanooga National	Ten
Dandridge	Knoxville National	Ten
David's Cross-Roads	Chattanooga National	Ten

BODIES REMOVED FROM TENNESSEE

Original Burial Site	Final Burial Site	
Dechard Station	Stone's River National	Ten
Decherd	Chattanooga National	Ten
Dickerson's Pike	Nashville National	Ten
Dixon Springs	Nashville National	Ten
Docktown	Chattanooga National	Ten
Dodsville	Chattanooga National	Ten
Dover	Fort Donelson National	Ten
Dyer's Station	Cornith National	Miss
Edgefield	Nashville National	Ten
Elk River	Stone's River National	Ten
Elkin Bridge	Nashville National	Ten
Elliott's Ferry	Chattanooga National	Ten
Elliott's Hospital	Elliott's Hospital	Ten
Elmwood	Memphis National	Ten
Estell Spring	Stone's River National	Ten
Fair Garden	Chattanooga National	Ten
Farmington	Cornith National	Miss
Farmington	Stone's River National	Ten
Fayetteville	Stone's River National	Ten
Fisherville	Memphis National	Ten
Florence	Stone's River National	Ten
Fort Donelson	Fort Donelson National	Ten
Fort Henry	Shiloh National	Ten
Fort Pickering	Memphis National	Ten
Fort Pillow	Memphis National	Ten
Fort Richardson	Fort Leavenworth National	Kan
Fort Rosecrans	Stone's River National	Ten
Fosterville	Stone's River National	Ten
Fountain Head	Nashville National	Ten
Franklin	Stone's River National	Ten
French Broad River	Chattanooga National	Ten
Friendship Church	Stone's River National	Ten
Fullen's Depot	Knoxville National	Ten
Gallatin	Nashville National	Ten
Gillem's Station	Nashville National	Ten
Glendale Station	Nashville National	Ten
Goose Creek	Knoxville National	Ten
Grand Junction	Cornith National	Miss
Granville	Chattanooga National	Ten
Gravelly Springs	Shiloh National	Ten
Green River Station	Nashville National	Ten
Green's Mills	Chattanooga National	Ten
Greenville #	Knoxville National	Ten
Gun Spring	Stone's River National	Ten
Guy's Gap	Stone's River National	Ten
Hackman	Memphis National	Ten
Hall's Mill	Nashville National	Ten
Hamberg	Shiloh National	Ten
Hamburg	Cornith National	Miss
Harding House	Stone's River National	Ten
Harpeth River	Nashville National	Ten
Harrison	Chattanooga National	Ten
Hartsville	Nashville National	Ten
Henderson	Nashville National	Ten
Hickory Hill	Stone's River National	Ten
Hillsboro'	Stone's River National	Ten
Hoover's Gap	Stone's River National	Ten
Humboldt	Cornith National	Miss
Humbolt Road	Memphis National	Ten
Hutton's Chapel	Nashville National	Ten

Original Burial Site	Final Burial Site	
Island No. 10	Memphis National	Ten
Island No. 40	Memphis National	Ten
Isler Landing	Memphis National	Ten
Jacksboro'	Knoxville National	Ten
Jackson	Cornith National	Miss
Jackson County	Chattanooga National	Ten
Jasper	Chattanooga National	Ten
Johnson's Depot	Knoxville National	Ten
Johnsonville	Nashville National	Ten
Jonesboro'	Knoxville National	Ten
Kelley's Landing	Chattanooga National	Ten
Kelly's Ferry	Chattanooga National	Ten
Kenton	Cornith National	Miss
Kingston	Chattanooga National	Ten
Kingston	Knoxville National	Ten
Kingston Springs	Nashville National	Ten
Knoxville	Knoxville National	Ten
Knoxville #	Chattanooga National	Ten
La Grange	Memphis National	Ten
Lafayette	Memphis National	Ten
Larkin's Landing	Chattanooga National	Ten
Larkinsville	Chattanooga National	Ten
Lavergue	Stone's River National	Ten
Lebanon	Stone's River National	Ten
Lenoir's Station	Knoxville National	Ten
Lewisville	Knoxville National	Ten
Lexington	Cornith National	Miss
Liberty Gap	Stone's River National	Ten
Lick Creek	Knoxville National	Ten
Limestone	Knoxville National	Ten
London	Chattanooga National	Ten
London	Knoxville National	Ten
Lookout Mount	Chattanooga National	Ten
Lookout Valley	Chattanooga National	Ten
Louden	Knoxville National	Ten
Lousiville	Knoxville National	Ten
Madison County	Chattanooga National	Ten
Madisonville	Cumberland Gap National	Ten
Magnolia	Fort Donelson National	Ten
Manchester	Stone's River National	Ten
Manny's Grove	Stone's River National	Ten
Mason Station	Memphis National	Ten
Maynardsville	Knoxville National	Ten
Maysville #	Chattanooga National	Ten
McEwen's Station	Nashville National	Ten
McGowan's Station	Nashville National	Ten
McMinnville	Stone's River National	Ten
Meadow Station	Cornith National	Miss
Memphis	Memphis National	Ten
Middlebury Station	Cornith National	Miss
Miffin	Cornith National	Miss
Mill Creek	Nashville National	Ten
Mission Ridge	Chattanooga National	Ten
Mitchelville	Nashville National	Ten
Monterecy	Shiloh National	Ten
Morristown	Knoxville National	Ten
Moscow	Memphis National	Ten
Mossy Creek	Knoxville National	Ten
Mount Pleasant	Memphis National	Ten
Mount Vernon	Memphis National	Ten

BODIES REMOVED FROM TENNESSEE

Original Burial Site	Final Burial Site	
Murfreesboro	Stone's River National	Ten
Nashville	Nashville National	Ten
Nashville	Spring Grove, Cincinnati	Ohio
New Market	Knoxville National	Ten
Newport	Chattanooga National	Ten
Nolensville	Nashville National	Ten
Normandy	Stone's River National	Ten
Ooltawah	Chattanooga National	Ten
Overalt's Creek	Stone's River National	Ten
Paris	Memphis National	Ten
Paris Landing	Shiloh National	Ten
Parker's X Roads	Cornith National	Miss
Perryville	Shiloh National	Ten
Philadelphia	Chattanooga National	Ten
Pike House Ferry	Nashville National	Ten
Pinson Station	Cornith National	Miss
Pittsburg Landing	Shiloh National	Ten
Pittsburg Landing	Spring Grove, Cincinnati	Ohio
Pittsburg Landing Road	Cornith National	Miss
Post Oak Springs	Post Oak Springs	Ten
Pulaski	Stone's River National	Ten
Purdy	Cornith National	Miss
Raccoon Mountains	Chattanooga National	Ten
Randolph's Forge	Fort Donelson National	Ten
Readyville	Stone's River National	Ten
Red River Bridge	Nashville National	Ten
Rheatown	Knoxville National	Ten
Richland Station	Nashville National	Ten
Rockford Ledge	Nashville National	Ten
Russellville	Knoxville National	Ten
Rutherford's Station	Cornith National	Miss
Rutledge	Knoxville National	Ten
Saltillo	Shiloh National	Ten
Saulsbury	Cornith National	Miss
Savannah	Shiloh National	Ten
Scotsboro' County	Chattanooga National	Ten
Scull Camp Bridge	Stone's River National	Ten
Seiverville	Chattanooga National	Ten
Senior Station	Chattanooga National	Ten
Seviersville	Knoxville National	Ten
Shelbyville	Stone's River National	Ten
Shell Mound	Chattanooga National	Ten
Shiloh	Shiloh National	Ten
Shiloh Church	Shiloh National	Ten
Signal Hill	Nashville National	Ten
Silas Creek	Chattanooga National	Ten
Silver Spring	Stone's River National	Ten
Smeedsville	Nashville National	Ten
Smyrna	Stone's River National	Ten
South Tunnel	Nashville National	Ten
Sparta	Stone's River National	Ten
Spring Hill	Stone's River National	Ten
Springfield	Nashville National	Ten
State Line Station	Nashville National	Ten
Steven's Gap	Chattanooga National	Ten
Stevenson County	Chattanooga National	Ten
Stewart's Creek	Stone's River National	Ten
Stone's River B.F.	Stone's River National	Ten
Strawberry Plain	Knoxville National	Ten
Suck Creek	Chattanooga National	Ten

77

BODIES REMOVED FROM TENNESSEE

Original Burial Site	Final Burial Site	
Summertown	Summertown	Ten
Swquatchie	Chattanooga National	Ten
Tantalon	Chattanooga National	Ten
Tazewell	Knoxville National	Ten
Thompson's Station	Stone's River National	Ten
Tiptonville	Memphis National	Ten
Trace Creek	Nashville National	Ten
Tracy City	Chattanooga National	Ten
Trenton	Cornith National	Miss
Triune	Nashville National	Ten
Troy	Cornith National	Miss
Tullahoma	Stone's River National	Ten
Tyrn Springs	Nashville National	Ten
Union City	Cornith National	Miss
Union Depot	Memphis National	Ten
Vernon	Nashville National	Ten
Waldon's Ridge	Chattanooga National	Ten
Walker's Ford	Cumberland Gap National	Ten
Wartrace	Stone's River National	Ten
Wauhatchie	Chattanooga National	Ten
Waverly	Nashville National	Ten
Waynesboro' Road	Shiloh National	Ten
White's Bluff	Nashville National	Ten
Whiteside	Chattanooga National	Ten
Winchester	Stone's River National	Ten
Wolf River	Memphis National	Ten
Wolf River Bridge	Memphis National	Ten
Woodbury	Stone's River National	Ten
Chattanooga	Chattanooga National	Ten
Decherd	Stone's River National	Ten

BODIES REMOVED FROM TEXAS

Original Burial Site	Final Burial Site	
Austin #	San Antonio National	Tex
Auston	San Antonio National	Tex
Barrancas	Brownsville National	Tex
Boerne	San Antonio National	Tex
Brazos, Santiago #	Brownsville National	Tex
Brownsville	Brownsville National	Tex
Camp Castroville	San Antonio National	Tex
Camp Del Rio	San Antonio National	Tex
Camp Eagle Pass #	San Antonio National	Tex
Camp Ford #	Alexandria National	La
Camp Guilford D. Bailey	San Antonio National	Tex
Camp Lincoln	San Antonio National	Tex
Camp Pena Colorado	San Antonio National	Tex
Camp Sterling	Galveston National	Tex
Camp Verde #	San Antonio National	Tex
Chappell Hill	Chappell Hill	Tex
Clarksville	Brownsville National	Tex
Corpus Christi	Corpus Christi	Tex
Cortinas Ranch	Brownsville National	Tex
Edinburg #	Brownsville National	Tex
Fort Belknap	San Antonio National	Tex
Fort Bliss	San Antonio National	Tex
Fort Brown #	Fort Leavenworth National	Kan
Fort Clark #	Fort Leavenworth National	Kan
Fort Clark #	San Antonio National	Tex
Fort Concho	San Antonio National	Tex

BODIES REMOVED FROM TEXAS

Original Burial Site	Final Burial Site	
Fort Davis	San Antonio	Tex
Fort Duncan	see Camp Eagle Pass	Tex
Fort Elliott	San Antonio National	Tex
Fort Ewell	San Antonio National	Tex
Fort Griffin	San Antonio National	Tex
Fort Hancock	San Antonio National	Tex
Fort Inge	San Antonio National	Tex
Fort Martin Scott	San Antonio National	Tex
Fort Mason	San Antonio National	Tex
Fort McDavit	San Antonio National	Tex
Fort McIntosh	Fort McIntosh	Tex
Fort McKavett	San Antonio National	Tex
Fort McPherson	San Antonio National	Tex
Fort Merrill	San Antonio National	Tex
Fort Richardson	San Antonio National	Tex
Fort Ringgold	Fort Ringgold	Tex
Fort Sam Houston	San Antonio National	Tex
Fort Stockson	San Antonio National	Tex
Galveston	Galveston National	Tex
Green Lake	Green Lake	Tex
Hempstead	Hempstead	Tex
Indianola #	Brownsville National	Tex
Jasper	Jasper	Tex
Jefferson	Alexandria National	Tex
Jefferson	Shreveport National	La
Lavaca #	Galveston National	Tex
Marshall	Shreveport National	La
Matagorda	Matagorda	Tex
Moedina River	Austin National	Tex
Placido River	Galveston National	Tex
Powderhorn Bayou	Powderhorn Bayou	Tex
Rancho Blancho	Brownsville National	Tex
Ringgold Barracks	Fort Ringgold	Tex
Roma	Roma	Tex
Salado Creek	Austin National	Tex
San Antonio	Austin National	Tex
Santa Maria	Brownsville National	Tex
Tyler	Alexandria National	La
Victoria #	Brownsville National	Tex
White's Ranch	Brownsville National	Tex

BODIES REMOVED FROM UTAH

Original Burial Site	Final Burial Site	
Camp Cameron	Camp Cameron	U T
Camp Douglas	Camp Douglas	U T
Fort Bridger	Fort Bridger	U T

BODIES REMOVED FROM VERMONT

Original Burial Site	Final Burial Site	
Battleboro	Battleboro	Vt
East Cornith	East Cornith	Vt
Montpelier	Montpelier	Vt

BODIES REMOVED FROM VIRGINIA

Original Burial Site	Final Burial Site	
18th Corps Hospital	Cold Harbor National	Va
6th Corps Hospital	Cold Harbor National	Va
Abingdon	Knoxville National	Ten
Adkin's Switch	Knoxville National	Ten
Aldie	Arlington National	Va
Alexandria	Alexandria National	Va
Alexandria County	Arlington National	Va
Amelia C. H.	Poplar Grove National	Va
Amelia Springs	Poplar Grove National	Va
Antioch Church	Seven Pines National	Va
Appomattox C.H.	Appomattox C.H.	Va
Appomattox C.H. #	Poplar Grove National	Va
Aquia Creek	Alexandria National	Va
Aquia Creek	Fredericksburg National	Va
Arlington	Arlington National	Va
Ashland	Richmond National	Va
Auburn	Arlington National	Va
Augusta County	Staunton National	Va
Baggs Farm	Winchester	va
Ball's Bluff	Ball's Bluff National	Va
Ball's Bluff #	Arlington National	Va
Banks of the Appomattox	City Point National	Va
Barborsville	New Albany National	Ind
Barbour's X Roads	Arlington National	Va
Barry Ford	Culpeper National	Va
Bath	Winchester National	Va
Bath County	Winchester National	Va
Bealton	Arlington National	Va
Bealton Station	Arlington National	Va
Beaver Dam Station	Richmond National	Va
Beaver Dam Station	Winchester National	Va
Belle Island (James River)#	Richmond National	Va
Belle Plain	Fredericksburg National	Va
Bentonville	Winchester National	Va
Bermuda Hundred	Poplar Grove National	Va
Berry's Ferry	Winchester National	Va
Berryville	Winchester National	Va
Bethesda Church	Cold Harbor National	Va
Beverly Ford	Arlington National	Va
Big Bethel B.F.	Hampton National	Va
Blackwell	Arlington National	Va
Blandford	Poplar Grove National	Va
Blandford Cemetery	Poplar Grove National	Va
Bolivar	Winchester National	Va
Bottom's Bridge	Richmond National	Va
Bower's Hill	Hampton National	Va
Brandy Station	Culpeper National	Va
Brick House Point	Yorktown National	Va
Bridgewater	Staunton National	Va
Brighton	Yorktown National	Va
Bristoe Station	Arlington National	Va
Brook's Station	Fredericksburg National	Va
Bull Run	Arlington National	Va
Bumpass Turnout	Richmond National	Va
Bunker's Hill	Winchester National	Va
Burgess' Mill	Poplar Grove National	Va
Burksville Junction #	Poplar Grove National	Va
Camback's Mill	Fredericksburg National	Va
Cameron	Arlington National	Va
Camp Casey	Camp Casey	Va

BODIES REMOVED FROM VIRGINIA

Original Burial Site	Final Burial Site	
Camp Hamilton	Hampton National	Va
Caroline County	Fredericksburg National	Va
Carr's Church	Yorktown National	Va
Cartersville	Richmond National	Va
Catlett Station	Arlington National	Va
Cedar Creek Bridge	Winchester National	Va
Cedar Mountain	Staunton National	Va
Ceder Mountain	Culpeper National	Va
Center Branch	Fredericksburg National	Va
Centerville	Arlington National	Va
Chancellorsville	Fredericksburg National	Va
Chapin's Farm	Fort Harrison National	Va
Charles City	Culpeper National	Va
Charles City	Hampton National	Va
Charles City	Richmond National	Va
Charlottesville	Charlottesville	Va
Cheeseman's Landing	Yorktown National	Va
Cherrystone	Hampton National	Va
Chestnut Grove Church	Seven Pines National	Va
Christiansburg	Staunton National	Va
City Point	City Point National	Va
Clark County	Winchester National	Va
Cloyd's Mountain	Staunton National	Va
Cold Harbor	Cold Harbor National	Va
Cold Harbor #	Richmond National	Va
Connor's Store	Staunton National	Va
Cool Spring	Winchester National	Va
Covington	Staunton National	Va
Craney Island	Hampton National	Va
Crater (Battle of)	Poplar Grove National	Va
Cross Keys	Staunton National	Va
Crump's X-Roads	Yorktown National	Va
Culpeper	Culpeper National	Va
Culpeper County	Culpeper National	Va
Cumberland	Yorktown National	Va
Dabney's Mill	Poplar Grove National	Va
Dabney's Mills	Richmond National	Va
Dangerfield	Dangerfield	Va
Danville	Danville National	Va
Darksville	Winchester National	Va
Deep Bottom	Fort Harrison National	Va
Dicord Bridge	Yorktown National	Va
Dinwiddle County #	Poplar Grove National	Va
Dry Creek	Staunton National	Va
Dublin	Knoxville National	Ten
Dutch Gap	Fort Harrison National	Va
Dutch Gap	Poplar Grove National	Va
Elkton Heights	Winchester National	Va
Ely's Ford	Fredericksburg National	Va
Enoch Church	Yorktown National	Va
Fair Oaks	Seven Pines National	Va
Fair Oaks Station	Richmond National	Va
Fairfax County	Arlington National	Va
Falls Church	Falls Church	Va
Falmouth	Fredericksburg National	Va
Farmville	Poplar Grove National	Va
Fayette Courthouse	Staunton National	Va
Five Forks	Poplar Grove National	Va
Fletcher Chapel	Fredericksburg National	Va
Fords of the Rapidan River#	Culpeper National	Va

81

BODIES REMOVED FROM VIRGINIA

Original Burial Site	Final Burial Site	
Fort Burnham	Fort Harrison National	Va
Fort Damnation	Poplar Grove National	Va
Fort Davis	Poplar Grove National	Va
Fort Gilman	Fort Harrison National	Va
Fort Gilmer	Fort Harrison National	Va
Fort Gilmore	Richmond National	Va
Fort Gregg	Poplar Grove National	Va
Fort Harrison	Fort Harrison National	Va
Fort Harrison #	Richmond National	Va
Fort Haskins	Poplar Grove National	Va
Fort Hell	Poplar Grove National	Va
Fort Johnson	Fort Harrison National	Va
Fort Monroe	Hampton National	Va
Fort Norfolk	Hampton National	Va
Fort Pocahontas	see Wilson's Landing	Va
Fort Steadman	Poplar Grove National	Va
Fort Stevens	Poplar Grove National	Va
Fort Yorktown	Yorktown National	Va
Franklin	Staunton National	Va
Frederick County	Winchester National	Va
Fredericks Hall Station	Richmond National	Va
Fredericksburg	Fredericksburg National	Va
Freeman's Ford	Arlington National	Va
Front Royal #	Winchester National	Va
Furrey's Furnace	Staunton National	Va
Fussel's Mill	Glendale National	Va
Gainsville	Arlington National	Va
Garrett's Crossing	Poplar Grove National	Va
Gauley	Staunton National	Va
Georgetown	Arlington National	Va
Gettie's Station	Hampton National	Va
Glouchester Point	Glouchester Point	Va
Gordonsville #	Culpeper National	Va
Gordonsville #	Richmond National	Va
Grafton Church	Yorktown National	Va
Gravelly Church	Poplar Grove National	Va
Great Bridge	Hampton National	Va
Greenwood Mills	Winchester National	Va
Griffin's Spring	Richmond National	Va
Ground Squirrel Bridge	Richmond National	Va
Guyandott	New Albany National	Ind
Hall's Shop	Cold Harbor National	Va
Halltown	Winchester National	Va
Hampton	Hampton National	Va
Hampton	Hampton VA Medical Center	Va
Hancock Station	Poplar Grove National	Va
Hancock Station	Richmond National	Va
Hanover C.H.	Cold Harbor National	Va
Hanover County	Richmond National	Va
Hanover Junction	Richmond National	Va
Hanson's Hill	Winchester National	Va
Harper's Ferry	Winchester National	Va
Harrisburg	Staunton National	Va
Harrison's Landing	Glendale National	Va
Harrison's Landing	Poplar Grove National	Va
Harrisonburg #	Staunton National	Va
Hartwood (Stafford County)	Fredericksburg National	Va
Hatcher's Run	Poplar Grove National	Va
Henrico County	Richmond National	Va
Henry and Emery College	Knoxville National	Ten

BODIES REMOVED FROM VIRGINIA

Original Burial Site	Final Burial Site	
Highland County	Staunton National	Va
Hope Landing	Fredericksburg National	Va
Hungry Station	Richmond National	Va
Jackson River Depot	Staunton National	Va
Jackson's Mill	Poplar Grove National	Va
Jamestown Island	Hampton National	Va
Jefferson county	Winchester National	Va
Jettersville	Poplar Grove National	Va
Jonesville	Knoxville National	Ten
Kearneyville Station	Winchester National	Va
Kelly's Ford	Arlington National	Va
Kelly's Ford	Culpeper	Va
Kernstown	Winchester National	Va
King and Queen's C.H.	Yorktown National	Va
King George County	Fredericksburg National	Va
King William's Church	Yorktown National	Va
Lacey Springs	Staunton National	Va
Lacey's Spring	Staunton National	Va
Laurel Hill	Fort Harrison National	Va
Laurel Hill	Fredericksburg National	Va
Leesville	Ball's Bluff National	Va
Lewisburg	Staunton National	Va
Liberty #	Arlington National	Va
Liberty Church	Poplar Grove National	Va
Liberty Hall	Richmond National	Va
Liberty Mills	Culpeper National	Va
Locust Grove	Fredericksburg National	Va
Lollersville	Richmond National	Va
London County	Winchester National	Va
Loudon County	Arlington National	Va
Loudon County	Winchester National	Va
Lovettsville	Winchester National	Va
Luray	Staunton National	Va
Lurray Church	Staunton National	Va
Lynchburg #	Poplar Grove National	Va
Madison C.H.	Culpeper National	Va
Malvern Hill	Glendale National	Va
Malvern Hill	Richmond National	Va
Manassas	Culpeper National	Va
Manassas B.F.	Arlington National	Va
Manassas Station	Arlington National	Va
Marion	Knoxville National	Ten
Marlboro' Point	Fredericksburg National	Va
Mary's Heights	Fredericksburg National	Va
Massannton Mount	Winchester National	Va
Massaponax Courthouse	Fredericksburg National	Va
McCool's Farm	Fredericksburg National	Va
Mead Station	Poplar Grove National	Va
Meade Station	City Point National	Va
Meadow Bluff	Staunton National	Va
Meadow Station	Seven Pines National	Va
Mechanicsville	Richmond National	Va
Mechanicsville	Yorktown National	Va
Melton Station	Richmond National	Va
Middletown	Winchester National	Va
Milford	Staunton National	Va
Mine Run	Fredericksburg National	Va
Mitchell's Station	Culpeper National	Va
Mocasin Gap	Knoxville National	Ten
Monterey	Staunton National	Va

83

Original Burial Site	Final Burial Site	
Morrisville	Arlington National	Va
Morrisville	Culpeper National	Va
Mount Airy	Knoxville National	Ten
Mount Carmell	Winchester National	Va
Mount Castle	Seven Pines National	Va
Mount Eary	Knoxville National	Ten
Mount Hebron	Winchester National	Va
Mount Holly	Arlington National	Va
Mount Jackson #	Winchester National	Va
Mount Solon	Staunton National	Va
Mountain Gap	Winchester National	Va
Munley's Mill	Richmond National	Va
Namozine Church	Poplar Grove National	Va
Naval Hospital	Hampton National	Va
Nazomi Church	Poplar Grove National	Va
Neawport	Winchester National	Va
Nelson's Farm B.F.	Glendale National	Va
New Baltimore	Arlington National	Va
New Market	Arlington National	Va
New Market	Winchester National	Va
New Point Light House	Yorktown National	Va
New River	Knoxville National	Ten
New River Bridge	Knoxville National	Ten
Newport News	Hampton National	Va
Newtown	Winchester National	Va
Noaksville	Arlington National	Va
Norfolk	Hampton National	Va
Norfolk	Naval Cemetery, Norfolk	Va
North Anna River	Fredericksburg National	Va
Nottoway County	Nottoway County	Va
Oak Grove	Poplar Grove National	Va
Oakland	Staunton National	Va
Olive Branch	Yorktown National	Va
Orange and Alexandria RR #	Arlington National	Va
Orange Court House #	Arlington National	Va
Orange Court House #	Culpeper National	Va
Orleans	Arlington National	Va
Page County	Staunton National	Va
Petersburg	Poplar Grove National	Va
Petersburg #	Winchester National	Va
Piedmont	Staunton National	Va
Pine Hill	Winchester National	Va
Pineview	Culpeper National	Va
Piping Tree	Richmond National	Va
Pippin Tree Ferry	Yorktown National	Va
Point of Rocks	City Point National	Va
Pole Green Church	Richmond National	Va
Port Republic	Staunton National	Va
Port Royal	Fredericksburg National	Va
Portsmouth #	Culpeper National	Va
Portsmouth #	Hampton National	Va
Pottiesville	Richmond National	Va
Prospect Hill	Winchester National	Va
Raccoon Ford	Culpeper National	Va
Raisher's Woods	Winchester National	Va
Rapidan Ford #	Culpeper National	Va
Rapidan Station	Culpeper National	Va
Rappahannock Station #	Arlington National	Va
Rappahannock Station #	Culpeper National	Va
Ream Station	Poplar Grove National	Va

BODIES REMOVED FROM VIRGINIA

Original Burial Site	Final Burial Site	
Rectortown	Arlington National	Va
Rectortown	Winchester National	Va
Rice Station	Poplar Grove National	Va
Richmond	Richmond National	Va
Robinson's Tavern	Robinson's Tavern	Va
Rocketts	Richmond National	Va
Rockingham County	Staunton National	Va
Romney	Winchester National	Va
Rose Hill Point	Fredericksburg National	Va
Safrona Church	Poplar Grove National	Va
Sailor's Creek	Poplar Grove National	Va
Salem	Arlington National	Va
Salem	Staunton National	Va
Salem Church	Fredericksburg National	Va
Salem Church	Glendale National	Va
Saltville	Knoxville National	Va
Samaria Church	Glendale National	Va
Savage Station	Richmond National	Va
Savage Station	Seven Pines National	Va
Sawyer's Lane	Hampton National	Va
Seven Pines	Seven Pines National	Va
Seven Pines #	Richmond National	Va
Shenandoah County	Winchester National	Va
Ship Point	Yorktown National	Va
Sir John's Run	Winchester National	Va
Sleepy Creek	Winchester National	Va
Smithfield	Hampton National	Va
Snicker's Ferry	Winchester National	Va
South Mills	Hampton National	Va
Southampton	Southampton	Va
Sperryville	Culpeper National	Va
Spotsylvania Courthouse #	Fredericksburg National	Va
Springfield	Winchester National	Va
Stafford Court House	Fredericksburg National	Va
Staunton	Staunton National	Va
Stevensburg	Culpeper National	Va
Stony Creek	Poplar Grove National	Va
Strasburg	Winchester National	Va
Sudley Mills	Arlington National	Va
Suffolk #	Hampton National	Va
Summit Point	Winchester National	Va
Summit Station	Seven Pines National	Va
Sussex Court House	Poplar Grove National	Va
Sutherland Station	Poplar Grove National	Va
Sweet Run Swamp	Winchester National	Va
Taylorsville	Richmond National	Va
Thoroughfare Gap	Arlington National	Va
Trevilian Station	Culpeper National	Va
Trevillian's Station	Richmond National	Va
Union Mills	Arlington National	Va
United States Ford	Fredericksburg National	Va
Upper Grafton Church	Yorktown National	Va
Wade's Depot	Winchester National	Va
Wade's Station	Winchester National	Va
Wallace Farms	Fredericksburg National	Va
Warren County	Winchester National	Va
Warrenton	Arlington National	Va
Warrenton	see Ball's Bluff National	Va
Warrenton Junction	Arlington National	Va
Warrington Springs	Arlington National	Va

BODIES REMOVED FROM VIRGINIA

Original Burial Site	Final Burial Site	
Warwick C.H.	Yorktown National	Va
Washington C.H.	Culpeper National	Va
Waterford	see Ball's Bluff National	Va
Waterloo	Arlington National	Va
Waynesboro	Staunton National	Va
Weaterly Chapel	Winchester National	Va
Weaversville	Arlington National	Va
Weid's Station	Winchester National	Va
West Point	Yorktown National	Va
Westmoreland Courthouse	Fredericksburg National	Va
White House Landing	Yorktown National	Va
White Oak Church	Fredericksburg	Va
White Oak Swamp	Richmond National	Va
White Plains	Arlington National	Va
White Springs	Knoxville National	Ten
White Sulphur Springs	Staunton National	Va
Whitehall	Hampton National	Va
Wilderness Battlefield #	Fredericksburg National	Va
Williams' Ferry	Yorktown National	Va
Williamsburg	Yorktown National	Va
Williamsburg Road (near)	Richmond National	Va
Wilson's Landing #	Glendale National	Va
Winchester	Winchester National	Va
Woodstock	Winchester National	Va
Woodville	Culpeper National	Va
Wytheville	Knoxville National	Ten
Yorktown	Yorktown National	Va
Young's Mills	Yorktown National	Va
Zion's Church	Yorktown National	Va

BODIES REMOVED FROM WASHINGTON STATE

Original Burial Site	Final Burial Site	
Fort Sopkane	Fort Sopkane	Was
Camp Harney	San Francisco National	Calf
Camp Steele	Camp Steele	Wash
Fort Colville #	San Francisco National	Calf
Fort Steilacoom #	San Francisco National	Calf
Fort Townsend	San Francisco National	Calf
Fort Vancouver	Fort Vancouver	Wash
Fort Walla Walla	Fort Walla Walla	Wash

BODIES REMOVED FROM WEST VIRGINIA

Original Burial Site	Final Burial Site	
Alderson	Staunton National	Va
Allegheny Mountains	Grafton National	W Va
Berkley County	Winchester National	Va
Beverly	Grafton National	W Va
Beverly	Spring Grove, Cincinnati	Ohio
Carrick's Ford	Grafton National	W Va
Charleston	Grafton National	W Va
Charlestown	Winchester National	Va
Cheat Mountain	Grafton National	W Va
Clark County	Winchester National	Va
Clarksburg	Grafton National	W Va
Cloyd Mountain B.F.	Grafton National	W Va
Droup Mountain B.F.	Grafton National	W Va
Fairmont	Grafton National	W Va
Garrick's Ford B F	Grafton National	W Va

86

BODIES REMOVED FROM WEST VIRGINIA

Original Burial Site	Final Burial Site	
Gauley	Gauley	W Va
Grafton	Grafton National	W Va
Greenbriar River	Grafton National	W Va
Harper's Ferry	Antietam National	Md
Harper's Ferry	Winchester National	Va
Hutt	Grafton National	W Va
Huttersonville	Grafton National	W Va
Huttonsville	Grafton National	W Va
Kanawha	Grafton National	W Va
Laurel Hill B.F.	Grafton National	W Va
Lewisburg	Staunton National	Va
Martinsburg	Arlington National	Va
Martinsburg	Winchester National	Va
Massanutton Mountain	Winchester National	Va
Moorefield	Winchester National	Va
New Creek	Grafton National	W Va
New River Bridge B.F.	Grafton National	W Va
Parkersburg #	Grafton National	W Va
Petersburg	Winchester National	Va
Philippi	Grafton National	W Va
Piedmont	Arlington National	Va
Piedmont	Staunton National	Va
Rich Mountain B.F.	Grafton National	W Va
Romney	Winchester National	Va
Shaffer Mountain B.F.	Grafton National	W Va
Sheppardstown	Antietam National	Md
Shepperdstown	Winchester National	Va
Summit Point	Winchester National	Va
Walker Mountain	Grafton National	W Va
Wheeling #	Grafton National	W Va

BODIES REMOVED FROM WISCONSIN

Original Burial Site	Final Burial Site	
Fond du Lac	Fond du Lac	Wis
Green Bay	Green Bay	Wis
Janesville	Janesville	Wis
Kenosha	Kenosha	Wis
Madison	Madison	Wis
Milwaukee	Milwaukee	Wis
Prairie du Chen	Prairie du Chen	Wis
Racine	Racine	Wis
Ripon	Ripon	Wis

BODIES REMOVED FROM THE WYOMING TERRITORY

Original Burial Site	Final Burial Site	
Camp Medicine Butte	Camp Medicine Butte	Wyo
Camp Pilot Butte	Fort D. A. Russell	Wyo
Fort Bridges	Fort McPherson National	Neb
Fort Canby	Fort Canby	Wyo
Fort Fetterman	Fort McPherson National	Neb
Fort Laramie #	Fort McPherson National	Neb
Fort McKinney #	Fort Leavenworth National	Kan
Fort Phil Kearney #	Custer National	M T
Fort Reno #	Custer National	M T
Fort Russell	Fort Russell	Wyo
Fort Sanders	Fort McPherson National	Neb
Fort Sterle	Fort McPherson National	Neb
Fort Washakie	Fort Leavenworth National	Kan

BODIES REMOVED FROM THE WYOMING TERRITORY

Original Burial Site	Final Burial Site	
Fort Yellowstone	Fort Yellowstone	Wyo
Gratton	Fort McPherson National	Neb
Independence Rock	Fort McPherson National	Neb
Yellowstone National Park	Fort Yellowstone	Wyo
Yellowstone National Park #	Custer National	M T

SECTION 3

DESCRIPTIONS OF CEMETERIES
Listed by State

**On Fame's eternal camping ground
Their silent tents are spread**

BODIES DELIVERED TO FRIENDS

Volume 10 of the Roll of Honor has a listing of 721 White soldiers and 12 colored soldiers "who were interred in the Department of the East, and whose remains have been delivered to relatives, friends, or other interested parties." Volume one of the series lists colored soldiers who died at Washington and were buried by friends.

Volume 14 of the Roll of Honor lists POW's who were buried at unknown locations, who died aboard ships, or who died in Washington area hospitals after being exchanged.

CAHABA
Alabama

147 Union Soldiers died while prisoners at Cahaba, Alabama. Volume 14 of the Roll of Honor lists these soldiers. According to a letter written in 1890, these graves were moved to Marietta National Cemetery "long before" 1890. Many of the prisoners who survived the prison camp perished when the Federal steamer Sultana exploded on April 27, 1865. The ship had just left Vicksburg, Mississippi, on its way north.

DEMOPOLIS
Alabama

Volume 14 of the Roll of Honor lists one known POW who was buried at Demopolis. Apparently other soldiers were also buried here however. In a letter dated December 17, 1865, Lt. Jon. Swan reported "...the records have been seriously neglected by U.S. officers in transfers from one officer to another."

No other information has been found, however the Federal Government's position on Union graves in Alabama was: "to allow these graves to remain undisturbed..."

FORT MORGAN
Alabama

Bodies from Fort Morgan were moved to the Mobile National Cemetery after the war. The USS Tecumseh was lost with 92 sailors during the Battle of Mobile Bay (August 5, 1864). In 1967 divers from the US Navy and the Smithsonian recovered four bodies from the ship. These bodies were interred in the Arlington National Cemetery. The site of the ship is marked with a Coast Guard buoy.

GAINSVILLE
Alabama

An unknown number of Federal soldiers were buried in Gainsville's public cemetery located 1/4 mile west of town on the west side of the W G and T railroad. In 1865 the graves were marked by wooden headboards, but apparently no records of the burials survived.

HUNTSVILLE
Alabama

No accurate records exist of the Union burials in Huntsville. A July 1866 report reads: "no (sic) of graves supposed to be 670." A report in April of 1866 said: "all records to be found.... are very imperfect and meager." Apparently at that time a list of 265 known soldiers existed. Volume 14 of the Roll of Honor lists only one soldier (a POW) who died at Huntsville.

By February, 1867, a total of 654 bodies had been moved from Huntsville and vicinity to the Chattanooga National Cemetery.

JACKSONVILLE
Alabama

According to an 1865 report, Union Soldiers were buried in Jacksonville's Citizens Cemetery. No records of these burials can be found.

LIVINGSTON
Alabama

On February 8, 1876, Quartermaster General Meigs ordered that the bodies of two Federal soldiers who had died at Livingston were not to be moved to a national cemetery, but were to remain in Livingston. No reason for the refusal was given.

The two soldiers were apparently on occupation duty in Livingston. Their names were:

Pvt. James Martin Co A 2nd Inf
Pvt. James Grayson Co D 7th Cavalry

MOBILE NATIONAL CEMETERY
Alabama

Mobile National Cemetery was established in 1865 when the city of Mobile donated about three acres of land in the city's Magnolia Cemetery to the United States. Bodies were moved to the cemetery from Fort Morgan, Fort Gaines, and other parts of the state.

Few records of the burials at Mobile were published. Volume 14 of the Roll of Honor lists only burials of POW's. Col. Mack in his 1871 report stated: "There are no records in the office." Despite this, Mack reported a total of 902 burials:

white soldiers and sailors	646 (33 unknown)
colored soldiers	<u>256</u> (91 unknown)
	902

Four Confederate soldiers were buried at Mobile National Cemetery.

Mobile was not a desirable post in the 1860's. In fact Col. Mack wrote "...no superintendent has latterly (sic) been appointed since the death of the last two..."

MONTGOMERY
Alabama

Volume 14 of the Roll of Honor lists 198 Federal soldiers who died while prisoners at Montgomery. After the war the city of Montgomery donated the soldiers lot they were buried in to the United States. However on July 14, 1866, the bodies were moved to Marietta National Cemetery. In 1879 the United States Congress passed HR3434 which returned to soldiers lot to the city of Montgomery.

MOULTON
Alabama

E. Green, a private in Company M of the 9th Illinois Cavalry died of a gunshot wound on April 26, 1864, at Moulton. Green had been wounded when he was captured. No record of removal of Green's remains to a national cemetery has been found.

MOUTEVALLO
Alabama

An unknown number of U.S. Soldiers died at Moutevallo, Alabama. In 1865 the graves were marked by headboards. According to the report: "The ground is owned by Mr. Wills who makes no charge for the ground occupied by the soldiers."

No further records exist.

NAVY COVE
Alabama

On July 18, 1889, Dr. Semour Bullock, Jr., of Navy Cove wrote the War Department to report he had discovered a coffin that winds had blown on to the beach near his home. Dr. Bullock requested that the remains be removed to a National Cemetery.

The superintendent of Mobile National Cemetery was sent to investigate. He used the buttons found in the coffin to identify the body. He reported to the Quartermaster's office that the body "appears to be a Navy officer of rank." Apparently the superintendent forwarded the buttons with his report. Today they remain in the Quartermaster's file. On September 2, 1889, the body was reinterred in the Mobile National Cemetery. The total cost of removing the body was $8.40.

TALLADEGA
Alabama

A consolidated report dated December 1865 listed both Federal and Confederate burials in "citizens cemetery" on the south side of town. No other records were found.

FORT KODIAK
Alaska

According to an 1870 report, five known soldiers were buried at Fort Kodiak from 1868-9. No record of removal has been found.

CAMP DATE CREEK
Arizona

An undated list in the Quartermaster's cemetery file lists twenty-five known U.S. soldiers who died at Camp Date Creek between 1866 to 1873. Fourteen unknown civilians who were killed by indians were buried there also.

Thirty-nine bodies were moved from Camp Date Creek to the San Francisco National Cemetery sometime before 1909.

CAMP McDOWELL
Arizona

Camp McDowell was established as Camp Verde in 1865 by the 1st California Cavalry. The fort was located on the west bank of the Rio Verde River. Its mission was to help control Yavapai and Apache Indians.

Volume 19 of the Roll of Honor lists 13 burials at Camp McDowell. An 1873 statement showed a total of 64 burials in the post cemetery. Five of these were infants and fifteen were citizens (wives...). The records of San Francisco National Cemetery show that 48 bodies were moved there from Fort Verde.

EL PICACHO
Arizona

According to volume 8 of the Roll of Honor three troopers from the First California Cavalry died at El Picacho in April 1862. No further information on these burials has been found.

FORT BOWIE
Arizona

At least eighty-five United States Soldiers were buried in the Post Cemetery at Fort Bowie, Arizona Territory. Fourteen were unknown. Volume 12 of the Roll of Honor lists only seven names. No other records exist.

FORT GOODWIN
Arizona

Volume 12 of the Roll of Honor lists fourteen soldiers who died at Fort Goodwin. No information on removal of these remains to a national cemetery has been found.

FORT HUACHUCA
Arizona

At least three U.S. soldiers were buried in Fort Huachuca's post cemetery by 1891. These were not Civil War era soldiers.
No record of the moving of the remains has been found.

FORT LOWELL
Arizona

At least two United States soldiers died at Fort Lowell in the 1880's were buried in the post cemetery. No record of removal of these remains has been found.

FORT MASON
Arizona

Volume 12 of the Roll of Honor lists thirty-two soldiers who died at Fort Mason (Camp McKee). The post was founded in August 1865. It closed in October 1866 due to the high death rate among the troops.
These remains were moved to San Francisco National Cemetery sometime before 1909.

FORT MOJAVE
Arizona

Volume 12 of the Roll of Honor lists the burial of Pvt. William D. Fanning at "Fort Mojare", a misspelling of Fort Mojave. His remains were moved to the San Francisco some time before 1909.

FORT WALLEN
Arizona

Volume 12 of the Roll of Honor lists one soldier who died at Fort Wallen. Sometime before 1909, some bodies from the Fort Wallen post cemetery were moved to the San Francisco National Cemetery.

SAN CARLOS
Arizona

In 1886 the post quartermaster at San Carlos requested 12 headstones for soldiers buried in the post cemetery. There were four graves in the cemetery already marked with stones.

TUCSON
Arizona

Volume 8 of the Roll of Honor lists six known and twelve unknown soldiers buried at Tucson. No more information on these burials has been found.

WHIPPLE BARRACKS
Arizona

A 1873 report listed twenty-two known and fourteen unknown soldiers buried at Whipple Barracks. Some of the causes of death listed were:

    2 killed in action by Indians
    2 died of wounds

97

1 murdered
1 "accidental pistol shot"
1 wounded by pistol shot in Prescott, Arizona

At least eight more soldiers had died by 1893. These bodies were moved to the San Francisco National Cemetery by 1906.

BATESVILLE
Arkansas

Seventy Federal Soldiers were buried at Batesville, Arkansas, during the war. Volume 7 of the Roll of Honor lists twenty-four names. These bodies were moved to the Federal Cemetery at DeVall's Bluff, Arkansas, and later to the Fort Smith (Arkansas) National Cemetery.

CAMDEN
Arkansas

Thirty-eight white and three colored (83rd USCT) soldiers were buried in Camden, Arkansas. Volume 8 of the Roll of Honor lists the names of all forty-one. These bodies were moved to Baton Rouge National Cemetery after the war.

DeVALL'S BLUFF
Arkansas

Volume 8 of the Roll of Honor lists 403 white and 89 colored soldiers who were buried at DeVall's Bluff. Most of the white soldiers died in 1864 or 1865. Almost all the colored troops died in 1865 and 1866.

After the war these bodies were removed to the Little Rock National Cemetery.

FAYETTEVILLE NATIONAL CEMETERY
Arkansas

The first burials in Fayetteville National Cemetery were made in the spring of 1867. The U.S. Government purchased about five acres of land from David Walker and Mr. and Mrs. Stephen Stone. Most of the dead buried here came from the Fayetteville area, Prairie Grove Battlefield, and the Pea Ridge Battlefield.

According to a 1909 report a total of 253 bodies were moved to Fayetteville from the Pea Ridge (Elkhorn Tavern) Battlefield. According to Volume 10 of the Roll of Honor, a total of 702 Union soldiers were buried at Pea Ridge. See the Pea Ridge, Arkansas, entry for more about Pea Ridge (Elkhorn Tavern). Colonel Folsom's report (1868) says that bodies were moved from Pea Ridge to Springfield National Cemetery also. The Veterans Administration's data also supports this.

Names of the men buried at Fayetteville can be found in volumes 10, 14, 18, and 26 of the Roll of Honor series. However only thirty-seven known soldiers are listed in volume 26. The volume also records the reinterments of 744 unknown soldiers. By the time volume 26 of the Roll of Honor was published (1871) a total of 1,975 soldiers were buried at Fayetteville. Only 465 (23.5%) were known. Apparently very few colored troops were buried at Fayetteville.

FITZHUGHS WOODS
Arkansas

In 1872 the Quartermaster General received a report of unmarked graves near Fitzhughs Woods. Because no officer had confirmed the burial site, no further action was taken.

FORT HINDMAN
Arkansas

Fort Hindman was a Confederate stronghold at Arkansas Post on the Arkansas River in Southeastern Arkansas. It protected Little Rock from attack from the Southeast.

In early January 1863 Major General John McClernand, a "political" general, lead over 30,000 Federal troops up the Arkansas River. Rear Admiral David Porter's naval flotilla supported McClernand. Fort Hindman was held by around 5,000 Confederate troops under Brigadier General Thomas J. Churchill.

On January 11,1863, the Union Navy supported by infantry battered the fort into submission. McClernand reported losses of 134 killed and 898 wounded. According to Churchill the Confederates lost "sixty killed."

General Grant disapproved of McClernand's plans to proceed up river and ordered the force back down the river. According to the National Park Service's brochure, the post was never again garrisoned during the war.

Volume 12 of the Roll of Honor, dated March 1, 1867, lists exactly 100 burials "at Arkansas Post." There were 35 known and 65 unknown soldiers. This is close to the 134 killed in the official report. However Volume 2 of the Disposition lists 320 bodies removed from "near Fort Hindman" to the Memphis National Cemetery. The removals were done between April 1867 and February 1868. Where did the additional 220 bodies come from? Several possibilities exist.

First of all the figure in Disposition could be a typo. Second it could be that the officer who reported the graves to the Quartermaster's office could have made a mistake. However normally these reports were filled out by an officer at the post. (or in this case in the area).

A third possibility is that Confederate dead were also moved with the Union dead. In the damp environment headboards could have rotted away. It is very possible that Confederate dead could have been moved to Memphis National Cemetery and buried as Union unknowns. According to the National Park Service no Confederate Cemetery now exists at Arkansas Post. The river has changed course and the site of the fort is now under water.

A fourth possibility is that the Disposition is incorrect. A report on removals to be made in Arkansas dated February 4, 1867, listed 36 known and 158 unknown Union Soldiers that were to be moved to Pine Bluff, Arkansas. Brevet Colonel C.W. Folsom's 1868 report listed a cost of $5.00 per body for removing bodies from Arkansas Post to Pine Bluff in 1867. If these soldiers were reinterred at Pine Bluff, they were later moved to Little Rock National Cemetery.

FORT SMITH NATIONAL CEMETERY
Arkansas

The original Fort Smith was founded in December 1817 by Major William Bradford. The fort's purpose was to keep the peace between local Osage Indians and emigrating Cherokee Indians. The first post was abandoned in 1824. However in 1838 a second fort was built near the site of the first fort. This fort acted as a supply base until 1871. Confederates held Fort Smith from during the early years of the Civil War (April 1861 to September 1863). No major battles were fought in the area, but many skirmishes were.

The first burial in the post cemetery was made in 1832. By 1868 the cemetery contained about 5 1/2 acres of land. Volume 18 of the Roll of Honor lists 1,579 burials in the cemetery. Volume 26 (1871) lists 199 additional burials.

When Col. Mack inspected the cemetery he noted problems with the drainage system. It was too small to handle the run off when heavy rains occurred and gullies developed. Only $12,275.17 had been spent on the cemetery by August 31, 1871.

Col. Mack noted that 162 women, children, and other civilians had been buried in the cemetery along with 125 Confederate Prisoners of War. Only 17 of the Confederates were known. Col. Mack listed other burials:

	Known	Unknown
officers	20	3
white Union Soldiers	477	993
colored Union soldiers	68	3
	565	999

Fort Smith closed in 1871. The next year the Federal Court for the Western District of Arkansas took over the buildings. In December 1875, Congress gave the city of Fort Smith all of the fort's land, except for the National Cemetery and one acre for the court, to sell. The proceeds were to be used for "free schools."

The court at Fort Smith had jurisdiction over both western Arkansas and Indian Territory. Indian courts could not try white men and criminals flocked to Indian Territory. In 1875 Judge Isaac C. Parker was appointed to the bench. In 21 years Judge Parker heard over 13,000 cases. He sentenced 160 men to hang, and 79 were hung. He died in 1896 and was buried in grave # 4000 of the National Cemetery.

HELENA
Arkansas

A report dated May 14, 1865, listed 499 known and 1285 unknown burials at Helena for a total of 1784 burials. Volume 8 of the Roll of Honor lists 831 white and 36 colored soldiers buried "at Helena."

Volume 2 of the Disposition listed 980 bodies removed from Helena to Memphis National Cemetery in 1867 and 1868. A letter dated January 11, 1887, reports that over 1,000 bodies were moved from Helena to Memphis "soon after the close of the war." It is possible some of the bodies moved to Memphis were Confederate, not Union soldiers.

JACKSONPORT
Arkansas

Six white Union soldiers were buried at Jacksonport according to volume 7 of the Roll of Honor. These bodies were removed to the Little Rock National Cemetery after the war.

LITTLE ROCK NATIONAL CEMETERY
Arkansas

On June 29, 1866, the U.S. Army purchased 8 3/4 acres of land for $150.00 from the city of Little Rock. The site for new cemetery was on the Pine Bluff road about two miles southeast of the Arkansas Statehouse. Most of the burials in the cemetery came from hospitals in Little Rock. However other bodies were moved to the cemetery from Devall's Bluff, Arkansas Post, Pine Bluff, and other sites throughout central and southeastern Arkansas.

Col. Mack, who inspected the cemetery in 1871, noted a total of 5,439 burials:

	known	unknown
white soldiers	2,724	1,953
colored soldiers	438	324
	3,162	2,277

Col. Mack was not impressed with the condition of the cemetery. Drainage was a problem and some graves only had two or three inches of dirt covering them. Even the cistern was leaking. The superintendent needed more help to keep the cemetery in"first-rate order." A total of $42,356.86 had been spent on the cemetery by August 31, 1871.

Volumes 8, 18, and 26 of the Roll of Honor list burials in the cemetery.

MADISON
Arkansas

In 1889 the graves of nine Federal occupation troops who had died in Madison were marked with headstones.

102

MADISON COUNTY
Arkansas

In December 1884 the local GAR Post requested eleven headstones for Union Soldiers buried in the Saint Paul Cemetery in Madison County. The same letter requested twelve markers for the Whilty (?) Cemetery. Residents of northwestern Arkansas had divided loyalties during the war. These might have been casualties of the war or former soldiers who died after the war. No dates of death were given.

This letter was misfiled in an envelope labeled "Apalachicola, Florida."

OZARK HOSPITAL
Arkansas

Private A.S. Neff, a POW, died at Ozark Hospital on December 17, 1862. No other information on this burial has been found.

PEA RIDGE
Arkansas

On March 7 and 8, 1862, Union Troops under Brig. General Samuel Curtis defeated confederate troops under Major General Earl Van Dorn at Pea Ridge (Elkhorn Tavern). The Union victory drove the Confederates from northern Arkansas and kept Missouri in the Union.

Volume 10 of the Roll of Honor lists a total of 702 Union troops buried "at Pea Ridge". Of this only 81 (11.5%) were known. 621 were unknown. However the Official Records of the War of the Rebellion gives the Union loss as 203 killed, 972 wounded, and 174 missing. Most union troops left the Pea Ridge area soon after the engagement. Many of the unknown listed in the Roll of Honor must actually be Confederate dead.

Col. Folsum's report (1868) states that Union dead from Pea Ridge were buried at Springfield National Cemetery. The Springfield National Cemetery's information sheet (written by the Veterans Administration) also says this. However in a 1909 report the superintendent of the Fayetteville National Cemetery listed 253 bodies moved from Pea Ridge to Fayetteville. This information apparently came from a burial roster. Because the figure of 702 bodies buried at Pea Ridge apparently contains the Confederate dead, it seems reasonable to conclude that less than 100 Union soldiers were moved to Springfield from Pea Ridge. The majority of dead were moved to Fayetteville.

PINE BLUFF
Arkansas

Volume 8 of the Roll of Honor lists 499 white and 21 colored soldiers buried at Pine Bluff. These bodies were moved to the Little Rock National Cemetery after the war.

PRAIRIE GROVE
Arkansas

The Battle of Prairie Grove ended the last attempt of the Confederacy to wrest control of northern Arkansas from the Union. On December 7, 1862, Union forces turned back Confederate forces under Major General Thomas Hindman. The Union loss was placed at 167 dead with 798 wounded and 183 missing. Volume 10 of the Roll of Honor lists a total of 382 soldiers buried "at Prairie Grove". Of these 161 were known and 221 unknown. It seems that some of the unknowns were Confederate dead.

A 1909 report lists 191 bodies moved from Prairie Grove to Fayetteville National Cemetery. This means the rest of the graves might have been Confederate graves.

ALCATRAZ ISLAND
California

Volume 12 of the Roll of Honor lists eight known soldiers who were buried "at Alcatraces (sic) Island." However, in a 1886 report the post quartermaster wrote: "there is not any post cemetery at this station, our dead being buried in the National Cemetery at Presidio, San Francisco, Cal." (The San Francisco National Cemetery)

ANGEL ISLAND
California

Twenty-seven soldiers (24 known) were buried at the Federal Post on Angel Island, California, according to a 1868 report. No record of the names can be found in the Roll of Honor. This post was still active in 1889.

BENECIA BARRACKS
California

Volume 8 of the Roll of Honor lists fifteen burials at Benecia Barracks. However volume 12 of the series lists only six burials. One name appears to be new, the others are apparently corrected names.

In 1887 the War Department supplied fourteen headstones to mark graves at Benecia Barracks.

CAMP ANDERSON
California

Volume 12 of the Roll of Honor lists four soldiers who died at Camp Anderson. No information on removal of these remains to a national cemetery has been found.

CAMP BABBITT
California

Volume 12 of the Roll of Honor lists five soldiers who died at Camp Babbitt. No information on removal of these remains to a national cemetery has been found.

CAMP INDEPENDENCE
California

David Joyce and Jabez Lovejoy, both privates in Company G of the 2nd California, died at Camp Independence in 1863. These bodies were moved to the San Francisco National Cemetery around 1910. Volume 8 of the Roll of Honor lists these burials.

CAMP JAQUA
California

Volume 12 of the Roll of Honor lists three soldiers who died at Camp Jaqua. No information on removal of these remains to a national cemetery has been found.

CAMP LINCOLN
California

Volume 12 of the <u>Roll of Honor</u> lists five soldiers who died at Camp Lincoln. No information on removal of these remains to a national cemetery has been found.

DRUM BARRACKS
California

Volume 12 of the <u>Roll of Honor</u> lists twenty-nine soldiers who died at Drum Barracks. No information on removal of these remains to a national cemetery has been found.

FORT BIDWELL
California

Two troopers of the Second California Cavalry died at Fort Bidwell in early 1866. Volume 8 of the <u>Roll of Honor</u> lists the names. Volume 12 of the <u>Roll</u> refers to Camp Bidwell. U.S. Senate bill 5.1845 (1884) was introduced to transfer the cemetery to the members of Northeast Lodge number 165 Free and Accepted Masons and the members of Morilla Lodge number 291 Independent order of Odd Fellows.

The cemetery consisted of nine acres and was to be named: the Civic and Military Cemetery of Fort Bidwell, Modoc County, California.

FORT GASTON
California

Volume 12 of the <u>Roll of Honor</u> lists eight soldiers who died at Fort Gaston. No information on removal of these remains to a national cemetery has been found.

FORT GRANT
California

Volume 12 of the <u>Roll of Honor</u> lists one soldier who died at Fort Grant. No information on removal of these remains to a national cemetery has been found.

FORT HUMBOLDT
California

Volume 12 of the <u>Roll of Honor</u> lists fourteen soldiers who died at Fort Humboldt. No information on removal of these remains to a national cemetery has been found.

FORT POINT
California

Volume 12 of the <u>Roll of Honor</u> lists four soldiers who died at Fort Point. (later Fort Winfield Scott) No more information on these burials has been found.

FORT ROSECRANS NATIONAL CEMETERY
California

Over 1,000 acres of land at "New San Diego" was set aside as a military post in February 1852. Volume 8 of the <u>Roll of Honor</u> lists eighteen burials (nine known) in the post cemetery. In 1899 the post was named Fort Rosecrans in honor of Major General William S. Rosecrans.

In 1874 the bodies of seventeen United States soldiers and one civilian who were killed at the Battle of San Pasqual during the Mexican War were moved to the post cemetery. A large boulder from the battlefield was moved to the cemetery in 1922. The names of the dead are listed on a bronze tablet affixed to the boulder.

The U.S.S. Bennington was anchored in San Diego's harbor on the morning of July 21, 1905, when a boiler explosion ripped through the ship. One officer and sixty-five crew members died. Many of the dead were buried in the Bennington plot of the post cemetery. A 75-foot granite monument was erected over the graves by surviving shipmates.

On October 5, 1934, the eight acre post cemetery was designated Fort Rosecrans National Cemetery.

FORT WRIGHT
California

Volume 8 of the Roll of Honor names two soldiers from Company F of the 2nd California who died at Fort Wright. These bodies were moved to the San Francisco National Cemetery sometime before 1908.

FORT YUMA
California

Camp Independence was founded on the opposite side of the Colorado River from Yuma, Arizona. In 1851 the camp was moved to higher ground. The post was renamed Fort Yuma after the move. Volume 12 of the Roll of Honor lists twenty-six soldiers buried at Fort Yuma. Almost all of these soldiers belonged to various California units.

The post closed in May 1883. A total of 159 bodies were moved from Fort Yuma to the San Francisco National Cemetery in September 1890.

MONTERRY BARRACKS
California

Volume 12 of the Roll of Honor lists one soldier who died at Monterry Barracks. No information on removal of these remains to a national cemetery has been found.

SAN FRANCISCO NATIONAL CEMETERY
California

In 1882, Brig. General D.B. Saekeh inspected the graves of California Volunteers at Fort Yuma, Arizona. The headboards were in poor condition. General Saekeh suggested that a cemetery be built at the Presdio of San Francisco for burials of soldiers on the west coast. General Saekeh concluded: "the Pacific States deserve some such show of consideration."

Quartermaster General Samuel Holibird recommended the cemetery be constructed on March 15, 1884. Bids were let on the lodge in July, 1884. A stone wall was built in 1885.

Bodies were moved to the cemetery from Arizona Territory, California, Nevada, Oregon, and Washington. By the end of December, 1908, a total of 5,855 interments had been made:

4,954	known soldiers
405	unknown soldiers
496	civilians (about 60 unknown)
5,855	

Sometimes members of a family were buried in a common grave. The headstone would simply give the family name, i.e. the "Dumbly Family."

CAMP COLLINS
Colorado Territory

The 1st Colorado Cavalry first occupied Camp Collins in the fall of 1863. The post was moved after a flood in 1864. The post was renamed Fort Collins in 1864 also. The fort was abandoned early in 1867.

Eleven soldiers were buried at Camp Collins, Colorado Territory, during the war. Their names are listed in volume 7 of the Roll of Honor. In the 1880's the local GAR post requested help in moving 25 or 30 graves to a new cemetery the GAR had established. The War Department's reply was "...there is no appropriation available for such purpose. This office has no authority to remove the remains of deceased soldiers, except to a national cemetery in cases where there is danger of disturbance, or desecration of the graves."

CANTONMENT ON THE UNCOMPAHARE
Colorado

This camp was established in Montrose County on July 21, 1880. the post's name was later changed to Fort Crawford. According to an 1886 headstone request, ten known soldiers were buried in the post cemetery between 1881 and 1885.

The post was abandoned on December 31, 1890. These bodies were moved to Fort McPherson National Cemetery sometime before 1909.

COLORADO SPRINGS
Colorado

In 1884 the War Department supplied headstones for seventeen white and one colored soldier buried at Colorado Springs. The War Department did not supply markers for twelve other graves because the headstone request did not identify the regiment to which they belonged. The War Department could not verify service during the war by name only. There was never an index of names of Union soldiers. This still hampers genealogists.

DENVER
Colorado

Volume 8 of the Roll of Honor (1866) lists twenty-five known soldiers buried at Denver. Volume 13 of the Roll of Honor (1867) lists only one known (not listed in the earlier volume) and thirteen unknowns.

In 1886 the local GAR post had moved "all known bodies" from City Cemetery to a lot they had purchased in Riverside Cemetery for $960. The bodies had come from Valverde, Apache Canyon, and Sand Creek.

The GAR post requested headstones to mark the graves in 1887. The Quartermaster Generals office replied that they had "no money left for markers."

The 1909 report of Fort Leavenworth National Cemetery listed three bodies moved to Fort Leavenworth from Denver. These may have been soldiers who died after the war.

FORT GARLAND
Colorado

Fort Garland was active from June 1858 to 1883. It was located near the present day town of Fort Garland. Volume 19 of the Roll of Honor lists three burials there.

In 1889 the Quartermaster General declined to move the graves from old post cemetery because of a lack of funds. However a total of fifty graves were moved from Fort Garland to Fort Leavenworth some time before 1909.

FORT GASTON
Colorado

On March 8, 1887, the post cemetery quartermaster at Fort Gaston requested twelve headstones for soldiers buried in the post cemetery. The soldiers had died between 1864 and 1884.

No record of the removal of these bodies to a national cemetery has been found.

FORT LEWIS
Colorado

A total of nineteen U.S. soldiers died at Fort Lewis according to lists in the Quartermaster General's files. No record of removal of these bodies have been found.

FORT LYON
Colorado

The first fortification on the site of Fort Lyon was a trading post known as Brent's New Fort. The post, started in 1853, was leased to the Army in 1859. Flooding caused the fort to be moved in 1866. In 1889 the post was abandoned.

Volume 19 of the Roll of Honor lists twenty-four soldiers buried in the post cemetery. A total of 176 bodies had been moved to Fort Leavenworth National Cemetery by 1906. Fort Lyon became a VA hospital in 1934.

FORT MORGAN
Colorado Territory

Volume 19 of the Roll of Honor lists three known and seven unknown soldiers who died at Fort Morgan. The fort was abandoned in 1868, but no information on removals of these bodies has been found

111

FORT SEDGWICK
Colorado

Volume 7 of the <u>Roll of Honor</u> lists twenty-three burials (all but two known) buried at Fort Sedgwick. These bodies were later moved to the Fort McPherson National Cemetery in Nebraska.

JULESBURG
Colorado

On the morning of January 7, 1865, a detachment of soldiers from Fort Rankin, near Julesburg, rode into an Indian Ambush. Fifteen soldiers and four civilians died. According to an undated endorsement to a letter of inquiry these bodies were never moved to a national cemetery.

DANBURY
Connecticut

Filed under Danbury, Connecticut, in the national cemetery files (RG92-576) is an undated list of Union soldiers buried in the Danbury area. The local GAR compiled this list of soldiers who died during the war. Most of these were "removed from southern locations."

The burial sites were:

Wooster Cemetery	45 soldiers
Wooster Street Burying Ground	3 soldiers
North Burying Ground	1 soldier
Catholic Cemetery	8 soldiers
Stan's Plain Burying Ground	2 soldiers (1 USCT)
Mina Brook Burying Ground	1 soldier
Pembroke Burying Ground	1 soldier
Hawleyville, Conn. Burying Ground	2 soldiers

The <u>Roll of Honor</u> does not record these burials.

HARTFORD
Connecticut

Volume 9 of the <u>Roll of Honor</u> lists two deaths at Hartford. However both bodies were "removed by friends."

According to an undated list, the following cemeteries contain graves of Union soldiers. Most of these bodies were removed from the South.

Old North Cemetery	21 graves
Spring Grove Cemetery	30 graves
Ceder Hill Cemetery	1 grave
Lion's Hill Cemetery	9 graves
Catholic	1 grave

NEW HAVEN
Connecticut

According to volume 9 of the <u>Roll of Honor</u>, 232 white and two colored soldiers were buried "at New Haven." It appears that many of these bodies were "removed by their friends" to private cemeteries or private lots.

In 1874, Col. Mack reported 220 burials at New Haven. 117 known soldiers were buried in a soldiers lot owned by the State of Connecticut in Evergreen Cemetery. These soldiers died in the hospital at New Haven. Seventy other soldiers were buried "with their friends in this cemetery."

Eight soldiers were buried in Saint Bernard's Catholic Cemetery in a 10 foot by 12 foot lot. The United States was supposed to own the lot but no deed had been received. Twenty-five other Union soldiers were buried in this cemetery "with their friends."

Some bodies from New Haven were moved to the Cypress Hills National Cemetery at an unspecified time.

FORT ABERCROMBIE
Dakota Territory

Thirty-four soldiers died at Fort Abercrombie, Dakota Territory, from 1859 to 1865. The names were listed in volume 9 of the <u>Roll of Honor.</u> In October 1885, seventy-nine bodies were moved from Fort Abercrombie to Fort Abraham Lincoln, Dakota Territory. These remains were again moved in August 1890. The final burial site was Custer Battlefield National Cemetery.

FORT ABRAHAM LINCOLN
Dakota Territory

Fort Abraham Lincoln was located on the Missouri River near Bismarck. Established in 1872, the post was used as a supply base for campaigns against the Sioux and Cheyenne Indians. Wounded from the 7th Cavalry were brought here by steamship after Custer's ill-fated 1876 attack on the Sioux at Little Big Horn.

The post closed in 1890. In August, 1890, 166 bodies were moved to Custer Battlefield National Cemetery. No list of the names of the soldiers buried here has been found. However 107 of these bodies came from Fort Abercrombie and Fort Stevenson, Dakota Territories.

FORT BUFORD
Dakota Territory

Fort Buford was founded in 1866. It was located on the Missouri River near the mouth of the Yellowstone River.

Volume 19 of the Roll of Honor lists five burials in the post cemetery. The post closed in 1895. In May 1896, 151 bodies were moved from Fort Buford's post cemetery to Custer National Cemetery.

FORT CASPER
Dakota Territory

Volume 10 of the Roll of Honor lists thirty-eight burials (only ten known) in Fort Casper's post cemetery. No record of removal of these remains to a national cemetery has been found.

FORT DAKOTA
Dakota Territory

Volume 19 of the Roll of Honor lists two burials (all known) in Fort Dakota's post cemetery. No record of removal of these remains to a national cemetery has been found.

FORT RANDALL
Dakota Territory

Fort Randall was established in 1856 on the Missouri River. Volume 19 of the Roll of Honor (1868) listed 44 burials in the post cemetery. Volume 9 of the Roll of Honor contains an earlier list. In 1886 the acting assistant post Quartermaster requested 28 headstones for known soldiers buried in the post cemetery. Fort Randall closed in 1892. Sixty-eight bodies from the post cemetery were moved to Fort Leavenworth National Cemetery sometime before 1909.

FORT RENO
Dakota Territory

Volume 9 of the Roll of Honor lists eight burials in Fort Reno's post cemetery. Volume 19 of the series lists 33 names (three unknown). These remains were later moved to the Custer National Cemetery.

FORT RICE
Dakota Territory

Volume 9 of the Roll of Honor lists 119 burials (only 102 known) in Fort Rice's post cemetery. Volume 19 of the series contains what appears to be a corrected list of only 51 names.

Wawble Wau-Kauth-ah (High Eagle), a former chief of the Unkpapas Sioux Indians, was buried in the center of the cemetery by permission of the post commander. High Eagle had selected his own burial site.

These remains were later moved to the Custer National Cemetery.

FORT SCULLY
Dakota Territory

Volume 19 of the Roll of Honor lists twenty-two burials (all known) in Fort Scully's post cemetery. These remains were later moved to Fort Leavenworth National Cemetery.

FORT THOMPSON
Dakota Territory

Volume 19 of the <u>Roll of Honor</u> lists three burials in Fort Thompson's post cemetery. No record of removal of these remains to a national cemetery has been found.

FORT WADSWORTH
Dakota Territory

Volume 19 of the <u>Roll of Honor</u> lists 16 burials in Fort Wadsworth's post cemetery. No record of removal of these remains to a national cemetery has been found.

YANKTON
Dakota Territory

Corporal C.T. Bundy of the 6th Iowa Cavalry died at Yankton, Dakota Territory, on March 2, 1865. No record of removal of Bundy's remains to a national cemetery has been found.

BRANDYWINE HUNDRED
Delaware

Twenty-two Union Soldiers were buried in or near Brandywine Hundred, Delaware. According to an undated list, most graves were not marked with wooden headboards. Most of the soldiers died during or shortly after the war.

BURIAL LOCATIONS:

Mount Lebanon M.E. Church	2 graves
Newark Union M.E. Church	1 grave
Mount Pleasant M.E. Church	3 graves
New Port M.E. Church	1 grave
Scranton "Friends" Burying Ground	1 grave
Saint James Episcopal Church	6 graves
Red Clay Presbyterian Church	2 graves
Mount Salem M.E. Church	3 graves
Saint Peters (Colored) M.E. Church	3 graves

WILMINGTON
Delaware

Volume 7 of the <u>Roll of Honor</u> lists a total of 82 burials (all white) at Wilmington:

Wilmington and Brandywine Cemetery	68 burials
Catholic Cemetery	10 burials
Asbury M.E. Church Graveyard	4 burials

BATTLEGROUND NATIONAL CEMETERY
Washington, D.C.

Battleground National Cemetery is a unique cemetery. It is the only Civil War era National Cemetery without unknown dead. All 41 Union soldiers buried here are known. No bodies were moved here after the war. 40 of the soldiers buried here were killed in the Battle of Washington on July 12, 1864. This battle occurred near Fort Stevens during General Jubal Early's raid on Washington. In 1864 the cemetery was about 4 miles from the outskirts of the capitol. Volume 1 of the <u>Roll of Honor</u> lists these burials.

In 1933 the cemetery was transferred from the War Department to the National Park Service.The only veteran buried here is Major Edward R. Campbell who was buried here on March 12, 1936. Campbell was 92 when he died.

CONGRESSIONAL CEMETERY
Washington, D.C.

The land for the Congressional Cemetery was purchased for $1,115 in 1807. A brick wall was built around the cemetery in 1824 at a cost of $2,000.

At least 62 soldiers were buried in the cemetery during the war. General D.H. Rucker of the Quartermaster Department arranged with J.W. Plant, a local undertaker, to bury the soldiers. In April 1868, 46 of these bodies were moved to Arlington National Cemetery. The rest of the bodies were removed by friends. Still the Government owned 924 burial sites in the cemetery.

Seventy-five sailors were buried in the Congressional Cemetery between 1867 and 1878. In 1885 the Navy requested tombstones for these known sailors.

117

Senate Document 72 (1902) lists 16 senators, 68 Congressmen, and 25 other officials buried in the cemetery. One of the other officials was the first Vice President to die in office, George Clinton (1811). Pushmatahaw, a Choctaw Indian Chief, was also buried here.

SOLDIERS' HOME NATIONAL CEMETERY
Washington, D.C.

According to a 1909 report: "Total interments is (sic) 7265-4744 of these interments was (sic) made during the War of Southern Rebellion 1861 to 1865 from the hospitals in Washington." Volume 1 of the Roll of Honor lists 5,211 burials in the United States Military Asylum Cemetery. The first burial was made in the cemetery on August 3 (or 1) ,1861. The last Civil War burial was made on May 13, 1864. On that day Arlington National Cemetery opened.

By the time Col. Mack inspected the cemetery in 1871, it had been enlarged from six acres to nine acres by enclosing the cemetery reserved for "inmates of the home" with a new stone fence. By August 31, 1871, a total of $69,816.28 had been spent on the cemetery.

The interments in 1871 were:

	known	unknown
officers	20	0
enlisted men	5,070	278
U.S. soldiers	2	0
employees, citizens ...	117	0
Rebel prisoners of war	125	0
	5,334	278

APALACHICOLA
Florida

Volume 9 of the Roll of Honor lists two white and twelve colored soldiers who died at Apalachicola. These bodies were later moved to Barrancas National Cemetery.

BALDWIN
Florida

James M. French, a private in the 111th Illinois, died at Baldwin on April 28, 1865. No record of reinterment of this soldier in a national cemetery has been found.

BARRANCAS NATIONAL CEMETERY
Florida

Fort Barrancas was one of three forts built to guard Pensacola's harbor. On January 10, 1861, Florida seceded from the Union. Lieutenant Adam Slemmer, the United States Commander at Pensacola, only had 81 men to garrison's all three forts. He abandoned Fort Barrancas and nearby Fort McRae and concentrated his forces at Fort Pickens.

Fort Pickens was never taken by the Confederates, who abandoned Pensacola in April 1862. After the war Barrancas National Cemetery was established nine miles from Pensacola. When Col. Mack inspected the cemetery in 1871, he reported the cemetery was slightly over seven acres in size. It was divided into two sections. The east section had 337 graves of U.S. Navy officers and sailors. Only 112 of these sailors were known. 1,042 soldiers were buried in the west section:

	known	unknown
white Union soldiers	379	271
colored Union soldiers	154	98
citizens	21	47
Rebel soldiers	60	12
	614	428

Burials at Pensacola are listed in volumes 7 and 14 of the Roll of Honor. The Apache Chief Geronimo and his tribe were held at Fort Pickens in the late 1880's. Ga-ah, Geronimo's wife, died while a prisoner at Fort Pickens. She is buried in Barrancas National Cemetery.

In 1927, 468 bodies from Key West and 21 bodies from Fort Dade were moved to the cemetery.

CHATTAHOOCKE
Florida

Volume 7 of the Roll of Honor lists one known U S colored soldier buried at Chattahoocke. No other records exist.

119

FORT JEFFERSON
Florida

Volume 9 of the Roll of Honor listed 58 known white soldiers and 5 known colored soldiers buried at Fort Jefferson. A list dated April 15, 1873, gave the names of 32 known soldiers buried in the post cemetery. 19 unknown soldiers and two citizens were also buried in the cemetery. According to the report, one unknown soldier was buried "with a woman named Charlotte in the same grave."

GAINSVILLE
Florida

A 1866 report stated that about 15 unknown soldiers, mostly 15th Ohio, were buried near Gainsville. The report stated the graves were: "supposed to be in Alachua Co., on the line of the Fenandina and Gulf R.R."

The land the graves were on was to be purchased but no other records can be found.

JACKSONVILLE
Florida

Volume 9 of the Roll of Honor lists 61 white (2 unknown) and 30 U.S. colored troops who died at Jacksonville. Most of these died in 1865. Volume 14, the Roll of Honor's POW listing, lists what appears to be a corrected list of 42 white soldiers who were buried at Jacksonville. These graves were moved to Beaufort National Cemetery.

KEY WEST
Florida

Volume 9 of the Roll of Honor lists 50 white and 77 colored soldiers (all known) buried at Key West. The cemetery was not maintained. Once a sergeant paid $25 from his own pocket to repair the cemetery's fence. He did so because horses and cows were grazing on the graves. He eventually was reimbursed.

In January 1886 the Government purchased land known as the Mallory Lot for a cemetery. A total of 214 bodies were moved to the cemetery. In 1927 a total of 468 bodies were moved from Key West to Barrancas National Cemetery.

LAKE CITY
Florida

Volume 9 of the Roll of Honor lists the burials of eleven white and one colored soldier at Lake City. No other information about these burials has been found.

QUINCY
Florida

A letter, dated 1866, listed two known U S Colored Troops buried at Quincy. No other records exist.

SAINT AUGUSTINE NATIONAL CEMETERY
Florida

When the United States gained control of Florida in 1821, the St. Francis Barracks was established on the outskirts of Saint Augustine. A plot of land was set aside as a post cemetery. The first burial took place in 1828.

In December 28, 1835, 109 men under Major Francis L. Dade were attacked by Seminole Indians while they were en route from Fort Brook (Tampa) to Fort King (Ocala). Only one man survived the massacre. The Seminole War ended in 1842. Shortly afterwards the bodies were moved to the Saint Augustine Post Cemetery and buried with other victims of the Seminole War The mass graves were marked with three pyramids of native coquia stone.

In 1912 Superintendent Rowland Osborn estimated that a total of 1460 soldiers killed in the "Florida War" were buried at Saint Augustine. His report listed a few names. Osborn also stated: "some (bodies) were recently reinterred in (the) Beaufort S. C. National Cemetery."

Confederate forces seized the post in 1861, but in March 1862, Union Naval forces recaptured the town. A burial register dated 1864, listed 61 burials in the post cemetery between 1862 and 1864: seven officers, 42 enlisted men, and seven unknowns.

By 1881 the neglected post cemetery had fallen into disrepair. At the

121

urging of the post commander, Quartermaster General Meigs proposed making the post cemetery a National Cemetery. Meigs pointed out that Saint Augustine was resort city and many ex-soldiers died there. Also in 1881 the soldiers and officers of the post erected a monument to the memory of those who died in the "Florida War" by "voluntary subscription." Each man donated one day's pay to build the monument.

In 1884 a letter signed by the mayor and local citizens asked for appointment of a superintendent for the cemetery. Quartermaster General Holabird replied that until recently the cemetery had been a post cemetery. A superintendent would be too expensive. However a superintendent had been appointed by 1912. In 1906 bodies from Jacksonville and Lakeland were moved to the cemetery.

A separate post cemetery was active at Saint Francis Barracks in the 1880's.

SAINT FRANCIS BARRACKS
Florida

The Quartermaster of Saint Francis Barracks requested six headstones for the post cemetery in 1886. One was for "an inmate of the soldier's home." Two burials were recorded in 1889. One was apparently a veteran, a member of the GAR.

This appears to be a separate cemetery from Saint Augustine National Cemetery.

SANTA ROSA ISLAND
Florida

Volume 7 of the Roll of Honor lists 61 white and two colored soldiers who were buried on Santa Rosa Island during the Civil War. All but ten bodies were moved to Barrancas National Cemetery after the war. The ten who were not moved had died of yellow fever in 1863.

In 1876 Major T. Seymour of the 5th Artillery requested that these bodies also be moved to Barrancas National Cemetery. Quartermaster General Meigs refused the request citing other examples of not moving bodies of yellow fever victims. He wrote: "...even if it can be done without danger it will disturb men's minds, who do not know that such a transfer is safe."

TALLAHASSEE
Florida

Volume 9 of the <u>Roll of Honor</u> (1866) names ten soldiers, one sailor, and eleven U.S. Colored Troops who died at Tallahassee in 1865 and 1866. However the Quartermaster General's records have an 1866 list showing 41 known burials in Tallahassee's City Cemetery. No record of removal of these bodies to a National Cemetery has been found.

ANDERSONVILLE NATIONAL CEMETERY
Georgia

Andersonville was the main Confederate prison camp during the last year and a half of the war. Southern officials feared that the Confederate prisons near Richmond might be captured by Union troops. Late in 1863 they began searching for a better site. In January, 1864, Confederate soldiers and negro slaves began clearing land near Andersonville in Southwestern Georgia. This site was far from Union troops in Tennessee and Virginia. In August 1865, Captain James Moore, the quartermaster in charge of the Union reburial party, described the location: "The country is covered mostly with pines and hemlocks, and the soil sandy, sterile, and unfit for cultivation..." Moore continued: "It is said to be the most unhealthy part of Georgia and was probably selected as a depot for prisoners on account of this fact."

Moore continues with a description of the local residents: "The inhabitants of this sparsely-settled locality are, with few exceptions (are) of the most ignorant class, and from their haggard and shallow faces the effect of chills and fever are distinctly visible."

The work on the prison continued until the first 500 prisoners arrived on February 25, 1864. By August over 32,000 prisoners had arrived. In that time over 7,400 died. Overcrowding, lack of sanitation, wounds, and disease killed most. Guards shot those who crossed a rail fence known as a "deadline."

Prisoners even killed each other. Several hundred who formed gangs were known as the Andersonville raiders. These gangs stole from their fellow prisons. In early May the problem became worse as the Raiders took to robbing new prisoners that had just arrived with their veteran bounties. On June 29 Captain Henry Wirz, the prison commander, ordered the Confederate guards to "clear the stockade" of the raiders.

The guards began to seize the raiders that prisoners pointed out to them. The next day General John H. Winder, Captain Wirz's superior ordered the accused raiders tried by a court of prisoners. Six raiders were found guilty of murder by the court and hanged late in the evening on July 11, 1864. They are buried separately from other prisoners in the national cemetery.

Although the executions stopped the raider killings, the prisoners continued to die at an alarming rate. Malnutrition was a contributing cause to many deaths. When Union troops occupied Atlanta, Confederate authorities moved many prisoners to Millen, Georgia, and Florence, South Carolina. Over 12,900 Federal Troops died at Andersonville. About 45,000 prisoners were held there during the war. The mortality rate was about 28%. About 24% of some 12,000 Confederate prisoners at Elmira, New York, died during the war.

The largest Union prison was Camp Douglas, Ill. Of about 30,000 Confederates imprisoned here during the war, officially 4,454 died. This gives a mortality rate of about 15%. Surprisingly only twelve Union prison guards at Camp Douglas died during the war. However 115 prison guards died at Andersonville during the war. If poor food weakened the prisoners it also weakened the guards. These guards bodies were moved to Oak Grove Cemetery in Americus, Georgia, in 1900.

The horrors of Anderson lead to the first war crimes trial. Of the survivors Walt Whitman wrote: "The dead there are not to be pitied as much as some of the living that come from there--if they can be call'd living--." Wirz was arrested on May 7, 1865. When he was sent north ex-pow's tried to kill him.

Wirz was "tried" by a military commission headed by Major General Lew Wallace. The outcome was never in doubt. Wallace wrote his wife before the "trial" began: "I hear also that the prisoner's defense will be that he obeyed orders received from his superiors--in other words, it is expected that out of this investigation will come proof of Jeff. Davis' connection with that criminality. Quien Sabe!" Wriz's defense attorneys finally withdrew from the case in October. They had been stymied in their efforts to prove that Northern prisons were as bad as Andersonville. On October 24, 1865, Wriz was found guilty. He was hanged on November 10, 1865. No conspiracy was ever proven.

Major James D. Jones, CSA, served as drillmaster and ordinance officer at Andersonville. In his memoirs he wrote: "Andersonville was no worse than northern prisons. There was suffering at Johnson's Island; there are hardships in all prisons. Thirty thousand men in a stockade are apt to suffer more or less." Jones stated that: "The prisoners got fully as much, and as good rations as our guards." He related stories of his servant buying food from prisoners when the guard's rations were small.

Major Jones pointed out the major reason for the large number of deaths in Andersonville (and all Civil War prisons). He wrote: "And may I ask, whose fault was it that there was no exchange of prisoners? We would gladly given 10 for 1 (and we had them to give) but no! The policy of the Federal government was to exhaust the South. That was General Grant's policy; and the only one that was a success." Jones is correct. The failure of the prisoner exchange cartel in late 1863 caused many deaths on both sides.

While the charges against Wriz were being prepared, plans were made to mark the graves at Andersonville. On July 8, 1865, Captain James Moore left Washington with 34 men to mark the graves. Accompanying Moore was Clara Barton and a 19 year-old ex-soldier, Dorence Atwater.

Atwater had served in the Federal Cavalry for almost two years before being captured in July 1863. He was imprisoned at Belle Island, then Richmond. In March, 1864, he was sent Andersonville. He was sick and sent to the prison hospital in May. On June 15, he was paroled and assigned to work as the "clerk of the dead" in Wirz's office. Atwater recorded the names, date of death, disease, and burial site of each dead soldier. Each entry in the "book of the dead" was numbered and each grave was marked with a board with the same number. Atwater kept a duplicate death register, which he hid in his coat lining when he was released in March 1865. His copy contained 12,920 names. Atwater contacted the War Department when he arrived home. On April 15 he met with Major Samuel Beck to discuss the rolls. Beck offered Atwater $300 for the rolls. Atwater stated he did want to sell the rolls, he only wanted the names published. Beck told Atwater if he refused to sell the rolls they would be declared contraband and be confiscated. Atwater realized he could not win so he told Beck: "Give me $300, a clerkship, and my rolls back as soon as they are copied and you can take them." Atwater began his clerkship on June 1st, but he could not get his rolls back. Beck, after consulting with this superiors, told Atwater: "The rolls shall not be copied for any traffic whatever."

Because the prison death register captured at Andersonville contained only about 10,500 names, Atwater was given his original rolls back to use on the expedition to Georgia. Atwater again copied his list. This list would be his downfall.

Clara Barton had learned of Atwater's list and hounded Secretary of War Stanton and Quartermaster General Meigs until they allowed both Atwater and her to accompany Moore to Andersonville. Because of the destruction of Georgia's railroads it took the expedition six days to travel from Savannah to Andersonville. Two companies of U.S. Troops were detailed to help Moore. When he arrived at Andersonville he found Mr. W.A. Griffin of Fort Valley, Georgia, who had brought 20 negroes to the cemetery to work. Moore's official report neglects to mention Griffin's help.

The dead had been buried in trenches that ranged from fifty to one hundred and fifty yards in length. Although the bodies had been buried two to three feet deep, the rain had washed most of the dirt of some of the graves. However no bodies were exposed. Clara Barton reported: "The place was found in much better condition than had been anticipated."

The bodies were buried side by side without coffins. In fact each body took up only about a foot in the trench. Moore's group piled more dirt on the graves and marked them with headboards. 120,000 feet of pine lumber was used to mark the graves. 12,461 graves were marked with the names. 461 graves were unknowns. Volume 3 of the Roll of Honor lists the burials. Volume 14 of the roll lists 141 additional known and 167 unknown burials at Andersonville. Volume 17 of the Roll of Honor lists 580 interments of bodies made after the war. Most of these bodies came from southwestern Georgia and Alabama. By 1871 a total of 13,712 burials had been made. Of these 12,778 were known.

Moore left Andersonville in mid-August. His report fails to mention either Clara Barton's or Atwater's contributions to the success of the expedition. Moore did report that he was having a copy of "the record" of burials made for the use of the superintendent. Apparently Atwater took this copy with him when he left for Washington. Upon his arrival Major Beck demanded return of the copies of the roll. When Atwater refused he was jailed.

Atwater was quickly court-martialed and found guilty. He was dishonorabled discharged and sentenced to 18 months at hard labor. Clara Barton, Horace Greeley, and others began to push for Atwater's release. He served about two months before being released. Because the list of names had still not been published, Atwater made arrangements with Greeley to publish the list of names. On February 14, 1866, the Tribune Publishing Company published Atwater's list. The War Department was publicly embarrassed. In a letter dated February 17th, Meigs asked Major Moore to give a date of publication of the official list. Moore's answer was "in a few days." This list became volume 3 of the Roll of Honor. Atwater was made a U.S. Consul to the Seychelles in 1868. President Grant transferred him to Tahiti in 1871. Atwater married a native princess and became a successful businessman. Congress set aside the court martial verdict in 1898. Atwater died in 1910.

Although Col. Moore's expedition had covered and marked the graves, a plan was proposed to move the bodies to a new cemetery on a nearby hill. "W.D.", a special correspondent to the Boston Thursday Spectator and Weekly Advertiser, reported this plan in April, 1868. He had visited the cemetery and was indigent that the proposal was not carried out. Instead the graves were remounded with dirt like some "species of Indian mounds" and the headboard raised. The writer ended his argument with: "To leave them (the dead soldiers) were they lie and bury them under a hill of clay, when a spot capable of remarkable beauty lies close by, would be anything but creditable to the nation." W.D.'s pleas fell on deaf ears. The graves were not moved.

Although the government improved the cemetery, it did not have title to the land. Benjamin B. Dykes, the original land owner, filed a petition for possession of the land and a writ of ejectment of the superintendent of the cemetery in August 1869. In March 1872, Quartermaster Meigs wrote the Secretary of War about the case: "the land and property consist of a rebel stockade and slaughter house,and some ditches into which they tumbled the bodies of those there starved and murdered. Dykes is reported to have boasted that he would plant a vineyard, and that the dead Yankees would make good wine."

Meigs believed that "our title" is "complete by capture and occupation." He stated: "No government money will be paid with good will to such a person (Dykes) for the ground consecrated by the sufferings of the martyrs of Andersonville."

In a letter written February 7, 1873, Meigs wrote: "I have no idea that anything could be done, in reason with Mr. Dykes, of whom very offensive expressions towards 'dead Yankees'" (have been attributed).

On February 20, 1875, Dykes sold 120 acres of land to the Federal Government. On September 25, 1875, Dykes sued in Federal Court for $65,848.50 for damages. He claimed over $24,000 damages for lack of use of the land. Also included were 900 cords of wood, 300,000 feet of lumber, and 250,000 brick. A note dated March 24,1881, reads: "Dept. of Justice: Case of B.B. Dykes vs. the U.S. (Andersonville Cemetery) has been decided in favor of the Govt."

The site of the prison was purchased by the Georgia Department of the Grand Army of the Republic in 1890. The Woman's Relief Corps, the National Women's Auxiliary of the GAR, later purchased the land for one dollar. The site was donated to the United States in 1910. In 1971 the National Park Service took over administration of the Andersonville National Historic Site from the Department of the Army.

ATLANTA
Georgia

Volume 14 of the Roll of Honor lists 124 Union POW's who died at Atlanta. These bodied were moved to Marietta National Cemetery after the war.

AUGUSTA
Georgia

Seventy-nine known Union soldiers died while prisoners at Augusta, according to volume 14 of the Roll of Honor. Records at the National Archives state these bodies were moved to Andersonville National Cemetery, however other records state that all bodies at Augusta were moved to Marietta National Cemetery.

CASSVILLE
Georgia

Corporal George W. Lanam of the 45th Ohio died at Cassville on December 7, 1863, while a prisoner. No records of removal of his remains have been found.

COVINGTON
Georgia

Volume 14 of the Roll of Honor lists two burials of Federal prisoners at Covington. These bodies were moved to Andersonville National Cemetery after the war.

KINGSTON
Georgia

A total of two Federal and 250 Confederate soldiers are buried in Kingston's Confederate Cemetery. The Confederates had hospitals in Kingston until May 1864. After that the Union forces operated the hospitals. Other Federal bodies from the area were moved to the Marietta National Cemetery.

LAWTON NATIONAL CEMETERY
Georgia

For two months in 1864 a Confederate POW camp was operated just west of Lawton, Georgia. Because the camp was five and one half miles north of Millen, Georgia, the camp was known as the Millen prison.

The prison was located at Magnolia Springs a source of pure water. Confederate authorities had begun moving prisoners from Andersonville to Millen in October 1864. In November, as Sherman's army approached, the prisoners were sent back to Andersonville.

About 7,000 POW's were held at Millen and 725 died. 491 were buried in three trenches near the Savannah and Augusta Railroad. Two trenches near the hospital held 234 more bodies.

When Federal authorities began reinterring the dead, they noticed that each body was marked by a wooden stake and every 50th stake was numbered. Only two stakes had names. J.T. Shephard was written on the 138th stake. The 257th board bore the name: J.B. Northrup. Apparently, a record of deaths in the camp had been kept but no record seemed to exist. A former prisoner who had served as a clerk verified that careful records had been kept. But where were they?

A Captain Cameron, described as a gentlemen of character and humanity, had devised the record keeping system. The description of Captain Cameron is unique in the Roll of Honor. Normally "rebels" are described in a very negative way. In the same paragraph the commander of the prison pen is described as "...under the charge of one Vowels, described by the citizens of that neighborhood as 'a vagabond without home or friends either before or since the war'..."

When questioned about the missing records Captain Cameron said he packed muster rolls, records of interments, and ration returns in a wine box to send to General John H. Winder, the Confederate Commissary General of prisons. Cameron took the package to the railroad office at Waynesboro 14 miles away. The package was to be sent to the Georgia Adjutant General in Augusta to forward to General Winder at Columbia, SC. Apparently the records never reached General Winder.

The railroad station at Waynesboro had been burned by Kilpatrick's calvary and no record of the box remained. However, in 1865, the United States Christian Commission obtained what appeared to be the lost dead register. A Presbyterian clergyman found the lost records in Savannah in December 1864. After the war he took the records to the United States Christian Commission who published them. Because the records listed both J.T. Shephard and J.B. Northrup in the correct graves, the roll was determined to be authentic.

How the roll ended up in Savannah is a mystery. Did the railroad agent misdirect the box? Did soldiers or bystanders remove the box before the railroad office was burned? Perhaps they thought the box still held wine. In any event the records were saved and the graves marked.

From November 1866 to February 1867, 380 bodies from the Macon, Georgia, vicinity were moved to Lawton National Cemetery. Volume C of the Disposition lists original burial sites of 748 soldiers interred in Lawton National Cemetery. Volumes XIV and XVII of the Roll of Honor lists the names of Union soldiers buried at Lawton.

Before the end of 1868 the bodies were disinterred and moved to Beaufort National Cemetery in South Carolina.

MACON
Georgia

Volume 14 of the <u>Roll of Honor</u> lists 236 Union Prisoners of War who died at Macon. According to volume 1 of the <u>Disposition</u> a total of 380 bodies were moved from Macon and vicinity to Lawton National Cemetery between November 10, 1866, and February 28, 1867. Lawton National Cemetery was later moved to <u>Beaufort National Cemetery.</u> The same page of the <u>Disposition</u> lists a total of 102 bodies moved from Macon and vicinity to Andersonville National Cemetery in March 1867. Volume 2 of the <u>Disposition</u> lists a total of 490 removals from Macon to Andersonville. These removals occurred between January 1867 and January 1868. 56 of these bodies came from the 137th U. S. Colored Infantry's regimental cemetery. The Quartermaster's files contain a list of eleven Federal occupation soldiers and one unknown child of a United States soldier who died at Macon. These bodies were moved Andersonville in 1873.

MADISON
Georgia

Twenty-three Union prisoners who died at Madison are listed in Volume 14 of the <u>Roll of Honor</u>. These bodies were reinterred in Andersonville National Cemetery.

MARIETTA NATIONAL CEMETERY
Georgia

Atlanta was the objective of Sherman's Army in 1864. After the war Mr. Henry G. Cole, a citizen of Marietta who had remained loyal to the Union, offered land in Marietta to use a cemetery for both Confederate and Union dead. Cole hoped that burying the war dead in a common cemetery would help heal wounds. But hostile feelings prevented a common cemetery, so in 1866 Mr. Cole donated some 20 acres to the Federal Government. When Mr. Cole died in 1875, he was buried in the family plot that had been reserved by Mr. Cole's deed.

Burials in the cemetery were made from Atlanta, Rome, and Dalton, Georgia and the Montgomery, Alabama National Cemetery. Volume 23 of the <u>Roll of Honor</u> lists burials in the cemetery.

When Col. Mack made his report in 1871, he reported a total of 10,069 burials:

	known	unknown
officers	223	16
white soldiers and sailors	6,632	2,950
colored soldiers	158	67
citizens	21	0
	7,036	3,033

By August 31, 1871, a total of $187,788.17 had been spent on the cemetery.

SAVANNAH
Georgia

Volume 14 of the <u>Roll of Honor</u> lists the names of two Federal soldiers who died in Savannah on November 30, 1864. These soldiers were prisoners of the war who died just three weeks before Sherman captured the city. Apparently other Union troops died in Savannah after Sherman captured the city, but no records of their names have been found.

On December 26, 1867, Mr. J.P. Low of Charleston, S.C., was awarded a contract to remove bodies from Savannah to the Beaufort National Cemetery.

WEST POINT
Georgia

A total of 76 Confederate and Union soldiers are buried in the Fort Tyler Cemetery. These soldiers died in the Battle of Fort Tyler on April 16, 1865.

CAMP LYON
Idaho Territory

Volume 8 of the <u>Roll of Honor</u> lists one burial in Camp Lyon's post cemetery. No record of removal of these remains to a national cemetery has been found.

CAMP WINTHROP
Idaho Territory

Volume 19 of the Roll of Honor lists one burial in Camp Winthrop's post cemetery. No record of removal of these remains to a national cemetery has been found.

FORT BOISE
Idaho Territory

Volumes 8 and 19 of the Roll of Honor list a total of eleven burials in Fort Boise's post cemetery. No record of removal of these remains to a national cemetery has been found.

FORT LAPWAI
Idaho

Fort Lapwai was active form 1863 until 1884. Volume 8 of the Roll of Honor, which calls the fort, Fort Laporai, lists three burials. The Quartermaster General's files include a list of 64 burials in the post cemetery. When the fort closed in 1884, the buildings were turned over to the Interior Department for use as a school. In 1890 the bodies from the post cemetery were moved to Fort Walla Walla, Washington, at a cost of $1,298.88.

ALTON NATIONAL CEMETERY
Illinois

Alton served as a major Federal supply depot during the war. A large Federal POW Camp operated here from 1863 to 1865. In 1863 a smallpox epidemic swept the area. At least 1,354 Confederate POW's died in prison. Many died in the smallpox hospital on "Smallpox Island" in the middle of the Mississippi River. In 1910 the Federal Government erected a 58 foot granite obelisk to mark the Confederate graves. By then the names of 684 Confederates buried in the Confederate Cemetery had been lost.

The Federal Soldiers who died in and near Alton were eventually buried in the Alton National Cemetery located in the Alton City Cemetery. Volumes 9, 12, and 13 of the Roll of Honor list a total of 226 Union

Soldiers buried at Alton. However several bodies were removed by friends. Several graves were not found when the bodies were moved to the National Cemetery.

BUNKER HILL
Illinois

A 1870 request for tombstones listed 15 Union Soldiers buried in the Bunker Hill Cemetery. It is unclear if these soldiers died during or after the war.

CAMP BUTLER NATIONAL CEMETERY
Illinois

The site for Camp Butler was chosen by General William T. Sherman in 1861. Sherman was seeking a site for training camp near Springfield. The camp was named for William Butler the Illinois State Treasurer who assisted Sherman in his search for a site for the camp.

The first trainees arrived on May 5, 1861. Even though the site was well chosen, morality ran high. They were buried in what became Camp Butler National Cemetery. Few bodies were moved to Camp Butler, but about one hundred bodies were moved to Camp Butler from Springfield. Volume 9 of the Roll of Honor lists 1,054 white and 9 colored soldiers buried at Camp Butler. Four of the colored soldiers were substitutes.

Camp Butler also served as a Union POW Camp. Over 2,000 Confederates captured at Fort Donelson, Ten, arrived on February 16, 1862. Most of these were exchanged before the POW exchange system broke down in 1863. However over 800 Confederate POW's died at Camp Butler. The Official Records do not list the total number of Confederate death because of missing records. However 848 Confederates are buried at Camp Butler.

CARBONDALE
Illinois

An unsigned list dated June 15, 1870, gave the names of 26 known soldiers buried "at the penitentiary" at Carbondale. No other information exists.

CARLINVILLE
Illinois

Volume 13 of the <u>Roll of Honor</u> lists eight Union soldiers who died at Carlinville between 1862 and 1864. No record of removal of these remains to a national cemetery has been found.

CHESTNUT
Illinois

A letter dated October 22, 1883, requested a tombstone for a Union soldier who died in April 1865. The exact burial location was not given.

CHICAGO
Illinois

Federal soldiers were interred in at least two cemeteries in Chicago during the war. Volume 18 of the <u>Roll of Honor</u> lists 303 known and 14 unknown soldiers buried at Rose Hill Cemetery. In 1868 Rose Hill was six and one-half miles north of Chicago on the Chicago and Milwaukee Railroad. It was also "...accessible by two good wagon roads-one along the lake, the other the prairie road."

Volume 9 of the <u>Roll of Honor</u> lists another 159 soldiers buried "at Chicago." These names are not included in the 317 listed for Rose Hill Cemetery but the index to volume 18 states that these are in addition to volume 9. Record Group 92-E576 had the <u>Roll of Honor</u> for Rose Hill Cemetery filed under "Oakland, Chicago."

Chicago was also the site of Camp Douglas, a large Union POW Camp. Epidemics of both smallpox and choler claimed many lives. A December 1866 report listed 655 Confederate POW's buried at the city cemetery. A letter dated May 1, 1867, listed plans to move the "rebel" POW's from City Cemetery to Oak Woods Cemetery. The charges were: $1.90 to move each body, $1.00 to rebury the body, and $2.00 for the plot each body was reinterred in. According to volume 1 of the <u>Disposition</u> a total of 3,384 bodies were moved from City Cemetery to Oak Woods. These graves were not individually marked.

In 1895 the United Confederate Veterans received permission to construct a monument on the "Confederate Mound." On May 30, 1895, the granite monument was dedicated. In 1910 the United States Government provided a sub-base for the monument. Sixteen bronze tablets attached to the base list the names of 4,243 known Confederates buried in the mound. Thirty-two unknown Confederate soldiers are also buried in the mound. Oak Woods Cemetery Association literature states: "The Government's records show the number of Confederate soldiers buried to be 4,275, although conservative estimates based on cemetery records show the number to be considerably higher. The Placque (sic) on the Mound (erected by the UCV) estimates 6,000."

Twelve unknown Union soldiers are buried at the Confederate Mound. They were apparently prison guards who died of disease.

DECATUR
Illinois

In 1889 headstones were requested for 48 soldiers who had died in Decatur. The majority of these were "sick and wounded from the railroad." They were buried in Glenwood Cemetery. The list of names is not filed with the request. Apparently it was sent to the headstone contractor.

Twenty of these soldiers were unknown. The Quartermaster General explained: "...headstones for the graves of unknown soldiers, in private, village, and city cemeteries, have not heretofore been furnished by the Department unless the soldiers were buried in a soldier's Lot or in a plot, in a regular city cemetery, devoted exclusivly (sic) to the burials of soldiers." However the policy was to be changed. The headstones for the unknowns were "to be shipped in the next list."

DIXON
Illinois

Volume 18 of the Roll of Honor lists 16 burials in Dixon's Town cemetery. In 1883 James Sanfomr requested headstones for four of these graves.

DUNDEE
Illinois

Volume 18 of the Roll of Honor lists ten known and two unknown members of the 8th and 17th Illinois Cavalry buried at Dundee.

ELGIN
Illinois

Fifteen white soldiers were buried in Elgin's City Cemetery according to volume 18 of the <u>Roll of Honor</u>. Apparently these bodies were never moved to a national cemetery.

GALESBURG
Illinois

One known Union soldier is buried in Hope Cemetery in Galesburg.

JOLIET
Illinois

Two white soldiers listed in volume 18 of the <u>Roll of Honor</u> were buried at Joliet.

MOUND CITY NATIONAL CEMETERY
Illinois

The first burials in Mound City National Cemetery were made in 1862. A total of 1,644 burials were made from hospitals in Mound City. The ten acre land was purchased from the Cairo Land Company. The site was located near Mound City's Naval Yard and a strong dike completely surrounded the cemetery to keep out the Ohio River's backwaters.

After the war bodies from Cairo, Belmont, Paducah, Columbus, and other locations were brought to the cemetery. Removals from Kentucky cost an average or $6.60. Removals from Illinois and Missouri cost an average of $6.75. Four iron cannon were used as monuments beside a "very poor (small and crooked) flagstaff." One worker, paid $1.75 a day, assisted the superintendent. A total of $53,944.96 had been expended on the cemetery by August 31, 1871.

A total of 4,868 interments had been made by 1871:

	known	unknown
white soldiers and sailors	2,060	2,460
colored soldiers and sailors	307	0

136

Rebel prisoners of war	0	41
	2,367	2,501

Volumes 9, 18, and 26 of the <u>Roll of Honor</u> lists these interments.

QUINCY NATIONAL CEMETERY
Illinois

A 150 by 200 foot soldiers' lot in Woodland Cemetery was donated to the United States by Ex-Governor Wood of Quincy. Volume 9 of the <u>Roll of Honor</u> lists 287 burials (274 white) at Quincy. When Col. Mack inspected the cemetery in 1870, he noted a total of 242 burials:

white Union soldiers, known	209
white Union soldiers, unknown	6
colored Union soldiers, known	27
	242

These burials were made from the general hospital at Quincy, but when Col. Mack inspected the cemetery he could locate no records of burials at the cemetery, "and no one connected with it (the cemetery) knows anything about them" (the records). Only $1,266.25 had been spent on the cemetery by May 31, 1871.

In July 1882, the cemetery was declared a National Cemetery at the request of the Grand Army of the Republic (GAR). Martin Easley was appointed superintendent at a salary of $720. However soon it was charged that superintendent Easley had agreed to share his salary with the Quincy G.A.R. post. Easley supposedly kept only $200 of the $720 salary. On January 30,1883, superintendent Easley's appointment was canceled by the Secretary of War.

Congressman C.A. Anderson pushed for appointment of another superintendent. On January 16,1888, Congressman Anderson introduced House Resolution #4934 that would establish a National Cemetery at Quincy. In a brief prepared for the Secretary of War, Quartermaster General S.B. Holabird pointed out that the order declaring Quincy a National Cemetery had not been revoked. Holabird also pointed out that the cemetery was being cared for at a cost of $25 per year, so some $900 per year was being saved.

ROCK ISLAND NATIONAL CEMETERY
Illinois

In 1863 part of Rock Island, located in the Mississippi River between

Illinois and Iowa, was chosen as a Union POW Camp. The island already housed the Rock Island Arsenal. On November 25, 1863, the first of what would amount to over 12,000 prisoners arrived. Most were captured in the Chattanooga, Tennessee area. One of the first POW's to arrive also brought smallpox. 1,952 Confederate prisoners died of disease and wounds. Union guards, most of them either members of the Veteran's Reserve Corps or the 108th U.S. Colored Troops, also died.

According to Volume IX of the Roll of Honor, a total of 153 Union soldiers were originally buried at Rock Island. 95 were white and 58 were colored. A 1868 report lists 136 interments in the cemetery: 74 white soldiers, 49 colored soldiers, 6 women and children and 7 unknowns.

Between 1868 and 1871 the cemetery was moved to allow for expansion of the arsenal. Shortly thereafter 159 bodies from Oakdale Cemetery near Davenport, Iowa, were moved to the cemetery. These were soldiers who died at Camp Black Hawk, a calvary training camp. They are listed in Volume XII of the Roll of Honor. At least 19 bodies were left in the Oakdale Cemetery.

Today the VA classifies Oakdale Cemetery as a soldier's lot and the Confederate Cemetery as a Confederate Cemetery.

ROCKFORD
Illinois

Seventeen soldiers were buried in Rockford are listed in volume 18 of the Roll of Honor.

SAINT CHARLES
Illinois

Volume 18 of the Roll of Honor lists twelve (ten known) members of the 8th and 17th Illinois Cavalry buried at Saint Charles.

SPRINGFIELD
Illinois

Most of the Union soldiers who died at Springfield were later buried in Camp Butler National Cemetery near Springfield. Volume 9 of the Roll of Honor lists 22 burials in private cemeteries in Springfield. 19 soldiers were buried in Oak Ridge Cemetery. Three soldiers, all Illinois troops, were buried in Hutchinson's cemetery. The Union Commander-in-Chief, Abraham Lincoln, is buried in Oak Ridge Cemetery also.

FORT GIBSON
Indian Territory

Fort Gibson was founded in 1824. It was active until 1857. During the Civil War Confederates occupied the fort until the Union Army captured the fort on April 5, 1863. The army abandoned Fort Gibson in 1890.

The Quartermaster department advertised for bids to move bodies to the New National Cemetery at Fort Gibson on April 18, 1868. The contract called for moving 2,050 bodies from 21 locations in Arkansas, Missouri, Kansas, the Cherokee Nation. 1,400 of these bodies were within an eight mile radius (including the old post cemetery). Although the bid required: "The bodies are to be removed carefully and decently; all marks and inscriptions found with the body will be carefully recorded...", few bodies were identified.

When Col. Mack inspected the cemetery in 1871 he reported 156 graves and 1,967 unknown graves. Volume 25 of the Roll of Honor lists 151 names. Most of these were from various Indian units. Mack reported a total of $1,700.23 spent on the cemetery by August 31, 1871.

FORT RENO
Indian Territory

Fort Reno was established in July 1874 to protect the nearby Darlington Indian Agency. At least 27 burials had been made in the post cemetery by 1889 according to lists in the Quartermaster General's files. After the post closed in the early 1900's, the Quartermaster Department used the facility as a supply depot. Later the site became an agriculture research station.

The old post cemetery was used as a burial site for 62 German and eight Italian POW's, who died during World War II. These graves are in a section of the cemetery separated from the main cemetery by a stone wall. The last burial in the cemetery was made in 1948.

In 1960 a Senate committee studied making Fort Reno Post Cemetery a national cemetery. However the cemetery remains an army post cemetery. The old cemetery is located just west of El Reno, Oklahoma, just north of I-40.

VARIOUS SITES
Indiana

A report from Brevet Brigadier General J.D. Bingham dated April 24, 1868, lists a total of 396 interments at 97 different locations in Indiana. This report misses the burials of several hundred soldiers at Evansville. It also does not list the Madison and Jeffersonville cemeteries that were moved to New Albany. Bingham's report is in the Appendix. Volume 18 of the Roll of Honor lists 402 known soldiers buried in "various places" in Indiana.

CROWN HILL NATIONAL CEMETERY
Indiana

The first public cemetery in Indianapolis was Greenlawn Cemetery located in downtown Indianapolis. During the Civil War Greenlawn was filled with graves, so in 1863 a new civic group was formed to seek a site for a new cemetery. In 1863 Martin Williams, a local farmer sold 166 acres to the newly formed Crown Hill Cemetery Association.

In 1866 Governor Oliver P. Morton suggested that 708 bodies of Union soldiers be moved to Crown Hill. The cemetery association offered to donate the land to the United States if the government would "expend a certain sum on improvements." Because no appropriation had been made for improvements to national cemeteries the government paid the cemetery association $5,000 for the land. The cemetery association then spent the $5,000 on improvements. Still by June 30, 1871, only $12,127 had been spent on the cemetery.

Most of the burials in the cemetery came from Camp Carrington and hospitals in the area. Volume 8 of the Roll of Honor lists a total of 1,248 white and 40 colored soldiers buried at Indianapolis. Volume 18 of the series adds 330 names. However when Col. Mack inspected the cemetery in 1870, he reported only 702 interments:

	known	unknown
officers	1	0
white soldiers	641	36
colored soldiers	30	0
	672	36

1,556 Confederate POW's were buried in Greenlawn Cemetery. Later their bodies were exhumed and buried in a separate Confederate plot in Crown Hill.

EVANSVILLE
Indiana

There were Union soldiers buried in the Soldier's Lot of Oak Hill Cemetery in Evansville. That much is known. The number of soldiers buried there is unclear.

Volume 8 of the Roll of Honor (1866) lists 86 known white and 33 known colored soldiers buried "at Evansville". A data sheet dated September 16, 1868, listed: one known officer, 554 known white soldiers, 8 unknown white, and 33 known US Colored Troops for a total of 596 graves. No list of names was with the data sheet. Brevet Brigadier General J.D. Bingham's report of Union soldiers interred in Indiana only lists one grave at Evansville.

The lot was purchased by the United States on February 28, 1871, for $300. The lot was supposed to hold 540 bodies. However in a letter dated March 12, 1880, the Quartermaster's Department reported that no record of the names exist.

JEFFERSONVILLE
Indiana

Volume 17 of the Roll of Honor lists two burial sites at Jeffersonville. 126 known soldiers were buried in the City Cemetery. All of these soldiers died in hospitals in Jeffersonville. 584 more soldiers (570 known) were buried in the "Soldiers' Burial Lot." These soldiers had also died in hospitals.

This Roll of Honor (1868) reports that both these cemeteries were moved to New Albany National Cemetery. Apparently this had been done by the time Col. Mack made his report in 1871.

In 1890 the city of Jeffersonville moved some soldier's graves when the road through the cemetery was widened. These graves were marked with stones after they were moved. Apparently these graves, about 70, were soldiers who died at "Old Fort Finney."

MADISON
Indiana

One hundred thirty-five Union soldiers died in hospitals at Madison, Indiana. These soldiers were originally buried in Madison's City Cemetery but they were moved to New Albany National Cemetery around 1868. A report dated 1869 states these soldiers were moved to Jefferson, Indiana.

That report appears to be in error because the bodies at Jefferson were also moved to New Albany.

Volume 8 of the Roll of Honor lists 132 burials. Volume 17 of the Roll of Honor has a corrected list of 135 burials. The names were copied from the headboards as no official cemetery burial list was found.

MOUNT VERNON
Indiana

In May 1888 Post # 491 of the GAR requested "a number" of headstones for Union soldiers buried in the Black Township Cemetery. Forty-seven of these were for unknown soldiers. Apparently these soldiers died during the war. This is the first time that headstones were furnished for unknown soldiers not buried in a soldiers lot.

These burials do not appear on Brig. Gen. J.D. Bingham's list of burials in Indiana.

NEW ALBANY NATIONAL CEMETERY
Indiana

Many of the bodies at New Albany came from hospitals in Indiana, Kentucky, West Virginia, and Virginia. The cemetery covered almost 5 1/2 acres in 1871. Colored soldiers from the Eastern Cemetery in nearby Louisville, Kentucky, were moved to New Albany rather than the white-only Cave Hill National Cemetery in Louisville. Even at New Albany these soldiers were "buried in a section by themselves."

When Col. Mack inspected the cemetery in 1871, he noted 2,807 burials:

	known	unknown
white soldiers	1,341	490
colored soldiers	757	208
employees	11	0
	2,109	698

Burials in New Albany National Cemetery are recorded in volumes 17 and 24 of the Roll of Honor.

VARIOUS SITES
Iowa

Volume 18 of the Roll of Honor lists a total of 443 burials at "various sites" in Iowa. Most of the soldiers listed were from Iowa units.

CLEAR LAKE
Iowa

In 1884 eight headstones were requested for graves in Clear Lake, Iowa. It is unclear if the soldiers died during or after the war.

CLINTON
Iowa

The War Department supplied 12 headstones for deceased Union soldiers in 1885. It is unclear if these soldiers died during or after the war. However an undated sheet in the same file listed two known and five unknown Federal soldiers buried at Clinton. These soldiers were "shot by Whulins (?) Cavalry."

OAKDALE CEMETERY
Davenport, Iowa

Camp Black Hawk was a Union Calvary training camp in Scott County near Davenport, Iowa. A total of 173 white and 5 colored soldiers were buried in 3 areas of Oakdale Cemetery. Volume XII of the Roll of Honor lists the names.

159 bodies were moved to Rock Island National Cemetery between 1868 and 1871. Today the VA classifies Oakdale as a soldiers' lot with a total of 76 interments in 75 grave sites in the Oakdale Cemetery Soldiers' Lot.

DES MOINES
Iowa

Volume 10 of the Roll of Honor lists eleven soldiers who were buried in Woodland Cemetery. No other information on these burials has been found.

KEOKUK NATIONAL CEMETERY
Iowa

Keokuk National Cemetery was once part of Keokuk's Oakland Cemetery. Keokuk's city officials donated some of the cemetery to the United States in 1866 but additional land was purchased in 1870. Most of the burials in the cemetery were from the general hospital in Keokuk, but a few bodies were moved to the cemetery from Iowa City and Memphis, Missouri.

Col. Mack reported that 600 known white and 27 unknown white soldiers had been buried in the cemetery by 1871. Volume 12 of the Roll of Honor (1867) listed 596 white and 24 colored interments.

On November 13 and 14, 1908, 73 bodies that had been removed from Fort Yates, N.D., were reinterred in the cemetery.

SIOUX CITY
Iowa

Volume 9 of the Roll of Honor lists five known soldiers who died at Sioux City in 1865. No record of removal of the bodies to a national cemetery has been found.

VARIOUS SITES
Kansas

Volume 18 of the Roll of Honor lists soldiers buried at "various sites" in Kansas. The bodies listed as buried at the Mine Creek Battlefield were moved to the Mound City Soldiers Lot after the war.

BARNESVILLE
Kansas

Volume 18 of the Roll of Honor lists 18 burials in the Barnesville Cemetery at Barnesville, Kansas. Eight were known, the rest unknown. All but two were members of the 5th Kansas Cavalry. 15 died in 1862. Volume 2 of the Disposition lists 14 burials in the cemetery. Eight bodies were moved from Camp Denver on Indian Creek near Barnesville. A brief note on a sheet of paper used as a "place marker" in the National Cemetery file reads: "Barnsville, Kan, see Ft. Riley, Kan." No record of when the bodies were moved to Fort Riley exists.

BAXTER SPRINGS
Kansas

On the morning of October 6, 1863, a force of Confederate Guerrillas under Quantrill surprised a force of about 100 troops escorting Major General James Blunt near Baxter Springs, Kansas. According to a letter written in 1883:"...some 80 or 90 Union soldiers (were) killed. The remains of these soldiers are now buried in a soldier's lot at that place, having been removed from the trenches in which they were originally interred." A list of 26 names of the soldiers is also in the file. However, in 1871 Col. Mack reported a total of 124 known burials.

In 1885 the Congress authorized $4,000 for a monument to mark the graves of 82 soldiers. The city of Baxter Springs had donated a 60 foot by 80 foot lot to the United States.

Today Baxter Springs is classified as a Soldiers Lot. By 1987 a total of 291 burials had been made in 153 grave sites.

FORT AUBREY
Kansas

A. Grooms of the 14th Mississippi Cavalry died at Fort Aubrey on September 6, 1865. No record of removal of this grave to a national cemetery has been found.

FORT DODGE
Kansas

Fort Dodge was an important US Fort during and after the Civil War. Volume 9 of the Roll of Honor listed two known and six unknown burials. Volume 10 of the series reported the known burials. Volume 18, published in 1868, listed 84 burials. At least 14 of these were Quartermaster's Department employees. One was a child. 23 were unknown. One was listed as a "colored citizen." Two worked for a stage company and one was listed as a "haymaker."

Isadore Bowman, who died August 1, 1867, was listed as the wife of Major H. Douglas, 3rd Infantry. Why she was listed by her maiden name is not clear. Perhaps she was an example of an early liberated woman.

In May 1889 the Quartermaster General refused a request from the local GAR chapter for money to move these graves to the GAR Cemetery. Instead he sent a headstone order form. These graves were moved to Fort Leavenworth National Cemetery before 1909.

FORT ELLSWORTH
Kansas

Fort Ellsworth was founded in August, 1864, by units of the 7th Iowa Cavalry. According to Robert's Encyclopedia of Historic Forts, Fort Ellsworth was renamed Fort Harker on November 11, 1866. The post closed in 1873.

Volume 9 of the Roll of Honor lists the names of seven soldiers buried at Fort Ellsworth. Volume 10 adds one name for a total of eight burials.

Fort Leavenworth National Cemetery's 1909 report lists 16 bodies removed from Fort Ellsworth and 201 bodies removed from Fort Harker.

FORT FLETCHER
Kansas

Volume 9 of the Roll of Honor lists two burials at Fort Fletcher. Volume 10 adds two names for a total of four burials. No further information on these graves has been found.

FORT HAYS
Kansas

Volume 18 of the Roll of Honor lists 45 burials in Fort Hay's Post Cemetery during 1867. Eleven of these were employees of the quartermaster department. Most died of cholera during August. By the early 1880's, 168 burials had been made in the post cemetery. 70 of these were known. 180 bodies were moved from the post cemetery to Fort Leavenworth National Cemetery sometime before 1909.

FORT LARNED
Kansas

Volume 9 of the Roll of Honor lists 40 white (only 11 known) and six colored soldiers buried in Fort Larned's Post Cemetery. In 1867, volume 18 listed a total of 36 names. These bodies were later moved to the Fort Leavenworth National Cemetery.

FORT LEAVENWORTH NATIONAL CEMETERY
Kansas

Fort Leavenworth National Cemetery is one of the original twelve national cemeteries established in 1862. When Congress empowered President Lincoln to purchase land for national cemeteries, Fort Leavenworth's post cemetery was proclaimed a national cemetery. The cemetery initially covered about 14 acres, but subsequent transfers of land from Fort Leavenworth increased the cemetery to 36.1 acres.

Volume 9 of the Roll of Honor lists 197 interments in the cemetery from 1861 to 1866. Five interments prior to the Rebellion were listed. The oldest burial listed is that of Private George Thompson of the 4th U.S. Artillery who died March 16, 1851. However the VA data sheet lists Captain James Allen who died in 1846 as the oldest burial. Both volumes 18 and 26 of the Roll of Honor list additional burials at Fort Leavenworth.

A June 30, 1875, data sheet listed burials in the cemetery:

	known	unknown
officers	15	0
white soldiers	366	751
colored soldiers	25	0
civilians	223	0

Rebels	7	0
	636	751

Total   1387

Many of the 751 unknown soldiers were reinterments from Kansas City, Lexington, Mo, Saint Joseph, Mo.,and Westport, Mo. In the 1880's the Quartermaster's Department began to consolidate bodies in National Cemeteries. Because of the ease of shipping bodies by railroad, bodies from many post cemeteries were shipped to Fort Leavenworth. Bodies were shipped to the cemetery from over 80 locations including Pine Ridge, S.D., Fort Supply, Ok., Fort Union, N.Mex., and Fort Wallace, Kan. One of the most famous removals was Captain Thomas W. Custer, brother of George Armstrong Custer. Custer was killed with his brother at the battle of the Little Big Horn. Capt. Custer was the first American to receive two Congressional Medals of Honor. Fort Leavenworth National Cemetery is closed to interments except for family members of people buried in the cemetery.

Leavenworth National Cemetery is Leavenworth's second national cemetery. Originally this cemetery was a part of the Western Branch, National Home for Disabled Volunteer Soldiers. The first burial took place on January 22, 1886.

In addition to the two national cemeteries located in Leavenworth, the US Army also has a post cemetery at Fort Leavenworth. No additional data has been found about this cemetery.

FORT RILEY
Kansas

Fort Riley was established in 1853 in what is now Riley County, Kansas. In August 1855, a cholera epidemic claimed some 75 to 100 lives. Most victims were apparently buried in unmarked graves. Volume 9 of the Roll of Honor (1866) lists only 21 burials in the post cemetery. A second cholera epidemic in the summer of 1867 claimed 67 lives. Volume 18 of the Roll of Honor lists 96 burials in the post cemetery.

An 1880 report listed burials:

- 131   known soldiers
- 32   family members (known and unknown)
- 4   known officers
- 6   known employees
- 21   unknown employees

The post cemetery was almost designated a National Cemetery in 1889, but Quartermaster General S.B. Holabird disapproved. At least two

148

bodies had been moved from Fort Riley to Fort Leavenworth National Cemetery by 1909. However apparently most of the bodies were left in the post cemetery. Today there are at least 150 unknowns buried in Fort Riley's post cemetery.

FORT SCOTT NATIONAL CEMETERY
Kansas

Fort Scott National Cemetery was one of the twelve original National Cemeteries, having been designated a National Cemetery on November 15, 1862. Fort Scott was founded in May 1842. By 1853 (some sources say 1855) it had been abandoned. However in 1862 it was reestablished as a supply depot. It closed for good in 1873.

The first recorded burial in Fort Scott's post cemetery was Captain Alexander Morrow who died in 1851. In 1862 the local Presbyterian Church purchased about five acres of land about one and one-half miles south of the post for a cemetery. In 1862 this "Presbyterian Graveyard" and about three acres of adjoining land owned by the Town of Fort Scott were designated the Fort Scott National Cemetery. The United States finally secured title in 1875.

Volumes 10 and 18 of the Roll of Honor list interments in the cemetery. The colored soldiers were buried in a separate section. 15 Confederate soldiers who died while prisoners of war at Fort Scott were buried in a row in section four. At least 16 Indian soldiers who died during the Civil War are buried in the cemetery.

When Col. Mack inspected the cemetery in 1871, there was no road to the cemetery. It could be reached only by railroad. The cemetery was not laid out in any "perceptible plan" nor were the burials made in any order. Col. Mack could not locate the superintendent. The cemetery's grass had been neatly cut, but the headboards were in very poor condition. A few graves were marked with fieldstones.

Col. Mack reported a total of 421 burials in the cemetery:

officers (known)	2
Union soldiers - known	304
Union soldiers - unknown	<u>101</u>
	407
Rebel soldiers	<u>14</u>
	421

FORT WALLACE
Kansas

Volume 18 of the Roll of Honor lists 48 burials (including civilians and employees) in Fort Wallace's Post Cemetery. Most of these deaths occurred during a cholera epidemic that occurred in July and August. Bodies from at least five other locations were moved to the post cemetery. A list in the Quartermaster's records lists 39 known soldiers who died at the post in 1867 and 1868. Bodies from the Fort Wallace Post Cemetery were moved to Fort Leavenworth National Cemetery in 1886.

GENEVA
Kansas

Volume 10 of the Roll of Honor lists four Union soldiers buried at Geneva. Volume 18 of the series lists only two names. No record of removal of the remains to a national cemetery has been found.

IOLA
Kansas

Volume 10 of the Roll of Honor lists 12 Union soldiers buried at Iola. Volume 18 the series lists 13 names. No record of removal of these remains to a national cemetery has been found.

LAWRENCE
Kansas

On August 21, 1863, William Quantrill lead about 450 guerrillas (really bush whackers) on a raid at Lawrence, an abolitionist strong hold and headquarters of the Red Legs, a gang of Jayhawkers. Quantrill's raiders killed about 150 men including two squads of Union recruits who had been asleep in their tents.

Volume 10 of the Roll of Honor lists 27 soldiers buried at Lawrence. Volume 18 of the series adds 27 names, 17 of them are listed "14th Kansas Cavalry, massacred by Quantrill." However an unsigned, undated report states that about 120 soldiers including 20 negroes were buried at Lawrence.

In 1880 Mr. L.J.Bee requested 17 headstones to mark the graves of the 14th Kansas Cavalry troopers.

LITTLE RIVER BATTLEFIELD
Kansas

In 1889 the War Department received a request to move the bodies of 17 soldiers who were killed fighting the Indians some 18 years before to Fort McPherson National Cemetery. The frugal War Department replied that they had no money to move the bodies. However, the next year the War Department moved over 300 bodies from post cemeteries to Custer Battlefield National Cemetery. Why the Little River bodies were not moved this is a mystery. Perhaps the request had been filed away and forgotten.

LOUISVILLE
Kansas

Private William S. Seymour, a private in Company K of the 11th Kansas Cavalry, was buried three miles south of Louisville in Pottowattamie County. At least one unknown was moved to this site in February 1868.

MARMATON CITY
Kansas

Six members of the Kansas State Militia, who were buried at Marmaton City, are listed in Volume 18 of the Roll of Honor.

MONUMENT STATION
Kansas

Volume 10 of the Roll of Honor lists 11 Union soldiers (two unknown) buried at Monument Station. Volume 18 of the series (1867) lists only two names. No record of removal of the remains to a national cemetery has been found.

MOUND CITY
Kansas

On October 25, 1864, Confederates under General Sterling Price were defeated at the battle of Mine Creek. Some 25,000 men were engaged in the battle, the largest fought in Kansas. In 1865, bodies from the battlefield were moved to a soldier's lot in nearby Mound City.

Volume 10 of the Roll of Honor lists seven soldiers buried at Mound City during 1864-5. Volume 18 of the series adds 12 names and lists 15 more unknown graves. Apparently at least 27 soldiers were buried there during the war. Today Mound City is a soldier's lot with 91 burials in 87 graves. Other records in the Quartermaster General's records show that at least some bodies from Mound City were moved to the Fort Scott National Cemetery.

OLATHE
Kansas

Volume 10 of the Roll of Honor lists six Union soldiers (all known) buried at Olathe. Volume 18 of the series lists eleven names. No record of removal of the remains to a national cemetery has been found.

OSSAWATAMIE
Kansas

Volume 18 of the Roll of Honor lists four known and two unknown soldiers buried at Ossawatamie. These bodies were later moved to Fort Riley, Kansas.

OTTUMWA
Kansas

Seven members of Kansas units who died at Ottumwa are listed in volume 18 of the Roll of Honor. No more information about these burials has been found.

PARSONS
Kansas

In February 1887 the Quartermaster's Department furnished 34 stones to Parson's GAR Post for soldiers who died after the war. In 1890 Congress passed Senate Bill 3374 appropriating $5,000 to improve Parson's "Soldiers' Cemetery."

POALA
Kansas

Volume 10 of the Roll of Honor lists six burials at Poala. Volume 18 of the series lists 13 known (3 colored) and 9 unknowns buried at Poala. In 1871 the Secretary of War ordered the "25 or 30 graves" at Poala fenced.

SPRING HILL
Kansas

Five members of the 1st Kansas Infantry who died at Spring Hill are listed in Volume 18 of the Roll of Honor.

TOPEKA
Kansas

Volume 10 of the Roll of Honor lists twenty Union soldiers (all known) buried at Topeka. However volume 18 of the series only lists three names.These remains were moved to the Fort Leavenworth National Cemetery.

TOWNER'S STATION
Kansas

A 1867 report listed three burials at Towner's Station. No other information can be found on these burials.

ASHLAND
Kentucky

According to a letter dated April 18, 1866, 190 Union Soldiers were buried in the town cemetery at Ashland, Kentucky. Fifty of these were U.S. Colored Troops. No record of removals of these bodies can be found. They are not listed in the Roll of Honor nor can a headstone request for them be found.

CAMP DICK ROBINSON
Kentucky

Camp Dick Robinson, the first Federal Army recruiting station south of the Ohio River, was established in 1861 over the protests of Kentucky's governor. The camp was located south of Nicholasville in Jesssamine County. 84 Union soldiers were buried at the camp according to an 1867 report. No further information on these burials has been found.

CAMP NELSON NATIONAL CEMETERY
Kentucky

Camp Nelson National Cemetery was located about six miles from Nicholasville on the Danville Turnpike. During the war Camp Nelson was located on a hill to defend the crossing of the Kentucky River. Camp Nelson was rendezvous for forming colored troop units so many of the burials (almost 46%) were of colored troops.

Because most of the original burials were made from the hospital at Camp Nelson, only 104 of the 1,611 original burials were of unknown dead.(about 6.5%) Captain E.B.W. Restieaux, acting Quartermaster of the United States Volunteers, kept very good records. Burials in Camp Nelson National Cemetery are listed in volume 17 of the Roll of Honor.

Dead from the Perryville National Cemetery were moved to Camp Nelson in the late 1860's. By the time Col. Mack inspected the cemetery in 1871, a total of 3,638 burials had been made in the cemetery:

	known	unknown
white soldiers	1,494	1,184
colored soldiers	867	5
employees	80	0
	2,449	1.189

154

CAVE HILL NATIONAL CEMETERY
Louisville, Kentucky

During the war Louisville contained many hospitals. It was far enough in the rear of the front lines to be secure but still close enough to the front for easy transportation. Many of the soldiers who died at Louisville were removed by friends. Others were buried in Cave Hill National Cemetery. According to Colonel Folsom's report (1868) the land was purchased from the Cave Hill Cemetery Company. However a 1977 Veteran's Administration data sheet states that the company donated land to the U.S. Government in 1861 and 1897. Purchases of additional land were made in 1863, 1864, and 1867.

All of the original interments were identified. In the spring of 1867, 732 additional interments were made. Most of these bodies were found south of Louisville. Twelve bodies were removed from Fort Willich near Mumfordsville. The stone tablet marking their graves was also removed to Cave Hill. The statue was inscribed in German. The inscription is translated:

"Here rest the first heroes of the 32rd Indiana German regiment, who laid down their lives for the preservation of the constitution of the Republic of the United States of North America. They were killed December 17,1861, in a fight with the rebels at Rowlett Station, Kentucky, in which one regiment of Texan rangers, two regiments of infantry and a battery of six cannon, over 3,000 strong, were defeated by 500 German soldiers."

The cemetery was "...handsomely adorned with shrubbery and roses..." with funds raised by the ladies of Louisville and the United States Sanitary Commission. In 1867 a total of 3,871 Union soldiers were buried in the cemetery. Of the 536 are unknown. Also 37 Confederates were buried in the cemetery. Roll of Honor, volume 17, lists interments in Cave Hill National Cemetery.

Not all former soldiers were happy with the burial arrangements in Cave Hill. In September nine former soldiers requested removal of "...thirty-six (36) other infamous Guerrillas and spies hung by the military authorities..." Their graves were "...within 2 feet of graves of the Union dead, and with no mark to distinguish them..." The letter was marked "no action needed."

Not all Union soldiers who died in Louisville were buried at Cave Hill. 506 colored soldiers who were originally buried in Eastern Cemetery in Louisville were removed to New Albany National Cemetery in Indiana. No official reason for the colored soldiers not being buried in Cave Hill is given in Colonel Folsom's report but it appears the Federal officials did not want colored soldiers buried in a private, "white" cemetery.

Care Hill National Cemetery is maintained by contract with the Cave Hill Cemetery Company. In 1977 the contract paid $12,600 per year for maintenance. The superintendent of Zachary Taylor National Cemetery (also in Louisville) supervises the cemetery. By 1977, a total of 5,684 interments had been made in 5,621 grave sites.

COVINGTON NATIONAL CEMETERY
Kentucky

Volume 17 of the Roll of Honor lists a total of 440 soldiers (435 known) buried in Covington's Linden Grove Cemetery. Because the Federal Government had problems obtaining tittle to the lot, these bodies were moved to the Camp Nelson National Cemetery.

DANVILLE NATIONAL CEMETERY
Kentucky

The first record of the Danville National Cemetery is a note showing that a contractor was paid $2.00 each to bury 44 bodies in the Danville City Cemetery. In July 1867 the U.S. Government purchased 18 lots from the city of Danville. Most of the dead in the cemetery came from hospitals located in and near Danville.

By the time Volume 17 of the Roll of Honor was published in 1868 a total of 355 burials had been made. Only eight of the dead were unknowns. Their bodies were removed from Milledgeville and Middleburg, Ky. They were "supposed to have belonged to the 32d (sic) Kentucky volunteer infantry."

Col. Mack's report (1871) listed a total of 358 burials in the cemetery. He listed a total of $18,843 spent on the cemetery through January 31, 1869. He also noted: "Hogs have been lately rooting over this part of the cemetery; probably got in by accident."

EASTERN CEMETERY
Louisville, Kentucky

506 US colored troops were buried in Eastern Cemetery. 500 were known, 6 were unknown. The names of the known soldiers are listed in volume XVII of the Roll of Honor. In 1868, the graves were ordered moved to New Albany, Indiana, National Cemetery despite the fact that room for the

bodies was available in the Louisville's Cave Hill National Cemetery. It appears the War Department did not wish to offend the Cave Hill Cemetery Association by burying colored soldiers in a "white" cemetery.

FLOYD COUNTY
Kentucky

A 1866 report listed 14 Union and eight "rebel" graves in Floyd County. No other records exist in the file, however some bodies from Floyd County were moved to the New Albany National Cemetery after the war.

FRANKFORT
Kentucky

112 Union soldiers (one colored) died in or near Frankfort. Most died in hospitals but a few died while passing through the area. Volume 17 of the Roll of Honor listed 92 names. These bodies were reinterred in Camp Nelson National Cemetery after the war.

A 1866 report listed 30 "rebels" also buried at Frauksfort (sic).

LEBANON NATIONAL CEMETERY
Kentucky

Over 500 soldiers, who died in hospitals in Lebanon during the war, were buried in a two acre plot. On April 6, 1867, the War Department purchased the plot from James and William E. McElroy for $50.00. In 1868 Quartermaster General Meigs decided to allow the graves to remain "for the present". In 1868 work on the Lebanon National Cemetery began. 374 bodies from 41 locations in a 50 mile radius were moved to the cemetery.

Volume 17 of the Roll of Honor lists a total of 1,058 burials, however only 864 graves existed. The discrepancy was explained: "Eighty-one Indiana names...should not be counted, as there is no knowledge of their now being here."

The lodge was built in 1875 at a cost of $2,961.50. By 1888 a total of 869 burials had been made in the cemetery.

LEXINGTON NATIONAL CEMETERY
Kentucky

The United States purchased a site for a cemetery 2 1/2 miles from Lexington during the war. Volume 17 of the Roll of Honor lists 864 interments in the cemetery. A Mr. Vance, the government undertaker, buried about 200 soldiers in the cemetery. After the war bodies were moved to the cemetery from a 2,400 square mile including Bardstown, Lebanon, and Crab orchard.

Col. Mack (1871) counted 929 graves, but the Quartermaster's records showed 948 burials. The cemetery was maintained by the cemetery association in "fine order." Col. Mack reported a total of $16,811.74 on the cemetery by January 31, 1869.

LONDON NATIONAL CEMETERY
Kentucky

Volume 17 of the Roll of Honor lists a total of 269 soldiers (only 87 known) buried in London.Because of the remoteness of the area, these bodies were moved to the Camp Nelson National Cemetery.

MILL SPRINGS NATIONAL CEMETERY
Kentucky

Mill Springs National Cemetery is located at the site of the Battle of Logan's Cross Roads in Pulaski County, Kentucky. In fact the Quartermaster Department filed its correspondence with the cemetery under the name Logan's Cross Roads National Cemetery. Mr. William H. Logan donated about 3 acres to the U.S. Government to construct the cemetery. Bodies from a radius of about 40 miles were brought to the cemetery. Volume 17 of the Roll of Honor lists a total of 701 interments. 368 of the interments were of unknown soldiers. No records of the hospital burials at Somerset, Columbia, or Burnside Point that were moved to the cemetery were found. Identity of soldiers could be made only from headboards or "inscriptions cut on trees." However of the 43 Union soldiers killed at Logan's Crossroads in 1862, only two could not be identified.

Logan's Crossroads was not an easy place to reach in 1867. A potential visitor could take a train from Louisville to Stanford, Ky. A stage ran from Stanford to Somerset, eight miles from the cemetery. The visitor had to make arrangements for their own transportation from Somerset to the cemetery. Ex-sergeant James Burke, who had lost his arm in the war, was the first "keeper" (superintendent) of the cemetery. Mr. Logan and Mr. Burke did not get along well. In 1875 Mr. Burke wrote Quartermaster General Meigs that: "I have gotten into a spot of trouble...." Logan had sued Burke for trespass because the superintendent ordered his laborer to cut down blackberry briers near the cemetery's stone wall. Burke planned to whitewash the fence. Meigs dispatched an investigator who discovered that Logan had sued Burke twice before but lost both times.

Twice Secretary of War William W. Belkap and Quartermaster Meigs requested that the Attorney General appoint counsel to defend Burke. Meigs wrote: "The alleged trespass occurred while the superintendent was attending to his official duties. The cost of defense, may, perhaps, be more than the damages claimed; but the superintendent, out of his small compensation, can afford to pay neither, nor does it seem right that he should be compelled to."

Attorney General Charles Davis disagreed. He said that Burke was "very independent and illdisposed to conciliate." Also Burke had "no official duty" that would allow him to trespass on private property. Burke lost the case and damages were assessed at one cent plus cost. Altogether the suit cost Burke $180.90. In 1878 Burke requested transfer and was set to Danville National Cemetery.

Meigs wrote: "I think that a wrong has been done Burke under the color of law, and that his claim is just; but I know of no appropriation under control of the War Department which could be properly drawn upon to indemnify him." Meigs suggested perhaps Congress could vote to reimburse Burke. In 1882 the Senate's Committee on Military affairs decided that "this was manifestly a 'spite suit.'" Congress then voted to reimburse Burke.

159

Burials in Mill Spring National Cemetery - 1868

State	Known	Unknown	Total
Illinois	3	1	4
Indiana	25	3	28
Kentucky	95	4	99
Michigan	24	1	25
Minnesota	19	0	19
Ohio	49	2	51
Pennsylvania	1	0	1
Rhode Island	1	0	1
Tennessee	6	1	7
United States Army	2	0	2
Colored Troops	19	11	30
New Jersey	6	16	22
New Hampshire	5	0	5
Employees	1	1	2
Miscellaneous	77	0	77
Unknown	0	328	328
	333	368	701

RICHMOND NATIONAL CEMETERY
Kentucky

Volume 17 of the Roll of Honor lists a total of 241 soldiers (only 38 known) buried in the Richmond National Cemetery. These bodies were moved to the Camp Nelson National Cemetery.

TOMPKINSVILLE NATIONAL CEMETERY
Kentucky

A total of 115 Union soldiers buried at Tompkinsville are listed in volume 17 of the Roll of Honor. Mr. J.B. Evans, a loyal citizen of Tompkinsville, donated a cemetery plot to the Federal Government. Burials were made from 21 sites including several small battlefields and the Glasgow area.

Because of the remoteness of the cemetery the graves were moved to the Nashville National Cemetery before 1871.

ALEXANDRIA NATIONAL CEMETERY
Louisiana

The National Cemetery at Pineville was located on the north side of the Red River across from Alexandria, Louisiana. About eight acres of land was purchased from a Mrs. Poussius for $150.00. First interments were made in June, 1867. Bodies were moved to the cemetery from Pineville, Alexandria, Marksville, Fort De Russy, Yellow Bayou, and Semmesport, Louisiana. In March, 1868, 76 bodies were moved from the former Shreveport (Louisiana) National Cemetery.

Volumes 9, 14, and 25 of the Roll of Honor list interments. By the time volume 25 had been printed (1870) a total of 1280 interments had been made. 14 sailors, one employee, and 11 "citizens" were buried here.

Access to the cemetery was a problem until the late 1880's. As early as 1882 the State Central Express of Alexandria editorialized that: "Congress should not overlook the most obscure village in the Union, if they desire to carry out the intentions of those who first conceived the idea of creating National Cemeteries...." In 1888 congress appropriated $11,000 to construct a road to the cemetery from the river.

In 1896 two bodies were moved to the cemetery from Pleasant Hill, Louisiana, and one from Tyler, Texas. In 1911 over 3,100 bodies from the Brownsville National Cemetery and the Fort Ringgold Post Cemetery were moved to the cemetery.

BATON ROUGE NATIONAL CEMETERY
Louisiana

The interments in Baton Rouge National Cemetery were completed in the summer of 1868. Most of the bodies came from the immediate vicinity of Baton Rouge, although 116 bodies were moved from Camden, Arkansas. Volumes A, B, and D of the Disposition lists the original burial sites.

The original cemetery covered seven and one half acres and was located about one mile from the steamboat landing. In 1868, 2,891 graves were in the cemetery. Volumes 9 and 19 of the Roll of Honor lists the known dead. Volume 8 of the Roll of Honor lists 42 soldiers who died at Camden, Arkansas.

BRASHER CITY
Louisiana

Seventy white and two colored troops who died at Brasher City are listed in volume 7 of the Roll of Honor. These bodies were later moved to the Chalmette National Cemetery.

CAMP MOORE
Louisiana

Camp Moore was a Confederate camp of instruction located near the Tangipahoa River. Started in 1861 raw Confederate recruits were trained in drill before being sent to front line units. A measles epidemic in 1861 cost the lives of many recruits. In November 1864 a surprise Union cavalry raid destroyed the camp.

In July 1886 U.S. Senator J.B. Eustis wrote the War Department asking for $1,000 to mark the graves of Union soldiers at Camp Moore. Apparently these were soldiers killed in the 1864 raid. The state of Louisiana had already appropriated $1,000 for marking the graves of Louisiana soldiers. Quartermaster General Samuel B. Holabird requested more information on the Union soldiers' graves. The file contains no further correspondence, but today Louisiana operates Camp Moore as Camp Moore State Commemorative Area.

CHALMETTE NATIONAL CEMETERY
Louisiana

12,241 Union soldiers were buried in Chalmette National Cemetery by 1869. Captain N.S. Constable, US QM Corps, began construction of the cemetery in May 1864. The land (13.6 acres) had been purchased by the city of New Orleans in 1861. It was donated to the United States in May 1868.

The cemetery is located near the site where General Andrew Jackson defeated the British in the Battle of New Orleans in 1815. Volume 21 of the Roll of Honor lists the cemetery as Monument National Cemetery because the monument to Jackson's victory was about 600 yards from the cemetery.

Volumes 7 and 21 of the Roll of Honor list the burials in the cemetery.

The majority of the soldiers buried here did not die at New Orleans. Volumes 1,2,and 3 of the Disposition list the original burial sites of 8,784 soldiers moved to Chalmette. Less than 4,500 of these were buried at New Orleans or Jackson Barracks (one mile north of Chalmette). Colonel C.W. Folsom's report (1868) described the cemetery as: "Although naturally not very picturesque...." It went on to describe improvements such as fencing, planting trees and shrubs, and grading roads. The average cost of moving a body to the cemetery by rail was $4.85.

The Ladies Benevolent Association of New Orleans requested permission to remove the remains of Confederate soldiers buried in the cemetery in December 1868. A report dated July 14, 1884, stated that the remains of 134 Confederate soldiers were removed to Cypress Grove Cemetery. No date of the removal was given.

FORT MACOMB
Louisiana

Eight white soldiers from the 13th Maine and six colored soldiers died at Fort Macomb according to volume 9 of the Roll of Honor. These bodies were moved to the Chalmette National Cemetery after the war.

FORT SAINT PHILLIP NATIONAL CEMETERY
Louisiana

Fort Saint Phillip was located in the Mississippi River Delta some 60 miles below New Orleans. It along with Fort Jackson across the river was designed to protect New Orleans. However in early 1862 a fleet under Rear Admiral David Farragut captured both forts.

Fort Saint Phillip (some sources say Philip) National Cemetery was begun in April 1867. A levee was constructed around the entire two acre plot to hold back the river. Most of the bodies in the cemetery came from Fort Jackson. A total of 326 bodies were buried in the cemetery. Volume 19 of the Roll of Honor lists 56 known burials.

The cemetery was in a remote, swampy site. On April 9, 1878, the Secretary of War approved removal of 349 remains from Fort Saint Phillip to Chalmette National Cemetery, however "the condition of appropriations will not at this time justify the requisite expense." The endorsement on the letter was "bring up next year."

In March 1879 the bodies were moved at a cost of $1,050.26.

163

GRAND TERRE ISLAND
Louisiana

Two white and five colored soldiers were buried at Fort Livingston on Grand Terre Island according to volume 7 of the Roll of Honor.

MONROE
Louisiana

Private W.G.Lucan, 97th Illinois, died while a POW at Monroe. No more information about Lucan's burial has been located.

PETTUS FARILLO
Louisiana

Private A.L. Hill died at the "Pettus Farillo Parish" Hospital in December, 1862. No other records have been found.

PORT HUDSON NATIONAL CEMETERY
Louisiana

Although Grant's siege of Vicksburg is better remembered, Port Hudson was the last Confederate fortification blocking the Mississippi River to fall to Union troops. General Nathaniel Banks bottled the Confederate defenders inside their fortifications on May 27, 1863. The Confederates surrendered on July 9th. The Union had gained control of the entire Mississippi, cutting the Confederacy in two.

Volume 9 of the Roll of Honor lists 107 white and 444 colored soldiers buried "at Port Hudson." Volume 18 of the Roll of Honor contains a revised list of burials. Several of the U.S. colored troops were white officers. In 1869 the cemetery consisted of eight acres of land from Mr. James H. Gibbons.

When Col. Mack inspected the cemetery in 1871, he reported that: "the location is bad; but it is understood that it was selected on account of its being the burial-place of the dead of General Banks's investing army." The almost level land was poorly drained and damp. Mack suggested that a ditch be dug to drain the cemetery into a nearby ravine, but the hostile owner of the adjoining land "would grant no favors except for money." Expenditures on the cemetery totaled $21,287.43 by August 31, 1871. Burials in the cemetery were:

officers	7
white soldiers and sailors	274
colored Union troops	256
citizens	4
unknown and unclassified	3,262
	3,803

In 1888 W.H. Owen, a civil engineer, inspected the cemetery for the Quartermaster's Department. He reported a total of 3,827 interments. The privy needed replacing and "the cemetery is not looking as well as it should, and probably because of the shortness of labor." One man was paid $1.00 for about ten months to assist the superintendent. Mr. Owen suggested the allocation of $270 for labor needed to be increased.

SHREVEPORT NATIONAL CEMETERY
Louisiana

Seventy-one bodies from Shreveport, Marshall, Texas, and Jefferson, Texas, were buried in Shreveport in May 1867. In March, 1868, the cemetery was closed and 78 bodies were moved from Shreveport to the Alexandria National Cemetery in Louisiana.

AUGUSTA
Maine

Forty-two soldiers died in Augusta, Maine, during the war. 41 were white and one was colored. The Quartermaster's office received a headstone request for these graves in 1880. The names are listed in Volume 7 of the Roll of Honor .

Today the VA lists Mount Pleasant Cemetery as a soldiers' lot with 39 interments in 88 (sic) occupied grave sites.

165

BUCKSPORT
Maine

Eleven soldiers were who died from 1862-1867 were buried in Oak Hill Cemetery in Bucksport, Maine. Their names were found on a request for tombstones.

CALAIS
Maine

Seventeen Union Soldiers were buried at Calais, Maine, according to an undated tombstone request. However these might be soldiers who died after the war. The Roll of Honor does not list these burials.

DANVILLE
Maine

William Webb, an unassigned recruit of the 17 U.S. Infantry, died at Danville on May 30, 1865, according to volume 7 of the Roll of Honor.

ETUA
Maine

According to a tombstone request dated June 29, 1887, one Union soldier died at Etua in April 1865. The request did not give the cemetery the soldier was buried in.

FORT PREBLE
Maine

Volume 7 of the Roll of Honor lists four soldiers buried "outside Fort Preble." These recruits died in March and April 1864.

NAUTUCKET
Maine

The Quartermaster's files contain a list of 32 soldiers buried at Nautucket. The 1866 list was never listed in the Roll of Honor series.

PORTLAND
Maine

Volume 9 of the Roll of Honor lists three burial sites of soldiers in Portland:

Cemetery	Number of Graves
C.E. Churchyard	2
Mackey Island	10 (all unknown)
Forest	20

WALLINGFORD
Maine

John W. Webb, an unassigned recruit of the 17th U.S. Infantry, died at Wallingford on August 8, 1865. No more information on this burial can be found.

ANNAPOLIS NATIONAL CEMETERY
Maryland

Annapolis National Cemetery was founded in 1862 to bury Union soldiers who died in hospitals located in Annapolis during the war. Volume 7 of the Roll of Honor listed 468 burials from the U.S. General Hospital no. 2 located at Saint John's College. 23 other burials were listed in the citizen's grave yard. 449 burials had been made at the Camp Parole Hospital. Volume 14 of the Roll of Honor listed 13 other names.

When Col. C.W. Folsom inspected the cemetery on November 18, 1867, he reported that 2,293 interments had been made. A work force of 35 was employed to build the cemetery. Folsom noted that "payment should be more prompt."

Col. Mack noted a total of 2,343 known (14 USCT) and 134 unknown

167

(five USCT) burials. 14 citizens and "others" were also buried at Annapolis. One of the "others" was a Russian sailor from a Russian man-of-war who died at Annapolis in 1864. Nine known and one unknown Confederate POW's are also buried here.

NAVAL CEMETERY
Annapolis, Maryland

Two U.S. Sailors who died at Annapolis were buried in the "Naval Cemetery." Their names appear on a request for 27 headmarkers dated March, 18, 1867.

ANTIETAM NATIONAL CEMETERY
Sharpsburg, Maryland

On September 17, 1862, Robert E. Lee's first invasion of the "North" ended at Sharpsburg, Maryland. Lee's army of little over 40,000 men were met by over 87,000 Federals under Major General George McClellan. Technically the battle was a draw because Lee was not driven from the field, but he was forced to withdraw two days later. McClellan lost 2,010 killed in the one day battle. Combined with Lee's loss of 1,546 killed in action this made Antietam (or Sharpsburg) the bloodiest one day battle of the war.

In March 1865 the "Antietam National Cemetery Association" was formed by "members from the different loyal states whose dead are represented in the cemetery..." Approbations from state legislatures were supposed to purchase the land, build a lodge and stonewall, and reinter the dead. However in 1866 the Federal government began paying for moving the dead. The cemetery was dedicated on September 17, 1867.

1,475 bodies were moved to the cemetery from the Antietam battlefield. Other bodies were moved to the cemetery from the South Mountain, and Monocacy Junction Battlefields. Also dead were moved from Harper's Ferry, West Virginia. Roll of Honor volume 15 lists a total of 4,695 burials, 2,903 were known and 1,792 were unknown.

In 1884 Congress approbated money to pay off the debts of the cemetery association. The title for the land was then transferred to the Federal Government. No Confederates are buried at Sharpsburg. In September 1992 two bodies were discovered by relic hunters near the battlefield. No identification of the bodies was possible. They were buried in Washington Cemetery in nearby Hagerstown.

BLADENSBURG
Maryland

In 1873 four bodies were moved from the Fort Bladensburg Cemetery to the U.S. Military Asylum Cemetery in Washington, D.C. One body was soldier, one body was a wife, and two were unknowns. The <u>Roll of Honor</u> does not list these burials.

CUMBERLAND
Maryland

The local GAR chapter requested that 87 bodies be moved from Hooks Cemetery to Antietam National Cemetery in 1887. Twelve bodies were moved but 75 were left. The Quartermaster General's office wrote the local GAR chapter to explain that only one of the soldiers not moved had died during the war.

196 bodies had been moved from Cumberland to Antietam National Cemetery between October 15, 1866 and August 15, 1867.

FORT McHENRY
Maryland

An 1866 list in the Quartermaster's files lists 127 known soldiers (five colored) buried at Fort McHenry. The graves were marked with headstones in 1874. The post cemetery was still active as late as 1893.

FORT WASHINGTON
Maryland

Volume 10 of the <u>Roll of Honor</u> lists six soldiers (one unknown) buried at Fort Washington. No other records on these burials have been found.

FREDERICK
Maryland

1,084 soldiers were buried in Mount Olivet Cemetery in Frederick. Volume 7 and 12 lists the names of the soldiers. These soldiers were moved to Antietam National Cemetery after the war.

LAUREL
Maryland

At least 11 Union soldiers were buried in Laurel during the war. In 1866, six bodies were moved to Arlington National Cemetery. The other six were left to "be carried for by their friends."

After the bodies were moved, Mr. John Webb wrote the War Department requesting the return of the body of his sister-in-law. Webb stated that the contractors moving the bodies apparently removed his sister-in-law's body by mistake. After several exchanges of letters, the body was returned to Laurel. Mr. Webb never named his sister-in-law.

Cemeteries in Laurel with known Union dead are:

St. John's Church yard	3 burials
Catholic Church yard	2 burials
Methodist Church yard	1 burial

LAUREL CEMETERY
Baltimore, Maryland

Volume 7 of the Roll of Honor lists six U.S. colored troops buried in 1865 and 1866 in Baltimore's Laurel Cemetery. Volume 19 of the Roll of Honor lists a total of 229 burials of U.S. Colored Troops (including the names in volume 7).

Neither Col. Moore (1869) nor Col. Mack (1871) inspected this cemetery. In 1875 the U.S. Government purchased "Strangers Lot" in the cemetery and moved the bodies to it. An 1881 report stated: "A man is paid $15. (sic) per quarter for hoisting and taking down the flag, which he is required to do every day.."

An 1883 letter from the Superintendent of Loudon Park National Cemetery stated he had found no record of interments in the Laurel Cemetery. The Quartermaster General's office endorsement states: "It is presumed... two hundred and forty interments..."

In 1884 about 200 bodies were moved from Laurel Cemetery to Loudon Park National Cemetery.

LOUDON PARK NATIONAL CEMETERY
Maryland

Two separate, segregated cemeteries were established in Baltimore during the war. On October 18, 1861, the Federal Government purchased about 1/4 acre of land from the Loudon Park Cemetery Association. This lot, located in the northeast section of the cemetery became Loudon Park National Cemetery.

Volume 19 of the Roll of Honor (1868) lists 1,785 burials of white Union soldiers buried in the cemetery. Most of these burials were made from hospitals in Baltimore. Other burials were made from Relay House and Elkridge Landing. 31 Confederate Prisoners of War and four Confederate citizen detainees who died at Fort McHenry were also buried at the cemetery.

A total of $10,682.25 had been spent on the cemetery by August 31, 1871. When Col. Mack inspected the cemetery in July 1871 he found that thistles and weeds covered part of the graves, apparently the grass had not been cut all year. The headboards were faded and decayed. Some had fallen down. The former Superintendent had been discharged and the Fort McHenry Quartermaster had responsibility for the upkeep of the cemetery. A new superintendent had been appointed by 1874, but the cemetery still was not properly maintained.

The 229 colored soldiers who died in Baltimore were buried in the "Laurel National Cemetery" in Baltimore. A proposal to move these bodies to Loudon Park was rejected in June 1868. Laurel's upkeep suffered, so in 1879 Quartermaster Meigs decided that Loudon Park's superintendent should also care for Laurel Cemetery. Finally the graves that could be identified (about 200) were moved to Loudon Park in 1884. Laurel National Cemetery was then dropped from the National Cemetery rolls.

POINT LOOKOUT
Maryland

Volume 9 of the Roll of Honor lists 425 white and 22 colored soldiers buried at Point Lookout. All of these burials were of known soldiers. After the war these bodies were moved to the Arlington National Cemetery.

A total of 3,384 Confederate soldiers died while prisoners at Point

171

Lookout. These bodies were later moved to a common grave because fire had destroyed the wooden headstones. The Federal Government marked the graves with a 85 foot high granite monument in 1911. Twelve bronze tablets on the monument listed the names of 3,383 Confederate soldiers buried there.

PRESTON
Maryland

One Union soldier is buried in the M.E. Churchyard at Preston. A headstone for this soldier was furnished in 1885.

ABINGTON
Massachusetts

At least eleven Union soldiers died in Abington during the war. They were buried in Mount Vernon Cemetery. In December 1870, the local GAR post requested tombstones for these soldiers.

BOSTON
Massachusetts

Two sites in Boston Harbor were used as cemeteries during the Civil War.

Volume 9 of the Roll of Honor lists 12 white and one colored soldier buried on Gallop's Island.

An 1866 report listed one unknown soldier buried on Long Island. No record of removals of these bodies has been found.

BROOKLINE
Massachusetts

Four Union Soldiers were buried in Holywood (sic) Cemetery at Brookline, Massachusetts. Volume 9 of the Roll of Honor lists one name while Volume 16 lists three different names.

CAMBRIDGE
Massachusetts

Nineteen known Federal Soldiers were buried in the soldiers lot in Cambridge Cemetery. Volume 16 of the Roll of Honor lists these burials. One soldier was buried in Cambridge's Cemetery according to Volume 9 of the Roll of Honor.

CHELSEA
Massachusetts

Two Cemeteries at Chelsea, Massachusetts, hold Union War dead.

Private James Miller of the 58th Massachusetts died on April 16, 1865. He was buried in the Woodlawn Cemetery according to the Volume 9 of the Roll of Honor.

16 known Union Soldiers were interred in the Garden Cemetery at Chelsea. Three of these soldiers were removed from Yorktown, Va. The other 13 died in hospitals or at home from wounds.

In June 1867, a monument was erected at a cost of about $3,500. The inscription reads: **"A memorial in honor of the citizen soldiers of Chelsea, who, at the call of their country, and in defense of freedom and the American Union, sacrificed their lives in the Civil War of 1861-1865."**

Burials in Garden Cemetery are listed in volume 16 of the Roll of Honor.

DEDHAM
Massachusetts

Volume 9 of the Roll of Honor lists 29 white and 40 colored troops buried "at Dedham." No other information can be found on these burials.

EASTHAMPTON
Massachusetts

In 1880 the Town of Easthampton raised funds to mark the graves of five Union soldiers. Although the Town Council wrote the War Department that the graves had been marked, the letter does not state if the soldiers died during or after the war.

ROXBURY
Massachusetts

Volume 9 of the <u>Roll of Honor</u> lists four soldiers buried in the Mount Hope Cemetery at Roxbury. An undated list in the National Archives gives the location as West Roxbury.

WORCHESTER
Massachusetts

Volume 16 of the <u>Roll of Honor</u> lists a total of 60 soldiers buried in private lots in the Worcester area:

Cemetery	Number of Graves
Hope	18
Rural	22
Saint John's	19
Pine	1

MEXICO CITY NATIONAL CEMETERY
Mexico

Mexico City National Cemetery was the first cemetery established by Congress to protect the final resting place of United States soldiers. However it was not considered a national cemetery for almost a quarter century.

According to Edward Steere, General Winfield Scott failed to make arrangements for the proper burial of the casualties of the Mexican War. In 1850, Congress allocated $10,000; " for purchasing, walling, and ditching a piece of land near the city of Mexico, for a cemetery or burial-ground for such of the officers and soldiers as fell in battle or died in and around said city, and for the interment of American citizens who have died or may die in said city..."

R.P. Letcher, the United States minister to Mexico, wrote the Secretary of State on January 10, 1852:

"The burial-ground contains about two acres, and it affords me great pleasure to say' (sic) has been admirably chosen. The situation in every respect is decidedly beautiful. I have very rarely seen, in the course of my life, a spot better suited for the purpose intended.

"The entire lot is inclosed by a high, thick wall, remarkably well constructed. The work is exceedingly well executed.

"The cottage designed as a residence for the sexton within the inclosure is a comfortable building and of good size.

"The remains of some four hundred and seventy or eighty officers and soldiers who fell in battle or died here during the late war with Mexico have been transferred from the commons and re-interred in the cemetery.

"The agent could not take up the remains of a greater number for the want of means, and I am sorry, very sorry, for it."

The cemetery never had an allocation for upkeep and was almost forgotten until General Rosecrans (U.S. Minister to Mexico) complained about its poor condition. A small amount was spent for repairs. On March 3, 1873, Congress authorized maintenance of the cemetery from the appropriation for national cemeteries. The cemetery was to be "subject to the rules and regulations affecting United States National Military Cemeteries..." that the president decided applied to the cemetery.

By 1874 about 470 soldiers and 238 "mostly citizens" had been buried in the Mexico City National Cemetery. A total of $7,908.22 was spent in repairs to the cemetery in 1873-74.

The American Battle Monuments Commission was established by Congress in 1923 to maintain the overseas burial sites of American Armed Forces personnel who died during World War 1. The Mexico City National Cemetery was transferred to the commission.

Today the Mexico City National Cemetery is a one acre plot with a mass grave and small monument. Inscribed on the monument is:

TO THE HONORED MEMORY OF 750 AMERICANS, KNOWN BUT TO GOD, WHOSE BONES, COLLECTED BY THEIR COUNTRY'S ORDER, ARE HERE BURIED.

The remains of 813 "Americans and others" are buried in wall crypts.

DETROIT
Michigan

Volume 8 of the Roll of Honor lists 120 white and 15 colored soldiers buried "at Detroit." No other information can be found on the burial site of these soldiers.

According to volume 18 of the Roll of Honor, 62 known soldiers were buried in lots owned by the Elmwood Cemetery Association. These burials were made between October 9, 1862, and July 29, 1865.

FORT DETROIT
Michigan

An 1869 report on the possible sale of the land Fort Detroit's post cemetery concluded: "we should not sell our dead." Quartermaster General Meigs endorsement reads: "Should not be sold, but if so ... move to Fort Wayne near Detroit."

No additional information on this cemetery exists in the Archive's file. In 1871, the Fort Wayne Cemetery had 24 burials.

FORT GRATIOT
Michigan

According to a letter dated October 21, 1881, the Fort Gratiot Post Cemetery was established about 1828. Because many graves were unmarked, "the number of interments cannot therefore be accurately ascertained."

The graves were moved to Lakeside Cemetery near Port Huron in 1884.

FORT MACKINAC
Michigan

An undated report in the Quartermaster's files lists 67 burials in Fort Mackinac post cemetery. In 1889 the Superintendent of Fort Mackinac "National Park" wrote the Quartermaster General requesting that the United States mark the graves of United States soldiers killed in battles with the British.

In 1906 Congress allocated $1,000 to mark and repair the post cemetery at old Fort Mackinac, Michigan.

FORT WAYNE
Michigan

Volume 18 of the Roll of Honor lists 24 Union soldiers buried in Fort Wayne's Post Cemetery. After the war bodies from Flint, Kalamazoo, Niles, and Ypsilanti were moved to the post cemetery. In 1886 Fort Wayne's acting assistant quartermaster requested headstones for 115 known soldiers buried in the post cemetery.

FORT WILKENS
Michigan

The only information in the Quartermaster General's files about the post cemetery at Fort Wilkens is a 1870 report stating that the post commander had ordered the burial of the illegitimate child of a soldier's wife. The child was given "full military honors."

GRAND RAPIDS
Michigan

Sixty-one Union soldiers were buried in a soldiers lot in Grand Rapid's Oak Hill Cemetery. Most of the burials were made in late 1863 and early 1864. Volume 18 of the Roll of Honor lists the names of 35 known interments. In 1886 the Quartermaster's department processed a request for 61 headstones for the cemetery. Only 21 names were known in 1886.

An undated report in the same envelope in the Archives listed 105 known soldiers buried in the city cemetery near the Detroit and Milwaukee railroad tracks. No other information on these burials have been found.

JACKSON
Michigan

Twenty-nine U.S. soldiers were buried in Jackson's City Cemetery's soldiers lot. The two 20 foot by 30 foot lots were donated to the United States. By September 1868, $187.00 had been spent on the cemetery. Volume 18 of the Roll of Honor lists 26 known and three unknown burials. However one of the unknown burials is apparently that of Corporal William George of Company H,125th U.S.C.T. George is listed in volume 8 of the Roll of Honor with a date of death of December 2, 1865.

NILES
Michigan

Private E. Nelson, 12th Wisconsin Infantry, died at Niles on March 15, 1864. His remains were moved to Fort Wayne at an unknown date.

ALEXANDRIA
Minnesota

Volume 7 of the Roll of Honor lists three burials at Alexandria. No other information on these burials has been found.

FORT RIDGELY
Minnesota

Fort Ridgely was founded on April 29, 1853, near Lower Sioux Agency. On August 18, 1862, the Santee Sioux under Chief Little Crow began massacring white people in and near the agency. A relief force from Fort Ridgely was cut to pieces. The Sioux almost overran the fort until they were beaten back by three rusty cannons maned by a ragtag group of amateur artillerymen. The Minnesota Historical Society believes at least 644 civilians and 113 soldiers died during the uprising before Col. Henry Sibley defeated the Sioux in September at the Battle of Wood Lake.

Volume 8 of the Roll of Honor (1866) lists 57 soldiers "interred at Fort Ridgely...previously to and during the Rebellion." Volume 19 of the Roll of Honor (1868) lists only 25 soldiers buried at Fort Ridgely. A letter dated June 7, 1881, reported that 18 known soldiers were moved to Rock Island National Cemetery. Bodies of two civilians were left.

FORT RIPLEY
Minnesota

A total of twenty-one soldiers (all known) were buried at Fort Ripley between 1862 ad 1867 according to volume 19 of the Roll of Honor. These bodies were moved to Rock Island National Cemetery in the mid-1870's.

FORT SNELLING NATIONAL CEMETERY
Minnesota

In 1820 a permanent fort was established near the junction of the Minnesota and Mississippi Rivers by Col. Josiah Snelling. The post was named Fort St. Anthony, but on January 7, 1825, the fort was renamed Fort Snelling in honor of Col. Snelling.

The post closed in 1857, however the site was used as a training center (Camp Coldwater) by Minnesota troops during the Civil War. The fort served as a supply base from 1866 to 1946. Volume 9 of the Roll of Honor lists 64 soldiers buried at Fort Snelling (all known). Volume 19 of the Roll of Honor lists only 9 burials! (These were all named in volume 9). Local veteran groups in the Saint Paul-Minneapolis area petitioned Congress to establish a National Cemetery in the area. Congress authorized the use of part of Fort Snelling as a National Cemetery in 1937. The first burial was made on July 5, 1939, when the body of Captain George H. Mallon was reinterred in the cemetery. Captain Mallon, who died in 1934, had been awarded the Congressional Medal of Honor for his actions in the Meuse-Argonne drive in 1918.

On July 14, 1839, the first of the 680 bodies buried in the old post cemetery was moved to the National Cemetery. Unfortunately none of the graves in the post cemetery was marked with a headstone, so all were buried as unknowns.

POMME de TERRE
Minnesota

Volume 7 of the Roll of Honor lists four burials at Pomme de Terre. No more information on these burials has been found.

SAUK CENTRE
Minnesota

Volume 7 of the Roll of Honor lists six burials (one unknown) at Sauk Centre. No other information on these burials has been found.

CORINTH NATIONAL CEMETERY
Mississippi

Corinth served as a Confederate supply depot during the ill-fated Shiloh campaign. After Shiloh the Confederates evacuated Corinth, but they recaptured the town in late 1862 after a two day battle.

After the war 5,688 Union soldiers were reinterred in Corinth National Cemetery. The 20 acres of land were "purchased by appraisement" from "Walker, White, and Vance." Because many of the dead were moved to Corinth from other sites, only 1,793 burials were of known soldiers.

(3,895 were unknown). The burials were from 273 regiments from 15 different states.

Volume 20 of the Roll of Honor lists the burials. Three Confederate soldiers were buried in Corinth National Cemetery.

GRENADA
Mississippi

Five Union soldiers, who died while prisoners of war at Grenada, are listed in volume 14 of the Roll of Honor. These bodies were moved to Vicksburg National Cemetery after the war.

GREENWOOD ISLAND
Mississippi

An 1887 report stated the graves at Greenwood Island Reservation and Military Asylum were in good condition. No more information can be found in the Quartermaster's files.

HOLLY SPRINGS
Mississippi

In 1889 the Quartermaster Department supplied headstones for four known U.S. soldiers buried in the City Cemetery. Apparently these soldiers, members of the 38th U.S. Infantry, were Federal occupation troops who died in Holly Springs. Other U.S. troops who died at Holly Springs were reinterred in the Corinth National Cemetery.

JACKSON
Mississippi

Volume 6 of the Roll of Honor lists six burials (five known) at Jackson. These burials were made in the summer of 1863 after Grant's army burned almost all of Jackson. His men jokingly called Jackson, "Chimneyville."

No record of removal of these bodies to a national cemetery has been found.

NATCHEZ NATIONAL CEMETERY
Mississippi

Natchez National Cemetery was started as a cemetery of convenience. No major battle was fought at Natchez. Nor was there a large Union hospital or a Confederate prisoner of war camp nearby. Instead Natchez was the only decent sized town on the Mississippi River between the National Cemetery at Port Hudson, Louisiana and Vicksburg National Cemetery.

Quartermaster General Meigs informed Secretary of War Stanton in June 1866 that a national cemetery would be established at Natchez. But because of the danger of spreading disease in hot weather, no bodies would be moved until the fall. One reason Meigs chose to establish the cemetery at Natchez was a report written by Chaplain E.B. Whitman in May 1866. Chaplain Whitman described the city cemetery at Natchez, where some burials of Union soldiers had been made, as "deplorable."

The site chosen for the cemetery was on a high bluff overlooking the Mississippi River. The 11.7 acres of land for the cemetery was appropriated in 1866. In 1867 a total of $1,800 was paid to Margaret Case, T.D. Purnell, and others. Col. Mack in his 1871 report criticized the layout of the cemetery. He said the plan showed " a good deal of taste", but he thought too much labor would be required because of washing caused by rain. In 1871, 20 men with four mules and carts were finishing work on the cemetery. Mack estimated that six laborers at $35 a month would be required after the cemetery was finished. By August 31, 1871, a total of $68,865.74 had been spent on the cemetery. Some of the removals to the cemetery were contracted. The contractor disinterred the body, furnished a coffin, dug the grave, and filled the grave for 90 cents. Cost of transporting the body was extra.

Many of the 34 sites from which bodies were moved to Natchez were remote. Because the graves had not been cared for in several years, most of the bodies could not be identified. Volume 27 of the Roll of Honor (1871) lists a total of 3,073 interments in the cemetery. Only 302 were of known soldiers (less than 10%). Col. Mack reported eleven officers and 2,484 colored soldiers buried in the cemetery. Only 50 of the colored soldiers (2%) were identified.

OXFORD
Mississippi

Two Union soldiers, who died while POW's at Oxford, are listed in volume 14 of the Roll of Honor. These bodies were moved to the Cornith National Cemetery after the war.

SHIP ISLAND
Mississippi

Volume 9 of the Roll of Honor lists 226 white and five colored soldiers who were buried at Ship Island. These bodies were later moved to Chalmette National Cemetery.

STARKVILLE
Mississippi

Private A. Laurson, of Company E of the 2nd Iowa, died of a result of wounds while a prisoner of war at Starkville. After the war, his remains were reinterred in the Vicksburg National Cemetery.

VICKSBURG
Mississippi

Vicksburg was the most important Confederate stronghold on the Mississippi River in the Fall of 1862. Grant proposed to move against Vicksburg but political interference, the swampy terrain, and the Confederate defenders all managed to stymie Sherman's advance in late December.

In January Major General John McClernand took most of Sherman's army and overwhelmed the Confederate defenders at Fort Hindman, Arkansas Post. Grant had to regroup for his next attempt. He even tried to bypass Vicksburg by cutting a channel around the town, but failed. He was forced to regroup again.

Regroup Grant did. He moved his men down the river, running the Vicksburg batteries at night. He landed near Grand Gulf some 25 miles below Vicksburg. On May 16 Grant defeated Philadelphia-born John Pemberton's Confederates at Champion Hill. Vicksburg was doomed. Grant tried two general assaults on Vicksburg on May 19 and May 22, but he was repulsed. Both sides settled into a siege. Pemberton had no hope of relief, so on July 3 he asked for terms. "Unconditional surrender" Grant agreed to parole Pemberton's command, so on July 4, 1863, Vicksburg fell. Port Hudson surrendered five days later.

In 1866 the United States purchased 40 acres of land for the Vicksburg National Cemetery from Aloy H. Jaynes and wife for $9,000. The site was selected by Major General T.J. Wood and Brevet Brigadier General H.M. Whittelsey, AQM. By the time volume 24 of the Roll of Honor was written (1869) a total of 15,508 Union soldiers had been buried in the cemetery. Of the 5,553 colored troops, only about 2% were known. Bodies were brought to the cemetery from at least 99 different locations including the Champion Hill Battlefield, Raymond, and Grand Gulf in Mississippi. Bodies from Bayou Boeuf, Lake Providence, and Milliken's Bend, Louisiana, were also moved to the cemetery. Some bodies were brought to the cemetery from extreme Southeastern Arkansas. Volume 27 of the Roll of Honor lists 889 additional burials (only 34 known) in the cemetery. By the time Col. Mack inspected the cemetery in 1871, he noted a total of 16,586 burials:

	known	unknown	% known
white Union soldiers	3,482	6,953	33.3%
colored Union soldiers	147	8,004	2.4%
	3,629	12,957	21.9%

The original burials were made on hillsides overlooking the Mississippi. Col. Mack reported that the site selected was "very injudicious." In 1869 after the burials had been made, a rain and snow storm caused much of the hill side to slide down the hill. A Mr. Gall, "a competent civil engineer," was hired to salvage the cemetery. He began to install drains to carry the water that was "constantly oozing out of the bluff." Then gutters and culverts were installed to handle rain water. Two years later Gall still employed a work force of 60 men, 14 mules, and 2 horses. By August 31, 1870, a total of $261,239.59 had been spent on the cemetery and Col. Mack reported that upkeep would be expensive. In his 1874 report, Col. Mack reported that some graves had fallen in and were in danger of causing more mudslides. A total of $289,421.03 had been spent on the cemetery by June 30, 1874, with an estimate of $5,000 for repairs during the 1875-6 fiscal year.

BLOOMFIELD
Missouri

Volume 13 of the Roll of Honor lists burials of Union soldiers in and near Bloomfield. After the war bodies from this area were moved to the Jefferson Barracks National Cemetery and the Springfield National Cemetery.

BRUNSWICK
Missouri

Two soldiers from Company X of the 49th Missouri Volunteers died at Brunswick according to volume 10 of the Roll of Honor. These bodies were moved to Jefferson City National Cemetery after the war.

CAMP COLE
Missouri

An 1886 letter requested a monument to mark the graves of Union soldiers who were killed in the "Camp Cole fight." The War Department's reply was written in ink on tissue thin paper. It is now unreadable. However no other paperwork exists, so it is doubtful these graves were marked

Volume 3 of the Disposition listed one grave, 2 1/2 miles south of Camp Cole moved to Jefferson Barracks National Cemetery between March and May 1868.

CAPE GIRARDEAU
Missouri

Volume 9 of the Roll of Honor lists 247 Union soldiers buried at Cape Girardeau. After the war these bodies were moved to Jefferson Barracks National Cemetery.

CASSVILLE
Missouri

Volume 9 of the Roll of Honor lists one hundred known soldiers buried at Cassville. After the war bodies from Cassville were moved to both the Fayetteville National Cemetery and the Springfield National Cemetery.

CENTRALIA
Missouri

The battle of Centralia may have been the shortest battle of the Civil War. Some historians say it only lasted two minutes. The stage was set when a band of guerrillas under Bloody Bill Anderson waylaid a train at Centralia on September 27, 1864. Twenty-four discharged and furloughed Union soldiers were shot down.

A short time later Major A.V.E. Johnson approached Centralia with some 130 raw militia. Johnson apparently thought his poorly trained men could fight the guerrillas on foot. He was wrong. The militia's single shot muskets were no match for the mounted guerrilla's six-shot pistols. When the guerrillas attacked the militia fired one volley, broke , and ran. The result was a slaughter. Jesse James claimed to have killed Johnson. After the battle one guerrilla hopped from one body to the next. He explained it was the quickest way to count them. All together he stepped on 124 corpses. Two of the guerrillas were killed.

After the "battle" most of the dead were buried in a trench in Centralia. Some bodies were taken to Mexico, Missouri, for burial. These bodies were moved to Jefferson Barracks National Cemetery after the war. Other bodies from Centralia were also moved to Jefferson Barracks National Cemetery after the war.

The United States Government erected a 15 foot high monument of knipper stone sometime before 1871 at Cenralia. The monument is inscribed: **"The remains of Companies A, G,and H, Thirty-Ninth Regiment, Missouri Volunteer Infantry, who were killed in action at Centralia, Missouri, on the 27th day of September, 1864, are interred here."** In June, 1874, 89 bodies and the monument were moved from Centralia to Jefferson City National Cemetery. The Roll of Honor series does not record these names.

CLINTON
Missouri

A list dated December 17, 1870, listed eight known Union soldiers buried at Oak Grove Cemetery near Clinton. A 1884 letter requested removal of "a number" of Federal soldiers who were killed-in-action or who died of disease to a lot purchased by the government. No other records were found concerning these graves, but in light of the War Department policy of not moving bodies it is unlikely the graves were moved.

185

DALLAS
Missouri

Volume 13 of the Roll of Honor lists five known and one unknown soldiers buried at Dallas in Ballinger County. These bodies were moved to Jefferson Barracks National Cemetery.

FRANKLIN
Missouri

Thirteen known and 59 unknown soldiers were buried in a cemetery one half of a mile north of the railroad depot at Franklin. According to volume 12 of the Roll of Honor, three more graves (unknown) were located outside the cemetery. These bodies were moved to Jefferson Barracks National Cemetery in 1868.

FREDRICKTOWN
Missouri

According to volume 12 of the Roll of Honor, five soldiers (all known) were buried at Fredricktown. No record of removal of these bodies to a national cemetery after the war has been found.

GLASGOW
Missouri

According to volume 10 of the Roll of Honor, 23 soldiers (11 known) were buried at Glasgow. These bodies were moved to Jefferson City National Cemetery after the war.

GREENFIELD
Missouri

In 1887, John A. Davis, a resident of Greenfield, requested a headstone for a soldier who apparently died at Greenfield in 1864. The stone was to be set in the local cemetery. Other bodies from Greenfield had been moved to the Springfield National Cemetery.

GREENVILLE
Missouri

According to volume 13 of the Roll of Honor a total of 19 soldiers (11 known) were buried at Greenville. These bodies were moved to Jefferson Barracks National Cemetery after the war.

HUNTSVILLE
Missouri

Volume 10 of the Roll of Honor lists three known Union soldiers buried at Huntsville. These bodies were moved to Jefferson Barracks National Cemetery in 1867.

INDEPENDENCE
Missouri

A 1866 report stated that of the 55 graves at Independence, "only 26 can be identified." Volume 12 of the Roll of Honor lists these names. These bodies were moved to Fort Leavenworth National Cemetery after the war.

IRONTON
Missouri

A total of 248 Union soldiers were buried in and around Ironton according to volume 12 of the Roll of Honor. These soldiers were moved to Jefferson Barracks National Cemetery in 1868.

JACKSON
Missouri

One known and four unknown soldiers were buried at Jackson according to volume 13 of the Roll of Honor. These graves were moved to Jefferson Barracks National Cemetery.

JEFFERSON BARRACKS NATIONAL CEMETERY
Missouri

Jefferson Barracks National Cemetery roots go back to 1826 when the first burial was made in the post cemetery at Jefferson Barracks not far from present day Saint Louis. Elizabeth Ann Lash, an officer's child, was the first recorded burial, however other burials may have been made first. By the Civil War 726 burials had been made in the post cemetery.

Volume 10 of the Roll of Honor lists 3,078 burials "at Saint Louis", 290 in Christ Church Cemetery, and 339 burials (240 white) at the smallpox hospital on Arsenal Island. After the war more land near the post cemetery was developed for cemetery use. by 1871 the cemetery covered slightly over 20 acres. In 1987 the cemetery consisted of 306.98 acres, with 160 developed.

By the time volume 20 of the Roll of Honor was published (1869), 6,134 known and 4083 unknown burials had been made. However in 1871 Col. Mack's report listed the burials:

white Union soldiers - known	6,693
white Union soldiers - unknown	843
colored Union troops - known	23
colored Union troops - unknown	1,044
Buried in Old Post Cemetery:	
mostly unknown	726
Rebel prisoners of war	1,010
others, not of military service	_556_
	10,895

The VA data sheet on Jefferson Barracks (1987) lists 1,140 Confederate dead. 161 were male civilians. Mrs. Jane N. Foster from Randolph County, Arkansas, was a "Confederate civilian" who died at Jefferson Barracks.

A total of $142,287.46 had been spent on the cemetery by August 31, 1871. Coffins cost 90 cents a piece in 1869.

An obelisk in section 57 honors the memory of 175 soldiers and noncommissioned officers who died of cholera at Jefferson Barracks in August 1866.

Jefferson Barracks National Cemetery has had its share of wild rumors. On December 29, 1867, the Washington Sunday Herald ran a short article: "Many of the coffins of soldiers, buried by contract at St. Louis, have been found filled with sticks and stones. Their bodies were doubtless (sic) sold by the contractors for anatomical purposes." Nothing else is included in the file with this article. Normally such an article is attached to a report denouncing the article as totally false. Perhaps a report was made and not filed, or perhaps the contractors decided to add to their profits by appearing to move more bodies than they found.

In 1913 the superintendent wrote: "Section 29 is not the locality (sic) of Philippines, dishonorably discharged, or disgraced soldiers." Apparently he was responding to charges in the local press. He did state at least one Philippine civilian who died at the Louisiana Purchase Exposition was buried in section 30 of the cemetery.

JEFFERSON CITY NATIONAL CEMETERY
Missouri

Jefferson City National Cemetery almost was never built. In 1867 plans were made to move the 315 bodies listed in volume 10 of the Roll of Honor to Jefferson Barracks National Cemetery at Saint Louis. Bodies from the surrounding area could have been moved to the Springfield National Cemetery. However the decision was made to build a cemetery at Jefferson City.

Two acres of land was purchased from "Mr. Israel B. Reed and wife." The lot chosen was near the state prison about one mile east of the Missouri State Capitol Building. The location near the prison allowed the superintendent to use convict labor to maintain the grounds. By August 31, 1871, only $11,577.15 had been expended on the cemetery. Construction began in December 1867, was completed in 1868.

Volume 19 of the Roll of Honor (1869) listed a total of 644 interments:

U.S. soldiers - known	328
U.S. soldiers - unknown	307
prisoners of war	3
citizens	1
children	_5_
	644

The bodies of 87 Union soldiers who were killed in the Battle of Centralia, Missouri, on September 27, 1864, were moved to Jefferson City in June 1874. The Roll of Honor series does not list their burials.

KANSAS CITY
Missouri

According to volume 10 of the Roll of Honor, 140 soldiers (only 22 known) were buried at Union City Cemetery near Kansas City. No record of removal of these bodies to a national cemetery after the war has been found.

LEBANON
Missouri

Volume 9 of the Roll of Honor lists 66 burials (18 known) at Lebanon. After the war these bodies were moved to Springfield National Cemetery.

LEXINGTON
Missouri

The Battle of Lexington is also known as the "Battle of the Hemp Bales." The bales of hemp played a big part in almost forgotten battle. On September 12, 1861, an army of 12,000 Confederates under Major General Sterling Price besieged some 3,500 Union troops at Lexington. After waiting for his ammunition train to arrive, Price launched an attack on the Union lines (September 19th). Price managed to encircle the Union's fortifications, but was unable to break the Union lines. The morning of September 20, Price's men used bales of hemp they had found in a nearby warehouse as a sort of movable breastworks. Today the Battle Of Lexington is often called the battle of the hemp bales. Realizing that his lines would be breached, Col. James A. Mulligan, the Union Commander surrendered.

Volume 12 of the Roll of Honor lists 36 Union soldiers (10 known) buried by citizens at Lexington. After the war these bodies were moved to Fort Leavenworth National Cemetery. However in 1932 five bodies of unknown Union soldiers were uncovered on the battlefield. They are believed to have been members of Col. Thomas A. Marshall's Cavalry. Today their graves are marked. The battlefield is now operated as a state historic site.

McDOWELL
Missouri

Mr. W.J. Allock wrote the War Department on April 10, 1879, asking that the bodies of three Union soldiers in the McDowell area be moved to the Springfield National Cemetery. The Quartermaster's Department wrote back asking for more information. No other correspondence exits in the file.

NEWONIA
Missouri

According to volume 12 of the Roll of Honor, 13 soldiers (only five known) were buried at Newonia. These bodies were moved to Springfield National Cemetery after the war.

OTTERVILLE
Missouri

According to volume 12 of the Roll of Honor, 16 soldiers (all known) were buried at Otterville. These bodies were moved to Jefferson City National Cemetery after the war.

PATTERSON
Missouri

Volume 13 of the Roll of Honor lists 56 burials (only seven known) in seven different sites within five miles of Patterson. These bodies were moved to Jefferson Barracks National Cemetery after the war.

REEVES STATION
Missouri

Volume 13 of the Roll of Honor lists two known soldiers and 19 unknown soldiers buried at Reeves Station. A Lieutenant Bronner of the 3rd Mo. S. M. Calvary was buried "15 miles from Reeves Station."

In 1866 a recommendation was made to move these bodies to Patterson, Missouri. However this recommendation was not carried out. Later the bodies were moved to Jefferson Barracks National Cemetery.

SEDALIA
Missouri

According to volume 12 of the Roll of Honor, 53 soldiers (19 known) were buried at Sedalia. These bodies were moved to Jefferson City National Cemetery after the war.

SPRINGFIELD NATIONAL CEMETERY
Missouri

On August 10, 1861, the first major battle of the Civil War west of the Mississippi was fought at Wilson's Creek some ten miles southwest of Springfield, Missouri. Although the Confederates under General Sterling Price defeated the Union forces under Brigadier General Nathaniel Lyon, Price failed to follow up his victory, and Missouri remained in the Union. Lyon was killed in the battle along with about 220 of his men. Springfield National Cemetery was established in 1867. It was located three miles southeast of Springfield on the Kickapoo Prairie. The five acres of land was purchased from the City of Springfield. Burials were made from Wilson Creek, Pea Ridge Battlefield, Newtonia, and other locations in the surrounding area. Volume 9 of the Roll of Honor (1866) lists a total of 529 burials "at Springfield." Volume 18 of the series lists 1,0333 additional burials for a total of 1,514. 795 were known. 710 were unknown. In 1884 headstones were supplied to mark the graves of 30 government employees buried at Springfield.

A Confederate Cemetery was established next to the National Cemetery in 1870. In 1911 the Confederate Cemetery Association of Missouri deeded the six acre cemetery to the United States provided the land be used only to bury Confederate Veterans. Congress accepted the land on March 3, 1911. In 1948 the association lifted burial restrictions on four acres of the land. In 1957, Congress amended its acceptance of the land so that veterans of all wars could be buried there.

Volume 2 of the Disposition lists 110 soldiers' bodies moved from "the public graveyard 1/2 mile NE of the court-house at Springfield" to Jefferson Barracks National Cemetery at Saint Louis. These removals took place on March 20, 1868, a year after the Springfield National Cemetery was established. No explanation of why these bodies were moved across the state has been found. One possibility is that the bodies were moved by contractors who were paid by the body. In fact in 1867 the Washington Sunday Herald charged that coffins buried by contract at Saint Louis were filed with sticks and stones. Perhaps the "bodies" never actually existed.

A second possibility is that the Springfield superintendent who was in charge that year failed to have the bodies moved. Col. Mack's 1872 report stated that the "worthless" former superintendent had "sadly neglected" the cemetery. Six bodies from the Springfield area were moved to the cemetery in 1871. Volume 3 of the Disposition reports 303 bodies moved to the cemetery in early 1868, but none from the "public cemetery."

TIPTON
Missouri

According to volume 12 of the Roll of Honor, 108 soldiers (only 14 known) were buried at Tipton. These bodies were moved to Jefferson Barracks National Cemetery in 1867.

WARRENSBURG
Missouri

Volume 12 of the Roll of Honor lists 19 soldiers (eight known) buried at Warrensburg. These soldiers were moved to either Jefferson City National Cemetery or Jefferson Barracks National Cemetery. Different Quartermaster records state that all the bodies were moved to both cemeteries.

WARRENTON
Missouri

According to volume 12 of the Roll of Honor, 17 soldiers (only one known) were buried at Warrenton. No record of removal of these bodies to a national cemetery after the war has been found.

WAYNESVILLE
Missouri

According to volume 12 of the Roll of Honor, four soldiers (all known) were buried at Waynesville. These bodies were moved to Jefferson Barracks National Cemetery in 1867.

WESTON
Missouri

According to volume 12 of the Roll of Honor, 23 soldiers (only two known) were buried at Weston. These bodies were moved to Fort Leavenworth National Cemetery after the war.

CAMP COOKE
Montana

Camp Cooke was the first "permanent" post in Montana. The post was founded by the 12th and 13th Infantry on July 11, 1866. The post was located on the Missouri River near the Judith River. Fifteen privates of the 13th United States Infantry died at Camp Cooke in late 1866 and 1867. Volume 19 of the Roll of Honor listed the causes of death along with the names. The causes of death ranged from: "morbiss brightes" to consumption to scalded foot to rheumatism. One citizen who committed suicide was buried there. Pitanista, the chief of the Pirgan Indian tribe, was buried here also.

The post closed on March 31, 1870. No record of removals of bodies from this post exists.

CUSTER NATIONAL CEMETERY
Montana

On June 25, 1876, five companies of the United States Seventh Cavalry under Col. George Armstrong Custer were defeated by the Sioux and Cheyenne Indians at the Battle of the Little Bighorn (also known as Custer's last stand). About 225 soldiers and civilians died with Custer. Custer's brothers Thomas and Boston, his brother-in-law James Calhoun, and his nephew Harry Reed were killed along with Custer.

Custer's subordinates, Major Marcus Reno and Captain Frederick Benteen also engaged the Indians. They were forced to retreat with casualties of 53 killed and 60 wounded.

Custer's men were hastily buried on the battlefield. In the summer of 1877, the bodies of most of the officers were moved and the soldiers reburied where they fell. Custer's body was moved to West Point. Remains of Captain Tom Custer, winner of two Congressional Medal of Honor during the Civil War, were moved to the Fort Leavenworth National Cemetery.

In 1879 the site was declared a national cemetery. As forts in the area closed, bodies from the fort's post cemetery were moved to the national cemetery. In 181 a marble monument engraved with the names of Custer's troops, was erected on Custer Hill. The bodies of Custer's troops were reburied in a common grave on Custer Hill.

In 1888 bodies from Fort Phil Kearny were moved to the cemetery. Bodies from nineteen posts were moved to cemetery in the 1890's and early 1900's. Often civilians buried in post cemeteries were moved to the cemetery, but in 1890, the bodies of 19 civilians were left at Fort Rice, North Dakota. In 1890, 338 bodies from six posts were moved to the cemetery at a cost of $4,378.10 ($12.95 per body). Surprisingly the graves of the 53 soldiers killed at the Reno-Benteen Battle site were never marked or moved to the cemetery.

A report dated December 31, 1908, listed interments in the cemetery:

865   known
263   unknown
236   civilians

The cemetery was transferred from the War Department to the National Park Service on July 1, 1940. In 1946 the sites name was changed to the Custer Battlefield National Monument. In 1991, the battlefield was renamed Little Bighorn Battlefield National Monument. The cemetery became Custer National Cemetery.

FORT CUSTER
Montana

In March 1889 the post quartermaster of Fort Custer ordered 25 headstones for the post cemetery. By 1909 the post had closed. When it closed 66 bodies were moved to Custer Battlefield National Cemetery.

FORT ELLIS
Montana Territory

In 1886 the post quartermaster requested six headstones for Fort Ellis's post cemetery. The six soldiers died between 1880 and 1886. In 1889, thirty-nine bodies from the deactivated Fort Ellis to the Fort Missoula post cemetery.

FORT MISSOULA
Montana

Nine known U.S. soldiers were buried at Fort Missoula between 1878 and 1885. The list of names is in the Quartermaster's records. No record of removal of the bodies has been found.

FORT SHAW
Montana Territory

Volume 19 of the Roll of Honor lists three soldiers and two "citizens" who died at Fort Shaw in late 1867. Three died of typhoid dysentery, one died of exposure while drunk, and one "shot himself through the head." Sometime before 1909, 77 bodies from Fort Shaw were moved to Custer National Cemetery.

VARIOUS SITES
Montana Territory

In the early 1880's the War Department considered erecting a monument "to the officers and soldiers killed, or who died of wounds received in action, while clearing the District of the Yellowstone of hostile Indians." One sketch of the proposed monument was received by the Quartermaster General's office on April 22, 1881. This sketch, preserved in box #196 of RG92-E376, listed a total 39 names:

5th Infantry	9 soldiers
22th Infantry	1 soldier
7th Cavalry	22 troopers

The soldiers were killed in the following battles in the Montana Territory:

Bear Paw Mountains
Clark's Fork
Mispah Creek
O'Fallen Creek
Pumpkin Creek
Rosebud Creek
Tongue River
Wolf Mountains

It appears that these bodies were never recovered and moved to a national cemetery. This red granite monument was first erected at Fort Keogh, Montana. However no records exist showing when it was erected. When Fort Keogh closed the contractor attempted to move the monument to the Custer Battlefield National Cemetery. The monument was delivered to Crow Agency in 1908, however it was not erected in the cemetery until 1910.

FORT McPHERSON NATIONAL CEMETERY
Nebraska

Volume 7 of the <u>Roll of Honor</u> lists a total of 17 soldiers buried in Fort McPherson's post cemetery. As other frontier posts were abandoned it was difficult to preserve the post's cemeteries. In 1873, the Fort McPherson Post Cemetery was designated a national cemetery. As other posts closed, the bodies in the abandoned post cemeteries were removed to Fort McPherson National Cemetery. In 1873 the cemetery contained 389 bodies. By 1889 a total of 551 interments had been made:

	known	known
soldiers	254	273
civilians	4	20

FORT OMAHA
Nebraska

Fort Omaha never had a post cemetery according to a 1877 "brief" in the Quartermaster's files. A total of 43 interments were made in the Prospect Hill Cemetery in Omaha. 31 of the interments were soldiers, the other 12 were civilians. In 1877 the United States purchased the lot in Prospect Hill Cemetery where the burials had been made. The graves had been marked with headstones sometime before 1877. Volume 7 of the <u>Roll of Honor</u> lists three known and two unknown burials in the "Omaha Cemetery."

FORT ROBINSON
Nebraska Territory

In 1886 Fort Robinson's assistant quartermaster requested headstones for 25 known soldiers buried in the post cemetery. Four of these bodies had been moved from Camp Sheridan, Nebraska Territory, in 1880.

CAMP DUN GLEN
Nevada

Volume 12 of the Roll of Honor lists one soldier who died at Camp Dun Glen. No information on removal of these remains to a national cemetery has been found.

CAMP McKEE
Nevada

Volume 12 of the Roll of Honor lists two soldiers who died at Camp McKee. No information on removal of these remains to a national cemetery has been found.

CARSON
Nevada

In 1879 the local GAR Post requested headstones for 19 unmarked graves at Carson, Nevada. These soldiers may have died during the war, but that is strictly conjecture.

FORT CHURCHILL
Nevada

Volume 12 of the Roll of Honor lists eleven soldiers who died at Fort Churchill. No information on removal of these remains to a national cemetery has been found.

FORT McDERMIT
Nevada

Fort McDermit was located in the Santa Rosa Mountains of Nevada. It was first occupied as Camp McDermit in August 1865. The post closed in December 1888. Volume 12 of the Roll of Honor lists two burials at the post. No record of removal of these bodies has been found.

FORT RUBY
Nevada

Burials at Fort Ruby are listed in volumes 8 and 12 of the Roll of Honor. The bodies were moved to San Francisco National Cemetery in October 1901.

CANDIA
New Hampshire

In May 1879 tombstones were requested for about 120 graves of soldiers buried in Candia. According to the letter some of these soldiers had served in American Revolution. No list of names could be found in the Archives' files. It is unclear if any of these soldiers actually died during the Civil War.

CONCORD
New Hampshire

Ten Union soldiers died of disease in hospitals in Concord. They were buried as unknowns in Concord's "old cemetery."

MANCHESTER
New Hampshire

Volume 9 of the Roll of Honor lists 38 burials in Manchester. It appears that almost all of the burials were of New Hampshire troops.

Cemetery	Number of burials
Valley	20
"Hospital Grounds"	6
Merrill's	3
Pine Grove	4
Stowell's	2
Gopp's Falls	2
Piscataquax	1

199

PORTSMOUTH
New Hampshire

According to a 1886 report from Mr. John W. Hogg, Chief Clerk of the Navy Department, eight known and about 40 unknown sailors were buried in the Portsmouth, N.H., Navy Yard Cemetery. The first recorded interment was made in 1842.

BEVERLY NATIONAL CEMETERY
New Jersey

All of the 147 Federal Soldiers who are buried in the Beverly National Cemetery died in the Union hospital located in the "Wall Rope Factory." According to a 1875 Statement of Interments, 139 were known white soldiers, 7 were unknown white soldiers, and one known colored soldier.

Mr. Christian Weymann donated one acre of "low flat" land for the cemetery. In 1855 seven unknown Revolutionary Soldiers were removed from behind the 5th and Arch Street Fire Station in Camden, N.J., and buried in a mass grave.

Volume 12 of the Roll of Honor lists 197 white and 2 colored soldiers buried "at Beverly." It is possible the sixty "missing" soldiers were removed by friends or buried in private cemeteries.

BRIDGETON
New Jersey

S.J. Fogg of the 3rd New Jersey was buried at Bridgeton on June 1, 1862. The records contain no more information on this burial.

BURLINGTON COUNTY
New Jersey

A list, dated September 1868, gave the names of 12 soldiers who were buried at or near Tuckerton, New Jersey. Seven were buried in the Tuckerton Cemetery. Three were buried in N.E. Churchyard. One was buried in the "Friends Ground". The last was buried at West Creek.

FINN'S POINT NATIONAL CEMETERY
New Jersey

A major Union Civil War POW camp was Fort Delaware, Delaware. The fort was on Pea Patch Island in the Delaware River about 1 1/2 miles from Finn's Point, NJ. 1,260 Confederate POW's were "on hand" on June 30, 1862. Only 17 POW's were "on hand" on January 31, 1863. However the breakdown of the POW cartel caused the prison population to soar. By the end of July, 1863, the prison held 8,932.

One hundred sixty-nine prisoners died that month. Over 2,400 Confederates died on Pea Patch Island during the war.

Because of the high water table on Pea Patch Island, most of the dead Confederates were shipped across the river to the military post cemetery at Finn's Point, New Jersey.

In 1875 Governor James Kemper of Virginia wrote the Secretary of War concerning the neglected Confederate graves at Pea Patch Island. Adjutant General E.D. Townsend wrote Governor Kemper that: "Most of the bodies of the confederate prisoners of war who died at Fort Delaware (some 2,500 in all) are interred in the soldiers burial ground at Finn's Point on the New Jersey shore... and while not as in good order as might be desired, is reported as presenting a more respectable appearance than most country church-yards." The cemetery was named a National Cemetery in 1875 and the Quartermaster General was instructed to transfer any soldiers' remains on Pea Patch Island to the national cemetery.

A "brief" in the Finn's Point file (RG92-576) dated August 3,1888, summarized an inspection report. 135 Union and 2,509 Confederates were buried at Finn's Point. The first allotment of money for the cemetery was $90.00.

In 1879 the U.S. Government erected a ten foot marble monument over the mass grave of the 135 Union soldiers. The monument lists 105 names. The Roll of Honor series does not list these names.

In 1910 the U.S. Government erected an 85 foot granite obelisk to mark the mass graves of the confederates. Bronze tablets list the names of 2,436 confederates who died on Pea Patch Island.

NEWARK
New Jersey

One hundred twenty-five white soldiers and three colored soldiers were buried in Newark's Fairmont Cemetery. All but two were private soldiers. The graves were marked by headstones in 1880. Volume 9 of the Roll of Honor lists these names.

ALBUQUERQUE
New Mexico

Volumes 8 and 19 of the Roll of Honor list a total of twelve burials (one unknown) at Albuquerque. No record of removals of these bodies to a national cemetery has been found.

APACHE CANYON
New Mexico

Thirty-five unknown soldiers were buried at Apache Canyon. It appears these bodies were never moved to a national cemetery.

FORT APACHE
New Mexico

In 1886 The Post Commander of Fort Apache,New Mexico, requested 45 headstones for the post cemetery. None of these soldiers died during the Civil War.

FORT BASCOM
New Mexico

Fort Bascom, also called Camp Easton, was in operation from August 1863 to December 1870. The fort was located on the Canadian River eight miles north of Tucumcari. Volume 8 of the Roll of Honor lists eight soldiers who died at Fort Bascom in 1864 and 1865. Nine additional names are listed in volume 19 of the series. Thirty-five graves were moved from Fort Bascom to Fort Leavenworth National Cemetery before 1909.

FORT BAYARD NATIONAL CEMETERY
New Mexico

Volume 19 of the Roll of Honor lists three burials at Fort Bayard. It appears that bodies from Fort Bayard were moved to both the San Antonio National Cemetery and the Fort Leavenworth National Cemetery.

In 1900 Fort Bayard was decommissioned as an active post and converted to an army hospital. In the early 1920's the United States Public Health Service operated the hospital for the treatment of tuberculosis. In 1922 the VA assumed control of the hospital. It appears that the burials in the Fort Bayard National Cemetery date from 1922.

FORT CRAIG
New Mexico

A 1866 report listed 121 known and 25 unknown Union soldiers buried in Fort Craig's post cemetery. Sixty-seven of the known soldiers and all 25 unknown soldiers were "supposed to have been killed at the Battle of Val Verde." Volume 19 of the Roll of Honor lists 49 names and seven unknowns buried at Fort Craig.

In March 1876, 147 bodies were moved from Fort Craig to Santa Fe National Cemetery. The post closed in 1885.

FORT CUMMINGS
New Mexico

Six soldiers, five from Company G of the 1st California Infantry and one from Company D of the 125th U.S.C.T., died at Fort Cummings. Their names are recorded in volume 19 of the Roll of Honor. The fort was deactivated in 1873, but reoccupied twice during the war with the Apaches. The fort was last occupied in 1886. No records of removals of the graves have been found.

FORT FILMORE
New Mexico

A 1867 report stated that the graves at Fort Filmore were in "poor condition." Apparently vandals had damaged the headboards. No estimate at the number of dead was included in the report nor is there any additional information to be found in the files of the Quartermaster General.

203

FORT MARCY
New Mexico

Fort Marcy was founded in 1846. Volume 8 of the <u>Roll of Honor</u> lists 46 burials (16 known) in the post cemetery. Volume 19 of the series lists three additional names. At least 167 bodies were moved from the post cemetery to the Santa Fe National Cemetery.

FORT McRAE
New Mexico

Volumes 8 and 19 of the <u>Roll of Honor</u> list a total of eleven burials at Fort McRae. These bodies were later moved to the Santa Fe National Cemetery.

FORT SELDEN
New Mexico

A total of thirteen burials at Fort Selden are listed in volumes 8 and 19 of the <u>Roll of Honor</u>. These bodies were later moved to the Fort Leavenworth National Cemetery.

FORT STANTON
New Mexico

Volume 12 of the <u>Roll of Honor</u> lists 19 burials at Fort Stanton. Volumes 8 and 19 of the series repeat some of the names listed in volume 12. These bodies were later moved to Santa Fe National Cemetery.

FORT SUMNER
New Mexico

Volumes 8 and 19 of the <u>Roll of Honor</u> list a total of 15 burials at Fort Sumner. The five names in volume 8 are not repeated in volume 19. These bodies were moved to the Santa Fe National Cemetery.

FORT UNION
New Mexico

Volume 19 of the Roll of Honor lists 56 burials in Fort Union's post cemetery between June 27, 1854, and November 18, 1867. Lt. Joseph Maxwell was the first recorded burial. Two privates from the 125th U.S.C.T. both died on November 18, 1867. Some bodies from the post cemetery were moved to the Santa Fe National Cemetery at an unknown date. However 293 bodies were moved to the Fort Leavenworth National Cemetery before 1906.

FORT WINGATE
New Mexico

The first Fort Wingate was founded in October 1862 near present day town of Grants, New Mexico. This post closed in July 1868. Volume 8 of the Roll of Honor lists 12 burials in the post cemetery between 1864 and 1866. Volume 19 of the series lists five burials between 1866 and 1867. An 1868 report states that 18 U.S. soldiers were buried in the post cemetery from 1863 to 1868. However only eight of the bodies could be identified. The post was to be closed and the bodies moved to Fort Lyon, a new fort some 68 miles north west. The post closed in July 1868.

Sometime thereafter a second Fort Wingate was established near Bear Springs in McKinley County. This post closed in 1912, but remained an army depot. An 1886 headstone request listed 29 known burials in Fort Wingate's post cemetery. Because the dates of death on the list range from 1866 to 1885, it appears that the remains from the original post cemetery were transferred to this cemetery instead of Fort Lyon.

At least one body from Fort Wingate was moved to Fort Leavenworth National Cemetery. The existing records do not indicate any other removals.

LAS CRUCES
New Mexico

An 1868 report named three of the 12 Union soldiers buried at Los Cruces. The cemetery was reported in "good order." The Quartermaster's files contain no further information on these burials.

LOS PINOS
New Mexico

In November 1870, a total of 73 bodies were moved from Los Pinos to the Santa Fe National Cemetery. Volumes 8 and 19 of the Roll of Honor list about 20 burials at Los Pinos.

SANTA FE NATIONAL CEMETERY
New Mexico

Fort Marcy was established at Santa Fe in 1846. Volume 8 of the Roll of Honor lists 16 known and 30 unknown burials in the post cemetery. However two years later volume 19 of the Roll of Honor listed only three burials at Fort Marcy. The names were different.

An 1868 report by Brevet Lt. Col. M.L. Sudington stated that the post cemetery at Fort Marcy was a lot about one-half acre in size that "will be donated by the Catholic Church to the United States." Col. Sudington also stated: "The site is the best which could be selected." Bodies were moved to the cemetery from Pigeons Ranch's Battlefield and Glorieta Battlefield.

In early 1875 the enlarged post cemetery was designated a National Cemetery by the Secretary of War. The idea was to move bodies from cemeteries at abandoned posts would be moved to the cemetery. In March 1876, 147 bodies were moved from Fort Craig to the cemetery. However by the early 1880's it proved easier to ship bodies from posts in New Mexico and Arizona to Fort Leavenworth (Kansas) National Cemetery on the Atchison, Topeka, nd Santa Fe Railroad than to Santa Fe National Cemetery.

An 1875 post cemetery roster lists a total of 265 burials (only five known) in 191 graves. As many as seven bodies were buried to the grave. By the mid-1880's, only 15 bodies were known, however the cemetery contained at least 604 graves.

ALBANY
New York

Seventy-Eight Union Soldiers are buried in the "Soldiers' Lot" of Albany's Rural Cemetery. Volume 10 of the Roll of Honor lists the names. The Department of Veteran's Affairs today lists this cemetery as a Soldiers' Lot with 149 interments.

BROOKLYN NAVAL CEMETERY
New York

Two hundred twenty three (223) sailors were buried in the Brooklyn (NY) Naval Cemetery from 1861 to December 28, 1864. According to a 1886 tombstone request, all were known burials.

BUFFALO
New York

Volume 16 of the Roll of Honor lists burials in three Buffalo cemeteries.

Twelve known soldiers were buried in Pine Hill Cemetery.

Six known and four unknown soldiers were buried in the Limestone Hill (Catholic) Cemetery.

26 known Federal soldiers were reinterred in Forest Lawn Cemetery. 18 of the soldiers were commissioned officers. Three were non-commissioned officers, and five were privates.

Bodies were removed to Forest Lawn from:

Cedar Creek, Virginia
Fort William, Louisiana
Fredericksburg, Virginia
Five Forks, Virginia
Fort Wayne, South Carolina
Donaldsonville, Louisiana
Gettysburg, Pennsylvania
Seven Pines, Virginia

CHERRY CREEK
New York

Ten Federal soldiers who died during the Civil War were buried in Cherry Creek Cemetery. At least two of these were killed in action in the South. According to volume 16 of the Roll of Honor these soldiers' graves were marked by marble monuments.

CYPRESS HILLS NATIONAL CEMETERY
New York

Cypress Hills National Cemetery was one of the twelve original National Cemeteries authorized by President Lincoln in 1862. The first burials were of Confederate POW's and their guards who died in a train wreck. A.J. Case, whose letterhead read "undertaker for the U.S. Army", made many of the burials.

After the war bodies "from the various hospitals and camps in and around New York City" were reburied in the cemetery. Col. C.W. Folsom (1868) noted the cemetery was located "three miles east of the city of Brooklyn, Long Island,..." The cemetery consisted of two acres in the "city cemetery."

Col. Folsom reported the reinterments from the area cost $10.00 per body. However in 1868, 312 bodies "more or less" were moved to Cypress Hills from Portsmouth Grove, RI, at a cost of $6.00 per body.

Volume 13 of the Roll of Honor lists a total of 3,151 burials in Cypress Hills National Cemetery. Volume 16 of the Roll of Honor (a revised list) lists 3,277 burials:

officers - known	5
white soldiers - known	3,002
colored soldiers - known	190
white soldiers - unknown	78
colored soldiers - unknown	2
	3,277

Not all the Union soldiers who were buried in the New York City area were moved to Cypress Hills during the 1860's. At least 31 soldiers were buried at Fort Columbus on Governor's Island. By the time burials on Governor's Island were halted in 1873, as many as 1,000 soldiers may have been buried there. It appears that these bodies were moved to Cypress Hills in the 1880's.

According to the Department of Veteran's Affairs a total of 488 Confederate POW's were buried at Cypress Hills.

When Cypress Hills was first made a national cemetery, a small burial plot called the Mount of Victory Plot was not included in the cemetery. This plot, about 2,400 square feet, contained 49 graves. Forty-one were graves of veterans of the War of 1812 and eight were graves of relatives of War of 1812 veterans. One grave was that of Hiram Cronk, who was "generally acknowledged to be the last survivor" of the War of 1812.

In 1940 the House Committee on military affairs investigated adding the Mount of Victory Plot to Cypress Hills. Secretary of War Harry H. Woodring opposed the plan for two reasons. First he thought the addition of the plot would set a precedent for the acceptance of private cemeteries into the national cemetery system. Secondly the War Department could only find service records of eight of the "veterans."

Congress voted to add the plot to the cemetery.

DUNKIRK
New York

Three Union soldiers died in the hospital at Dunkirk during the war. After the war the Quartermaster's Department refused to supply headstones because the soldiers' regiments were unknown. The War Department had no "name index" to service in the war.

ELMIRA
New York

Elmira became the location for a Union training camp in 1861. In addition at least two hospitals operated in Elmira. In July 1864, Confederate prisoners were moved to Elmira. Some 12,000 POW's were confined at Elmira. About 2,950 died, many during the severe winter of 1864-1865. They were buried in a two and one half acre plot in Elmira's Woodlawn Cemetery. Volume 7 of the Roll of Honor lists 106 white and 10 colored Union soldiers buried in the Woodlawn Cemetery.

In 1877 the Federal Government paid the City of Elmira $1500.00 for the plot which was renamed Woodlawn National Cemetery.

FORT NIAGARA
New York

Twenty soldiers and two children were buried at Fort Niagara near Youngstown, New York, according to volume 16 of the Roll of Honor. Two of these were soldiers killed during the War of 1812: Col. John Christie of the 23rd United States Infantry was killed at Lewiston, Kentucky, on July 23, 1813. Lieutenant Thomas Poe of the Pennsylvania Volunteers was killed in action at Lundy's Lane on July 23, 1813. At least four of the soldiers died of cholera in 1850.

FORT ONTARIO
New York

In 1886 the Quartermaster's Department marked the graves of 13 English soldiers buried at Fort Ontario with headstones. The headstones were marked "unknown soldier."

FORT WADSWORTH
New York

In 1886 the acting assistant quartermaster of Fort Wadsworth requested three headstones for soldiers who died at Fort Wadsworth between 1867 and 1870. The Roll of Honor series does not list these burials.

GOVERNOR'S ISLAND
New York

Over 500 soldiers were buried on Governor's Island. The exact dates of burials are unknown, but Record Group 92-E576 has a list of 500 names of soldiers buried on the island. The list also includes the names of 20 Confederates and 14 women and children buried in the "little cemetery."

These bodies were moved to Cypress Hills National Cemetery in 1886.

ITHACA
New York

On June 1, 1877, Dr. R.G. Gilbert wrote the War Department requesting headstones: "A large number (about twenty) of the deceased soldiers of the late war rest in our cemetery here with no headstones." No other information about these burials has been found.

JAMESTOWN
New York

The Quartermaster's Department furnished eight headstones to mark graves in Jamestown in the 1880's. At least one of the stones was furnished to mark the grave of a POW who died in Libby Prison.

LANSINGBURGH
New York

Volume 10 of the Roll of Honor lists sixteen soldiers buried at Lansingburgh between 1864 and 1865. No more data on these burials has been found.

LOCKPORT
New York

Eight known and one unknown soldier were interred in Lockport's Cold Spring Cemetery during the war. At least four of the soldiers died of wounds according to volume 16 of the Roll of Honor. Three of the soldiers were officers.

LODI
New York

Two officers and three private soldiers were buried in Lodi Cemetery in Lodi, New York. Volume 16 of the Roll of Honor lists the names. Two of the soldiers buried here were killed in action in the South.

MADISON BARRACKS
New York

Madison Barracks' post cemetery was begun in 1814 with one and a half acres of land purchased from a Mr. Luff. Soldiers from the War of 1812 and the border difficulties of 1837 are buried in the cemetery. Volume 16 of the Roll of Honor lists 26 known burials and five unknown burials in the post cemetery. 542 unknown graves were listed with the notation: "not enclosed. No marks for recognition."

The exact number of burials is unknown. The same volume of the Roll of Honor listed 35 known graves and 365 unknown graves for a total of 400 graves. As late as 1889 burials were still being made in the cemetery.

NEWBURG
New York

Some Union soldiers who died during the war are buried in Newburg. However the sketchy records do not indicate if they died at Newburg or were moved there from other sites. The Quartermaster's files contain a list of soldiers who died in Newburg during and after the war. This list was the report of the cemetery committee of Ellis Post #52 of the GAR.

NEW ROCHELLE
New York

Twenty-nine known and one unknown soldier were buried in Beechwood Cemetery in New Rochelle according to a 1866 report. Most if not all of these burials came from David's Island in New York City's harbor. After 1862 the dead from David's Island were buried at Cypress Hills National Cemetery.

NEW YORK CITY HARBOR
New York

Burials of deceased Union soldiers were made at least five forts located in New York City's Harbor. Volume 10 of the Roll of Honor lists these burials:

Fort Hamilton	30 known and 100 unknown burials
David's Island	12 known white and 1 known USCT
Willett's Point	4 unknown burials
Fort at Sandy Hook	4 known burials
Fort Columbus	31 known burials

Bodies from the first four sites were apparently moved to Cypress Hill National Cemetery shortly after the war. However burials continued on Governor's Island near Fort Columbus until stopped by the Quartermaster's General Order 11 in 1873. In 1886 these bodies (between 500 and 1,000) were moved to Cypress Hills National Cemetery.

A 1881 report states that troops who died on David's Island before 1862 were buried in Beechwood Cemetery in New Rochelle, N.Y. One "rebel" was buried on David's Island. The report also stated that 48 known Federal soldiers and one "rebel" had been buried on Hart Island.

ONEIDA COUNTY
New York

A total of twenty-two soldiers who were removed from the South were buried in Oneida County. The burial locations were:

New Fork Mills	7
Whitesboro	3
Oriskany	12

No more information is available.

PLATTSBURG BARRACKS
New York

Volume 16 of the Roll of Honor lists six burials in the "Soldiers Cemetery at Plattsburg Barracks." The four known burials were of members of the 42nd Infantry who drowned between May and September 1867.

ROCHESTER
New York

Volume 16 of the Roll of Honor lists nine officers and five soldiers buried in Rochester's Mount Hope Cemetery. However in 1871 Col. Mack reported: "there are said to be one hundred and fifty Union soldiers buried in this cemetery; nearly all being buried with their families." However ten soldiers were buried in the "Potter's field" without headboards.

In 1881 the War Department supplied 47 headstones for soldiers buried in the Holy Sepulchre Cemetery. The records are unclear if these burials were made during or after the war.

SENECA FALLS
New York

Andrew J. Rosenburg, from Company K of the 50th New York, died August 25, 1862. He was buried at Seneca Falls.

WEST POINT
New York

In 1886 the acting assistant post quartermaster requested 12 headstones for Federal soldiers buried in West Point's Post Cemetery. Five of these soldiers died during the Civil War.

WEST TROY
New York

In 1887 the acting assistant quartermaster of Watervliet Arsenal requested an unspecified number of headstones for a "small cemetery" at the arsenal. No other information can be found in the files.

CAROLINA CITY
North Carolina

24 Federal soldiers were buried at Carolina City according to volume 10 of the Roll of Honor. The eleven known soldiers were all U.S. Colored Troops. These bodies were moved to the Newberne National Cemetery after the war.

CHARLOTTE
North Carolina

Volume 10 of the Roll of Honor lists 90 soldiers buried in and near Charlotte. The graves were moved to Salisbury National Cemetery after the war.

FORT MACON
North Carolina

In 1873 the Fort Macon post cemetery held 12 bodies according to a list in the Quartermaster's files. Ten soldiers, one child, and one prisoner who died in 1872 were buried in the cemetery. No further information on these bodies has been found, but bodies at Fort Macon just after the Civil War were moved to the Newberne National Cemetery.

GOLDSBORO
North Carolina

After the war bodies from Goldsboro were moved to both the Raleigh and Newberne National Cemeteries. Burials at Goldsboro are listed in volumes 10 and 14 of the Roll of Honor.

GREENSBORO
North Carolina

Sixty-one Union soldiers who died at Greensboro are listed in volume 10 of the Roll of Honor. These bodies were reinterred in the Raleigh National Cemetery.

LENOIR
North Carolina

In 1882 Dr. J. M. Spainhour, a local dentist, requested headstones for "two sick soldiers who were left here." Dr. Spainhour continued: "Several humane citizens did all they could to restore them to health, but they died..." The official reply was that no stone could be furnished without "more definite data" to identify the soldiers. The official policy in 1882 was not to furnish headstones for unknown soldiers not buried in soldier's lots or national cemeteries.

It is possible that the two soldiers, who were buried in Lenoir's Fairfield Cemetery, were members of General Stoneman's command who raided through Lenoir in March and April 1865.

MOREHEAD CITY
North Carolina

Burials of 87 white (67 known) and 65 colored (45 known) soldiers at Morehead City are listed in volume 10 of the Roll of Honor. These bodies were moved to the Newberne National Cemetery after the war.

215

MORGANTON
North Carolina

Six Federal occupation troops died at Morganton during 1866 and 1867. Volume 10 of the Roll of Honor lists four names, but no other information on these burials has been found.

NEW BERNE NATIONAL CEMETERY
North Carolina

In January 1862, General Ambrose P. Burnside sailed from Hampton Roads, Va., toward the North Carolina coast. Burnside had some 15,000 men under his command. In early February Burnside captured Roanoke Island and began to move inland. On March 14, his troops overran General L. O'B. Branch's 4,000 troops and seized New Berne, North Carolina's second largest coastal city. New Berne would remain in Federal Hands for the rest of the war.

Volume 10 of the Roll of Honor (1866) lists a total of 1274 soldiers buried at New Berne. A yellow fever epidemic in 1864 caused many deaths. On February 1, 1867, New Berne National Cemetery was established. The 7 1/2 acre site was one mile north of the railroad station. Burials were made in 18 sections by state. Bodies were brought to the cemetery from Beaufort, Morehead, Kinston, Hatteras Island, Roanoke Island, and other places on the North Carolina coast.

One interment is that of Miss Carrie E. Cutter. Miss Cutter died Mar 24, 1862. She was buried in plot 41, section 10. She was "betrothed to unknown no. 40. Buried by his side at her request." Her fiance was from the 25th Massachusetts. His body was brought to the cemetery from Roanoke Island.

Volume 19 of the Roll of Honor lists additional interments in New Berne National Cemetery. By 1871 a total of 3,250 burials had been made in the cemetery:

	known	unknown
commissioned officers	22	1
white Union soldiers	1,726	806
white Union sailors	130	49
colored Union soldiers	209	195
employees and citizens	112	0
	2,119	1,051

Col. Mack who inspected the cemetery in 1870 reported that the wooden picket fence needed replacing. He also reported: "The tool-house and privy are under one roof, and present a much more respectable appearance than is usually found in such matters at the government cemeteries."

Removals to the cemetery cost $9.00 each. By May 31, 1871, a total of $36,723.66 had been spent on the cemetery.

RALEIGH NATIONAL CEMETERY
North Carolina

Burials in what became the Raleigh National Cemetery began in the spring of 1865 when troops under General Sherman began burying Union soldiers in a 4 1/2 acre plot of ground appropriated from the state of North Carolina. Burials were made by states if the soldier was known.

After the war bodies were brought to the cemetery from the Averysboro (sic) and Bentonville battlefields and other areas in central and eastern North Carolina including: Goldsboro, Greensboro, and Smithville. Volumes 10 and 18 of the Roll of Honor list burials in the Raleigh National Cemetery. Volume 14 of the series lists Union soldiers that were prisoners of war who died in Raleigh.

The total expenditure on the cemetery was $16,552.08 on April 30, 1871. The title to the land had not been secured however. A 1875 report lists the interments:

	known	unknown	total
officers	19	0	19
white Union soldiers and sailors	580	543	1123
black Union soldiers and sailors	20	6	26
citizens	3	4	4
	622	553	1,175

SALISBURY NATIONAL CEMETERY
North Carolina

No one doubts that a lot of Union soldiers died at the Salisbury Prison Camp, the only question is how many, 3,504? 5,000? 12,700? The only problem is that all of these figures were given as "official" by the War Department. No one knows the real figure.

The Salisbury Prison was begun in December 1861. The sixteen acre prison had good water wells, even oak trees. At first, with the prison exchange cartel working, prison life wasn't so bad. Major Otto Boetticher even drew a picture of a baseball game played in the prison in 1863. In fact, very few prisoners died during the prison's first three years of operation.

Apparently only 109 prisoners died before August 1864. However as the POW exchange cartel collapsed, the prison rapidly filled. Over 8,500 prisoners were "on hand" during November. On November 25, 1864, a group of prisoners rushed the guards trying to escape. This seems an unplanned attempt motivated by hunger rather than a premeditated escape attempt. Guards broke up the escape attempt with cannon fire. One Union soldier killed was Rupert Vincent, a private from New Hampshire. Vincent was really Robert Livingstone, son of Dr. David Livingstone, missionary to Africa.

One prisoner at Salisbury was B.F. Booth. Booth kept a diary while in the prison. He reported that on November 7, 1864, he received his daily ration of food: one pint of corn meal including the cob. He reported that the dead were buried in coffins, but the prisoners secretly marked a coffin. It was reused a few days later. The dead were stripped of their clothes by the prisoners then carried to the cemetery by the "dead-wagon" daily about 2 p.m.

When the prisoners were told on February 21, 1865, they would be released,Booth went to the deadhouse and copied the number of soldiers dying each day directly from the burial register. The register Booth copied listed deaths from October 6, 1864, to February 21, 1865, a total of 138 days:

October	267
November	969
December	164
January	942
February	458
	3800

No one died between October 1 and October 6. Booth believed that some prisoners, perhaps as many as 500, had been sent to hospitals outside the prison and died. He had no idea where they were buried.

Volume 10 of the Roll of Honor (1866) lists 12 soldiers buried in a cemetery southwest of the prison grounds. Another 22 Federal occupation troops who died were buried in Salisbury's Lutheran Cemetery.

Volume 14 of the Roll of Honor lists 3,504 soldiers buried at Salisbury. The bodies were buried in thirteen trenches, without coffins and with no means to identify individual graves. Apparently sixteen Masons were buried in marked graves. Although the Roll of Honor lists 3,504 burials, it claims "...over five thousand fell victim..." The Roll does not state where the names listed in this volume came from. This roll was published in 1868, but it was written in 1867.

Sometime before Col. Mack inspected the cemetery in 1871, someone "discovered" five additional burial trenches. Mack wrote: "These trenches are eighteen in number, parallel to each other, and average about 240 feet in length. The bodies were placed one above another, and mostly without coffins. From the number of bodies exhumed from a given space it was estimated that the number buried in these trenches was 11,700. The number of burials from the prison pen cannot be accurately known, as no records have been found; but the above estimate is considered as being under the real number of deaths." Mack says that death was a release from unnecessary suffering in this "Golgotha."

Mack went on to recommend the United States erect a monument to the "Union dead, who here molder into dust." Congress agreed with Col. Mack and appropriated $10,000 for a monument in 1873. The monument's inscription reads:

"THIS MONUMENT WAS ERECTED BY ACT OF CONGRESS APPROVED MARCH 3, 1873, TO THE MEMORY OF THE UN-KNOWN UNION SOLDIERS WHO DIED IN THE CONFEDERATE PRISON AT SALISBURY, N.C. THEY DIED THAT THEIR COUN-TRY MIGHT LIVE. IN 18 TRENCHES, JUST SOUTH OF THIS SPOT, REST THE BODIES OF 11,700 SOLDIERS OF THE UNITED STATES ARMY, WHO PERISHED DURING THE YEARS 1864 AND 1865 WHILE HELD BY THE CONFEDERATE MILITARY AUTHORI-TIES AS PRISONERS OF WAR IN A STOCKADE NEAR THIS PLACE. FOR OUR COUNTRY 'TIS A PLACE TO DIE."

The only problem with the monument, is that it is wrong. 11,700 soldiers did not die at Salisbury. Louis Brown was the first to document the deaths at Salisbury. In The Salisbury Prison, A Case Study of Confederate Military Prisons 1861-1865, he writes that less than 4,000 prisoners died at Salisbury. I concur.

Several things led me to this conclusion:

First of all, even the bitter, anti-Southern B.F. Booth published his copy of the numbers from the burial register, 3,800 deaths from October 6, 1864, to February 21, 1865. As Brown points out, the prison was not overcrowded before October 6, 1864. In fact several Confederate sources say only 109 prisoners died before October 1864.

Secondly, there is no record of an exhuming detail that found five more trenches at Salisbury. Not one piece of a report can be found that states more bodies or trenches had been located. And this is in the files of a Quartermaster Corps that had six different letters on what to do with a sick mule!

During research on this book, the author discovered a letter on a crude letterhead from "Salisbury National Cemetery." This appears to be the text for volume 14 of the Roll of Honor. However someone had crossed out "thirteen" trenches and substituted "18." The word "five" thousand were stuck out and "twelve" thousand was inserted. These changes were in blue crayon, in the same handwriting as changes in reports on other cemeteries. It appears that the report was changed in Washington.

Finally, there is the matter of the names listed in the Roll of Honor. Col. Mack states "...no records have been found...." This is untrue! Volume 14 of the Roll of Honor was published in 1868, three years before Mack's report. It appears that Mack conveniently "forgot" about the earlier report. During the author's research for this book, he discovered what appears to be the rough draft of the list of names for volume 14 of the Roll of Honor. It was filed under Raleigh National Cemetery.

The only question remaining is why did the Quartermaster's Department decide that 11,700 soldiers were buried at Salisbury? It is possible that in mounding the graves with dirt to sow grass, workers did dig into the mass grave and find bodies on top of each other. However it is surprising that no record of a report on finding additional burial trenches exist.

Booth did print a letter written by Martin Burke, Superintendent of Salisbury National Cemetery. In 1894 Burke wrote: "The rebel commandant of the prison failed to turn over any record of the prisoners, or the deaths, at Salisbury Prison Pen. We had to open about fifty feet of each trench and count the skulls or bodies, then measure the whole trench and made (sic) an estimate according to the number found in proportion to the length of the whole trench. It is supposed by the best of authorities that 15,000, instead of 11,700 are buried in the 18 trenches alone." Exactly how Burke knew how the graves were opened is unclear. He was not the superintendent in 1874, and it appears he was not at the cemetery before then.

Could it be that the War Department invented the deaths? During the last years of the war, the Northern press carried stories about the authorities in Southern prisons. Northerners sent food to "our starving soldiers in Southern prisons." As Louis Brown pointed out in 1980, if only 4,000 prisoners died at Salisbury, only 11% of the Union prisoners held by the Confederates died in captivity. About 12% of Confederates held in Northern prisons died. It would be unthinkable to have a higher death rate in Northern POW camps than Southern camps.

No one will ever know the truth about the deaths at Salisbury. The answer lies buried in the trenches.

SHELBY
North Carolina

The removal of three bodies of unknown Union soldiers from Shelby to Salisbury National Cemetery was approved on December 18, 1871, according to notes on the back of an envelope found in the Quartermaster's records. However five unknown Union soldiers and four unknown Confederate soldiers are buried side by side in Shelby's Sunset Cemetery. It is possible that these unknown Union soldiers were Union occupation troops stationed in Shelby, county seat of Cleveland County. Thomas Dixon, Jr., who observed these troops as a youth in Shelby. His book about Reconstruction, The Clansman, was made into the movie Birth of a Nation by D.W. Griffith in 1915. Dixon is buried a few yards from these soldiers.

WASHINGTON
North Carolina

Volume 10 of the Roll of Honor lists 88 burials at Washington. Several of these were of gunboat crew members. These bodies were moved to Newberne National Cemetery after the war.

WELDON
North Carolina

Volume 14 of the Roll of Honor lists seven prisoners of war who died at Weldon. No further information has been found.

WILMINGTON NATIONAL CEMETERY
North Carolina

Wilmington was the last major Atlantic seaport to fall to Union Forces. Fort Fisher kept the port open for blockade runners until it fell to a combined land-sea force on January 15, 1865.

The first burials in Wilmington National Cemetery were made on February 1, 1867. The five acres of land for the cemetery were purchased from Isaac D. Ryttenburg on February 20, 1867.

Bodies were moved to the cemetery from cemeteries in Wilmington, Fort Fisher, Saltville, and other sites in Southeastern North Carolina. The average cost of disinterring, recoffining, and reburying the bodies was $6.45. However local residents charged that many bodies moved to the cemetery were not Union troops. On November 12, 1881, the former Confederate

Commander at Fort Fisher, Col. William Lamb, charged in the Philadelphia Times: "on revisiting Fort Fisher after the war I found that the post burial ground, where my soldiers who died previous the battle were buried, had been robbed of all its dead, and was told that a contractor for the government had stolen their bodies in order to be paid for supplying them with coffins under any appropriation to bury the dead of the Union dead." Some four hundred unknown Confederate dead from the Wilmington area had been buried in Wilmington's Oakdale Cemetery in 1866.

Wilmington did not quickly accept the cemetery. Brevet Major General Lorenzo Thomas, who inspected the cemetery in 1868, reported: "The feeling of the community is not favorable to the cemetery, and shrubbery, though abundant, cannot be obtained except at high prices... at one time it was contemplated to discontinue the public road on which the cemetery fronts, and locating it in a different direction, but I judge the people owning land on this highway prevented the measure..."

In 1871 Col. Mack reported that a total of 2,057 graves at the cemetery were marked by headboards. However the burial register recorded only 2009 burials:

	known	unknown
officers	12	1
white soldiers and sailors	631	838
colored Union soldiers	55	502
	698	1,341

Burials in the cemetery are listed in volume 18 of the Roll of Honor. Volume 14 of the series lists 83 Union prisoners of war who died at Wilmington.

Twenty-eight Puerto Rican civilians who died during the 1918 influenza epidemic are also buried in the cemetery. These men were part of 1,900 laborers who stopped in Wilmington en route to Camp Bragg. By the time they arrived in Wilmington, some 300 had fallen ill. The other laborers returned home because their services were no longer needed at the construction site.

WILSON
North Carolina

One federal soldier died while a prisoner of war at Wilson according to volume 14 of the Roll of Honor. No record of removal of this body to a national cemetery has been found.

CAMP DELAWARE
Ohio

A 1879 letter requested the U.S. Government bury the U.S. colored troops who died at Camp Delaware during 1863 and 1864 in a common plot. No action was recorded.

CAMP DENNISON
Ohio

Volume 18 of the Roll of Honor lists 327 known and 17 unknown soldiers buried at Camp Dennison. Because the United States did not own the land were these soldiers were buried, the bodies were moved to the Spring Grove Cemetery in Cincinnati.

CLEVELAND
Ohio

Volume 9 of the Roll of Honor lists a total of 530 white and two colored soldiers (all known) buried "at Cleveland." The burial sites of these soldiers are not given. It may be that most of these soldiers died at home and were buried by their friends and relatives in private lots.

Volume 26 of the Roll of Honor lists 38 burials in Cleveland's Westside Cemetery. These burials included 12 bodies originally buried in Cleveland's Woodland Cemetery. However both Col. Mack's 1871 and 1874 reports list 27 burials in the Soldier's Lot in Cleveland's Woodland Cemetery. The 40 by 16 foot lot was purchased by the United States for $150. Sixteen other soldiers were buried in a lot near the main entrance gate. This lot was owned by the City of Cleveland. 102 other Union soldiers were buried "with their friends" in this cemetery. Most of these died after the war but a few had been removed from the South. Today Woodland is a soldiers' lot (48 burials) cared for by the Department of Veterans' Affairs.

Col. Mack's report does not mention Westside Cemetery, however he reported that three officers and nine soldiers were buried in Cleveland's Roman Catholic Cemetery.

COLUMBUS
Ohio

Volume 26 of the Roll of Honor lists a total of 492 burials (449 known) in the "Soldiers Burial Lot" in Columbus's Green Lawn Cemetery. Some time before 1879 the Green Lawn Cemetery Association requested 495 headstones for the graves. The association offered to deed the United States the soldier's lot if the War Department would erect the headstones. The every cost-conscious Quartermaster declined the offer.

Volume 9 of the Roll of Honor lists 348 white soldiers and 15 colored soldiers buried "at Columbus." The names listed do not match the names in volume 26 of the Roll of Honor. Nothing else about these burials can be found in the War Department records.

CRESTLINE
Ohio

In 1879 the War Department furnished headstones for seven unknown soldiers who "took sick" and died while passing through Crestline.

DAYTON
Ohio

112 Union soldiers, all known, were buried in Dayton's Woodlawn Cemetery. The majority belonged to Ohio units according to Volume 26 of the Roll of Honor. Most apparently died in hospitals in the Dayton area. None of these bodies were ever moved to the Dayton National Cemetery.

The first burial in what became the Dayton National Cemetery was made on September 11, 1867. This cemetery was for burials at the Central Branch of the National Asylum for Disabled Volunteer Soldiers. This cemetery was never under control of the Quartermaster's department.

In 1870 the local GAR chapter requested markers for five known soldiers who died of disease or who were moved "home" after the war. These markers were placed in Glade Run Cemetery in Dayton.

GALLIPOLIS
Ohio

One hundred fifty-seven Federal soldiers were buried in a soldiers' lot in Gallipolis's town cemetery. In 1871 Col. Mack reported that a total of $1,232.75 had been spent on the cemetery but the title to the lot had not been conveyed to the United States. It appears the United States never gained title.

The burials were:

	known	unknown
white Union soldiers	76	0
colored Union soldiers	4	77
citizens	1	0
	81	77

Volume 26 of the <u>Roll of Honor</u> lists 156 burials.

HARMON
Ohio

In 1884 the Harmon GAR post requested headstones for eight soldiers buried in the Harmon Cemetery. Two of these stones were for soldiers who died in 1862-1863.

JOHNSON'S ISLAND
Ohio

During the Civil War both sides segregated captured officers from captured enlisted men. This segregation reduced the risk of the officers leading the enlisted men in a prison break. Most Confederate officers were confined in the Johnson's Island Stockade in Lake Erie's Sandusky Bay. At least 206 Confederates died while prisoners on the island.

In September 1889 a group of Georgia newspaper men, fruit growers, and farmers visited Johnson Island. They were appalled at the neglected state of the cemetery. They arranged to have the graves marked with headstones of Georgia marble. These headstones were installed in 1890 after a fund raising drive.

In 1906 the Robert Patton Chapter of the United Daughters of the Confederacy (UDC) of Cincinnati, Ohio, purchased the cemetery. The UDC erected a large bronze statue of Confederate soldier at the cemetery in 1910.

The 1931 Congress authorized the Secretary of War to accept the cemetery. The Robert Patton Chapter of the UDC deeded the cemetery to the United States on June 6, 1932.

Volume 9 and 26 of the Roll of Honor lists a total of 14 burials of Union soldiers on Johnson's Island. However both Col. Mack's 1871 and 1874 reports list only the burials of 206 "rebels" on Johnson Island with eleven Federal soldiers buried in Sandusky's Oakwood Cemetery.

MARION
Ohio

In May 1889, Mr. John W. Thew of Marion wrote the War Department about improving the "burial place of soldiers who fought in the early Indian Wars." Mr. Thew thought the site, just west of Marion, was owned by the Government. Apparently it was not. The letter is marked "received for information," no action was taken.

SPRING GROVE CEMETERY
Cincinnati, Ohio

Volume 9 of the Roll of Honor lists a total of 797 white and six colored soldiers were buried "at Cincinnati." Most of these burials were made in three soldiers' lots in Spring Grove Cemetery. The cemetery was six miles north of the city. The first burial was made in the cemetery in August 1866.

Early records indicate two of the lots were donated to the United States by the State of Ohio. The other was donated by the cemetery association. However in 1871 Col. Mack could not determine if the tittle had been transferred. Records at the cemetery verify transfer of tittle at an unknown date.

Volume 18 of the Roll of Honor lists a total of 655 burials in the cemetery. A separate list gives the names of 54 soldiers who were originally buried at Spring Grove but later removed by friends and relatives. Some time late in the 1860's, 322 (or 339) bodies were moved from Camp Dennison to Spring Grove.

When Col. Mack inspected the cemetery in 1869, he reported a total of 994 burials in 932 graves:

	known	unknown
officers	19	0
white Union soldiers	945	28
colored Union soldiers	2	0
	966	28

Col. Mack reported that the graves were marked by numbered wooden pegs driven into the ground. No information on when these graves were permanently marked with flat headstones has been found. Mack reported a "very handsome marble monument" had been erected near the lot by "patriotic citizens." The statue cost $25,000. By April 30, 1870, the Federal Government had spent a total of $16,345.50 on the cemetery.

Volume 18 of the Roll of Honor (1868) lists the cemetery as Spring Grove National Cemetery. However both Col. Folsom (1868) and Col. Mack (1871) refer to it as a soldiers lot. Volume 26 of the Roll of Honor (1871) lists 1,005 "burials in (the) Soldiers' Lot in Spring Grove Cemetery. This is a corrected list of names.

CAMP C.F.SMITH
Oregon

Private Charles Denny of the 14th U.S. Infantry died at Camp C.F. Smith on January 8, 1867. No record of removal of this body to another cemetery has been found.

CAMP WARNER
Oregon

Two soldiers were buried at Camp Warner according to volume 19 of the Roll of Honor. No record of reinterment of these bodies in a national cemetery has been found.

FORT DALLES
Oregon

Two soldiers were buried at Fort Dalles according to volume 9 of the Roll of Honor (1866). These bodies were moved to Fort Vancouver by 1889.

FORT KLAMATH
Oregon

Fort Klamath's Quartermaster requested headstones for 50 known and eight unknown soldiers buried in the post cemetery. Fifteen of these soldiers died on April 26, 1873. Volume 9 of the Roll of Honor lists three soldiers who died from 1863 to 1865.

In October 1892, 56 bodies were moved from Fort Klamath's post cemetery to San Francisco National Cemetery.

FORT WATSON
Oregon

Volume 9 of the Roll of Honor lists three soldiers who died at Fort Watson in 1866 and 1867. These bodies were later moved to the Fort Vancouver Post Cemetery.

VARIOUS SITES
Pacific Military District

Volume 12 of the Roll of Honor lists fourteen soldiers who died at various sites in the Pacific Miliary District. Two soldiers were buried at Fort Cook. One was buried at Fort Mojare. No place of burial is given for eleven of these burials.

No information on removal of these remains to a national cemetery has been found.

BRISTOL
Pennsylvania

Federal Soldiers were buried in two cemeteries near Bristol, Pennsylvania. At Saint James Episcopal Cemetery there were: "...18 graves all known, on which marble slabs will be erected...." No names were found with this undated report.

Whitehall National Cemetery (AKA China Hall National Cemetery) was established about two and one half miles from Bristol on the Whitehall Landing Road. This small cemetery was used for burying the dead from the general hospital near Whitehall. The one acre plot was purchased in August

1864 from George Rental and wife.

A total of 61 Union Soldiers were buried at Whitehall: 59 known whites, one unknown white, and one known black. Children from the nearby Soldiers' and Sailors' Orphan Asylum were buried here also with the War Department's permission. This was a direct violation of Federal law which limited burials in national cemeteries to soldiers. In December 1891 and January 1892 these bodies were moved to Philadelphia National Cemetery. The cemetery site was later sold.

Volume 12 of the Roll of Honor lists a total of 85 soldiers buried "near Bristol." It appears that this list includes the names of soldiers buried in both cemeteries.

CAMELTON
Pennsylvania

In May 1880 tombstones were requested for 16 unmarked graves at Camelton, Pennsylvania. It is unclear if these soldiers died during or after the war. No record of these burials can be found in the Roll of Honor.

CAMP CADWALADER
Pennsylvania

An undated list in Record Group 92-E576 listed 114 white and two colored soldiers buried at Camp Cadwalader. No other record exists.

CARLISLE
Pennsylvania

The soldier's lot at Carlisle, Pennsylvania, illustrates the problem with researching Civil War Cemeteries. According to Volume 7 of the Roll of Honor, 35 Union Cavalry men were buried at Carlisle. Three were later removed by relatives. These names are on a list in an envelope labeled: "Carlisle, Penn." This envelope is listed in Record Group E92-576 as Ashland Cemetery. However an undated list records: 17 known burials (7 with stones) and 53 unknown at Carlisle Barracks.

A file card dated February 6, 1874, states"...most remains in this lot were removed from the Post Cemetery at Carlisle Barracks and interred in the Ashland Cemetery...." A file card dated March 25, 1878, gives the number of bodies as 313 and states: "I can find no evidence that the lots are owned by the U.S." However these file cards are in an envelope with the note: "deed filed with title papers." A letter in the envelope dated January 31, 1866, appears to be a transmittal letter sent with the deed.

A "brief" (a note written on a file card) dated March 7, 1890, reported that GAR Post #201 of Carlisle wanted the cemetery to bury "old soldiers." This request was refused. This brief states that 41 soldiers were buried at Carlisle Barracks.

The cemetery remains under VA control as a soldier's lot. According to a 1987 "Station Data" sheet Ashland Cemetery has a total of 523 interments but only 24 occupied grave sites. The total area of the lot is listed as .198 acres.

Today the mass grave is marked by a bronze tablet. The inscription reads: "**500 US SOLDIERS OF THE CIVIL WAR ARE HERE IN-TERRED**". Thirty-five names are listed. The inscription ends: "**THE REST ARE KNOWN BUT TO GOD.**"

The United States Army also lists Carlisle Barracks as a post cemetery.

CHAMBERSBURG
Pennsylvania

Forty-three Federal soldiers were buried at Chambersburg during the war according to volume 10 of the Roll of Honor. A list dated April 23, 1866, states that 42 were buried at Cedar Grove Cemetery. Most of these soldiers died in either 1862 or 1864. Very few, if any, of these soldiers were wounded at Gettysburg.

CHESTER
Pennsylvania

Roll of Honor, volume 12, lists 87 known Federal soldiers buried "at Chester." An undated list found in the post cemetery file reported 244 burials of known soldiers in the Rural Cemetery at Chester. This land had been donated to the United States.

Three known soldiers were buried in the Sairrh (?) Michaels Cemetery located 1/4 mile from town.

In 1880 a letter sent to the War Department referred to "digging up the Confederate Lot" in Chester. No other information can be found on the possible Confederate burials at Chester.

DOYLESVILLE
Pennsylvania

According to a list dated 1868, 21 known soldiers were buried at Doylesville. No other information is in the file.

DUCANSVILLE
Pennsylvania

The local GAR chapter requested a headstone to mark the grave of one soldier who died in 1862. The cemetery where the stone was placed was not mentioned.

EASTON
Pennsylvania

A total of 46 Union soldiers were buried in and near Easton, Pennsylvania, according to an undated list. All the soldiers were known but no list of names has been located.
The cemeteries were:

First Presbyterian Cemetery	2 graves
German Reformed Cemetery	4 graves
German Catholic Cemetery	3 graves
Easton Cemetery	27 graves
Arudt's Cemetery	6 graves
Hay's Cemetery	4 graves

ELK CREEK
Pennsylvania

The Elk Creek GAR post requested a headstone for a Union soldier buried in Elk Creek in 1865. The request, dated June 17, 1887, did not list the cemetery.

FORT MIFFLIN
Pennsylvania

William Fisher of the 56th Pennsylvania died at Fort Mifflin on August 28, 1864. No other information on this burial has been found.

GETTYSBURG NATIONAL CEMETERY
Pennsylvania

Gettysburg was, of course, the largest battle of the Civil War. For 3 days General Lee tried to break Meade's army. When he failed, the Confederacy failed. Over 3,100 Union troops were killed and over 5,000 were reported missing.

Because the battlefield was behind Union lines, many civilians came to Gettysburg and removed their relative's bodies. No one knows exactly how many bodies were removed from Gettysburg. Because the civilians were digging up hastily buried soldiers Col. H.C. Alleman issued an order banning disinterment of bodies during August and September. One woman from Massachusetts was reported to have opened 20 graves before she identified her husband by a button on his coat.

Some families made arrangements to have their relatives buried in the Evergreen Cemetery in Gettysburg. Volume 16 of the Roll of Honor lists 66 such burials.

Governor Andrew J. Curtin of Pennsylvania visited the battlefield a week after the battle. He was shocked by thousands of wounded and hundreds of unburied dead. Curtin made arrangements with a local attorney, David Wills, to ship home the bodies of Pennsylvania soldiers killed in the battle. Later McCurtin spear-headed a drive to create a "Soldiers National Cemetery" at Gettysburg. Wills became the local representative of the group.

Wills purchased 17 acres on Cemetery Hill. A local man, E.E. Biesecker, submitted the low bid of $1.59 per body to disinter the bodies, move them to the new cemetery, and reinter the bodies. He started exhuming bodies on October 27, 1863. The ground froze in winter, but by March 19, 1864, the job was completed. The work was overseen by Samuel Weaver. Weaver attempted to identify all the bodies by articles found with the bodies...Bibles, names on clothing, letters,... Weaver reported 3354 reinterments. 158 Massachusetts soldiers had been moved by special arrangement. A total of 3512 bodies were moved to the cemetery. Of these 979 (27.8%) were unknowns. The names of the known dead are recorded in volume 16 of the Roll of Honor.

Samuel Weaver reported that he saw the graves of over 3,000

Confederate soldiers at Gettysburg. Most of these bodies were removed to the south in the 1870's.

The expert on burials at Gettysburg is John W. Busey. In his book, The Last Full Measure, he attempts to identify the graves of partially identified soldiers by using compiled service records. Busey identifies two Confederate soldiers buried in Evergreen Cemetery and lists eight Confederates that may have been buried in Gettysburg National Cemetery as Union soldiers. His book is recommended for anyone trying to locate a Federal soldier who might have died at Gettysburg.

Congress passed a joint resolution on July 14, 1870, agreeing to accept the national cemetery if the commissions and Board of Managers of the cemetery would transfer the title of the cemetery to the U.S. Government. On April 22, 1870, Quartermaster General Meigs informed the Secretary of War that David Willis had transferred the deed for the cemetery to the Federal Government.

Bodies from the battle were discovered long after the war. In 1914 four bodies were discovered and reinterred in the National Cemetery.

BURIALS IN GETTYSBURG NATIONAL CEMETERY (1864)

State	Number
Connecticut	22
Delaware	15
Illinois	6
Indiana	79
Maine	104
Maryland	21
Massachusetts	158
Michigan	166
Minnesota	56
New Hampshire	46
New Jersey	77
New York	860
Ohio	131
Pennsylvania	501
Rhode Island	12
Vermont	61
West Virginia	11
Wisconsin	71
United States Troops	136
Unknown	979
Total	3,512

HARRISBURG
Pennsylvania

Union and Confederate dead from Camp Curtin were buried in a soldier's lot in Harrisburg Cemetery. Col. Mack reported in 1871 that "They (the graves) are said to number 155, but as there are only a few grave-marks, ... it is difficult to determine, on the spot, their exact number and position." Mack concludes: "This lot has not received much attention." An 1881 report states "one hundred fifty to two hundred Union soldiers" are buried here. The lot was in poor condition.

Volume 12 of the Roll of Honor lists 69 burials (67 known) "at Harrisburg." However a list of 155 names of soldiers buried at Harrisburg is in the Quartermaster's Cemetery file in the Archives.

HOLLIDAYSBURG
Pennsylvania

A total of 23 soldiers who died during the Civil War were buried in private lots in Hollidaysburg. No listing of the names exists, however all were known soldiers.

Cemetery	Burials
Girliru	11
Presbyterian	9
Catholic	1
Asbury Chapel	1
Dunkand	1

LACKAWAXAN
Pennsylvania

Lackawaxan's Soldiers' Cemetery contains the remains of 16 Union soldiers and 48 Confederate prisoners of war. The list in the Quartermaster General's files named the Union soldiers, but the data never made it into the Roll of Honor series. Lackawaxan is located in Pike County in far eastern Pennsylvania.

LEBANON
Pennsylvania

Isaac Shay of the 93th Pennsylvania died August 16, 1862, at Lebanon. No more records of this burial exist.

MERCERSBURG
Pennsylvania

Volume 16 lists seven burials of Union Solders at Mercersburg:

Methodist Episcopal Cemetery	4 soldiers
Presbyterian Cemetery	3 Union Soldiers, one unknown "Rebel"

An unknown "Rebel" was buried in a field near Mercersburg.

ORANGEVILLE
Pennsylvania

In 1879 a resident of Orangeville requested a headstone for an unknown Union soldier "buried in our graveyard." The request was not granted due to "meager information." Headstones for unknown soldiers' graves not buried in soldiers' lots were not furnished until 1888.

PHILADELPHIA
Pennsylvania

Soldiers who died in hospitals in Philadelphia were buried in seven different cemeteries. These cemeteries were either donated to or purchased by the government. Burials in Philadelphia were covered in volumes 12 and 16 of the Roll of Honor. However the Roll of Honor does not list burials in individual cemeteries.

Glenwood Cemetery was at the corner of Ridge Ave. and Islington Lane. Two soldiers' lots contained 702 graves of Union soldiers' and nine Confederate prisoners of war.

Odd Fellow's Cemetery was located at Islington Lane and Twenty-fourth Street. 67 Union soldiers were buried in one lot and 196 were buried in another. Fourteen Confederates were also buried there.

United American Mechanics' Cemetery was supposed to have eleven Union soldiers' graves, but when Col. Mack inspected the cemetery in 1871 he could find only six graves.

Woodland Cemetery was located one mile west of the Schuylkill River. One hundred and sixteen Union soldiers were buried there.

Twenty-four Union soldiers were buried in Lafayette Cemetery. The Volunteer Refreshment Association of Philadelphia paid for the lot and burial expenses of the soldiers.

Colored soldiers who had originally been buried in the Glenwood and Odd Fellows' Cemeteries were moved to the Lebanon Cemetery, a "colored cemetery." 329 soldiers were moved to Lebanon, but the graves were marked by numbered stakes. Every sixth grave had a headboard with the names of all six soldiers.

Mount Moriah Cemetery contained three soldiers' lots. 401 Union soldiers and six Confederate prisoners of war were buried in the largest. The "Cooper-Shop Saloon" lot was purchased by the Cooper-Shop Saloon. The lot was fenced by an iron fence, but the individual graves of the 31 soldiers buried there were not marked. 33 ex-soldiers who died at the Volunteer Soldiers' Home were buried in a separate lot.

Because of widening of roads in Philadelphia several cemeteries needed to be moved in 1885. The government advertised for land near the existing cemeteries. On March 4, 1885, the Philadelphia National Cemetery was established. Bodies from Woodland, Odd Fellows, United American Mechanics, Lebanon, and Lafayette Cemeteries were moved to the new cemetery. In 1888 Glenwood Cemetery was moved.

By January 8, 1889, a total of 2,191 burials had been made in Philadelphia National Cemetery:

	known	Unknown
U.S. Officers, soldiers, sailors, and marines	1,975	25
Confederates	0	189
Citizens	2	0
	1,977	214

The bodies in Mount Moriah were never moved to the National Cemetery. Today the Mount Moriah plot is classified a soldiers' lot. The Mount Moriah Naval Cemetery, a soldier's lot in the cemetery, is also under the jurisdiction of the Department of Veteran's Affairs. This cemetery is believed to have "5,000 plus" burials.

236

PITTSBURGH
Pennsylvania

Four cemeteries were established in and near Pittsburgh during the war according to volume 7 of the Roll of Honor.

Seventy-one soldiers were buried in Allegheny Cemetery. One was unknown.

Twenty-four known and eleven unknown soldiers were buried at Braddock's Fields. The majority of these soldiers were "Pennsylvania drafted militia." In 1869 these bodies were removed to the Allegheny Cemetery at a cost of $15.00 per body.

Eight known soldiers were buried at "Stranger's Ground."

Two known soldiers of the 8th U.S. Colored Artillery were buried in the "United States Lot."

Apparently in 1874 bodies from all four cemeteries were moved to the Soldiers Lot in the cemetery at 4734 Butler Street in Pittsburgh. In 1987 the VA listed a total of 308 interments in 303 gravesites in the Allegheny Cemetery Soldiers' Lot.

READING
Pennsylvania

Volume 16 of the Roll of Honor lists ten burials in Reading:

Charles Evans Cemetery	seven soldiers
Aulenbach Cemetery	three soldiers

SCRANTON
Pennsylvania

Six known Union soldiers were buried in Scranton during the Civil War. Their names, however, were not recorded in the Roll of Honor series.

SPRING MILLS
Pennsylvania

C. Morrison of the 19th Pennsylvania Cavalry was buried at Spring Mill on July 31, 1865. No further information on this burial has been found.

TAMAQUA
Pennsylvania

Three "soldiers' cemeteries" at Tamaqua are listed in volume 16 of the Roll of Honor:

Catholic Cemetery	2 graves
Odd Fellows Cemetery	6 graves
German Reformed Lutheran Church	4 graves
Total	12 graves

YORK
Pennsylvania

163 Union soldiers who died at the U.S. Army General Hospital at York are buried in a soldiers lot in York's Prospect Hill's Cemetery. Volume 12 of the Roll of Honor gives 162 names. According to volume 16 of the series, three of the soldiers died of wounds received at Gettysburg. However many of the soldiers buried in Prospect Hills died in 1862.

Four Union soldiers were buried in York's Catholic Cemetery according to volume 12 of the Roll of Honor.

DUTCH ISLAND
Rhode Island

A 1870 report states that between 12 to 15 graves were removed from Dutch Island. However the report fails to state where the bodies were reinterred. In 1867 around 300 bodies were moved from Portsmouth to Cypress Hills National Cemetery. It is possible the bodies from Dutch Island were moved there also.

FORT ADAMS
Rhode Island

Five Union soldiers died at Fort Adams during the war. In 1886 the War Department supplied 31 tombstones for known soldiers buried at Fort Adams. The Roll of Honor does not list these soldiers.

PORTSMOUTH GROVE
Rhode Island

Volume 7 of the Roll of Honor lists 263 known white and 29 colored (3 unknown) Federal soldiers buried at Portsmouth Grove, Rhode Island. In 1868 a total of 312 bodies, "more or less," were moved from Portsmouth Grove to Cypress Hills National Cemetery at a cost of $6.00 per body.

AIKEN
South Carolina

Thirteen soldiers of the 5th US Cavalry died in Aiken, S.C., during 1867. These occupation troops and one soldier's wife were buried "near Aiken."

In May 1882 a "former comrade" requested headstones for these neglected graves. No record of these deaths appear in the Roll of Honor.

ANDERSON
South Carolina

Six members of the First Maine Battery who died in late 1865 while on occupation duty at Anderson are listed in volume 9 of the Roll of Honor. No record of removal of these remains has been located.

BEAUFORT NATIONAL CEMETERY
South Carolina

The first burial in Beaufort National Cemetery was made in 1863, possibly shortly after the United States purchased the twenty-nine acre site from the state of South Carolina at a "tax sale" for $75.00. Exactly why the state of South Carolina owed taxes on the land is unclear, but it appears that this was a subterfuge to avoid purchasing the land. In any event in March 1868, the United States Attorney General ruled the February 10, 1863, deed valid. By that time thousands of Union soldiers had been buried in the cemetery.

Burials in the cemetery came from the Charleston area, Port Royal, Hilton Head Island, the Pocotaligo Bridge Battlefield, and other sites. In

239

1868 around a thousand bodies were moved from the Lawton National Cemetery in Georgia. 748 of these were prisoners who died in the Millen POW Camp in 1864.

Burials in the Beaufort National Cemetery are listed in volume 27 of the Roll of Honor. (Volume 9 is an incomplete list) an unusual feature of the list in volume 27 is that only the burial sites of unknown soldiers are listed. The burial sites of the 5,465 known burials were not listed.

By August 31, 1871, a total of $72,190.50 had been spent on the cemetery. A brick lodge had been built but because of the danger of malaria the superintendent was forced to rent a house elsewhere.

In 1871, Col. Mack reported a total of 9,081 burials:

	known	unknown
commissioned officers	84	0
white soldiers	3,621	3,353
colored soldiers	795	950
sailors	91	109
employees and citizens	78	0
	4,669	4,412

Col. Mack also reported in 1871: "the records at the cemetery were imperfect."

CHARLESTON
South Carolina

Two cemeteries in Charleston held Union dead. Most of the prisoners who died at the "Race-course Prison" were buried near the prison. Volume 14 of the Roll of Honor reports that 251 Union soldiers were buried at the prison. Their graves were marked by numbered stakes. However no burial register was obtained. The volume listed 356 names of soldiers and 33 unknowns who died at the prison. No accounting was made for the 138 "missing" dead. Sometime between 1868 and 1871 the bodies were removed to the Beaufort (S.C.) National Cemetery and buried as unknowns.

The second cemetery in Charleston was started when in May 1865 when the Federal Quartermaster at Charleston took possession of a lot near the chapel of Charleston's Magnolia Cemetery. Apparently the 124 soldiers (one source says 109 soldiers) buried here had died during the Federal occupation of Charleston.

Major Mack's report (1871) reported: "The lot was in very poor condition, overgrown with weeds, and generally neglected." Mack continued: The headboards were very shabby, and contrasted badly with the white marble slabs marking the graves of the Confederate (sic) by a handsome hedge..." Mack concluded: "The remains of these Union soldiers should be transferred to a national cemetery, or else the lot in this cemetery should be kept in respectable order."

The Federal government never had purchased the land. The cemetery corporation wanted the Union troops bodies moved. In 1867, they offered to donate a lot to bury the soldiers in if the U.S. Government would move the bodies from the near chapel. Apparently the unkept Federal plot detracted from the beauty of the cemetery. The mater came to a head in 1872. The only surviving record about the cemetery is a letter written to Secretary of War W.W. Belknap on May 14, 1872. In this letter Quartermaster Meigs delineates his views on the burial of Union troops.

Meigs summarized the current state of affairs. He stated the plot "was taken possession of by the U.S., on the order of Brig. General John F. Hatch." The officers of the cemetery corporation claimed that when the cemetery was dedicated in 1850 that this spot "...was reserved as an appendage and belonging to the chapel and declared to be forever exempted from sale or interment." In June 1867 the cemetery president proposed to donate the U.S. Government a lot for the reinterment of the remains. This was reported to Meigs in May 1869. Meigs' letter reports that: "Considering the matter in the light of a local hostile sentiment against the loyal Union dead I gave the following instructions on June 5, 1869:

"I am of opinion that the soldiers buried during the war by military authority should not be kicked out as a consequence of the local sentiment. We have no right now to use a private cemetery as a post cemetery in time of peace against the wished of the 'owners', & c (sic)." Apparently Meigs believed the war was still raging in May 1865.

On another report of this case he said he wrote: "I am against spending money, on moving about the dead, where it is not absolutely necessary in order to collect the victims of the war into national cemeteries... These (bodies) seem to have been buried by proper authority and in a cemetery. Why not, if the owners of the ground are dissatisfied, leave to them the task of desecrating the graves. Do the dead bodies of our soldiers offend them?"

Meigs reported that the cost of removing the graves to the nearest national cemetery was $800. He then continued: "I do not incline to indulge the wish of the Cemetery Corporation, and do not like the looks (sic) of the thing." He continued: "These men were buried in a city which had been in revolt, and had been invested ... (the bodies) should stay there, and that this occupation is sacred." He ends by stating: "...but its occupation (the land) cost the U.S. millions of money and much blood."

Mr. Belknap's reply was that the government had not title to the land and "without any reference to the local hostile sentiment alluded to within..." the graves would be to the Florence National Cemetery "at the proper season of the year."

CHESTER
South Carolina

Charles F. Emerson of Pittson, Maine, died while on occupation duty at Chester. Emerson, 19, was a member of the 15th Maine Veteran Volunteers. He is buried along with 56 unknown Confederates in Chester's Evergreen Cemetery. Emerson died on March 14, 1866. It is unclear who purchased and erected his headstone, but it refers to Emerson as a "comrade."

COLUMBIA
South Carolina

Thirty-three Union soldiers died while Prisoners of War at Columbia according to volume 14 of the Roll of Honor. The exact burial site of the soldiers is unknown. However 14 union occupation troops died at Columbia between 1868 and 1870. They were moved to Florence National Cemetery in 1887. It is logical to assume the other soldiers were also moved to Florence.

FLORENCE NATIONAL CEMETERY
South Carolina

The Florence prison pen was constructed in 1864 about one and a half miles from the railroad station. The pen covered about 15 miles with a stream running through the middle of the pen. About one-third of the prison was too swampy to use, but at least the stream supplied "clear, cold" water.

According to Col. Mack's report (1871): "The Union prisoners of war confined at Florence were treated with decency and humanity, in striking contrast to the shameful barbarities practiced at Andersonville and Salisbury, and consequently the ratio of deaths is very small compared with the mortality at those places." Still 2,793 Union soldiers died at Florence, or about 15.5% of the 18,000 who were confined there. Andersonville's death rate was about 28.7%. Salisbury's was about 24%.

The cemetery register was missing, still volume 14 of the Roll of Honor listed 296 names of soldiers buried at Florence. Some of these names were also listed in the Salisbury National Cemetery burial list also. No source of this list is given. Volume 19 of the Roll of Honor lists 29 burials made in 1865 and 1866. Col. Mack's report (1871) listed 30 known and 2,773 unknown burials. The expenditures had reached $10,858.43 by August 31, 1871.

Both Col. Moore and Col. Mack stated that a reward had been offered for the burial records, but they were never recovered. They were not destroyed by Rebel authorities in a cover up attempt, but taken by a Union soldier! On August 11, 1885, the Washington, D.C., Evening Star published a letter from John G. Lemmon who had served as a private in Company E of the 4th Michigan Cavalry. Lemmon had been transferred from Andersonville in September 1864. He reported: "We found ourselves better circumstanced (than at Andersonville) as long as the wood inside the pen lasted and until we became over crowded.." Lemmon became ill in January. After he recovered he became a nurse and finally Chief Steward of the hospital under the direction " of the skillful, kind-hearted but often tipsy, rebel surgeon." As Chief Steward Lemmon kept the record of deaths.

As Federal troops nearer Florence the Confederate guards fled. The prisoners were transported by wagons to the Florence depot where they were loaded into box cars for the trip to Wilmington, N.C. Lemmon stated the book was too large to conceal from the "intensely bitter secessionists" in Florence. He removed the pages from the book and hid them in his trousers' pocket. While en route to Wilmington he tended the sick.

Although fed at Wilmington by ladies from the Sanitary Commission, the prisoners were unable to bathe or exchange their lice infested clothing until they arrived in Annapolis a week later. While undressing to bathe Lemmon realized he had lost the pages of the register.

Buried in grave # 2450 is Florena Budwin, a woman. According to local folklore Budwin was married to an Union officer. She enlisted as a man to be with him. He was killed and she was captured and sent to Florence. When she became ill the camp physician discovered she was a woman. After she recovered she nursed the sick. However she again became ill and died on January 25, 1865. She was buried in a separate grave instead of a trench. The Roll of Honor lists her burial as "Florence Baduine." A special report made in August 1889 also mentions the "grave of the woman prisoner."

HILTON HEAD
South Carolina

Volume 9 of the Roll of Honor lists 912 white and 92 colored soldiers who were buried on Hilton Head Island. Volume 14 of the series lists the names of nine "prisoners of war" who died at Hilton Head. However one of these POW's died in May 1865 AFTER the war had ended. After the war these bodies were moved to Beaufort National Cemetery.

ORANGEBURG
South Carolina

Orangeburg was the site of a skirmish in 1865 at the Edisto River. Sherman's troops burned the courthouse when they passed through. Volume 9 of the Roll of Honor (1866) lists eight soldiers who died while on occupation duty in Orangeburg. Five were members of the 54th New York Infantry and three were members of the 102nd U.S. Colored Troops.

In 1879 a local businessman requested that the twenty or so scattered graves of Union soldiers be marked. An inspector was dispatched to Orangeburg to report on condition of the graves. He visited with long-time residents and identified six graves. These bodies were then moved to Florence National Cemetery.

SUMTER
South Carolina

Volume 9 of the Roll of Honor lists eight soldiers who died at Sumter. Six of these soldiers were members of the 30th Massachusetts who died while on occupation duty. No record of removal of these bodies to a national cemetery has been found.

YORKVILLE
South Carolina

Nine troopers of the 7th Cavalry died while on occupation duty at Yorkville. One body was sent home, but the others were buried in Rose Hill Cemetery. In 1879 Thomas Vance, a discharged Union soldiers, wrote the Secretary of War reporting that "the graves are in a very bad condition." He had built a fence, but it was "broken up" with the gate off by the hinges. Mr. Vance requested that the bodies be moved to Florence National Cemetery. He reported that the cemetery was being used as a children's playground.

Major J.M. Belcher of the Charleston Quartermaster's Depot was dispatched to investigate. Major Belcher found no indication that children were using the cemetery as a playground. However two or three children were buried there. Belcher also requested that a new fence be built to enclose the graves and the graves of "a woman and child" (relatives of the soldiers?) buried there. The Yorkville Enquirer reported the investigation with the comment: "There is not a South Carolinian in this entire community who would be guilty of the act of desecrating the grave of a United States soldier; and in our cemetery, the graves of those soldiers have received the same floral tributes as were bestowed upon those who fell in the Confederate Service."

Later these bodies were marked by headstones, however the grave of the woman and child were not marked.

The author's Great-Great-Grandfather, Andrew Jackson Hughes, who served in the Cleveland Guards (12th NC Infantry CSA) is also buried in the same cemetery.

Captain George D. Wallace, 7th US Cavalry, who was killed in the Battle of Wounded Knee, South Dakota, on December 29, 1890, is also buried in the Rosehill Cemetery.

BEAR STATION
Tennessee

One federal soldier died while a prisoner of war at Bear Station according to volume 14 of the Roll of Honor. No record of removal of this body to a national cemetery has been found.

CHATTANOOGA NATIONAL CEMETERY
Tennessee

Chattanooga became a Union supply base on September 9, 1863, when Major General William S. Rosecrans took the town of about 3,000 without losing a man. However Rosecrans's army was badly mauled at the battle of Chickamauga on September 19 and 20. Rosecrans then fell back to Chattanooga where his army was besieged by General Braxton Bragg.

Bragg's army was driven from Lookout Mountain on November 24, 1863. The next day Bragg's troops were driven from Missionary Ridge. The door to Atlanta was open.

The dead from these battles, Northern Georgia, Northern Alabama, and Southeastern Tennessee were buried in the Chattanooga National Cemetery. Volumes 11, 14, and 23 of the Roll of Honor list a total of 12,863 interments. 7,936 of them were known.

Chaplain Thomas Van Horne writing in 1866 reported a total of 8,512 interments. A total of 1,952 bodies were removed from Chickamauga. Of these only 154 were identified. The cemetery consisted of seventy-five acres. However Van Horne estimated that about one-third of the cemetery was unusable for burials due to rock out-croppings. Van Horn reported that he used soldiers who were detailed to assist him instead of contracting the job of reinterment. This saved the taxpayer "a large sum." A coffin cost the government $4.00 while a "rough box" cost only $2.00 according to Colonel C.W. Folsom's report (1868).

According to Robert Paul Jordan (The Civil War), General George "Pap" Thomas was asked if the dead in the cemetery should be buried by states. Thomas, who was born in Southampton County, Virginia, replied: "No, mix 'em up, mix 'em up. I'm tired of state's rights."

In 1866 seven soldiers from the "Mitchell Raiding Party" were moved from Atlanta to Chattanooga. These men had stolen a train at Big Shanty, Georgia, on April 12, 1862. They were captured and seven were hung at Atlanta. Most historians refer to this as the J.J. Andrews Raid or the "great locomotive chase." The raider's graves are marked with a monument in the shape of a locomotive.

One surprising burial is that of Corporal Louis C. Stockton of Company E of the 68th Indiana Infantry. He died August 14, 1864, at Andersonville, Georgia. Nothing in the records explain why he was moved to Chattanooga. Considering the War Department's frugality, it is surprising his body was moved.

ELLIOTT'S HOSPITAL
Tennessee

One federal soldier died while a prisoner of war at Elliott's Hospital according to volume 14 of the Roll of Honor. No record of removal of this body to a national cemetery has been found.

FORT DONELSON NATIONAL CEMETERY
Tennessee

Fort Donelson was a massive earthen fort on the Cumberland River in Northern Tennessee. In early February 1862 Union ironclads had pounded Fort Henry on the Tennessee River into submission. However the ironclads were beaten off when they attempted to run Fort Donelson on February 14, 1862. The Union army under an obscure brigadier general began to encircle the Confederate lines. The Confederates almost broke through the Federal lines on February 15, but indecision of the Confederate ruined the chance to break out. Several thousand Confederates escaped including cavalry commander Col. Nathan Bedford Forest.

The next morning General Simon Buckner asked the Union Commander for terms. He replied: "no terms except an unconditional and immediate surrender can be accepted." The Union had won a major victory--and more importantly it had a new hero--"unconditional surrender" Grant.

The site for the Fort Donelson National Cemetery was selected by Chaplain W.B. Earnshaw, Major A.W. Wills, and Captain G.W. Marshall. The last two officers were members of the Quartermaster Corps. The fifteen acres of land was purchased for $474.00. The committee had selected a site a redoubt of Fort Donelson. General L. Thomas reported that the redoubt would have been "an interesting feature" but an "inexperienced officer" leveled the redoubt "at great expense." Stone walls had to be built to keep the ground from washing.

At one time the plan was to move bodies to the cemetery from the banks of the Cumberland from Smithland to Clarksville. In fact volume 23 of the Roll of Honor refers to the cemetery as the Cumberland River National Cemetery. This plan was abandoned and few bodies were moved to the cemetery from other sites. Col. Mack reported that bodies were moved to the cemetery from Clarksville, but this seems to be incorrect.

By 1871 a total of 670 burials had been made in the cemetery:

	known	unknown
white soldiers	153	503
colored soldiers	4	8
employees	1	18
	158	512

GREENVILLE
Tennessee

One federal soldier died while a prisoner of war at Greenville according to volume 14 of the Roll of Honor. This body was moved to Knoxville National Cemetery after the war.

KNOXVILLE NATIONAL CEMETERY
Tennessee

Knoxville was controlled by the Confederates until General Burnside captured it in mid-1863. General Longstreet besieged the city in late 1863, but he failed to retake the city.

Knoxville National Cemetery was located about three-fourths of a mile west of Knoxville in 1869. The plot covered about 10 acres. The land was appropriated from John Dameron. The United States received title for the land on June 5, 1867. Captain W.A. Wainwright had charge of the cemetery during its construction. In May 1866 he reported that headboards cost 75 cents each.

Volume 11 of the Roll of Honor (1869) listed a total of 1,256 bodies moved to the cemetery from parts of Kentucky, Tennessee, and Virginia. Only 413 (32.9%) of these interments were known. Volume 14 of the Roll of Honor lists 17 Union soldiers who died as prisoners of war in Knoxville. The Tennessee Historical Commission reports that about 50 Union POW's were buried in the Confederate Cemetery on Bethel Avenue. Over 1,600 Confederates were buried there. Volume 23 of the series adds 1,253 names of soldiers whose bodies were moved to the cemetery after the war.

Col. Mack reported that the lodge was in poor condition in 1871. It was replaced by a stone lodge in 1873. The 1873 lodge cost $4,450.00. Col. Mack also reported total expenditures for the cemetery of $18,310.28. He also reported that local farmers who agreed to move about fifty bodies to the cemetery for $3.00 a body in 1867, were still trying to collect their money in 1871.

By 1871 a total of 3153 burials had been made:

	known	unknown
commissioned officers	25	0
white Union soldiers	1,965	1,007
colored Union soldiers	73	68
employees	15	0
	2,078	1,075

MARYSVILLE
Tennessee

On April 2, 1879, W.H. Kirk, Marysville's postmaster, wrote the War Department advising them that at least two Union soldiers were buried in Marysville. Mr. Kirk thought the bodies should be moved to a national cemetery. Other bodies from Marysville had been moved to the Chattanooga National Cemetery. Mr. Kirk's request was marked: "Information ... no action required."

MEMPHIS NATIONAL CEMETERY
Tennessee

Memphis National Cemetery was located on the Memphis and Ohio Railroad at its intersection with the Memphis and Raleigh Plank Road. In 1869 the cemetery was located 6 miles from the city of Memphis. A board of three officers, Chaplain William Earnshaw, Lt. Col. A. W. Wills, and Major G.W. Marshall, chose the 38 acre site which was purchased from William Sider and others. Wills and Marshall were quartermasters not engineers and the site selected was flat. Over 29,000 feet of drains were required to drain off standing water. The main drain was over 1,700 feet long, five feet wide, and five feet deep. The drain system added to the expense of the cemetery. By the end of August 1871 a total of $204,449.41 had been spent on the cemetery.

Interments in the cemetery were made by states. The Navy and regular army were buried in separate sections. Volume 21 of the <u>Roll of Honor</u> calls the cemetery the Mississippi River National Cemetery because most of the bodies moved to the cemetery came from sites along the Mississippi. These sites ranged from Hickman, Kentucky, to Helena, Arkansas. By 1869 a total of 13,962 burials had been made. 5,148 (36.9%) were known. Of the 4,208 U.S. Colored Troops, only 250 (5.9%) were known.

BURIALS IN MEMPHIS NATIONAL CEMETERY - 1869

U.S. Army	108	4
Alabama	50	0
Arkansas	43	0
Connecticut	10	0
Delaware	1	1
Illinois	1,101	7
Indiana	557	2
Iowa	740	22
Kansas	54	2
Kentucky	29	0
Louisiana	4	0
Maine	16	0
Massachusetts	17	0
Michigan	57	1
Minnesota	165	0
Mississippi	46	0
Missouri	438	9
U.S. Navy	186	0
Nebraska	8	0
New Hampshire	30	0
New Jersey	48	8
New York	55	0
Ohio	322	1
Pennsylvania	28	2
Rhode Island	3	0
Tennessee	144	11
Texas	1	0
Vermont	2	0
West Virginia	8	0
Wisconsin	413	6
U.S. Colored Troops	250	3,958
Mississippi River Marine Brigade	10	0
Employees	45	8
Miscellaneous	159	0
Unknown	0	4,773
	5,148	8,814

NASHVILLE NATIONAL CEMETERY
Tennessee

Nashville fell to Federal forces in early 1862. Until the end of the war it served as a major Federal supply depot. Many hospitals operated in and around the city. In early December 1864, General John Bell Hood (CSA) besieged Nashville. In a two day battle (December 15 and 16), General "Pap" Thomas' Federal troops broke the siege and almost crushed Hood's command.

After the war the Federal Government purchased almost 64 acres of land near Madison Station for $9,658.65. The cemetery was located some six miles north of Nashville. Bodies were moved to the cemetery from 251 different sites ranging from Carthage to the east to Johnsonville to the west. Some 700 bodies were supposed to have been moved to the cemetery from the Franklin Battlefield. The Tompkinsville, Kentucky, National Cemetery was closed some time before 1871. All the bodies were exhumed and moved to Nashville.

However most of the soldiers buried in the cemetery had died in hospitals in Nashville. After the war these remains were removed to the cemetery. Volume 22 of the Roll of Honor lists 16,486 burials. 12,487 of these burials were of known soldiers. Volume 22 also contains a list of 4,472 "Union soldiers who died or were killed at Nashville, Tennessee, and different points in the vicinity, who have either been interred as unknowns in the Nashville, Tennessee, National Cemetery, or removed to their homes by their friends."

Col. Mack's 1874 report listed 16,538 burials:

	known	unknown	total
white Union soldiers	10,388	3,508	13,896
colored Union soldiers	1,447	463	1,910
Total soldiers	11,835	3,971	15,806
employees	703	29	732
	12,538	4,000	16,538

Col. Mack reported a total expenditure of $103,540.81 up to June 30, 1874. He estimated a total expenditure of $2,000 for the 1875-6 fiscal year, including $200.00 for trees and plants.

POST OAK SPRINGS
Tennessee

In November 1870, the Quartermaster General was informed of two or three bodies of Union soldiers buried at Post Oak Springs. The existing records do not indicate if these bodies were removed to a National Cemetery.

SHILOH NATIONAL CEMETERY
Tennessee

The Battle of Shiloh was really two battles in one. On Sunday, April 6, 1862, Confederates under General Albert Sidney Johnson surprised the Federals and almost pushed them into the Tennessee River. Almost-but a stubborn defense by Brig. Gen. Benjamin Prentiss's troops in the Hornet's nest, Johnson's death, and fire from Union gunboats held the shocked Union Army together. The next day Major General Don Buell's troops helped Grant drive the Confederates, now under the command of General P.G.T. Beauregard, from the field. Dead Union troops were hastily buried on the field near where they fell. The Confederates were buried in five burial trenches. The largest holds over 700 bodies.

Shiloh National Cemetery contained ten acres of "uneven land" in 1874. It had been purchased for $500.00. Because of the remoteness of the cemetery few bodies were moved to it after the war. Instead most bodies from Southwestern Tennessee were moved to the Corinth National Cemetery. The east side of the cemetery was on a bluff overlooking the river but the bluff had been washing away before Mr. Gall, the civil engineer who rebuilt the Vicksburg National Cemetery, reshaped it. The improvements were expensive, by June 30, 1874, a total of $115,175.85 had been spent on the cemetery.

Volume 20 of the Roll of Honor lists a total of 3,584 burials in the cemetery. There were twenty-nine "regimental group burials." These bodies had been buried on the battlefield "by their comrades, and great care has been taken to preserve the original arrangement."

In 1871 Col. Mack noted a total of 3,586 burials in the cemetery:

	known	unknown
white soldiers	1,227	2,358
colored soldiers	0	1
	1,227	2,359

One of these burials was that of Peter Jecko, Superintendent of the National Cemetery, who died August 18, 1870.

STONE'S RIVER NATIONAL CEMETERY
Tennessee

Late in December 1862, Major General Rosecrans's 47,000 man Army of the Cumberland left Nashville marching toward Chattanooga. General Braxton Bragg's army (38,000 men) blocked the road at Murfreesboro. The two armies collided on December 31, 1862. Bragg's army almost drove Rosecran's army from the field, but B.G. Philip Sheridan's stubborn defense blunted the Confederate attack. On January 2nd, Bragg again tried to drive Rosecrans from the field, but failed.

Major General George Thomas established Stone's River National Cemetery on March 29, 1864. The cemetery was designed by Captain John A. Means, 115th Regiment Ohio Volunteer Infantry. The original work of constructing the cemetery was done by soldiers. After most of the local garrison was mustered out, Thomas dispatched Chaplin William Earnshaw to finish the cemetery. Earnshaw was ordered to Stone's River in June 1865, but he could not resume disinterring bodies until October 1st because of the danger of disease. Earnshaw's party traveled up to 85 miles from the cemetery collecting bodies.

Volume 11 of the Roll of Honor lists of 4,646 burials (70% known) in the cemetery. Volume 23 of the Roll of Honor (1869) lists an additional 1,359 bodies moved to the cemetery from Rose Hill Cemetery at Columbia, Tennessee, and few scattered locations. Most of the dead at Columbia came from the Spring Hill and Franklin Battlefields.

The land for the cemetery was purchased from James M. Tompkins and Benjamin Lillard. By the time Col. Mack inspected the cemetery in 1871, the cemetery covered about 20 acres. The cemetery was enclosed by a wooden picket fence on three sides, with a new stone wall on the west. $19,426.67 had been spent on the cemetery by August 31, 1871.

56 men of Hazen's Brigade who died at Stone's River were buried in a separate cemetery some 300 yards south of the main cemetery. A "handsome stone monument dedicated to their memory and noble deeds" was erected in the center of the lot.

The older name of the cemetery and battle is Stone's River. Today the National Park Service uses the name, Stones River National Cemetery.

Burials in Stone's River National Cemetery-1869

	Known	Unknown	Total
United States Army	107	58	165
Connecticut	4	0	4
Illinois	729	36	765
Indiana	719	64	783
Iowa	14	0	14
Kansas	4	0	4
Kentucky	213	17	230
Maine	1	0	1
Massachusetts	1	0	1
Michigan	233	13	246
Minnesota	25	0	25
Missouri	63	0	63
New York	40	0	40
New Jersey	3	0	3
Ohio	867	46	913
Pennsylvania	117	11	128
Tennessee	248	9	257
Wisconsin	124	4	128
United States Colored Troops	86	100	186
Pioneer Corps	12	0	12
Employees	0	5	5
Miscellaneous	207	1,944	2,151
	3,817	2,307	6,124

SUMMERTOWN
Tennessee

On January 4, 1888, Mrs. Ellie Hyde of Summertown requested permission to move the bodies of three Union soldiers buried "near Summertown" to the cemetery at Summertown. Mrs. Hyde proposed to fence and care for the graves herself. The Quartermaster's department had "no objections... if no expense to the government." The Quartermaster's department also mailed a headstone application.

AUSTIN
Texas

Five members of the 1st Iowa Cavalry and the 6th U.S. Cavalry died while on occupation duty in Austin according to volume 9 of the Roll of Honor. After the war these bodies were moved to the San Antonio National Cemetery.

BRAZOS SANTIAGO
Texas

Volume 6 of the Roll of Honor lists 54 white and 191 colored soldiers buried at Brazos Santiago. These bodies were moved to the Brownsville National Cemetery after the war.

BROWNSVILLE NATIONAL CEMETERY
Texas

The Brownsville National Cemetery was on a small island near Fort Brown. The 25 1/2 acre island was purchased from the U.S. District Court for $5,000. The cemetery was reached by a ferry from the fort.

Bodies were moved to this cemetery from Galveston, Indianola, Lavaca, Victoria, Ringgold Barracks, and other locations in southern Texas. The first burials in the cemetery were made in February 1868. Volumes 6 and 18 of the Roll of Honor list a total of 1639 burials in the cemetery.

By 1875 a total of 2,942 burials had been made in the cemetery:

	known	unknown
white soldiers and sailors	540	245
colored soldiers	973	1,165
citizens	19	0
	1,532	1410

Because of the large number of colored troops stationed at Fort Brown, there was friction between the local citizens and the soldiers. In 1906 several negro soldiers stationed at Fort Brown were accused of killing a local bar keeper. When the soldiers involved in the "Brownsville Affair" could not be identified, President Theodore ordered that 167 black soldiers, including six Congressional Medal of Honor winners, be given dishonorable discharges. It appears that vandalism in the cemetery might had been a problem.

Fort Brown closed in 1911. The Quartermaster advised the quartermaster at Brownsville to advertise for bids on moving 3,007 bodies from the cemetery to the Alexandria (Louisiana) National Cemetery on May 19, 1911. This was the only time that a national cemetery was moved just because a fort closed. The post quartermaster was advised not to use the name "Brownsville National Cemetery" in advertising for bids or in discussing the project. Whatever the reason the army had for moving the cemetery, they did not want any publicity.

1,443 known bodies were moved in 26" x 10" x 10" boxes. 22 "recent burials" were moved in 72" x 16" x 16" boxes. A total of 1,537 unknown remains were moved in 51-84" x 24" x 18" boxes. (About 30 bodies per box). These unknowns were buried three boxes deep. A total of 3,007 bodies were moved.

CAMP EAGLE PASS
Texas

In 1890 the post quartermaster requested 32 headstones for known Union soldiers who died at Camp Eagle Pass from 1868 to 1878. Camp Eagle Pass remained an active U.S. Army Post until 1916 under the name Fort Duncan.

In April 1900, 73 bodies were moved to the San Antonio National Cemetery from Camp Eagle Pass.

CAMP FORD
Texas

Volume 6 of the Roll of Honor lists 232 Union soldiers who died at Camp Ford just outside Tyler, Texas. Camp Ford was the largest Confederate POW camp west of the Mississippi. Volume 12 of the Roll of Honor lists an additional 54 names of Union soldiers who died at Camp Ford. That brought the number of burials to 286.

These bodies were eventually moved to Alexandria (Louisiana) National Cemetery.

CAMP VERDE
Texas

Three POW's who died at Camp Verde are listed in volume 14 of the Roll of Honor. These bodies were moved to the San Antonio National cemetery after the war.

CHAPPELL HILL
Texas

The superintendent of the Brownsville National Cemetery asked permission to move bodies from Chappell Hill, Texas, in 1869. The Quartermaster General's office replied that an earlier report (not found) stated that no bodies were found at Chappell Hill.

The superintendent wrote back in late September that 20 Union soldiers were buried at Chappell Hill. On October 13, 1869, Quartermaster Meigs ruled: "Let the bodies be not disturbed; but be allowed to remain where they now lie." The quartermaster went on to say that it was "over five hundred miles to Brownsville." Apparently the cost of removing these remains was too great.

No other information exists on these graves. Chappell Hill is located in Washington County about 350 airline miles from Brownsville.

CORPUS CHRISTI
Texas

Thirty-five U.S. colored troops, one member of the Drum Corps, and one citizen died at Corpus Christi in 1865. Volume 6 of the Roll of Honor lists their names. Nothing else can be found in the records.

EDINBURGH
Texas

Volume 6 of the Roll of Honor lists 31 members of the U.S. colored troops buried at Edinburgh. A separate list gives the names of 18 colored soldiers whose exact burial site was unknown, but was supposed to be in or near Edinburgh.

These bodies were moved to the Brownsville National Cemetery after the war.

257

FORT BLISS NATIONAL CEMETERY
Texas

Nineteen soldiers who died at Fort Bliss from 1862 to 1866 are listed in Volume 18 of the Roll of Honor. According to an undated list found in the Archives about 10 unknowns were also buried at Fort Bliss from 1863 to 1866. The majority of the soldiers buried at Fort Bliss were from the 5th U.S. Infantry, the 1st California Volunteers, and the 5th California Volunteers. Fort Bliss's original post cemetery was moved in 1894 to another site in the post. The land it was on is now the site of a public library. In 1939 the post cemetery was designated Fort Bliss National Cemetery. Memorial markers for Cpl. Frank Bratling , 8th U.S. Cavalry and Private George Hooker , 5th U.S. Cavalry , are located in Fort Bliss National Cemetery. Both soldiers were awarded the Medal of Honor posthumously for their actions in battles with the Indians.

FORT CLARK
Texas

In 1886 the Post Quartermaster requested 47 head rocks for soldiers who died at Fort Clark. The first burial in the post cemetery was made in 1879. These bodies were moved to the San Antonio National Cemetery before 1909.

FORT DAVIS
Texas

At least 86 soldiers died at Fort Davis, Texas, from 1867 to 1886. They were buried in the post cemetery. After the fort was abandoned in 1891 it fell into disrepair. The National Park Service began restoring Fort Davis in 1961. Today it operates as Fort Davis National Historic Site.

83 bodies were removed from Fort Davis to the San Antonio National Cemetery before 1909.

FORT ELLIOTT
Texas

On September 14, 1886, the post quartermaster requested 19 headstones for burials in the post cemetery. Thirteen were for soldiers. Six stones were for citizens. These bodies were moved to San Antonio National Cemetery before 1909.

FORT McINTOSH
Texas

The only information in the Quartermaster's files on Fort McIntosh is a report made by the post quartermaster in 1886. The report stated that there were no unmarked graves in the post cemetery.

FORT RINGGOLD
Texas

Volume 6 of the Roll of Honor lists fifty United States Colored Troops who died at Fort Ringgold in late 1865. It appears that sometime before 1874 these bodies were moved from Fort Ringgold to the Brownsville National Cemetery. In 1911 a total of 146 bodies (16 unknown) where moved from the Ringgold Barracks Post Cemetery to Alexandria (Louisiana) National Cemetery.

GALVESTON NATIONAL CEMETERY
Texas

Volume 6 of the Roll of Honor lists 44 white and 9 colored troops buried "at Galveston." Volume 18 lists 383 burials (38 unknown). Although Col. C.W. Folsom's report (1868) lists these burials, Col. Mack's report (1871) does not.

An envelope in the Galveston file in the Archives reads simply: "Union soldiers removed to:." No other information exists in the file, but it appears that these bodies were moved to the Brownsville (Texas) National Cemetery sometime before 1874.

GREEN LAKE
Texas

Volume 6 of the Roll of Honor lists eleven burials at Green Lake. No record of removal of these graves to a national cemetery has been found.

HEMPSTEAD
Texas

A report dated July 12, 1867, listed "between 600 and (sic) 800" burials at Hempstead. The local cemetery corporation had donated five acres for a soldiers lot. According to the report one hundred of these soldiers were known, but no list of names is in the file.

Volume 6 of the Roll of Honor lists four soldiers from the 12th Illinois Cavalry who died on September 17, 1865, "near Hempstead." No other information on these burials can be found. Col. Mack's report (1871) does not list these burials.

HOUSTON
Texas

Volume 6 of the Roll of Honor lists the names of five soldiers from the 12th Illinois Cavalry who were interred at Houston in late 1865. A total of 35 bodies were moved from Houston to Galveston National Cemetery some time around 1868.

INDIANOLA
Texas

Volume 6 of the Roll of Honor lists three separate cemeteries at Indianola with a total of 110 burials. J.L. Pickard, the surgeon of the 115th U.S.C.T., was buried in the public cemetery. All the other dead were U.S. colored troops.

After the war these bodies were moved to the Brownsville National Cemetery. On September 17, 1875, a hurricane destroyed 3/4's of Indianola. Over 900 perished in the storm. The town rebuilt, however in 1886 an even more severe storm literally washed Indianola in to the sea. Today nothing remains except a historic marker and a statue of La Salle, the French explorer who landed near Indianola.

JASPER
Texas

Private Victor Arnault of the 12th Illinois Cavalry was buried at Jasper on August 16, 1865. No record of removing Arnault's body to a National Cemetery has been found.

LAVACA
Texas

Volume 6 of the Roll of Honor lists ten burials in the Lavaca Cemetery. These bodies were moved to the Galveston National Cemetery after the war.

MATAGORDA
Texas

Volume 6 of the Roll of Honor lists five US Colored Troops buried at Matagorda. No record of removal of these graves to a national cemetery has been found.

ROMA
Texas

Volume 6 of the Roll of Honor lists eleven members of the 116th US Colored Troops buried at Roma. No record of removal of these graves to a national cemetery has been found.

SAN ANTONIO NATIONAL CEMETERY
Texas

San Antonio National Cemetery was founded in December 1867, when bodies were moved to the cemetery from San Antonio's City Cemetery. Volume 6 of the Roll of Honor listed those burials.

Bodies were moved to the cemetery from Austin, Indianola, and "other places in the state." The cemetery was located on a hill about one mile east of San Antonio's plaza. The two acre lot was a limestone bed with little soil. The graves were dug in the limestone. Limestone blocks were used to mark the graves. This is the first National Cemetery to use a "permanent" grave marker. The blocks cost $3.95 each, which was cheaper than a wooden headboard in the arid Southwest.

Volume 18 of the Roll of Honor (1868) lists 193 burials in the cemetery. When Col. Mack inspected the cemetery in 1871, he reported 197 known and 85 unknown burials,. As the western posts closed, the bodies from these posts were moved to San Antonio National Cemetery. 83 bodies were moved from Fort Davis at an unspecified date. In February 184, 113 bodies were moved to the cemetery from Fort Concho, Texas.

A 1875 special report listed the interments:

	known	unknown	total
officers	19	1	20
white soldiers	191	166	357
colored soldiers	14	4	18
civilians	37	9	46
	261	180	441

VICTORIA
Texas

Volume 6 of the Roll of Honor lists 84 burials of Federal soldiers at Victoria. These bodies were moved to the Brownsville National Cemetery after the war.

CAMP CAMERON
Utah

Volume 12 of the Roll of Honor lists three soldiers who died at Camp Cameron. No information on removal of these remains to a national cemetery has been found.

CAMP DOUGLAS
Utah

Camp Douglas was founded on October 26, 1862. Its function was to protect overland mail routes from hostile Indians. President Lincoln suggested the camp be named for the late Senator Stephen A. Douglas. Douglas had lost the 1860 Presidential election to Lincoln.

Camp Douglas's post cemetery contained the remains of 63 known soldiers when volume 19 of the Roll of Honor was published in 1868. 15 of these were killed in the "Bear River Indian Fight" on January 29, 1863. The survivors of this battle erected a 25 foot high monument to the memory of their fallen comrades. Governor Dotoy's grave was marked by a "fire redstone monument, 11 feet high." A separate cemetery for soldier's families was beside the cemetery. Volume 13 of the Roll of Honor had listed 59 burials at Camp Douglas. No record of removals from Camp Douglas had been found. In 1970 the post cemetery at Camp Douglas was placed on the National Register of Historic Places.

BATTLEBORO
Vermont

Seventeen known and one unknown Federal soldiers were buried in the Soldiers' Lot in Battleboro's Prospect Hill Cemetery. The cemetery was on "Cemetery Hill." George Joyall who was described as a "nurse in (the) hospital" was also buried in the 1,500 square foot plot. Volume 16 of the Roll of Honor lists these burials.

Today the VA is in charge of the lot.

EAST CORNITH
Vermont

In 1884 a headstone was requested for a Union soldier who died during the war. The cemetery was not given on the request.

MONTPELIER
Vermont

Montpelier's soldiers' lot is a lot 15 feet square located in Montpelier's Green Mountain Cemetery. On March 28, 1866, the town of Montpelier deeded the lot to the United States for one cent. Volume 16 of the Roll of Honor lists two burials. Today the soldiers' lot remains the smallest soldiers lot in the Department of Veterans Affairs' system with only eight interments.

ALEXANDRIA NATIONAL CEMETERY
Virginia

Most of the dead in the Alexandria National Cemetery died in hospitals in the Washington, D.C., area. A few remains were moved here after the war. A total of 3,601 interments had been made by 1866:

white soldiers	3,367
U.S. Navy	2
citizen	1
white females	2
colored soldiers	229
	3,601

Volume 4 of the Roll of Honor lists the burials. In 1873 two unknown Union Soldiers were moved from the city cemetery to Alexandria National Cemetery. Earlier in the same year 50 graves that had been discovered near the cemetery on land owned by the O I and M railroad were to be moved to the cemetery. However a note by the Secretary of War explained: "The superintendent has changed his mind and now believes... colored employees of the Quartermaster's Department were buried in this place. It is not deemed advisable to disinter these remains, and remove them to the National Cemetery." However the superintendent could sod the graves, if he chose to.

The cemetery was not a healthy place to live during the 1870's. In January of 1876 the superintendent, J.V. Davis, was granted permission to rent quarters outside the cemetery due to the "unhealthiness of his present quarters." Besides marshes in the area the National Cemetery was located "a few feet from the city cemetery." There was no sexton to care for the city cemetery and "the graves (in the city cemetery) are not covered when they fall in." In May Mr. Davis still lived in the National Cemetery's lodge. He could not find a suitable house in Alexandria.

In 1884 the graves of four quartermaster employees who drowned on April 24, 1865, during the pursuit of John Wilks Booth were marked. The four were Samuel N. Gosnell, Christian Farley, George W. Huntington, and Peter Carroll.

APPOMATTOX COURT HOUSE
Virginia

On April 9, 1865, a brief skirmish at Appomattox Court House proved to General Robert E. Lee that his army was surrounded by Union troops. Lee remarked: "then there is nothing left for me to do but to go and see General Grant, and I would rather die a thousand deaths." Lee's surrender of 26,672 men effectively ended the Civil War.

After the war the remains of most of the Federal soldiers killed at Appomattox Court House were removed to the Poplar Grove National Cemetery near Petersburg. However one unknown Federal soldier is buried along with 18 Confederate soldiers in the United Daughters of the Confederacy Cemetery which is maintained by the National Park Service as part of the Appomattox Court House National Historical Park.

Chris M. Calkins lists both Union and Confederate casualties in The Battles of Appomattox Station and Appomattox Court House.

ARLINGTON NATIONAL CEMETERY
Virginia

It is ironic that Arlington, the flagship cemetery of the national cemetery system, belonged to Mrs. Robert E. Lee. Mrs. Lee had inherited the Arlington estate from her father George Washington Parke Custis, stepson of George Washington.

When the war began, President Lincoln offered Lee command of the Union Army. Lee declined, saying he could not fight against his native state, Virginia. Lee left for Richmond. Mrs. Lee was privately warned that the Union army would soon occupy the estate, so Mrs. Lee also went south. Many of the Custis-Lee Mansion's furnishings were stolen by troops stationed there before General Irvin McDowell had the remaining furnishings moved to the U.S. Patent Office for safekeeping.

In 1862 Congress passed a law that levied taxes on land in "insurrectionary" districts. Because the goal of the law was to seize land of Confederates, the tax commissioners refused to accept payment from anyone but the land's owner. Mrs. Lee was almost an invalid and unable to pay the $92.07 tax. A cousin tried to pay the taxes, but the commissioners refused. The estate was confiscated and sold to the "government" for $26,800.

A contraband camp was established on the estate in June 1863. Exslaves who had moved to Washington were housed in the camp. Some 3,800 contrabands died during the war and were buried on the 1,100 acre estate. Today their graves are marked with headstones labeled "citizen" or "civilian." This freeman's village existed until 1890.

Until May, 1864, burials were made in the Soldier's Asylum Cemetery in Washington. However this cemetery was rapidly filling. Quartermaster General Meigs ordered burials to be made in Mrs. Lee's rose garden near the Curtis-Lee Mansion. On May 13, 1864, Private William

Christman, Company G, 67th Pennsylvania Infantry was buried on the estate. However the officers at Arlington had Christman buried elsewhere on the estate not in Mrs. Lee's rose garden.

Exactly why Meigs ordered burials at Arlington is debatable. Most historians believe that Meigs wanted to destroy the value of the estate to spite Lee. John Hinkel claims that Meigs wanted to spite the Regular Army officers who were living in the Curtis-Lee Mansion. One story claims that President Lincoln was riding in a buggy with Meigs and told Meigs that Arlington would make a beautiful cemetery. Meigs biographer, Russell Weigley, simply states that Meigs recommended to Secretary of War Stanton that Arlington be made a national cemetery. Stanton agreed on the same day! (June 15, 1864)

Meigs also recommended that burials elsewhere on the estate be stopped and all new burials be made near the "Arlington Mansion." In fact he had all the white soldiers buried on the other parts of the estate moved to near the mansion. Colored soldiers were buried in a separate section. Whatever Meigs' motives were, he succeeded in destroying Lee's use of Arlington. Lee only saw his former home once again, while riding a train.

Lee's oldest son, Custis Lee, sued in 1877 for the return of the estate, claiming the right of inheritance. The United States Supreme Court ruled in his favor. However because the cemetery contained over 16,000 bodies, Lee decided to accept Congress's offer of $150,000 for the estate.

Volume 1 of the Roll of Honor lists a total of 5,003 soldiers who were buried in Arlington between May 13, 1864, and June 30, 1865. Most of these soldiers died in hospitals in the Washington Area.

Harmony Cemetery was located on the New Bladensburg Road, about one-half miles from the city. It was established on February 17, 1863, and was reserved for soldiers who died of contagious diseases. Volume 1 of the Roll of Honor lists 415 white and 37 colored burials in Harmony Cemetery. Apparently 25 of these soldiers's bodies were later removed by their friends. These bodies were moved to Arlington shortly after the war.

After the war bodies from Northern Virginia and Maryland were moved to the cemetery. Most bodies came from a 25 miles radius of the cemetery. Bodies from the Bull Run Battlefield were buried in a vault under a granite monument with the following inscription:

BENEATH THIS STONE REPOSE THE BONES OF TWO THOUSAND, ONE HUNDRED AND ELEVEN UNKNOWN SOLDIERS, GATHERED AFTER THE WAR FROM THE FIELDS OF BULLRUN, AND THE ROUTE TO THE RAPPAHANNOCK.
THEIR REMAINS COULD NOT BE IDENTIFIED,BUT THEIR NAMES AND DEATHS ARE RECORDED IN THE ARCHIVES OF THEIR COUNTRY; AND ITS GRATEFUL CITIZENS

HONOR THEM AS THEIR NOBLE ARMY OF MARTYRS.
MAY THEY IN PEACE !

SEPTEMBER, A. D. 1866

Of course the "Archives of their country" does not record these deaths. Volume 15 of the Roll of Honor lists 2434 additional burials at Arlington.
By the time Col. Mack inspected the cemetery in 1874, a total of 16.260 burials had been made:

	known	unknown	total
commissioned officers	55	1	56
white Union soldiers	7,529	3,847	11,376
colored Union soldiers	114	229	343
total Union soldiers	7,698	4,077	11,775
employees and citizens	371	0	371
contrabands	3,485	272	3,757
Rebel POW's	357	0	357
	11,911	4,349	16,260

Today a total of 482 people are buried in the Confederate Section:

- 46 officers
- 351 enlisted men
- 58 wives
- 15 civilians
- 12 unknowns

It appears that some of these burials occurred after the war. The Confederate Memorial was designed by Moses Ezekiel, a former Confederate soldier. The memorial cost $75,000. President Woodrow Wilson dedicated it on June 4, 1914.
By June 1874 a total of $368,321.50 had been spent on the cemetery. The estimated cost of operations for the 1875-6 fiscal year was $15,680. The superintendent, F. Kauffman, was paid $75.00 a month.

BALL'S BLUFF NATIONAL CEMETERY
Virginia

Ball's Bluff National Cemetery is the second smallest Civil War era National Cemetery in number of burials. It appears to be the only National Cemetery that contains only soldiers killed in action. The soldiers buried here were members of reconnaissance force under Colonel Edward D. Baker,

71st Pennsylvania, that crossed the Potomac River near Leesburg, Virginia. They had crossed on a few boats but were driven back by Confederates under Colonel Nathan (Shanks) Evans. Many Union troops drowned trying to recross the river. Their bodies drifted down the Potomac toward Washington.

Baker and at least 48 other Federals were killed. 158 were wounded and 714 missing. The Confederates suffered 149 total casualties. (33 killed in action). The Congressional Investigation that resulted called the affair: "the most atrocious military blunder in history."

Early records indicated 54 unknown burials at Ball's Bluff. Later reports indicated 25 unknown burials. Also the cemetery fell into "disrepair" because no superintendent had been appointed to care for the graves. In 1877 the War Department considered abandoning the cemetery because it had no clear title. However what appears to be a sample title dated June 24, 1874, is filed in Record Group 92-E576. A note dated 1877 reads: "it appears...there are 54 bodies in 25 graves instead of 25 bodies." By 1884 the cemetery was in good condition with 25 graves. The headstones were "set in the arc of a circle." The Roll of Honor does not list Ball's Bluff.

Ball's Bluff may be reached by turning on an unnumbered dirt road 1.9 miles north of Leesburg. Today 24 headstones read "unknown" while the middle (key) stone reads:

James Allen
Co H 15 Regt
Mass Inf
October 15, 1861

About 75 feet toward the Bluff from the cemetery is a CSA style (pointed top) marker that reads:

Col. Edward D. Baker
71 PA Inf
killed here in the battle of Ball's Bluff,Va.
October 21, 1861

Colonel Baker's body was moved to a private cemetery in San Francisco. In 1940 he was reinterred in San Francisco National Cemetery.

Some of the bodies that floated down the Potomac were recovered and buried at Washington. At least one is in Arlington National Cemetery. About 120 feet west of the cemetery's fence is a grey stone marker to one Confederate Soldier. It reads:

CLINTON HATCHER
1840-1861
Co F 8th VA REGT.
C.S.A.
FELL BRAVELY DEFENDING HIS NATIVE STATE.

Local legend says the Federal Government refused Hatcher's parents request to bury their son inside the cemetery's fence where the grave would be protected. However nothing to substantiate this story has been found in the Archives.

The earliest report on Ball's Bluff is a report by Captain John Kay dated April 9, 1866. He listed one known and 53 unknown burials at Ball's Bluff. However he also lists three other cemeteries that he recommended to be moved to Ball's Bluff: Leesburg (two known graves), Warrenton's Methodist Episcopal's Cemetery (six known graves), and Waterford Cemetery (six known graves). Although 22 bodies were moved from Warrenton Cemetery to Arlington National Cemetery no record exists of removals from the ME Church Cemetery or Leesburg or Waterford. However the 1877 report do not list these reinterments. Perhaps they were never made and the graves lost.

In 1902 a Mrs. Paxton agreed to donate land for an access road to the cemetery provided the Government would build a fence (not a barbed wire fence) beside the road. In the 1950's the Quartermasters' Department proposed moving the bodies at Ball's Bluff to the Culpeper National Cemetery which was "in the same battle area." Congress did not approve this request.

BELLE ISLAND
Virginia

Volume 12 of the Roll of Honor lists 154 known and 30 unknown POW's who died in the Belle Island prison. These bodies were moved to the Richmond National Cemetery after the war.

BURKVILLE JUNCTION
Virginia

Volume 15 of the Roll of Honor contains the names of 25 Federal soldiers buried at Burkville Junction. According to Volume 15: "All of their remains have, undoubtedly, been removed long ere this to the national cemeteries at Yorktown and Petersburg..."

These bodies appear to have been moved to the Poplar Grove National Cemetery.

CAMP CASEY
Virginia

Two unknown Union soldiers were buried at Camp Casey. No additional records have been located.

CHARLOTTESVILLE
Virginia

Volume 14 of the Roll of Honor lists one POW who died at Charlottesville. No record of removal of this grave to a national cemetery has been found.

CITY POINT NATIONAL CEMETERY
Virginia

City Point National Cemetery contains many Union soldiers who died during the siege of Petersburg. Most of the dead in this cemetery came from the City Point area, but some were moved from the hospital cemetery at Point of Rocks located on the Appomattox River.

A total of 5,142 burials were made at City Point. Because most burials were soldiers who died in hospitals, 3,758 were known. (1,384 unknown) City Point is the only National Cemetery in the Richmond-Petersburg area that has more known than unknown burials.

Reinterments began at City Point in July 1866. According to Colonel C.W. Folsom's report (1868) the land for the cemetery was purchased by appraisement from E. Comer on January 25, 1868. Volume 16 of the Roll of Honor lists burials in the cemetery. Volume 13 of the Roll of Honor (1867) is an earlier list of burials.

COLD HARBOR NATIONAL CEMETERY
Virginia

The first major Civil War engagement near Cold Harbor was the Battle of Gaines' Mill on June 26-27,1862. Gaines' Mills was one of the first of the Seven Days Battles that ended General George McClellan's Peninsula Campaign.

From June first to June third, 1864, General Grant tried to break

Lee's lines at Cold Harbor. A massive attack by Grant on June 3, 1864, cost over 6,000 casualties. Over one-third were killed in action. Grant was later to say: "I have always regretted that the last assault at Cold Harbor was made."

Cold Harbor National Cemetery was established in 1866. Most of the bodies were moved to the cemetery from the Cold Harbor and Gaines' Mills Battlefields. Volume 9 of the Roll of Honor lists burials in the cemetery. 1062 soldiers were buried in single graves and the remains of 889 soldiers were buried in two trenches. In 1877 a large white marble sarcophagus was erected by the United States to mark the mass grave. It's inscription reads: **"Near this stone rest the remains of 899 Union soldiers gathered from the battlefields of Mechanicsville, Savage Station, Gaines Mills, and the vicinity of Cold Harbor."** This is the second largest mass grave of Union Civil War soldiers.

In 1867 search parties again visited the Cold Harbor area. Over 1,000 bodies were discovered and removed to the Richmond National Cemetery.

Col. Mack inspected the cemetery on July 25, 1871. He reported 1,951 burials:

officers - known	45
officers - unknown	5
enlisted men - known	531
enlisted men - unknown	<u>1,270</u>
	1,951

At the time of Col. Mack's inspection a total of $18,007.17 had been spent on the cemetery. When Col. Mack inspected the cemetery the superintendent was "quite sick." He died several days after Mack's visit.

CULPEPER NATIONAL CEMETERY
Virginia

The six acres of land for the Culpeper National Cemetery was acquired by a Decree of Condemnation on April 27, 1867. Mr. Edward B. Hill, the former owner, was paid $1,400 for the land. Some 350 bodies were moved to the cemetery from the Ceder Mountain Battlefield. On August 9, 1862, Stonewall Jackson's army soundly thrashed the Federals under General Nathaniel Banks at Ceder Mountain. Other bodies were moved to the cemetery from Brandy Station, Trevilians Station, Gordonsville, and other locations.

By the time Col. Mack inspected the cemetery in 1871, he noted a total of 1349 interments:

	known	unknown
commissioned officers	20	0
white soldiers	428	901
	448	901

A memorial plaque at the cemetery, donated by the local VFW Post, lists 902 unknown burials. Groups from five states, Maine, Massachusetts, New York, Ohio, and Pennsylvania, later erected monuments to their fallen comrades in the cemetery. The Seventh Ohio Regimental Association's Monument is in honor of the 37 members of that unit killed at Cedar Mountain. The unit suffered 153 wounded for a total loss of 190 out of 307 present. (almost 62%). The 26th North Carolina Infantry suffered almost an 87% loss in three terrible days at Gettysburg.

Burials in Culpeper National Cemetery are listed in volumes 14, 15, and 26 of the Roll of Honor.

DANGERFIELD
Virginia

An undated list gave the names of eight Federal soldiers who were buried at Dangerfield. These soldiers were most likely moved to a national cemetery, but no record of removal can be found.

DANVILLE NATIONAL CEMETERY
Virginia

Danville had the two most desirable qualities for a POW camp site. It was on the railroad and it was far enough away from the front lines to be secure from Union Cavalry raids. Seven tobacco warehouses in Danville were converted into makeshift prisons. A smallpox epidemic cost many lives.

The first burials in the Danville National Cemetery were made by a crew working under Superintendent J.J. Johnson on December 15, 1866. The burials were completed by July 31, 1867. Almost all the burials in the cemetery were made from the prison camp cemetery. Only a few bodies were brought to the cemetery from the surrounding countryside. Volume 13 of the Roll of Honor lists 1,280 Union soldiers (1,175 known) were buried in the cemetery.

The three and one-half acres of land the cemetery was on was part of "the widow Greene's estate." In 1871 the land had not been paid for because of possible defects in the title. However $1,200 was paid for the cemetery before 1874. In 1874 Col. Mack noted that the stone wall around the cemetery had been completed. It enclosed the colored section of the cemetery. (The older picket fence did not.) By June 30, 1874, a total of $41,994.16 had been spent on the cemetery.

In his 1874 report Col. Mack reported 1,314 burials (including eight "citizens"):

	known	unknown
white Union soldiers and sailors	1,126	131
colored Union soldiers and sailors	37	12
	1,163	143

DINWIDDLE COUNTY
Virginia

The names of 40 soldiers buried in Dinwiddle County are listed in volume 15 of the Roll of Honor. These bodies were moved to the Poplar Grove National Cemetery after the war.

FALLS CREEK
Virginia

In February 1871, a Mrs. Rutdj applied for a fence to be built around a cemetery on her property that contained Union graves. The Quartermaster Department's replay is too faded to read however no other material on these graves can be found.

Neither the Roll of Honor or the Disposition lists any Union burials at Falls Church.

FORT HARRISON NATIONAL CEMETERY
Virginia

Forts Harrison and Gilmer were two Confederate forts located southeast of Richmond. Early in the morning of September 29, 1864, Union troops attacked both forts. Fort Harrison was captured but Fort Gilmer was not. Failure to capture Fort Gilmer blocked Grant's plan to take Richmond from the east. Grant then settled into siege operations at Petersburg.

In 1866 land near Fort Harrison was appropriated for use as a cemetery. It appears that most burials in the cemetery were made in 1866. Land purchases in 1869, 1872, and 1873 brought the area to 1.55 acres. Most of the bodies in the cemetery came from a five mile radius of the cemetery.

A 1867 report listed interments:

	known	unknown
officers	4	12
white soldiers	163	395
colored soldiers	61	167
sailors	_11_	_1_
	239	575

Of the 814 interments in the cemetery in 1867, almost 71% were unknown. Burials in Fort Harrison National Cemetery are listed in volume 18 of the Roll of Honor.

In 1867 a second search of the area was made. Bodies recovered by this search were moved to the Richmond National Cemetery.

FREDERICKSBURG NATIONAL CEMETERY
Virginia

Four major battles were fought near Fredericksburg: Fredericksburg (December 13, 1862), Chancellorsville (May 1-4, 1863), the Wilderness (May 5,6,7, 1864) , and Spotsylvania Court House (May 8-18, 1869).

No real effort was made to bury all the Union dead from these battles until after the war. Captain James Moore was dispatched to the wilderness on June 8, 1865. His party worked from June 12 to June 24 burying the dead. Two cemeteries were established with a total of 642 graves. Most bodies had not been buried and "by exposure to the weather for more than a year all traces of their identity were entirely obliterated."

At Spotsylvania Court House Moore found that a local resident, a Mr. Sanford, had been hired by General Sherman on his march to Washington. Over 700 Federal soldiers were buried at Spotsylvania Court House. Volume 2 of the Roll of Honor lists the names of soldiers buried at these two battlefields. These bodies along with the surrounding area were moved to the Fredericksburg National Cemetery between December 1866 and July 30, 1868.

Work on Fredericksburg National Cemetery was begun in July 1865. The cemetery was located on Marye's Heights. Marye's Heights had been an impregnable defensive point in Lee's line during the Battle of Fredericksburg in 1862. Volume 25 of the Roll of Honor, published in 1870, listed 15,068 Union dead in Fredericksburg, but only 2467 were known. (16%) Col. Mack reported a total of 15,241 interments in 1871:

	known	unknown
officers	98	35
white soldiers	2,293	12,807
white sailors	4	0
colored soldiers	2	2
	2.397	12,844

Mack also reported a total expenditure of $183,332.69 up to July 31. 1871.

FRONT ROYAL
Virginia

Volume 15 of the Roll of Honor contains the names of Federal soldiers buried at Front Royal. According to Volume 15: "All of their remains have, undoubtedly, been removed long ere this to the national cemeteries at Yorktown and Petersburg..." However it appears that these bodies were moved to the Winchester National Cemetery instead.

GLENDALE NATIONAL CEMETERY
Virginia

The Battle of Glendale (or Nelson's Farm) was fought on the afternoon of June 30, 1862. It was followed the next day by the Battle of Malvern Hill which ended Lee's Seven Day campaign against McClellan.

The site for the Glendale National Cemetery was 14 miles from Richmond and 2 miles from Malvern Hill. Work on the cemetery began May 7, 1866, and ended July 14, 1866. Brevet Lt. Col. James Moore oversaw the reburials.

Volume 16 of the Roll of Honor listed 1,197 burials: 237 known and 960 unknown.

Col. Mack's report (1871) listed only 1,189 burials:

	known	unknown
white soldiers	230	949
colored soldiers	6	4
	236	1,053

A total of $15,538.35 had been spent on the cemetery up to May 31, 1871.

GLOUCESTER POINT
Virginia

Volume 15 of the Roll of Honor contains the names of 22 Federal soldiers buried at Gloucester Point. According to Volume 15: "All of their remains have, undoubtedly, been removed long ere this to the national cemeteries at Yorktown and Petersburg..."

GORDONSVILLE
Virginia

Volume 15 of the Roll of Honor contains the names of 26 Federal soldiers buried at Gordonsville. Volume 14 lists 26 POW's who died there. According to Volume 15: "All of their remains have, undoubtedly, been removed long ere this to the national cemeteries at Yorktown and Petersburg..." However according to other sources, bodies from this area were moved to both the Culpeper and Richmond National Cemeteries.

HAMPTON NATIONAL CEMETERY
Virginia

Hampton Hospital was a 1,800 bed hospital operated by the Union at Fort Monroe. Fort Monroe was one of the few Federal Forts in the South that the Confederacy never controlled.

Burials at Fort Monroe had been made as early as 1855, however as the dead toll rose, more land was appropriated for a cemetery. By 1868, over 11 acres were being used as a cemetery, however only about four and one-half acres had been purchased. The rest of the land was condemned and purchased in 1870.

Most of the burials at Hampton were from the hospital, so most of the burials were of known soldiers. A June 1867 report listed 4103 total burials: 13 officers, 3,186 known white soldiers, and 703 US colored troops. Volume 5 of the Roll of Honor lists these burials with additional names in volumes 25 and 26. Some bodies were moved to the cemetery by a private contractor for $4.00 per body. Although "Rebel dead" were not to be moved to the cemetery, a total of 272 Confederates are buried in the cemetery.

Col. Mack reported that 5,129 burials had been made in the cemetery by 1871:

	known	unkown
officers	25	0
white soldiers	3,519	402
white sailors	66	6
colored soldiers	985	57
women, children,...	83	8
	4,678	465

The total expenditure had been $56,116.29 up to May 31, 1871. The Hampton Normal and Agricultural Institute sold 5 1/2 acres of land to the government in 1891. This land was about 3/4 of a mile northeast of the original cemetery near Phoebus, Virginia. Additional land purchases were made in 1894 and 1934.

HAMPTON VA MEDICAL CENTER NATIONAL CEMETERY
Virginia

During a yellow fever epidemic in 1894 Hampton Hospital was quarantined. 22 soldiers who died during the quarantine were buried in a .03 of an acre plot on the hospital grounds. Fear of contracting yellow fever from the bodies lead to establishment of a separate cemetery. This is the smallest national cemetery in the United States.

HARRISONBURG
Virginia

Volume 14 of the Roll of Honor lists 13 POW's who died at Harrisonburg. Bodies from this area were moved to the Staunton National Cemetery after the war.

LIBERTY
Virginia

Volume 15 of the Roll of Honor contains the names of nine Federal soldiers buried at Liberty. According to Volume 15: "All of their remains have, undoubtedly, been removed long ere this to the national cemeteries at Yorktown and Petersburg..." However it appears that these bodies were moved to the Arlington National Cemetery.

LYNCHBURG
Virginia

Volume 12 of the Roll of Honor lists 185 white soldiers, one colored soldier, and one "citizen" who died at Lynchburg. Volume 14 lists 25 soldiers who died as prisoners at Lynchburg. Most of the names in volume 14 are also listed in volume 12. Volume 15 of the Roll of Honor (1868) repeats volume's 12 list (with several changes). A note in volume 15 states: "All of their remains have, undoubtedly, been removed long ere this to the National Cemeteries at Yorktown and Petersburg...." The bodies from Lynchburg were moved to Poplar Grove National Cemetery at Petersburg.

In 1886 J.F. Wilson, Lynchburg's postmaster, wrote the War Department asking permission to move the bodies of ten Federal occupation troops who died in Lynchburg to Cypress Grove Confederate Cemetery. The soldiers, members of the 11th and 29th Infantry, had been buried in a private cemetery. The War Department approved the request in June 1886.

MOUNT JACKSON
Virginia

Volume 14 of the Roll of Honor lists five POW's who died at Mount Jackson. Bodies from this area were moved to the Winchester National Cemetery after the war.

NORFOLK NAVAL HOSPITAL CEMETERY
Virginia

At least 243 sailors were buried at the Norfolk Naval Hospital Cemetery from June 11, 1862 to 1865. According to a 1886 tombstone request 116 graves were unknowns and 127 were: "...marked by wooden headboards, more or less decayed."

NOTTOWAY COUNTY
Virginia

Volume 15 of the Roll of Honor contains the names of six Federal soldiers buried in Nottoway County. According to Volume 15: "All of their remains have, undoubtedly, been removed long ere this to the national cemeteries at Yorktown and Petersburg..."

ORANGE COURTHOUSE
Virginia

Volume 14 of the <u>Roll of Honor</u> lists one POW who died at Orange Courthouse. Bodies from this area were moved to the Arlington National Cemetery and the Culpeper National Cemetery after the war.

ORANGE and ALEXANDRIA RAILROAD
Virginia

Volume 12 of the <u>Roll of Honor</u> lists 1,078 Union soldiers who were buried "along the Orange and Alexandria Railroad and the fords of the Rapidan River." It appears that the soldiers buried on the railroad were later moved to the Arlington National Cemetery while the bodies at the fords of the Rapidan were reinterred in the Culpeper National Cemetery.

POPLAR GROVE NATIONAL CEMETERY
Virginia

Petersburg was the site of the longest siege of the Civil War. On the afternoon of June 15, 1864, the Union XVIII Corps under General William F. Smith almost captured Petersburg. Had Smith succeeded, Lee would have had to abandon Richmond. But after the Union disaster at Cold Harbor the cautious Smith failed. Even though Grant slipped safely across the James River with over 100,000 men, the small Confederate force in Petersburg managed to stalemate the Union army. The siege ended when Grant's army broke Lee's lines at Fort Gregg on April 2, 1865.

Poplar Grove National Cemetery was established about five miles southeast of Petersburg near the Weldon Railroad. Two tracts of land totaling 8.1 acres were purchased. About one third of the land was covered with tall pine trees, the rest was almost flat and open.

Bodies were moved to Poplar Grove National Cemetery from the Union trenches around Petersburg, Ream's Station, Amelia Court House, Lynchburg, and other locations. Volumes 13, 14, and 15 of the <u>Roll of</u>

279

Honor list names of Union troops who died in or near Petersburg. Volume 19 of the Roll of Honor lists 5,547 burials at Petersburg. Volume 26 of the series lists 58 additional names. Volume 15 of the Roll of Honor devotes 90 pages to names of soldiers originally buried at "miscellaneous locations in Virginia." The introduction to this section states: "All of their remains have, undoubtedly, been removed long ere this to National Cemeteries at Yorktown and Petersburg..." It appears the War Department could not identify where these soldiers were moved, if, in fact, they were reinterred.

When Col. Mack inspected the cemetery in 1871, he reported that the rails on the wooden picket-fence were "much decayed." Also many graves had fallen in and needed to be filled with dirt. Although $109,362.80 had been spent on the cemetery by May 31, 1871, the superintendent only had one helper.

By 1871 a total of 6,187 burials had been made in the cemetery:

	known	unknown
officers	60	25
white Union soldiers	1,906	3,863
white Union sailors	3	0
colored Union soldiers	60	226
citizens	6	0
Confederates	15	23
	2,050	4,137

PORTSMOUTH
Virginia

Volume 12 of the Roll of Honor lists 64 Union soldiers (four unknown) buried "at Portsmouth." It appears that most of these bodies were moved to the Hampton National Cemetery.

Portsmouth is also home to the United States Naval Hospital at Portsmouth. This cemetery holds some casualties of the battle between the CSS Virginia (formerly the USS Merrimack) and the USS Cumberland and the USS Congress. The Virginia destroyed both Union ships. The March 8, 1862, battle marked the end of wooden war ships.

A stone cairn on the hospital grounds honors the 337 Union sailors lost in the battle. T. Fay, killed on the Cumberland, is buried in a separate grave. At least 58 known Confederates are buried here. There are 113 unknown graves including at least 46 Confederates.

(FORDS of the) RAPIDAN RIVER
Virginia

Volume 12 of the Roll of Honor lists 1078 Union soldiers who were buried "along the Orange and Alexandria Railroad and the fords of the Rapidan River." It appears that the soldiers buried on the railroad were later moved to the Arlington National Cemetery while the bodies at the fords of the Rapidan were reinterred in the Culpeper National Cemetery.

RAPPAHANNOCK STATION
Virginia

Volume 15 of the Roll of Honor contains the names of Federal soldiers buried at Rappahannock Station. According to Volume 15: "All of their remains have, undoubtedly, been removed long ere this to the national cemeteries at Yorktown and Petersburg..." However according to other sources, bodies from this area were moved to both the Culpeper and Arlington National Cemeteries.

RICHMOND NATIONAL CEMETERY
Virginia

Only 12.4% of the interments in the Richmond National Cemetery are of known soldiers. The cemetery was located three miles from Richmond, on the Williamsburg turnpike, just beyond the first toll-gate. The cemetery was inside the defensive fortification line constructed around Richmond. The land for the cemetery was appropriated in 1866. Three acres of land were purchased by appraisement from William Slater and wife on July 29, 1867. About five additional acres were purchased in 1868. In 1906 another purchase increased the cemetery's size to 9.74 acres.

Bodies were moved to the cemetery from Oakwood and Hollywood Cemeteries and Belle Island Confederate Prison. Other bodies were brought to the cemetery from about seventy different sites within a 25 mile radius of the cemetery. Burial parties revisited Richmond area battlefields and recovered bodies missed by earlier search parties. Although some 1,700 bodies from the area near Cold Harbor Battlefield had been removed to the Cold Harbor National Cemetery in 1866, almost 1,000 bodies were moved from Cold Harbor to the Richmond National Cemetery in 1867. Fifteen bodies were moved from the Seven Pines area. 202 bodies were moved to the cemetery between July 1871 and April 1872. A few bodies were still to be moved to the cemetery in 1872. In 1871, Col. Mack reported the burials:

known white Union soldiers	803
unknown white Union soldiers	5,665
marines	2
citizens	8
employees	3
servants (colored)	2
	6,483

Col. Mack reported that Patrick Hart, the superintendent, was "quite an amateur florist." A small greenhouse was attached to the new lodge and flowering plants and shrubs were being planted. The new brick lodge cost $2,700 in 1871. By July 31, 1871, a total of $99,594.28 had been spent on the cemetery.

Volume 12 of the Roll of Honor lists burials in Hollywood and Oakdale Cemeteries and at Belle Island. Volume 14 of the Roll of Honor is unique in that it details the original burial sites of unknowns buried in the cemetery. For example the 39 unknowns buried in graves 109 to 147 of section 4 of division F were buried at the junction of the New Kent and Charles City roads, and were men of McClellan's army who were killed in a skirmish at that point, and were gathered together and thrown into a hollow, and then covered with rails and dirt." Other burials in Richmond National Cemetery are listed in volume 16 of the Roll of Honor.

ROBINSON'S TAVERN
Virginia

Volume 14 of the Roll of Honor lists one POW who died at Robinson's Tavern. No record of removal of this grave to a national cemetery has been found.

SEVEN PINES NATIONAL CEMETERY
Virginia

In March 1862 Union General George B. McClellan landed an army of over 100,000 men on the Virginia Peninsula and began his army creeping toward Richmond. Rain and McClellan's caution slowed the advance more than the Confederates. Never the less by late May the Union army was within twelve miles of Richmond. Union balloon observation crews could spy the church spires of Richmond.

The Union Army had corps on both sides of the Chickahominy Creek when spring rains flooded the creek. The rain washed away bridges connecting Union Army Corps. Confederate General Joe Johnson ordered an attack on the Union forces near Seven Pines. Poor staff work and confusion of orders blunted the attack in the battles of Seven Pines and Fair Oaks. (May 31, June 1, 1862) Later General Richmond Taylor, CSA, wrote: "Confederate commanders knew no more about the topography...within a day's march of Richmond than they knew about Central Africa." The Seven Pines Battle had two major outcomes: First McClellan was stopped. He could have destroyed the Confederates had he attacked. He didn't. Secondly, Robert E. Lee was appointed to replace Johnson who had been seriously wounded.

In 1866 Lt. Col. James Moore surveyed the area around Richmond for possible sites for National Cemeteries. Slightly over one acre was appropriated for the cemetery in 1866. In 1867 the Government paid the former owner $134.33 for the land. In 1873 a small strip of land was purchased for building a lodge.

Burials in the cemetery were made from the Seven Pines and Fair Oaks Battlefields and other sites in a four mile radius. In 1871 Col. Moore reported the interments:

	known	unknown
white Union soldiers	141	1,209
colored Union soldiers	0	7
	141	1,216

Only 10% of the original 1,357 burials could be identified. Volumes 12 and 15 of the Roll of Honor lists the burials in the cemetery.

Considering the low cost of the land Seven Pines was an expensive cemetery. By June 30, 1874, a total of $70,750.58 had been spent on the cemetery. By comparison only $3,078.58 had been spent on the Fort Gibson (Indian Territory) National Cemetery during the same time period. Fort Gibson had 2,296 burials.

SOUTHAMPTON COURTHOUSE
Virginia

Volume 14 of the Roll of Honor lists one POW who died at Southampton Courthouse. No record of removal of this grave to a national cemetery has been found.

SPOTSYLVANIA COURT HOUSE
Virginia

From May 8 to May 20, 1864, Grant and Lee's armies fought to a draw at Spotsylvania Court House. After the battle Grant moved southeastward, racing Lee to Richmond.

In June 1865 Captain James Moore of the Quartermaster Corps was dispatched to the Wilderness and Spotsylvania battlefields to bury the dead. At Spotsylvania his work crew found few unburied dead. Most had been buried by a Mr. Sandford who had been hired by General Sherman to bury the dead. Sherman had contracted with Mr. Sanford while his army was en route from North Carolina to Washington. Over 700 bodies were identified by Moore's group. Their names are listed in volume 2 of the Roll of Honor. Unidentified soldiers were buried in a grave marked with a wooden tablet labeled: "Unknown U.S. Soldiers, killed May 10, 1864."

These bodies were moved to the Fredericksburg National Cemetery after the war.

STAUNTON NATIONAL CEMETERY
Virginia

Bodies from Cross Keys, Port Republic, Waynesville, and the Staunton area were moved to the Staunton National Cemetery at the close of the war. The lot (a little over an acre) was purchased for $900.

Burials in the Staunton National Cemetery are listed in volumes 14 and 15 of the Roll of Honor. In 1871 Col. Mack reported the interments as:

	known	unknown
commissioned officers	12	4
white Union soldiers	219	514
	231	518

Col. Mack's 1871 report criticized the inferior quality of workmanship on the new lodge then under construction. By 1874 the lodge was "in good order and tidy", but rubble-stone wall was "badly done, and ought not to have been accepted by the government agent." A total of $77,413.62 had been spent on the cemetery by June 30, 1874.

284

SUFFOLK
Virginia

Volume 15 of the Roll of Honor contains the names of Federal soldiers buried at Suffolk. According to Volume 15: "All of their remains have, undoubtedly, been removed long ere this to the national cemeteries at Yorktown and Petersburg..." However it appears that these bodies were moved to the Hampton National Cemetery.

WILDERNESS BATTLEFIELD
Virginia

On May 4, 1864, General Grant's Army of the Potomac crossed the Rapidan River headed toward Richmond. Lee's Army of Northern Virginia met Grant in the Wilderness, a thickly wooded area just west of Fredericksburg. The author's great-great-grandfather, Andrew Jackson Hughes, fought in the 12th North Carolina Infantry. He later told his grandson: "They woke us up and lined us in the woods before breakfast. We shot at the Yankees all day. Their bullets went over our heads and tore leaves off the trees. By that night I was covered in leaves." Grant and Lee fought to a draw, but then Grant did something that no Union commander had ever done before, he moved south. Lee's army would race him to a small crossroads hamlet, Spotsylvania Court House, and another bloodbath.

In June 1865 Captain James Moore, U.S. Quartermaster Corps, was dispatched to the Wilderness to bury the Union dead. Moore established two cemeteries: one with 108 bodies and a second with 534 bodies. Moore reported these burials were made "where the scenes of carnage appeared the greatest." In one place skeletons of Union troops were found inside the Confederate trenches.

Moore was unable to rebury the partly buried bodies his work group found because ".....the weather being exceedingly warm, and the unpleasant odor from decayed animal matter so great, as to make the removal impracticable. They were, however, carefully re-covered with earth and entirely hidden from view." Moore reported that hundreds of graves were unmarked and could not be found until winter when rain and snow would wash dirt from the graves.

Moore listed the names of soldiers his party reburied in volume 2 of the Roll of Honor. These bodies were moved to the Fredericksburg National Cemetery sometime between December 1866 and July 30, 1868.

WILSON'S LANDING
Virginia

Volume 15 of the Roll of Honor contains the names of 22 Federal soldiers buried at Lynchburg. According to Volume 15: "All of their remains have, undoubtedly, been removed long ere this to the national cemeteries at Yorktown and Petersburg..." Other burials at Fort Pocahontas (near Wilson's Landing) are listed in Volume 12 of the Roll of Honor. These bodies were moved to the Glendale National Cemetery.

WINCHESTER NATIONAL CEMETERY
Virginia

Winchester was the key to the Shenandoah Valley, breadbasket of the Confederacy. Four major battles were fought nearby and the town was reported to have changed hands 72 times during the war.

Winchester National Cemetery was dedicated April 8, 1866. It was established on a five acre tract purchased from Jacob Baker, a farmer, for $1,500. The original burials in the cemetery came from a radius of 40 miles, including Winchester, New Market, Martinsburgh, (W Va.) and Front Royal. Volume 15 of the Roll of Honor lists these burials. Seven POW's who died at Winchester are listed in volume 14 of the series. Roll of Honor, volume 26, simply notes a reinterment of unknown Federal soldiers from Harper's Ferry, West Virginia. Col. Mack noted a total of 4,440 burials in his 1871 report:

	known	unknown
commissioned officers	53	9
white Union soldiers	2,030	2,323
colored Union soldiers	3	6
citizens, women, and children	16	0
	2,102	2,338

The high percentage of known burials (just over 47%) is surprising considering the remoteness of some of the areas visited by the burial parties.

YORKTOWN NATIONAL CEMETERY
Virginia

Yorktown fell to General McClellan's army on May 3, 1862, after a month long siege. McClellan moved "on to Richmond" and into disaster during Lee's seven day campaign.

The Yorktown National Cemetery was established near the site of the siege lines dug during the 1871 Battle of Yorktown during the American Revolution. The land (about 3 acres) was purchased for $490. Bodies were moved to the cemetery from 27 different places, some as far as 50 miles away. However most of the bodies came from Yorktown and the Williamsburg Battlefield. In 1874 Col. Mack reported the interments:

	known	unknown
white Union soldiers and sailors	713	1,410
colored Union soldiers and sailors	11	17
citizens	9	6
Rebel soldiers	16	1
	749	1,434

Burials in the cemetery are listed in volume 16 of the Roll of Honor. Other bodies that might have been removed to the cemetery are listed in volume 15 of the series. The Colonial National Historical Park, which maintains the cemetery, has a corrected list of burials in the cemetery.

CAMP STEELE
Washington

Volume 19 of the Roll of Honor lists four soldiers (only two known) buried in the Camp Steele Post Cemetery. No more information on these burials has been found.

FORT COLVILLE
Washington

Volume 19 of the Roll of Honor lists six known soldiers buried in the Fort Colville Post Cemetery. These bodies were moved to the San Francisco National Cemetery.

FORT SPOKANE
Washington

In 1886 the Quartermaster of Fort Spokane ordered six headstones for known Federal soldiers who died at Fort Spokane between 1881 and 1885. No information on these burials has been located.

FORT STEILACOOM
Washington

Volume 19 of the Roll of Honor lists two soldiers who died at Fort Steilacoom during the war. In 1885 the Quartermaster's Department shipped eight headstones to Tacoma, Washington, to mark graves in the old post cemetery. However Mr. David H. Lovejoy, a local resident, wrote the Quartermaster General requesting money to transport the headstones from the Tacoma Railroad Depot the 13 miles to the cemetery.

The reply to Mr. Lovejoy's letter has not been located, but the government policy was not to pay for transporting the stones nor setting them. At least some of these bodies were later moved to the San Francisco National Cemetery.

FORT VANCOUVER
Washington

Volume 8 of the Roll of Honor lists 20 soldiers who were buried at Fort Vancouver before and during the Civil War. Volume 19 of the series adds three names of soldiers who died in 1866.

On August 19, 1880, Brig. Gen. O.O. Howard recommended that the Vancouver Barracks Post Cemetery be designated a National Cemetery. Besides providing a new source of funding for cemetery improvements, national cemetery status would allow burials of veterans in the cemetery. The exact date that the cemetery was designated a national cemetery is unclear. (Edward Steere incorrectly gives 1875)

However the cemetery's new found status was short-lived. An endorsement dated November 15, 1882, states: "The Secretary of War decides (sic) that this is a 'post cemetery' and shall remain so." In a letter (5 Dec 1882) Quartermaster General Rufus Ingalls stated: "This cemetery was once designated a national cemetery but the order was revoked by the Secretary of War and it was restored to its former status."

In September, 1883, the post cemetery was moved to a new location in the northeast corner of the post. A plot was established in the new cemetery for the bodies of civilians who were buried in the old cemetery. Some historians believe that the original post burial list had been lost and no one bothered to copy the names from the old headboards so when the bodies were moved the names were lost.

However Bob Baerncopf, sexton of the cemetery, has discovered that many bodies were moved to other cemeteries by friends or relatives. Mr. Baerncopf has identified at least 21 bodies that were moved, but the names still appear on the cemetery records. At least 12 bodies were moved to the post from other cemeteries including: Fort Watson, "The Dalles," and Clearwater Indian Territories.

FORT WALLA WALLA
Washington

Volume 19 of the Roll of Honor lists 12 known and five unknown soldiers buried at Fort Walla Walla. This post was still active as late as 1889 when the post quartermaster requested corrections made on twelve stones.

GAULEY
West Virginia

A 1866 report listed the following burials of Union soldiers near Gauley:

Location	No. of Bodies
Mrs. Miller's Lot	5
Falls of the Kanawha	6 or 8
Not specified	3

No further information on these burials has been located.

GRAFTON NATIONAL CEMETERY
West Virginia

Grafton National Cemetery is one of only two Civil War era national cemeteries not listed in the Roll of Honor series. No reason for this omission has been found in the records. (Ball's Bluff, Virginia, with only one known burial is the other.)

According to a data sheet, circa 1866, interments were made from battlefields, camps, and hospital cemeteries in West Virginia, Kentucky, and "various places within a circuit of 200 miles." The data sheet listed the interments:

	known	unknown
officers	10	8
soldiers	618	608
employees	5	2
citizens	0	3
	633	621

Col. Mack's 1871 inspection report described the cemetery as a rectangular lot 387 feet by 285 feet. The ground sloped moderately. It had been cut into three terraces. The lodge and tool house were built on the upper terrace. The two lower terraces contained the graves. Mack reported a total expenditure of $80,348.08. However the land had yet to be purchased. An 1889 data sheet reports the land was purchased for $3,400 from "Wm. D. Mack and others."

PARKERSBURG
West Virginia

Volume 13 of the Roll of Honor lists 39 white and 13 colored soldiers buried at Parkersburg. Most of these deaths occurred in late 1864 and 1865. These bodies were moved to Grafton National Cemetery.

WHEELING
West Virginia

32 white soldiers, two colored soldiers, and one government employee were buried at Wheeling according to volume 13 of the Roll of Honor. The majority died in 1865. These bodies were interred in Grafton National Cemetery after the war.

FOND DU LAC
Wisconsin

Twelve Union soldiers were buried in Fond Du Lac's Rienzi Cemetery. Volume 18 of the Roll of Honor lists the names.

GREEN BAY
Wisconsin

Volume 18 of the Roll of Honor lists three soldiers buried in private lots in Green Bay's city cemetery.

JANESVILLE
Wisconsin

Thirteen soldiers were buried in private lots in Janesville's Oak Hill Cemetery according to volume 18 of the Roll of Honor,

KENOSHA
Wisconsin

Volume 18 of the Roll of Honor lists three Union soldiers buried in private lots in Kenosha's City Cemetery.

MADISON
Wisconsin

A large hospital operated in Madison during the war. Volume 9 of the Roll of Honor lists 264 known soldiers buried "at Madison." Over 90% of these were Wisconsin soldiers. Volume 18 of the Roll of Honor lists 198 soldiers buried in Forest Hill Cemetery. Not all of these names appear in volume 9. It appears some of the soldiers listed in volume 9 were buried in private lots.

Col. Mack's report (1871) listed 219 burials of white soldiers in Forest Hill. 196 soldiers were known. The lot was 160 by 74 feet. The land was supposed to have been donated to the United States but no title could be found in the files. 137 Confederate POW's were also buried here. Today Forest Hill is classified as a soldiers lot by the VA. 178 interments are made in 276 gravesites.

MILWAUKEE
Wisconsin

Volume 9 of the Roll of Honor lists 58 known soldiers buried "at Milwaukee." Volume 18 lists 56 different known and 12 unknown soldiers buried in the Forest Home Cemetery.

Col. Mack's report (1871) reported 24 known Union soldiers buried in Forest Home's soldiers lot. He also reported 41 soldiers (13 of them officers) buried in the same cemetery in private lots. Today Forest Home is a soldiers lot under VA control. The 1987 station data sheet lists 21 interments in 21 grave sites.

PRAIRIE DU CHIEN
Wisconsin

Volume 18 of the Roll of Honor lists four known and 13 unknown soldiers buried in Prairie du Chien's City Cemetery. All four of the known soldiers belonged to Minnesota units. They died in late 1864.

Today the Department of Veterans' Affairs administers the cemetery as Fort Crawford Cemetery Soldier's Lot. By 1987, a total of 64 interments had been made in 64 grave sites.

RACINE
Wisconsin

Forty United States soldiers were buried in the Mound City Cemetery in Racine. The cemetery was called Mound City because it was built on an ancient Indian mound. Five known and ten unknown soldiers were buried in a soldiers lot. The other 25 known soldiers were buried in private lots. Volume 18 of the Roll of Honor lists the burials.

By 1987 the Mound Cemetery was classified as a soldiers' lot by the Department of Veterans Affairs. Their 1987 data sheet listed a total of 14 burials in 14 grave sites.

RIPON
Wisconsin

Nine Union soldiers who were buried in private lots in Ripon's City Cemetery are listed in volume 18 of the Roll of Honor.

CAMP MEDICINE BUTTE
Wyoming

According to a letter dated November 4, 1886, the bodies of three regular army soldiers killed in action against the Indians were buried in a private cemetery. The letter continues: "Several bodies of volunteer soldiers (are) buried in the same cemetery."

FORT BRIDGER
Wyoming

Mountain man Jim Bridger established a fort on the Green River in the late 1830's. This site was near present day Utah. In the 1850's Bridger had problems with the Mormons who settled in Utah. Col. Albert Sidney Johnson of the 2nd U.S. Cavalry established a fort at the site in 1857. The post was abandoned in 1878 but reoccupied from 1880 to 1890. Volume 19 of the Roll of Honor listed 20 burials in the post cemetery. Volume 12 of the Roll of Honor listed 18 burials "at Fort Bridges." No record of removals of these graves has been found. Wyoming now operates the site as a state historic site.

FORT CANBY
Wyoming Territory

In 1879 the Commander of Fort Canby requested 18 headstones for the unmarked graves of soldiers who died from 1865 to 1879. No further information exists.

FORT LARAMIE
Wyoming

It is unclear just how many Federal Soldiers were buried at Fort Laramie. Volume 9 of the Roll of Honor (1866) lists 18 soldiers buried "at Fort Laramie, D.T." These soldiers died in 1865. However volume 19 of the series lists 12 burials in the "new cemetery" and 16 in the "old Cemetery." Burials in the new cemetery were begun in July 1867. The soldiers' names in volume 9 of the Roll of Honor are not repeated in volume 19, however about 143 graves were to be moved to the new cemetery.

According to a headstone request from the Fort Laramie's Post Quartermaster, 46 known soldiers were buried at Fort Laramie between 1867 and 1880. At least some of the bodies buried at Fort Laramie were moved to the Fort McPherson National Cemetery before 1909.

FORT PHIL KEARNY
Wyoming Territory

In July 1866 General Henry B. Carrington established Fort Phil Kearny to protect the Bozeman Trail. The Sioux under Chief Red Cloud began a campaign against the fort at once. Paul Wellman writes in Death on the Prairie that the Sioux killed 154 people near the fort from August 1st to December 31, 1866. Captain William F. Fetterman was almost decoyed into an ambush on December 6. His command was saved only by quick action by Carrington. Fetterman later boasted: "Give me eighty men and I'll ride through the whole Sioux Nation." On Friday, December 21st, Fetterman rode with 78 soldiers to relive a wood chopping party that had come under attack. Two civilians rode with Fetterman. Fetterman disobeyed Carrington's order not to pursue the Indians. His command was completely wiped out.

By the end of December, 1867, 87 soldiers, eight civilians, and one employee had been buried in the post cemetery according to volume 19 of the Roll of Honor.

Fort Fetterman was abandoned by the Army in August of 1868 as a result of a treaty closing the Bozeman Trail. Red Cloud had won. The same day the fort was abandoned, Red Cloud's braves burned the fort. The bodies from the post cemetery were eventually moved to Custer National Cemetery.

FORT RUSSELL
Wyoming

The Quartermaster's files contain a list of 79 soldiers buried at Fort Russell. The list, dated 1887, also reported nine unknown burials and 59 civilians buried in the post cemetery. No record of removal of these remains has been found.

Volume 19 of the Roll of Honor lists a total of eleven burials at the fort.

FORT YELLOWSTONE
Wyoming

Yellowstone National Park was established on March 1, 1872. The army provided protection for the park. Burials of soldiers and their dependents were made in the post cemetery located at Mammoth Hot Springs. Interments began in 1888. By 1909 a total of 25 non-soldiers had been buried in the cemetery. The cemetery was inactive from 1925 to 1957 when one burial was made. Today there are 57 grave sites in the cemetery, but only 37 are occupied. On July 4-5, 1917, the remains of 20 soldiers buried in the cemetery were moved to Custer Battlefield National Cemetery. The remaining 37 graves are of soldier's wives and children.

Fourteen civilians are buried on a knoll near the Mammoth Hot Springs Hotel. Not all the names of these civilians are known.

In 1910 the Quartermaster's Department furnished a headstone for the grave of an infant child of an employee of the Yellowstone Park Hotel Association.

Mr. Lee Whittlesey, a National Park Service Employee, is currently writing a book entitled Death in Yellowstone. This book contains stories of many of the people buried in Yellowstone.

APPENDIX

PHOTOGRAPHS

"BIVOUAC OF THE DEAD" (POEM)

COLONEL MACK'S LIST OF BURIALS (by state) - 1871

LIST OF NATIONAL CEMETERIES AND SOLDIERS' LOTS

LIST OF POST CEMETERIES

LIST OF BURIALS IN INDIANA

LIST OF BURIALS IN INDIANA AND IOWA

SAMPLE PAGES FROM THE <u>ROLL</u> <u>OF</u> <u>HONOR</u>

BIBLIOGRAPHY

LIST OF ABBREVIATIONS

ABOUT THE AUTHOR

And Glory guards, with solemn round
The Bivouac of the Dead

297

One of the over 140,000 Unknown Union Soldiers who died during the war. (All photographs by the author)

One of over 164,000 known Union soldiers who died during the war.

Monument marking the mass grave of Union soldiers killed by the bushwacker Quantrill at Baxter Springs, Kansas, on October 6, 1863. Scanty records indicate that between 80 and 124 soldiers are buried here.

Kill-Him, a private in company D of the 1st Indian Infantry, buried at Fort Gibson National Cemetery.

Fort Gibson National Cemetery

Fort Gibson National Cemetery

BIVOUAC OF THE DEAD

Theodore O'Hara (1820-1867) wrote this poem in 1847 in
of Kentuckians who died at the Battle of Buena Vista. Most Civil War era
cemeteries have plaques containing two lines of verse from this poem. Lines
from this poem were printed on the front cover of volumes of the <u>Roll of
Honor</u> and <u>Disposition</u>.

O'Hara's poem was the only memorial to these soldiers until the
United States Congress purchased a cemetery for the bodies in 1850.

The muffled drum's sad roll has beat
    The soldier's last tattoo;
No more on Life's parade shall meet
    That brave and fallen few.
On Fame's eternal camping-ground
    Their silent tents to spread,
And Glory guards, with solemn round,
    The bivouac of the dead.

No rumor of the foe's advance
    Now swells upon the wind;
No troubled thought at midnight haunts
    Of loved ones left behind;
No vision of the morrow's strife
    The warrior's dream alarms;
No braying horn nor screaming fife
    At dawn shall call to arms.

Their shriveled swords are red with rust,
    Their plumed heads are bowed;
Their haughty banner, trailed in dust,
    Is now their marital shroud.
And plenteous funeral tears have washed
    The red stains from each brow,
And the proud forms, by battle gashed,
    Are free from anguish now.

The neighing troop, the flashing blade,
    The bugle's stirring blast,
The charge, the dreadful cannonade,
    The din and shout, are past;
Nor war's wild note nor glory's peal
    Shall thrill with fierce delight
Those breasts that nevermore may feel
    The rapture of the fight.

Like the fierce northern hurricane
    That sweeps his great plateau,
Flushed with the triumph yet to gain,
    Came down the serried foe.
Who heard the thunder of the fray
    Break o'er the field beneath,
Knew well the watchword of that day
    Was "Victory or death."

Long had the doubtful conflict raged
    O'er all that stricken plain,
For never fiercer fight had waged
    The vengeful blood of Spain;
And still the storm of battle blew,
    Still swelled the glory tide;
Not long, our stout old chieftain knew,
    Such odds his strength could bide.

Twas in that hour his stern command
    Called to a martyr's grave
The flower of his beloved land,
    The nation's flag to save.
By rivers of their fathers' gore
    His first-born laurels grew,
And well he deemed the sons would pour
    Their lives for glory too.

Full many a mother's breath has swept
    O'er Angostaura's plain--
And long the pitying sky has wept
    Above its mouldered slain.
The raven's scream, or eagle's flight,
    Or shepherd's pensive lay,
Alone awakes each sullen height
    That frowned o'er that dread fray.

Sons of the Dark and Bloody Ground
 Ye must not slumber there,
Where stranger steps and tongues resound
 Along the heedless air.
Your own proud land's heroic soil
 Shall be your fitter grave;
She claim's from war his richest spoil--
 The ashes of her brave.

Thus 'neath their parent turf they rest,
 Far from the glory field,
Borne to a Spartan mother's breast
 On many a bloody shield;
The sunshine of their native sky
 Smiles sadly on them here,
And kindred eyes and hearts watch by
 The heros sepulchre.

Rest on, embalmed and sainted dead!
 Dear as the blood ye gave;
No impious footstep shall here tread
 The herbage of your grave;
Nor shall your glory be forgot
 While fame her records keeps,
Or Honor points the hallowed spot
 Where Valor proudly sleeps.

Yon marble minstrel's voiceless stone
 In deathless song shall tell,
When many a vanished ago hath flown,
 The story how ye fell;
Nor wreck, nor change, nor winter's blight,
 Nor Time's remorseless doom.
Shall dim one ray of glory's light
 That gilds your deathless tomb.

COLONEL OSCAR MACK'S LIST OF BURIALS - 1871

Source: "Report of the Inspector General of National Cemeteries"

GENERAL RECAPITULATION.

States and Territories.	White.		Colored.		Unknown and unclassified.	Total Union soldiers.	Citizens.	Rebel prisoners of war.
	Known.	Unknown.	Known.	Unknown.				
Maine	134	35				169		
New Hampshire	152	10				162		
Vermont	24					24		
Massachusetts	231		40			271		
Rhode Island								
Connecticut	220					220		
New York	3,438	69	199	3		3,709	8	3,429
New Jersey	316	12				328		1,434
Pennsylvania	4,151	1,776	340			6,271		213
Delaware	71	12	3	1		87		140
Maryland	6,717	2,088	243	1		9,053		2,298
District of Columbia	5,211	278		5		5,489	19	125
West Virginia	639	613				1,252	117	
Virginia	27,922	36,868	2,305	1,135		68,230	*4,069	565
North Carolina	3,206	14,255	284	703		18,448	113	
South Carolina	3,974	6,235	795	950		11,954	78	
Georgia	19,619	3,805	174	162		23,760	21	118
Florida	685	576	154	98		1,513	†405	72
Alabama	613	33	165	91		902		
Mississippi	5,590	10,826	197	8,726		25,339		
Louisiana	8,171	6,429	1,882	837	3,358	20,677	18	
Texas	750	346	980	954		3,030	38	
Arkansas	3,677	3,643	506	327		8,153	168	125
Tennessee	30,190	18,600	2,720	4,621		56,061	816	
Kentucky	6,820	2,335	940	177		10,272	127	
Ohio	1,682	111	18			1,811	1	2,337
Indiana	2,878	534	820	208		4,440	11	1,556
Illinois	3,679	2,667	388			6,734	6	7,957
Missouri	7,943	2,571	23	1,044		11,581	562	1,013
Kansas	897	858				1,755	178	14
Michigan	140	53				193		
Wisconsin	366	46				412		137
Iowa	1,042	27				1,069		
Indian Territory	156	†1,967				2,123		
Total	151,237	117,678	13,176	20,043	3,358	305,492	6,741	21,533

* Mostly colored refugees.   † Sailors mostly; died before the rebellion.
‡ From Old Post Cemetery; died before the rebellion.

The soldiers buried in the remaining States and Territories belonged almost entirely to the Regular Army, and their deaths were not incidental to the rebellion; they are therefore omitted from the above recapitulation.

ADDRESSES OF NATIONAL CEMETERIES AND SOLDIERS' LOTS

Not all national cemeteries have on site superintendents (directors). Many are supervised by directors from other cemeteries. The cemeteries without an on site superintendent have information on what cemetery to call for more information. Cemeteries marked with a # contain Civil War dead. The status of a cemetery is given:

VA	cemetery under control of the Department of Veterans Affairs
NPS	cemetery under control of the National Park Service
ARMY	cemetery under control of U.S. Army

This listing was current as of January 1, 1993

Fort Mitchell National Cemetery
P.O. Box 2517
Phoenix City, Alabama 36867
VA Cemetery

Mobile National Cemetery #
1202 Virginia Street
Mobile, Alabama 36604
contact Barrancas National
Cemetery for more information
VA Cemetery

Fort Richardson National Cemetery
P.O. Box 5-498
Fort Richardson, Alaska 99505
VA Cemetery

Stika National Cemetery
P.O. Box 1065
Stika, Alaska 99835
contact Fort Lyon National
Cemetery for more information
VA Cemetery

National Memorial Cemetery of
Arizona
23029 North Cave Creek Road
Phoenix, Arizona 85024
VA Cemetery

Prescott National Cemetery
VA Medical Center
Prescott, Arizona 86301
VA Cemetery

Fayetteville National Cemetery #
700 Government Ave.
Fayetteville, Arkansas 72701
VA Cemetery

Fort Smith National Cemetery #
522 Garland Ave.
Fort Smith, Arkansas 72206
VA Cemetery

Little Rock National Cemetery #
2513 Confederate Ave.
Little Rock, Arkansas 72206
VA Cemetery

Fort Rosecrans National Cemetery#
Point Lama, Box 6237
San Diego, California 92106
VA Cemetery

Los Angeles National Cemetery
950 South Sepulveda Boulevard
Los Angeles, California 92106
VA Cemetery

Riverside National Cemetery
22495 Van Buren Boulevard
Riverside, California 92508
VA Cemetery

San Francisco National Cemetery #
P.O. Box 29012, Presidio of San
Francisco
San Francisco, California 94129
VA Cemetery

San Joaquin National Cemetery
31053 West McCabe Road
Gustine, California 95322
VA Cemetery

Fort Logan National Cemetery
3698 South Sheridan Boulevard
Denver, Colorado 81038
VA Cemetery

Fort Lyon National Cemetery
VA Medical Center
Fort Lyon, Colorado 81038
VA Cemetery

Battleground National Cemetery #
Washington, DC
contact NPS, 5210 Indian Head,
Oxon Hill, MD 20021 for info.
NPS Cemetery

Soldiers Home National
Cemetery #
21 Harewood Road, N.W.
Washington, DC 20011
US Army Cemetery

Barrancas National Cemetery #
Naval Air Station
Pensacola, Florida 32508
VA Cemetery

Bay Pines National Cemetery
P.O. Box 477
Bay Pines, Florida 33504
VA Cemetery

Florida National Cemetery
P.O. Box 377
Bushnell, Florida 33513
VA Cemetery

Saint Augustine National
Cemetery#
104 Marine Street
Saint Augustine, Florida 32084
VA Cemetery

Andersonville National Cemetery #
Rte 1, Box 85
Andersonville, GA 31711
NPS Cemetery

Marietta National Cemetery #
500 Washington Ave.
Marietta, Georgia 30060
VA Cemetery

National Memorial Cemetery of the
Pacific
2177 Pouwaina Drive
Honolulu, Hawaii 96813
VA Cemetery

Alton National Cemetery #
600 Pearl Street
Alton, Illinois 62003
contact Jefferson Barracks National
Cemetery for more information
VA Cemetery

Camp Butler National Cemetery #
Route 1
Springfield, Illinois 62707
VA Cemetery

Danville National Cemetery
1900 East Main Street
Danville, Illinois 61832
VA Cemetery

Mound City National Cemetery #
Junction Highway 37 & 51
Mound City, Illinois 62963
contact Jefferson Barracks National
Cemetery for more information
VA Cemetery

Quincy National Cemetery #
36th and Maine Street
Quincy, Illinois 62301
contact Keokuk National Cemetery
for more information
VA Cemetery

Rock Island National Cemetery #
Rock Island Arsenal
Rock Island, Illinois 61299
VA Cemetery

Crown Hill National Cemetery #
700 West 38th Street
Indianapolis, Indiana 46208
contact Marion National Cemetery
for more information
VA Cemetery

Marion National Cemetery
VA Medical Center
Marion, Indiana 46952
VA Cemetery

New Albany National Cemetery #
1943 Ekin Ave.
New Albany, Indiana 47150
contact Zachary Taylor National
Cemetery for more information
VA Cemetery

Keokuk National Cemetery #
1701J Street
Keokuk, Iowa 52632
VA Cemetery

Oakdale Cemetery #
2501 Eastern Ave.
Davenport, Iowa 52807
contact Rock Island National
Cemetery for more information
Soldier's Lot

Baxter Springs Soldiers' Lot #
Baxter Springs, Kansas 66713
contact Leavenworth National
Cemetery for more information
Solder's Lot

Fort Leavenworth National
Cemetery #
Leavenworth, Kansas 66027
contact Leavenworth National
Cemetery for more information
VA Cemetery

Fort Scott National Cemetery #
P.O. Box 917
Fort Scott, Kansas 66701
VA Cemetery

Leavenworth National Cemetery
P.O. Box 1694
Leavenworth, Kansas 66027
VA Cemetery

Mound City Solders' Lot #
Mound City, Kansas 66506
contact Leavenworth National
Cemetery for more information
Soldier's Lot

Evergreen Cemetery
25 South Alexandria Pike
Southgate, Kentucky 41071
contact Camp Nelson National
Cemetery for more information
Solder's Lot

Camp Nelson National Cemetery #
6980 Danville Road
Nicholasville, KY 40356
VA Cemetery

Cave Hill National Cemetery #
701 Baxter Ave.
Louisville, KY 40204
contact Zachary Taylor National
Cemetery for more information
VA Cemetery

Danville National Cemetery #
377 North first Street
Danville, KY 40442
contact Camp Nelson National
Cemetery for more information
VA Cemetery

Lebanon National Cemetery #
R.R. #1, Box 616
Lebanon, KY 40033
VA Cemetery

Lexington National Cemetery #
833 West Main Street
Lexington, KY 40508
contact Camp Nelson National
Cemetery for more information
VA Cemetery

Mill Springs National Cemetery #
Rural Route #2, P.O. Box 172
Nancy, KY 42544
contact Camp Nelson National
Cemetery for more information
VA Cemetery

Zachary Taylor National Cemetery
4701 Brownsboro Road
Louisville, KY 40207
VA Cemetery

Alexandria National Cemetery #
209 Shamrock
Alexandria, Louisiana 71360
VA Cemetery

Baton Rouge National Cemetery #
220 North 19th Street
Baton Rouge, Louisiana 70806
contact Port Hudson National
Cemetery for more information
VA Cemetery

Chalmette National Cemetery #
St. Bernard Highway
Chalmette, Louisiana 70043
NPS Cemetery

Port Hudson National Cemetery #
Route 1, Box 185
Zachary, Louisiana 70791
VA Cemetery

Mount Pleasant Cemetery #
North Street
August, Maine 00433
contact Massachusetts National
Cemetery for more information
Soldier's Lot

Togus National Cemetery
VA Medical Center
Togus, Maine 04330
call Massachusetts National
Cemetery for more information
VA Cemetery

Massachusetts National Cemetery
Bourne, Mass 02532
VA Cemetery

Woodlawn Cemetery
Harvard Street
Ayer, Massachusetts 01432
call Massachusetts National
Cemetery for more information
Soldier's Lot

Annapolis National Cemetery #
800 West Street
Annapolis, Maryland 21401
contact Baltimore National
Cemetery for more information
VA Cemetery

Antietam National Cemetery #
Box 158
Sharpsburg, Maryland 21782
NPS Cemetery

Baltimore National Cemetery
5501 Frederick Ave.
Baltimore, MD 21228
VA Cemetery

Loudon Park National Cemetery #
3445 Frederick Ave.
Baltimore, MD 21228
contact Baltimore National
Cemetery for more information
VA Cemetery

Fort Custer National Cemetery
15501 Dickman Road
Augusta, Michigan 49012
VA Cemetery

Lakeside Cemetery
3781 Gratiot Street
Port Huron, Michigan 48060
contact Fort Custer National
Cemetery for more information
Soldier's Lot

Fort Snelling National Cemetery #
7601 34th Ave, South
Minneapolis, Minnesota 55450
VA Cemetery

Biloxi National Cemetery
P.O. Box 4968
Biloxi, Mississippi 39535
VA Cemetery

Cornith National Cemetery #
1551 Hotton Street
Cornith, Mississippi 38834
VA Cemetery

Natchez National Cemetery #
61 Cemetery Road
Natchez, Mississippi 39120
VA Cemetery

Vicksburg National Cemetery #
3201 clay St.
Vicksburg, Mississippi 39180
NPS Cemetery

Jefferson Barracks National
Cemetery #
101 Memorial Drive
St. Louis, Missouri 63125
VA Cemetery

Custer National Cemetery
P.O. Box 39
Crow Agency, Montana 59022
NPS Cemetery

Fort McPherson National
Cemetery #
HCO 1, Box 67
Maxwell, Nebraska 69151
VA Cemetery

Forest Lawn Cemetery
7909 Morman Bridge Road
Omaha, Nebraska 68112
contact Leavenworth National
Cemetery for more information
Soldier's Lot

Beverly National Cemetery #
Rd # 1, Bridge Boro Road
Beverly, New Jersey 08010
VA Cemetery

Finn's Point National Cemetery #
RFD 3, Fort Mott Road
Salem. New Jersey 08079
VA Cemetery

Fort Bayard National Cemetery
P.O. Box 189
Bayard, New Mexico 88036
contact Fort Bliss National
Cemetery for more information
VA Cemetery

Santa Fe National Cemetery #
P.O. Box 88
Santa Fe, New Mexico 87501
VA Cemetery

Albany Rural Cemetery #
c/o Albany Cemetery Association
Albany, New York 12204
contact Bath National Cemetery for
more information
Soldier's Lot

Bath National Cemetery
VA Medical Center
Bath, New York 14810
VA Cemetery

Calverton National Cemetery
210 Princeton Road
Calverton, New York 11933
VA Cemetery

Cypress Hills National Cemetery #
625 Jamaica Ave
Brooklyn, New York 11208
contact Long Island National
Cemetery for more information
VA Cemetery

Long Island National Cemetery
Farmingdale, L.I., New York
11735
VA Cemetery

Woodlawn National Cemetery #
1825 Davis Street
Elmira, New York 14901
contact Bath National Cemetery for
more information
VA Cemetery

New Bern National Cemetery #
1711 National Ave
New Bern, North Carolina 28560
VA Cemetery

Raleigh National Cemetery #
101 Rock Quarry Road
Raleigh, North Carolina 27610
VA Cemetery

Salisbury National Cemetery #
202 Government Road
Salisbury, North Carolina 28144
VA Cemetery

Wilmington National Cemetery #
2011 Market Street
Wilmington, North Carolina 28403
contact New Bren National
Cemetery for more information
VA Cemetery

Dayton National Cemetery
VA Medical Center
Dayton, Ohio 45428
Va Cemetery

Woodland Cemetery #
6901 Woodland Ave.
Cleveland, Ohio 44104
contact Dayton National Cemetery
for more information
Soldier's Lot

Fort Gibson National Cemetery #
R.R. #2, P.O. Box 47
Fort Gibson, Oklahoma 74434
VA Cemetery

Eagle Point National Cemetery
2763 Riley Road
Eagle Point, Oregon 97524
VA Cemetery

Roseburg National Cemetery
VA Medical Center
Roseburg, Oregon 97470
VA Cemetery

Willamette National Cemetery
P.O. Box 66147
Portland, Oregon 97266
VA Cemetery

Gettysburg National Cemetery #
P.O. Box 70
Gettysburg, Pennsylvania 17325
NPS Cemetery

Indiantown Gap National Cemetery
P.O. Box 187
Annville, Pennsylvania 17003
VA Cemetery

Philadelphia National Cemetery #
Haines Street and Limekiln Pike
Philadelphia, Pennsylvania 19138
contact Beverly National Cemetery
for more information
VA Cemetery

Allegheny Cemetery #
4734 Butler Street
Pittsburg, Pennsylvania 15201
call Indiantown Gap National
Cemetery for more information
Soldier's Lot

Ashland Cemetery #
Carlisle, Pennsylvania 17013
call Indiantown Gap National
Cemetery for more information
Soldier's Lot

Mount Moriah Naval Cemetery #
62nd Street and Kingsessing Ave.
Philadelphia, Pennsylvania 19142
contact Beverly National Cemetery
for more information
Soldier's Lot

Prospect Hill Cemetery #
700 North George Street
York, Pennsylvania 17404
call Indiantown Gap National
Cemetery for more information
Soldier's Lot

Puerto Rico National Cemetery
P. O. Box 1298
Bayamon, Puerto Rico 00621
VA Cemetery

Beaufort National Cemetery #
1601 Boundary Street
Beaufort, South Carolina 29902
VA Cemetery

Florence National Cemetery #
89 East National Cemetery Road
Florence, South Carolina 29501
VA Cemetery

Black Hills National Cemetery
P. O. Box 640
Sturgis, South Dakota 57785
VA Cemetery

Fort Meade National Cemetery
VA Medical Center
Fort Meade, South Dakota 57785
Contact Black Hills National
Cemetery for more information
VA Cemetery

Hot Springs National Cemetery
VA Medical Center
Hot Springs, South Dakota 57747
VA Cemetery

Andrew Johnson National
Cemetery
Depot Street
Greenville, Tennessee 37743
NPS Cemetery

Chattanooga National Cemetery #
1200 Bailey Ave
Chattanooga, Tennessee 37404
VA Cemetery

Fort Donelson National
Cemetery #
P. O. Box 434
Dover, Tennessee 37058
NPS Cemetery

Knoxville National Cemetery #
939 Tyson Street N.W.
Knoxville, Tennessee 37917
VA Cemetery

Memphis National Cemetery #
3568 Townes Ave
Memphis, Tennessee 38122
VA Cemetery

Mountain Home National Cemetery
P.O. Box 8
Mountain Home, Tennessee 37684
VA Cemetery

San Antonio National Cemetery #
517 Paso Hondo Street
San Antonio, Texas 78202
contact Fort Sam Houston National
Cemetery for more information
VA Cemetery

Alexandria National Cemetery #
1450 Wilkes Street
Alexandria, Virginia 22314
contact Quantico National
Cemetery for more information
VA Cemetery

Arlington National Cemetery #
Arlington, Virginia 22211
US Army Cemetery

Ball's Bluff National Cemetery #
Leesbug, Virginia 22075
contact Culpeper National
Cemetery for more information
VA Cemetery

City Point National Cemetery #
10th Avenue and Davis Street
Hopewell, Virginia 23860
contact Richmond National
Cemetery for more information
VA Cemetery

Cold Harbor National Cemetery #
Route 156 North
Mechanicsville, Virginia 23111
contact Richmond National
Cemetery for more information
VA Cemetery

Culpeper National Cemetery #
305 U.S. Avenue
Culpeper, Virginia 22701
VA Cemetery

Danville National Cemetery #
721 Lee Street
Danville, Virginia 24541
Contact Salisbury (NC) National
Cemetery for more information
VA Cemetery

Fort Harrison National Cemetery #
8620 Varina Road
Richmond, Va 23231
Contact Richmond National
Cemetery for more information
VA Cemetery

Fredericksburg National
Cemetery #
1013 Lafayette Blvd.
Fredericksburg, Va 22404
NPS Cemetery

Glendale National Cemetery #
8301 Willis Church Road
Richmond, Virginia 23231
contact Richmond National
Cemetery for more information
VA Cemetery

Hampton National Cemetery #
Cemetery Road at Marshall Ave.
Hampton, Virginia 23669
VA Cemetery

Hampton VA Medical Center
National Cemetery
VA Medical Center
Hampton, Virginia 23669
contact Hampton National
Cemetery for more information
VA Cemetery

Poplar Grove National Cemetery #
c/o Petersburg National Battlefield
Petersburg, Virginia 23804
NPS Cemetery

Quantico National Cemetery
P.O. Box 10
Triangle, Virginia 22172
VA Cemetery

Richmond National Cemetery #
1701 Williamsburg Road
Richmond, Virginia 23231
VA Cemetery

Seven Pines National Cemetery #
400 East Williamsburg Road
Sandston, Virginia 23150
contact Richmond National
Cemetery for more information
VA Cemetery

Staunton National Cemetery #
901 Richmond Ave.
Staunton, Virginia 24401
VA Cemetery

Winchester National Cemetery #
401 National Ave.
Winchester, Virginia 22601
VA Cemetery

Yorktown National Cemetery #
Box 210
Yorktown, Virginia 23690
NPS Cemetery

Green Mount Cemetery #
250 State Street
Montpelier, Vermont 05602
call Massachusetts National
Cemetery for more information
Soldier's Lot

Prospect Hill Cemetery #
94 South Main Street
Battleboro, Vermont 05301
call Massachusetts National
Cemetery for more information
Soldier's Lot

Grafton National Cemetery #
431 Walnut Street
Grafton, West Virginia 26354
VA Cemetery

West Virginia National Cemetery
Route 2, Box 127
Pruntytown, West Virginia 23654
contact Grafton National Cemetery
for more information
VA Cemetery

Wood National Cemetery
VA Medical Center
Milwaukee, Wisconsin 53295
VA Cemetery

Forest Hill Cemetery #
One Speedway Road
Madison, Wisconsin 53705
contact Wood National Cemetery
for more information
Soldier's Lot

Forest Home Cemetery #
2405 West Forest Home Ave.
Milwaukee, Wisconsin 53215
contact Wood National Cemetery
for more information
Soldier's Lot

Fort Crawford Cemetery #
413 South Beaumont Road
Prairie du Chien, Wisconsin 53821
contact Wood National Cemetery
for more information
Soldier's Lot

Fort Winnebago Cemetery
Portage, Wisconsin 53901
contact Wood National Cemetery
for more information
Soldier's Lot

Mound Cemetery #
1147 West Boulevard
Racine, Wisconsin 53405
contact Wood National Cemetery
for more information
Soldier's Lot

UNITED STATES ARMY POST CEMETERIES

Fort Richardson	Anchorage, Ak
Fort McClellan	Fort McClellan, Ala
Fort Huachuca	Fort Huachuca, Ariz
Benicia Arsenal	Benicia, Calf.
Presidio of Monterey	Presidio of Monterey, Calf.
Fort Benning	Fort Benning, Ga.
Schofield Barracks	Wahiawa, Hi.
Fort Sheridan	Fort Sheridan, Ill.
Fort Leavenworth	Fort Leavenworth, Kan.
Fort Riley	Fort Riley, Kan.
Fort Knox	Fort Knox, Ky.
Fort Devens	Fort Devens, Mass.
Aberdeen Proving Ground	Aberdeen Proving Ground, Md.
Edgewood Arsenal	Aberdeen Proving Ground, Md.
Fort George C. Meade	Fort George C. Meade, Md.
Fort Leonard Wood	Fort Leonard Wood, Mo.
Fort Missoula	Fort Missoula, MT
Fort Bragg	Fort Bragg, NC
El Reno Post Cemetery	El Reno, OK
Fort Sill	Fort Sill, OK
Fort Stevens	Fort Stevens, Org.
Carlisle Barracks	Carlisle Barracks, Pen.
Fort Douglas	Fort Douglas, Utah
Fort Lawton	Fort Lawton, Wash.
Fort Lewis	Fort Lewis, Wash.
Fort Worden	Fort Worden, Wash.
Vancouver Barracks	Vancouver Barracks, Wash.

List of Places in Indiana where Union Soldiers are Buried
Report of Brigadier General J. D. Bingham
April 24, 1969

County	Place (Cemetery)	no. of Graves
Allen	Fort Wayne (Linwood)	17
Bartholomew	Ohio Township	1
Clay	Center Point	4
Clay	Friendly Grove	1
Clay	Perry	1
Clay	Shiloh	1
Clay	SugarRidge	2
Crawford		6
Deaborn	Caser Creek	2
Deaborn	Harrison	4
Dearborn	Logan	1
Dearborn	Miller	3
Decatur	Greensburg (Methodist)	4
Decatur	Greensburg (City)	8
Dekalb		6
Dekalb	Spencerville	1
Fountain		4
Fountain	Portland	1
Franklin	Bloomington (Eb. Chapel)	1
Franklin	Metamora	1
Franklin	New Trenton	2
Franklin	Pepperton	1
Greene		2
Greene	Bledsoe Burying Ground	1
Greene	Bloomfield	5
Greene	Ellensworth Burying Ground	1
Greene	Harrah Burying Ground	1
Greene	Lebanon	3
Hancock		1
Harrison		1
Harrison	Bradford Cemetery	3
Harrison	Bradford	2
Harrison	Greenville	1

320

Henry	Blue River	3
Henry	Dublin	2
Henry	Dudley	3
Henry	Fall Creek	8
Henry	Franklin	5
Henry	Greensboro	2
Henry	Harrison	15
Henry	Henry	9
Henry	Jefferson	4
Henry	Lewisville	2
Henry	Liberty	2
Henry	New Lisbon	3
Henry	Praire	7
Henry	Spiceland	10
Henry	Stoney Creek	4
Henry	Wayne	11
La Grange	Wolcottsville	1
Lawrence		1
Lawrence	Springville	7
Madison	Alfont (near)	1
Madison	Mount Carmel	1
Marion		1
Marion	Cumberland	2
Martin		8
Monroe		1
Montgomery		12
Noble	Libson	1
Ohio	Evansville	1
Ohio	Rising Sun	18
Orange	Paoli	6
Owen		4
Owen	Gosport	8
Owen	Spencer	7
Parke		5
Parke	Catlin	4
Shelby	Shelbyville	2
Sullivan		5
Sullivan	Evansville	1

Sullivan	New Lebanon	3
Switzerland	Allinsville	1
Switzerland	Bennington	5
Switzerland	Patriot	1
Switzerland	Vevay	4
Vigo		5
Vigo	(City Cemetery)	3
Vigo	Terre Hate	28
Warren	Pine Village	3
Washington	(Hope Cemetery)	2
Wayne	(Hillsboro Cemetery)	3
Wayne		2
Wayne	(Elkhorn Cemetery)	1
Wayne	Abbington	1
Wayne	Cambridge City	6
Wayne	Centersville	1
Wayne	Dublin	1
Wayne	Hagerstown	1
Wayne	Harrison	1
Wayne	Milton	1
Wayne	Richmond	11
Wayne	Salton	1
Wayne	Washington	3
	Mount Zion	5
	Thorntown	19
	Union Bethel	2

BURIALS IN INDIANA AND IOWA
Listed by County

Volume 18 of the <u>Roll of Honor</u> lists burials in the following counties in Indiana and Iowa. However the exact burial site is not listed.

INDIANA

Boone	Marion	Switzerland
Clay	Ohio	Vigo
De Kalb	Owen	Warren
Dearborn	Parke	Wayne
Henry	Sullivan	

IOWA

Adams	Franklin	Muscatine
Appanoose	Guthrie	Page
Black Hawk	Jones	Polk
Bremer	Lousia	Pottawatomie
Buchanan	Lucas	Ringgold
Davis	Marshall	Scott
Decatur	Mitchell	Tama
Delaware	Monoa	Union
Floyd	Monroe	Wapello

PAGE FROM VOLUME 9 OF THE <u>ROLL</u> <u>OF</u> <u>HONOR</u>

United States Soldiers interred at various places in Maine during the Rebellion.

No.	Name.	Rank.	Regiment.	Co.	Date of Death.
	OUTSIDE FORT PREBLE.				
1	Abbott, David..........	Recruit....	17th U. S. inf.....	....	April 21, 1864
2	Graves, Henry H.......	Private....	17th U. S. inf.....	H	Mar. 20, 1864
3	Hartley, Stephen Z.....	Recruit....	17th U. S. inf.....	....	April 17, 1864
4	Kraus, George..........	Rejected re-cruit.	....	....	April 20, 1864
	CHURCHYARD C.E., ME.				
1	Frank, Frederick.......	Musician...	17th U. S. inf.....	....	May 13, 1865
2	Wells, Sarah..........	....	....	....	Feb. 28, 1863
	DANVILLE, ME.				
1	Webb, William F......	Unassigned recruit.	17th U. S. inf.....	....	May 30, 1865
	WALLINGFORD, ME.				
1	Webb, John W.........	Unassigned recruit.	17th U. S. inf.....	....	Aug. 8, 1865
	MACKEY ISLAND, PORT-LAND HARBOR.				
1	Unknown.............	Unknown..	Unknown........	Un.	Unknown....
2	....do.............	....do......	....do.........	.do.	.....do......
3	....do.............	....do......	....do.........	.do.	.....do......
4	....do.............	....do......	....do.........	.do.	.....do......
5	....do.............	....do......	....do.........	.do.	.....do......
6	....do.............	....do......	....do.........	.do.	.....do......
7	....do.............	....do......	....do.........	.do.	.....do......
8	....do.............	....do......	....do.........	.do.	.....do......
9	....do.............	....do......	....do.........	.do.	.....do......
10	....do.............	....do......	....do.........	.do.	.....do......

United States Soldiers interred in Forest Cemetery, Portland, Maine, during the Rebellion.

No.	Name.	Rank.	Regiment.	Co.	Date of Death.
1	Allen, George	Unknown..	Unknown	Un.	April 24, 1864
2	Barstow, Joseph.........	....do......	....do.........	.do.	May 31, 1863
3	Beckwoth, Joel..... ...	....do......	....do.........	.do.	July 28, 1865
4	Carter, Edwin N........	....do......	....do.........	.do.	Sept. 5, 1865
5	Chase, Franklin........	....do......	....do...........	.do.	Jan. 19, 1863

PAGE FROM VOLUME 14 OF THE <u>ROLL</u> <u>OF</u> <u>HONOR</u>

This page proves that the War Department had a list of Union Soldiers who died at the Salisbury (NC) Prison Camp.

NORTH CAROLINA—Continued.

Salisbury, Rowan county.

No.	Name.	Rank.	Co.	Regiment.	Died. When.	Died. Cause.	Remarks.
1	Abbott, Abner	Private	A	8th New Jersey	Jan. 10, 1865	Pleurisy.	
2	Abbott, James	do.	C	1st New Hampshire cavalry	Jan. 8, 1865	Diarrhœa chronic.	
3	Abel, Harlow	do.	L	14th Pennsylvania cavalry	Nov. 21, 1864	Diarrhœa.	
4	Achy, Sidney	do.	C	190th Pennsylvania	Nov. 15, 1864	Pneumonia.	
5	Acliar, S. W.	do.	F	76th Pennsylvania	Nov. 27, 1864	Pleurisy.	
6	Acome, John	do.	H	69th New York	Nov. 11, 1864	Diarrhœa.	
7	Acord, John	do.	A	69th Pennsylvania	Oct. 27, 1864	Fever int.	
8	Adams, I. P.	do.	D	7th U. S. C. T.	Jan. 15, 1865		
9	Adder, W.	do.	C	30th Illinois	Jan. 11, 1865	Diarrhœa chronic.	
10	Addy, Thomas	do.	G	170th New York	Nov. 11, 1864	Diarrhœa.	
11	Adkins, Stanton	do.	I	2d Delaware	Jan. 31, 1865	Do.	
12	Adkins, Stanton	do.	D	123d Ohio	Jan. 31, 1865	Do.	
13	Adlington, H. L.	do.	G	10th New Hampshire	Nov. 29, 1864	Do.	
14	Agan, James	do.	H	93d New York	Nov. 7, 1864	Do.	
15	Agan, William	do.	K	69th New York	Nov. 19, 1864	Do.	
16	Agnew, William	Corporal	I	140th Pennsylvania	Sept. 15, 1863	Diarrhœa.	
17	Abl, William H.	Private	B	Purnell Legion	Feb. 16, 1865	Do.	
18	Ahrens, Matis	do.	F	35th Massachusetts	Nov. 22, 1864	Do.	
19	Abraugh, John	do.	D	191st Pennsylvania	Feb. 10, 1864	Unknown.	
20	Albright, David	do.	C	191st Pennsylvania	Dec. 23, 1864	Diarrhœa.	
21	Aldrich, A. H	do.	A	4th New York artillery	Nov. 19, 1864	Pneumonia.	
22	Alexander, Ephraim	do.	G	5th New York cavalry	Jan. 10, 1865	Diarrhœa.	
23	Alexandria, James	do.	G	191st Pennsylvania	Oct. 28, 1864	Do.	
24	Allcott, William	do.	F	191st Pennsylvania	Jan. 8, 1865	Do.	
25	Allen, A. B.	Citizen		North Carolina	Feb. 19, 1865	Do.	
26	Allen, Ben. J	Private	E	4th New Hampshire	Nov. 22, 1864	Pneumonia.	
27	Allen, Frederick	do.	K	1st D. C. cavalry	Feb. 13, 1865	Unknown.	
28	Allen, James	do.	E	54th Massachusetts	Jan. 19, 1865	Typh. fever.	
29	Allen, James	do.	A	Purnell Legion	Feb. 15, 1865	Scabies.	

BIBLIOGRAPHY

National Archives Record Groups

RG92-576 "General Correspondence and Reports Relating to National and Post Cemeteries." 1865-1890

RG92-582 "Requests for Information Relating to Missing Soldiers, Received by James Moore, Quartermaster." 1863-1867

RG92-587 "Correspondence Relating to the Administration of National Cemeteries." 1907-1919

RG92-589 "War Department Orders and Circulars Relating to Cemeteries." 1866-1873

RG92-599 "Quartermaster General Orders and Circulars and Blank Forms Relating to National Cemeteries. 1874-1905"

RG92-682 "Abstracts of Officer's Reports Relating to Burial Places of Soldiers, Available Records, and Recommendations." 1866

RG92-683 "Descriptive List of National Cemeteries." 1867-1870

RG92-684 "Register of Transactions and Data Relating to Land Tittles of National Cemeteries." 1868-1869

RG92-685 "Journal of a Trip Through Parts of Kentucky, Tennessee, and Georgia for the Purpose of Locating the Scattered Graves of Union Soldiers." [ca 1866]

RG92-686 "Journal of a Trip Through Shiloh, Pittsburg Landing, Fort Donaldson (sic), Cornith, and Vicksburg for the Purpose of Locating the Scattered Graves of Confederate and Union Soldiers." [ca 1866]

RG92-687 "Miscellaneous Cemetery Records." 1867-1898

RG92-692 "Rough Draft of Table of Contents and Index to Schedule of Reports of Disinterments of Deceased Union Soldiers and Prisoners of War." n.d.

RG92-695 "Correspondence - Office of the Commissioner for Marking Graves of the Confederate Dead." n.d.

Government Publications

Quartermaster General's Department

Folsom, Col. C.W. Report of the Inspector General of the National Cemeteries. 1868.

Mack, Col. Oscar A. Report of the Inspector General of the National Cemeteries for the Years 1870 and 1871.

Mack, Col. Oscar A. Report of the Inspector General of the National Cemeteries. 1874.

Roll of Honor: Names of Soldiers Who Died in Defense of the American Union, Interred in National Cemeteries.... 23 Volumes, 1865-1873

Statement of the Disposition of some of the Bodies of Deceased Union Soldiers and Prisoners of War Whose Remains Have Been Moved to National Cemeteries. 4 Volumes, 1868.

Other Governmental Sources

The Medical and Surgical History of the War of the Rebellion. U.S. Surgeon-General's Office. 1870

"Station Data Sheets". Department of Veterans Affairs and National Park Service.

War of the Rebellion...Official Records of the Union and Confederate Armies. 128 Volumes, 1880-1901

Other Sources

Andersonville. Eastern Acorn Press. Harrisburg, Pen. 1983

Booth, B.F. Dark Days of the Rebellion. Indianola, Ind. 1897

Brown, Louis. The Salisbury Prison: A Case Study of Confederate Military Prisons 1861-1865. Wendell, N.C. 1980

Busey, John W. The Last Fell Measure Burials in the Soldier's National Cemetery at Gettysburg. Highstown, N.J. 1988

Hinkel, John Vincent. Arlington: Monument to Heroes. Englewood Cliffs, N.J.

Hoffsommer, Robert D. "The Aftermath of Gettysburg." Gettysburg. Harrisburg, Pen. 1981

Roberts, Robert. Encyclopedia of Historic Forts. New York 1987

Skoch, George F. "In the Shadow of the Valley." Civil War Times. Sept. 1984

Steere, Edward "Origins of the National Cemetery System." The Quartermaster Review. 1953

Weigley, Russell. Quartermaster General of the Army: M.C. Meigs. New York, 1959

Wellman, Paul I. Death on the Prairie. New York, 1947

Wiley, Bell I. The Common Soldier of the Civil War. Gettysburg, Pen 1973

ABBREVIATIONS USED IN THIS BOOK

Ala	Alabama	Minn	Minnesota
Ariz	Arizona Territory	Miss	Mississippi
Ark	Arkansas	Mo	Missouri
Ask	Alaska	M T	Montana Territory
B.F.	Battlefield	Neb	Nebraska
C.H.	Court House	Nev	Nevada
Calf	California	NH	New Hampshire
Col	Colorado Territory	NJ	New Jersey
Con	Connecticut	NM	New Mexico
D.C.	District of Columbia	NY	New York
D T	Dakota Territory	NC	North Carolina
Del	Delaware	Org	Oregon
Fla	Florida	P I	Philippine Islands
GAR	Grand Army of the Republic	Pen	Pennsylvania
Geo	Georgia	RI	Rhode Island
ID T	Idaho Territory	SC	South Carolina
Ill	Illinois	Ten	Tennessee
In T	Indian Territory	Tex	Texas
Ind	Indiana	U T	Utah Territory
Kan	Kansas	Vt	Vermont
Ky	Kentucky	Va	Virginia
Lous	Louisiana	Wash	Washington
Md	Maryland	W Va	West Virginia
Mass	Massachusetts	Wis	Wisconsin
Mich	Michigan	Wyo	Wyoming

ABOUT THE AUTHOR

Mark Hughes is an electronic technologist who enjoys historical research. He is a graduate of Gaston College (AAS-1971) and Southeastern Oklahoma State University (BS-1985, Master of Technology-1986). He grew up on his parents' turkey farms in the Carolinas. Before becoming a professional educator he was an electronic technician.

A former instructor at Southwestern Oklahoma State University, he returned to the Carolinas in 1989 to establish an Electronics Engineering Technology program at Orangeburg-Calhoun Technical College were he is currently Department Head of the program. This is his first nontechnical publication.

He married Patricia Ann McDaniel in 1970. They have one daughter: Anna Grace Hughes (born 1987).